To alan
RFK's right hand
man.

Roger C Lit
4/3/67

R. F. K.

The Man Who Would Be President

R. F. K.

The Man Who Would Be President

By RALPH de TOLEDANO

G. P. Putnam's Sons
New York

Contents

R. F. K.

The Man Who Would Be President

1

What Manner of Man?

WHAT manner of man is Robert Francis Kennedy? Hated and loved, feared and despised, self-sufficient, cold, secretive, and remote, openly heedless of others, aggressive and shy—and, above all, ruthless—this is what people say of Bobby. Every day he violates the rules of politics—making too obvious the drive of his ambitions. Those closest to him, the Kennedy contemporaries, discuss him in words that cannot hide the cutting edge of irony. The most pointed remarks come from his wife Ethel. Yet he remains a fact of life on the American political scene, a contender for the Presidency and a major force in a state that greeted him with the epithet "carpetbagger" when he invaded it as a candidate for the United States Senate. Bobby Kennedy does not take kindly to the armchair psychoanalysis of writers, associates, friends, or enemies.

In an unguarded moment, before her husband's assassination thrust her into continuous and close contact with Bobby, Jacqueline Kennedy remarked: "I sometimes wish that Bobby, because he is so wonderful, had been an amoeba and then he could have mated with himself."

But Oriana Fallaci, an experienced journalist for *L'Europeo* of Milan, found herself deeply disconcerted by Bobby—and a little frightened—after a half-hour interview. In Bobby's suite at the Carlyle, the New York hotel to which Jack Kennedy had brought a kind of feverish gaiety, she felt a strangeness that was heightened by the banks of pictures, some of family, but most of his dead brother. One very large picture of President Kennedy, framed heavily in silver, struck her because Bobby ritualistically touched it as he walked in. She was struck, too, by his young-old face, his head-down stance, the way in which his eyes were hidden from her. "The hand came out to meet mine as if hoping never to find it," she observed. "When he did find my hand, he shook it without enthusiasm." When he finally looked directly at her, she saw the cold blue eyes in their "implacable" stare, their "magnetism."

"They probed into your soul," Signorina Fallaci recalled. "One suddenly understood why during the campaign, in Harlem, in Brooklyn, people risked suffocation just to hear him speak, why many feared him at the Department of Justice, why he appeals both to men and women, although he has no warmth, no tact and no oratorical talents." Gore Vidal, Jacqueline Kennedy's cousin, had intercepted the same look and, with catlike intuition, had seen in it "a Torquemada." For Oriana Fallaci, however, it was a confrontation with the essential Kennedy. "It is said he will never take second place," she noted, "that he never gives up the attempt to impose his will, that he despises all the vanquished, that he does everything superlatively well, from games to politics, from writing to generating children. One thing is certain: I have never known a so-called shy person so capable of intimidating non-shy people. . . . As the minutes passed, he became more withdrawn, more secretive, more melancholy, never shifting position, never changing the tone of his voice, which is shrill and monotonous like a horn."

Others have seen another Robert Kennedy—arrogant and childish, brow-beating those who cannot strike back. This is the Kennedy who took great pride in his meeting with Joey Gallo, a New York hoodlum who had been summoned to Bobby's office for questioning. The room in which the Attorney General holds court is perhaps the most imposing and somber of any in official Washington. Even an ingratiating man cannot rid it of its doomful atmosphere. Gallo walked in to find Bobby seated at the king-size desk, his shirt sleeves rolled up and his collar loosened, one foot perched on an open lower drawer and the other on top of the desk. "So you're Joey Gallo the jukebox king," Bobby said. "You don't look so tough. I'd like to fight you myself." (There is little doubt that Bobby would have won the fight.) But the Joey Gallos are not the only ones who feel the prod of Bobby's temperament. Reporters who have angered Bobby are cut dead, harassed, or humiliated. He gave one an interview at his estate on Hickory Hill in Virginia while he swam in his private pool. When asked a question he didn't like, Bobby dived low, emerging at the other side of the pool. Then, without a word, he climbed out of the water and stalked off.

Yet at Washington's National Airport, on his return from a Latin American trip, he gently broke away from the press when his two-year-old son Christopher tugged at his sleeve and asked, "Can we go home now, Daddy?" "Yes, Chris darling," he answered. "Yes, my love, yes." This was not the Kennedy of whom a Washington quipster punned: "Bobby thinks humility is something you find in the atmosphere."

The comments, good and bad—but mostly acerbic—are many, varied, and contradictory, and they explain why Pat Anderson, a public-relations assistant and occasional speech writer during Kennedy's Justice Department days, said, "He has been called a simple man; it would be more accurate to say he is many simple men." The catalog of these comments may oppress or irritate Bobby Kennedy, but they are a clue to his character and therefore bear repeating. In combination, they serve as an introduction to the man who would be President:

Cassius Clay: "I see Robert Kennedy walking though the streets meeting everybody, shaking everybody's hands, and when he gets into office you gonna need a necktie to go and see him."

President Kennedy: "The Attorney General has not yet spoken, but I can feel the hot breath of his disapproval on the back of my neck."

A close friend: " 'Liberal' is still apt to be a dirty word to Bobby. But in the end, like his brother, Jack, he usually comes down on the liberal side for the purest of practical reasons."

Government girl (when Bobby was making a personal appearance) : "I have a grade twelve and an inspector watching my office and my coffee's getting cold, but I don't care. I've got to see him."

Fletcher Knebel, Washington correspondent and best-selling novelist: "Robert F. Kennedy, the second most powerful man in the United States government, is about as innocent as a Bengal tiger. His body is lean and hard and it is doubtful that he has shed a tear in thirty years."

A close friend: "Bobby has a strong sense of right and wrong. He's honest to a fault. His first instinct is always to tell the truth. He's gracious in small things, considerate, thoughtful. He sympathizes with the underdog. There's a little bit of the devil in him. He's a great leader. He hates to waste time. But what I admire most is his guts. If there were a fire in the third story, Bobby would be the one to dash through the flames and rescue someone."

Pat Anderson: "Kennedy's most obvious fault is his rudeness. His face, when it lacks that boyish photogenic grin, is not a pleasant sight. It has a certain bony hardness and those ice-blue eyes are not the smiling ones that Irishmen sing songs about. At best, he recalls (Scott) Fitzgerald's description of Gatsby: 'an elegant young roughneck.' . . . He is too preoccupied with the salvation of mankind to be polite to individuals."

President Lyndon Johnson: "A young whippersnapper."

Senator John F. Kennedy (in 1959, when he was launching his campaign for President): "Do you realize that that high-pitched, grating voice is going to be dinning at me night and day for the next twelve months?"

Melvin M. Belli, West Coast trial lawyer who defended Jack Ruby: "He's arrogant, rude, and even ignorant of the law. He's the moneyed Little Lord Fauntleroy of government. Every newspaperman knows what he is, and even Johnson can't stand him, but everybody's too scared of the son-of-a-bitch."

Ethel Kennedy, commenting on his sloppy clothes: "You'd never confuse him with Dean Acheson." On his reputation: "Bobby can be so sensitive, so compassionate. All sides occur to Bobby, too. But it's more his nature to get right into it. He's a doer."

Newsweek (summing up the popular attitude). "A disquieting figure, part Boy Scout and part muscleman, a Savonarola in short pants."

A Washington newspaperman who played touch football with Bobby: "I'd like to hit him right in the mouth. Everytime I went up for a pass, he gave me elbows, knees, the works. When our team got within one touchdown of his team, by God, he picked up the ball and said the game was over."

Gore Vidal: "Why am I against Bobby? Because he's a dangerous, ruthless man. He's a Torquemada-like personality with none of his brother's gift for seeing things in other than black and white. . . . If you intend to ask anything about my pet peeves, just put down Bobby Kennedy. . . . It would take a public-relations genius to make him appear lovable. He is not. His obvious characteristics are energy, vindictiveness, and a simple-mindedness about human motives which may yet bring him down. . . . He has none of his brother's human ease—or charity."

James Hoffa: "He's a young, dim-witted, curly-headed smart-aleck."

An old family friend: "You have to remember that Bobby's instinct is to act directly. Underneath his surface toughness, he gets emotionally involved in what he is doing. It may amuse so-called sophisticates, but he saw the corruption he uncovered in the rackets investigation as a truly evil force trying to strangle the country, and he moved against it. While I think he has mellowed a great deal, he isn't ever going to compromise basic principles."

Kenneth O'Donnell, White House aide in the Kennedy and Johnson Administrations and captain of the Harvard football team when Bobby was an undergraduate: "I can't think of anyone who had less right to make the varsity squad than Bobby, when he first came out for practice. The war was over and we had plenty of manpower, all of it bigger, faster, and more experienced than he was. But every afternoon, he would be down on that field an hour early, and he always stayed an hour later. He just *made* himself better."

President Kennedy: "Bobby is caught in a crosscurrent of labels we pin on people. We tend to check off an arbitrary list, add up the results, and come up with a liberal or a conservative. Bobby doesn't fit this. I could say that he is essentially conservative, but not on a matter like the minimum wage or a number of other issues. He acts pragmatically. I think he once might have been intolerant of liberals as such because his early experience was with that high-minded high-speaking kind who never got anything done. That all changed the moment he met a liberal like Walter Reuther."

Jacqueline Kennedy: "He's the one I'd put my hand in the fire for."

A former associate: "You know, Bobby headed a group helping the White Fathers—the Foundation for All Africa. But Bobby's interests came first. When the Teamsters offered the foundation $300,000 to be used to help African students in this country, it had to be turned down because it might "embarrass" Bobby—and this was before he became Attorney General—so the students did without."

A Washington news analyst: "I lost respect for Bobby Kennedy when I saw that he had the rich man's habit of being ready to spend anybody's money but his own. We were trying to raise money for a new playground for the Catholic school in our parish. The idea had been Bobby's and he was pretty excited about it. But when it came to getting the dough, Bobby made it clear that he wouldn't contribute a penny. We had to drop the project."

James A. Wechsler, editor of the New York *Post*: "The longer I have known and watched Robert F. Kennedy, the more it has seemed to me that some published critiques of him should bear the warning usually associated with works of fiction: they have little resemblance to the living character I have encountered. Perhaps some who knew him at any earlier stage of his life still cling to impressions that may have had greater validity at the time. . . .

"He has what must be ineffectively described as charisma, and from the moment he arrived in New York every hack politician knew a formidable figure was at hand and that things would never quite be the same. . . . His gifts, one might say, are also his trouble. He is a restless, impatient citizen who drums his fingers on the table when he has grasped a thought before the visitor has finished the sentence. He can be harsh and abrasive when confronted by what he regards as verbal filibuster or unjust criticism. . . . To a certain degree, he is a political puritan eternally staggered by the notion that he is regarded as a hatchet man or demagogue, and his impetuous responses in such situations have defiled his portrait. He is wounded by the feeling of being misunderstood, and too often exposes the scars."

A Capitol Hill political observer: "The most frightening thing about Bobby is his total inability to feel for individuals. Beyond that small and dedicatedly loyal group which caters to his vanity, people are abstractions to him. This is what makes him seem cruel. Bobby isn't so much cruel as incapable of realizing it when he inflicts pain on others. He is unaware that he uses people, whether they be statesmen or little slum kids gathered around him to make a good picture for the TV cameras or for the news photographers."

This capacity for using people, often as a public-relations gimmick, is best exemplified by a touch football "game" staged on December 3, 1965, at the 100 block of Eye Street in the heart of a Washington Negro slum. Captains of the two teams were Bobby and Senator William Proxmire. The major spectators were reporters, photographers, and Senate office workers. The Washington *Evening Star*'s David Braaten described the scene ironically: "With a police captain, a sergeant, and two patrolmen rerouting traffic, the two senators tossed a coin, haphazardly picked a few youngsters for their teams and arranged for a rather cramped scrimmage between the parked cars lining the street. On the first play, a pass receiver crashed into a television camera assistant. On the second play, it turned out the action had taken place beyond TV camera range, and so had to be done over. After about thirty seconds' elapsed time, the game was called by mutual consent by the captains, possibly because they heard a cameraman remark that he had run out of film."

Cynical motives were also attributed to Bobby when he rounded up the parents of children going to the parochial school one of his sons attended. Bobby was troubled because the gymnasium and play facilities were inadequate. At his instigation, plans were drawn up by an architect, and the parents met once more with Bobby to find ways to finance the project—only to learn that Bobby expected them to raise all the money themselves and refused to make any contribution himself, when they turned to him for the financing, Bobby's interest in the project vanished.

Yet the fact remains that Bobby really loves children, as he has repeatedly remarked, and that his involvement in some welfare legislation is at least as much a function of that love as of political self-interest. In the welter of contradictions that bewilder both his friends and his foes, the Bobby Kennedy at play, in the context of his home, and among his friends becomes as significant a factor as those public actions which make up the bulk of this account. It was the "personal" Bobby Kennedy that the young people of East Harlem saw when he made a visit to some of the youth gangs there. The young toughs said later that he "spoke nice and had good manners." "He looked like a bop himself," a member of the Viceroy gang said. "And he sounded like he really really wanted to do something about it."

No one can deny that Bobby has gone out of his way, frequently with no publicity, to help underprivileged youth. When his family of nine children left for their Hyannis Port vacation, he opened his pool at Hickory Hill to children who would never have had a chance to swim. Two pools in Washington's slum neighborhood, closed for eleven years for lack of funds, were reopened after Bobby had solicited the necessary financing from Protestant, Catholic, and Jewish groups. But his powerful desire to do something and do it right away has often compromised his actions and made them seem suspect. It was Bobby, for example, who rammed through proposals to build a John F. Kennedy memorial playground in Washington. But by so doing, without prior assessment of the situation, he deprived Washington of the land on which a desperately needed new school was to have been built. Bobby has since moved on to other activities, and the playground is now seedy and short of funds.

The home life of the Bobby Kennedys, except for its compulsive athleticism and its obsessively competitive spirit,[1] is above reproach. Since January 1957, Bobby and his family have lived at Hickory Hill in Virginia, an estate bought from brother Jack, who found that its seven-mile remove from Washington, D.C., and the Georgetown social round was an inconvenience. A swimming pool, tennis court, and additional stables were added to contain the bouncing and abundant life of Bobby, Ethel, and their rapidly growing brood. (In 1966, there were nine.) No matter how full his schedule, Bobby tries to be home for dinner and plunges into the family life with zest, catching up on what the children have been doing, what their concerns are. When it is bedtime, the Kennedys supervise the nightly prayers of the children—the traditional "Now I lay me down to sleep" and a short verse asking the angel of God to watch over them. There is a recitation of the Lord's prayer and ten Hail Marys, followed by a reading from the Bible. The Catholicism of the Bobby Kennedys is full and ritualistic all seven days of the week.

The Kennedy children spill all over the fifteen rooms of Hickory Hill, and when they were younger could be found underfoot or entangled with each other or the furniture. They have been brought up to ignore danger and resist fear. Ethel has said of them, "Joe rode and jumped when he was four. There are risks, certainly, but you've got to let them take those risks. Kathleen has broken a leg riding, and Joe broke his skiing. Courtney broke her arm when she fell out of a tree. I want my children to have as little fear as possible, so that they'll accomplish more in life. This outweighs the chances they take." And the risks have continued. In 1965 Bobby Jr. fell from a garage roof, requiring 100 stitches on his leg. That same summer, Kathleen was thrown from her horse and suffered a concussion, contusion of the bladder, and internal bleeding. Bobby and Ethel were sailing, an hour and a half out of Sag Harbor, New York, in high seas when a Coast Guard cutter hailed their boat to inform them of Kathleen's accident. With eight-foot waves and a thirty-knot wind, the boats could not heave to—and Bobby stripped down and swam the fifty yards to the cutter. At Ethel's insistence, and after his strenuous objections, he wore a small floater around his neck when he plunged into the heavy seas.

The Kennedy children are on hand as a cheering section whenever the family and guests play their now-famous touch football.

[1] In 1963, writing *Bobby and the President,* Marquis Childs said: "Ethel has shrewdly remarked that the Kennedy achievements are not so much for the outside world to admire as they are proof to each other that they can excel in whatever they do."

In this game, Ethel is considered a champion. Her speedy, swivel-hipped broken-field running has astonished the experts. Like all the Kennedys, she enjoys the outdoor life and plays a driving game of tennis. Tomboyish, bright, and irreverent, she is more inde-pendent of spirit than any of the Kennedys—and richer. (Her late father had a controlling interest in one of the biggest privately owned companies in America, the Great Lakes Carbon Corpora-tion.) She has stood up to Bobby, which he wryly and ruefully acknowledges, with a disarmingly quick wit and a mind that seeks its own answers. She is casual, unpretentious, and given to zany spoofs. For a formal St. Patrick's Day dinner, she dressed her table with fat, green, and very live bullfrogs. (There are well over 100 animals and other pets on the premises, including a burro.) At an-other dinner, she arranged the place cards so that all the women sat at one table and all the men at another—with her.

For a time, the most discussed aspect of the Kennedy family life was the practice of dunking the guests, fully dressed, in the swim-ming pool. At one evening party, Bobby pushed Pierre Salinger, press secretary to Presidents Kennedy and Johnson, into the pool. Salinger sank to the bottom, then slowly rose, his cigar still firmly clamped between his teeth. Senator Kenneth Keating, before Bobby challenged and defeated him in New York, was also pushed into the pool. During a black-tie dinner for brother-in-law Peter Lawford, while Lester Lanin's orchestra played and Harry Belafonte enter-tained, Ethel lost her balance and fell into the pool. Presidential assistant Arthur Schlesinger Jr., along with Mrs. Spencer Davis, was pushed in after Ethel. On still another occasion, in fifty-degree weather, Ted Kennedy took a running dive into the pool and then shivered for the rest of the evening in a soaking wet dinner jacket.

Barry Goldwater could remark, "When Bobby Kennedy sends out invitations for a formal dinner, they should read 'black tie and snorkel.'" But the spectacle of an Attorney General and other im-portant officers of the government disporting themselves like twelve-year-olds—and the conspicuous waste of expensive clothing—did not sit well with many people. There were, in fact, some representations from the diplomatic corps to the Secretary of State on the effect abroad of Bobby's aquatic entertainments. The image was wrong—and these highjinks had come to a halt long before the death of President Kennedy. But other less spectacular though equally child-ish games continued—kick-the-can or hide-and-seek—with all guests required, on pain of ostracism, to participate. When Robert Frost, an octogenarian, came to dinner, the Kennedys and their guests played a more sedate game—writing poems. The famous poet's verses, Ethel said, "were slightly better than ours."

Kennedy fun is not always spontaneous. Pat Anderson, writing of his days in the Justice Department under Bobby, was appalled by the preparations for some of these gatherings. In *Esquire* he wrote:

> "Although I have never attended a party at Hickory Hill, I some-times shared his guests' thrill vicariously as I helped Dave Hackett write the poems and paint the posters that played such a vital part in Kennedy merry-making. I remember one night helping Hackett rewrite a long poem which celebrated a yachting trip he had taken with Bob and Ted. The gist of the poem was simply that Robert Kennedy was a hell of a fellow. All the other party props—the posters and the funny games—had the same moral. I could not understand a man who would let his closest friends pay homage to him, or friends who would do such a thing, or people who needed props and poems to have a party. Perhaps it is pertinent to remember that Fitzgerald is usually misquoted. He did not say the 'rich' are different from you and me; he said the 'very rich.' I have friends who are rich, but the Kennedys are very rich and perhaps that is the difference. I know no better explanation."

The self-consciousness of the poems and slogans manifested itself in another way. The Kennedys, both Bobby and Ethel, have made no bones of what they consider their "lowbrow" tastes. ("I like films such as *South Pacific,* shows such as *My Fair Lady,* and books such as *The King Must Die,*" Ethel once said. "But *On the Beach,* I don't like. I like happy, jolly things. We do not feel easy in the company of highbrows and we do not understand the first thing about music.") At the same time, Bobby has compensated for this "cultural" lack by asking his ghost writers to salt his speeches with scholarly or literary quotations and bits of verse. But in the middlebrow intellectualism of the New Frontier, the Robert Kennedys felt a little out of it. Their answer to the problem was to set up regular seminars at Hickory Hill to which the Kennedy Administration's academic contingent was invited seriatim to lecture and otherwise disseminate culture. These seminars, competing with more extrovert activities, did not last very long.

But the desire to be on a par with the intellectuals—and even to beat them in their own field of endeavor—has led Bobby to exploit the speed-reading so favored on the New Frontier by gulping down the kind of books which President Kennedy laid aside in favor of Ian Fleming's James Bond stories—*John Quincy Adams and the Foundations of American Foreign Policy, Conquistadors in North American History,* and *Fifteen Decisive Battles of the World.* But even speed-reading consumed hours, and, as Ethel remarked, "He hates to waste time." Therefore, Bobby wired his bathroom for sound, and he now listens to long-playing records of Shakespeare's plays while he showers and shaves.

If he embraces an idea or a policy, he gives it a bear hug and holds it close until it is driven out by something else. His attitude toward the civil rights movement was hardly sympathetic until the movement became politically expedient. Then Bobby went all the way. He resigned from Washington's Metropolitan Club, the mecca of the Capital's status-oriented, because it did not accept Negroes and frowned on members who invited Negroes to its stately precincts. And he began inviting Negroes—the preeminent of their race, to be sure—to his home. There was, moreover, some stir when Ethel went out to dinner with Rafer Johnson, the Olympic decathlon champion and one of the country's outstanding Negro athletes. In the highly social "horse country" of McLean, Virginia, where the Kennedys live, this raised eyebrows—not because there was the slightest hint of impropriety but simply because it seemed like an ostentatious display of "civil rights" zeal.

This kind of excessive devotion has been noted in other areas. As one of the leaders of the New Frontier's anti-anti-Communist faction, Bobby set out to undo the whole security structure of the federal Establishment. In part this was ideological, based on the conviction that domestic Communism was no threat and that the rights of individuals subject to loyalty security checks were being abridged. It was also personal, particularly where the State Department was concerned. A number of Kennedy appointees had received gravely adverse reports from the security division, and from its conscientious chief, Otto Otepka. Otepka refused to withdrawn his reports, pointing out that the Attorney General could overrule them but that his duty as security chief compelled a scrupulous accounting of every employee. When a high-ranking State Department official discovered that he was under investigation, he complained to John F. Reilly, the Deputy Assistant Secretary for Security. Reilly called Bobby, and Otepka was placed under Justice Department surveillance—though his only "crime" was the meticulous application of department regulations. Taps were placed on Otepka's phone, his locked files were searched, and eventually he was removed—all under the personal order of Bobby Kennedy.

Some have seen a key to his character in his way of playing touch football. That he plays rough is well known. But he is also not above cheating, if defeat faces him. Friends who have been drafted to play say that he will frequently refuse to count a touchdown of an opposing team by "changing" the rules or arguing violently that the goal line set before the game is really somewhere else. Good sportsmanship, certainly one of the attributes of the rugged life he preaches, never enters into any consideration with him. He will rig the teams so that his is overwhelmingly superior, then boast of his "victories." More important in gauging Bobby is his utter lack of feeling for the host-guest relationship when he invites friends and acquaintances to Hickory Hill. They must all do exactly as *he* says, play the games *he* wants to play, run or jump or sit or stand as *he* orders. If they refuse, then they are treated with scorn or roughly hazed.

Even his dog Brumus, famous for the free rein he was given in the Justice Department during Bobby's Attorney Generalship days, is treated better than important guests. During meals, he is given the run of the dining room. With no admonition from Bobby, Brumus will demand food of the guests and, if this is ignored, will simply help himself, reaching into a plate with his paw for whatever it is that attracts his whim and appetite. "Once was enough for me," a visitor to Hickory Hill said. "That damned dog was all over me, and Bobby seemed to think that my objections were pretty stuffy if not downright unmannerly. Brumus got most of my meal and left paw marks all over my clothes." In any other household the dog would have been banished. But Bobby finds it difficult to understand or sympathize with those who do not accept his standards of behavior or his way of life. The ethics of respecting the sensibilities of others were never instilled in him.

This hardly matches Bobby's much-cited code of morality. In fact, his reputation for the Puritan approach to public and private morals was on a number of occasions compromised, though Bobby angrily and self-righteously turned on those who made the point. For example, at the time that he was under the most pressure from civil rights groups, and demanding of others that they must live like Caesar's wife, Bobby allowed the National Insurance Association (originally the National Negro Association), a group of individuals representing small Negro insurance companies, to pick up his bill at the famous Beverly Hills Hotel in California. His friendship with Marilyn Monroe, and the long-distance phone calls she made to him, were the subject of much whispered surmise in the movie colony and in Washington. It did not come out into the open until *Esquire,* in its July 1966 issue, published a revealing piece about Joe DiMaggio, Marilyn's ex-husband, which tossed into the hopper of public discussion one cryptic and disturbing sentence:

"[DiMaggio] no longer speaks to his onetime friend, Frank Sinatra, who had befriended Marilyn in her final years, and he also is cool to Dean Martin and Peter Lawford and Lawford's former wife, Pat [Kennedy], who once gave a party at which she introduced Marilyn Monroe to Robert Kennedy, and the two of them danced often that night, Joe heard, and he did not take it well."

Lawford and Dean Martin were members of the famous Sinatra "Rat Pack" which figured so prominently in the annals of the New Frontier—and the Washington press corps put two and two together, probably coming up with five, as all purveyors of gossip are likely to do. But even the suspicion of unwarranted interest somehow cast a shadow on Bobby's moralizing strictures.

In California, Bobby's reputation for Catholic piety was somewhat bruised when he engaged in debate with Monsignor Daniel J. Keenan over the problems of migratory labor. As a member of a Senate subcommittee investigating conditions in California vineyards, Bobby advocated strict unionism. Father Keenan argued that the answer was not that simple. "The problem," he said, "is to know how the Union is to represent people who are here today and gone tomorrow." Bobby wanted a solution *now,* and left the priest with the observation: "We are going to have to pray for you on Sunday."

On the other hand, Bobby can demonstrate an almost superstitious fear of going beyond the strict bounds of his religious practices. In Tokyo, during his 1962 Far East journey, he visited a Buddhist temple with Ambassador Edwin O. Reischauer. It is customary to burn incense sticks on these occasions, but Bobby demurred.

"What will it mean if I do this?" he asked Reischauer.

"You're just showing respect," the ambassador answered.

"But won't it look as if I'm praying to Buddha?" Bobby asked.

"Of course not," Reischauer told him.

Bobby burned the incense, but with a worried aside to Reischauer: "If I get into trouble for this . . ."

Given as he is to the short, jabbing answer, Bobby still seeks the universal love of his fellows. He can say, "I am so well aware of being disliked by many that it no longer surprises or upsets me. I no longer care." But he feels compelled to explain that dislike in terms that fit in with his vision of himself as a knight rescuing the enslaved. "I have been too closely involved in too many struggles, too many battles," he has argued. "But there are also people who do like me. They elected me, did they not? The poorer people like me. Negroes and Puerto Ricans, for instance. The deprived, if you like. They are for me, I know. For me also are the people who understood President Kennedy, our Administration during those two and a half years, and I did not expect to find so many of them. I did not expect them to be in the greater number. So let the others say whatever they like. Oh, I know what they are saying about me."

And so he does, to a remarkable extent. He has hardly slowed down, however, or softened his aggressiveness to meet the criticisms of those who hate him or fear him. Fletcher Knebel's description, written before John F. Kennedy's assassination, still fits him. "Thus Bobby moves upward and onward. He fidgets endlessly as he goes, swinging his glasses, gesturing with finger and thumb, perching on table tops, window ledges and sofa backs, propping feet on the desk, squatting on his haunches, wrenching his tie loose and kicking table legs."

In the strange and complex world of politics, Bobby Kennedy remains always the physical man, the protagonist of action, the perpetually casual juvenile who suddenly relinquishes the stage to the icy activist. Fascinating and bewildering, frustrating to those who cannot match the power that riches and determination give him, he commands the adulation of those who see him from a distance and angers those who must deal with him—whether they be Senators, Presidents, or newspapermen. Sullen, withdrawn, or boisterously involved, manic or depressive, he is a fixture on the political scene, a constant threat to those who stand between him and his ambition, and superbly aware that there is always room at the top. Until the hammer of time has broken open the locked chest of his real personality, he will be the focus and the locus of conjectures. But the test of the man and the gauge of his potential for good or evil in the nation's history are to be found in those observable acts which have made up his public life.

2

——◆◄◆►◆——

As the Twig Is Bent?

IN the syllabus of prejudice, there are three kinds of Irish: shanty, lace-curtain, and whisky-in-the-house-although-no-one-is sick. Each category has its built-in needle, for no member of this pugnacious, whimsical, ambitious, and endearing group is too far from the days when only a ghetto welcomed his forebears to American soil. The story of the Irish immigration, like the story of every immigration that enriched this country, is both shameful and inspiring. It is shameful in the treatment accorded to those enterprising enough to pay their $20 steerage passage and to accept the horrors entailed in reaching a growing empire that needed their muscle and their determination as much as they needed the economic and political opportunity that an opening continent offered. It was inspiring because the Irish—and the Italians and the Jews, to name but three of the ethnic groups which made America their own—rose from the ghetto to place and influence, but more important, to acceptance by a predominantly Anglo-Saxon culture.

Time and the river of Irish misfortune washed up Patrick Kennedy on the crowded shore of Noddle's Island in East Boston during that year of revolution and frustration, 1848, when modern Europe was born. A blighted potato crop and its concomitant famine drove the Irish peasantry to America. In addition to famine, cholera, typhus, and relapsing fever struck a nation whose chronic poverty had starved everything but its sense of drama and the dramatic and emotional Irish temperament. After six weeks in the hold of a transatlantic vessel, a journey that would have shocked any self-respecting cattleman, Patrick Kennedy found himself in a new country where conditions for the immigrant were stark and traumatic. A commission investigating conditions in Boston's Irish ghetto turned the light of compassion on what it saw. Its account understated the case.

"This whole district," the Committee of Internal Health reported in 1849, "is a perfect hive of human beings, without comforts and mostly without common necessities; in many cases huddled together like brutes, without regard to sex or age, or sense of decency; grown men and women sleeping together in the same apartment, and sometimes wife and husband, brothers and sisters in the same bed. Under such circumstances, self-respect, forethought, all high and noble virtues soon die out, and sullen indifference and despair, or disorder, intemperance and utter degradation reign supreme." But the New World, for all its cruelty and disdain, gave the Irish two necessities which they had fled from Ireland to find—work and food. Alien to the Bostonians, the Irish could piece together the remnants of their own culture and look ahead with hope to a day when life would give them more than their daily bread, their drink of whisky, and the social blandishments of the corner saloon. Sentiment, Mother Machreeism, and violence went hand in hand. If they were lucky, four of every ten children they bore would live beyond the age of five and eventually became part of a labor market which the Yankee Brahmins despised but used.

Patrick Kennedy lived frugally, but at thirty-five he was dead, no richer than he had been when he landed in Boston. He left a wife, three daughters, and a son to fend for themselves in the asphalt wilderness of the Irish ghetto. The son, Patrick Joseph Kennedy, took the first steps out of the anonymous servitude of his people when, as a young man, he achieved the status of saloonkeeper. The times were propitious. Industry, numbers, and a natural genius for politics were giving the Irish in Boston and New York the kind of power which in a few decades would place in their hands the control of big-city machines and open the doors to advancement and eminence in every field of American life. The Democratic party, challenging the seemingly permanent hold of the Protestant Establishment on the nation's political life, could absorb the Irish vote and use it as the fulcrum for toppling the entrenched owners of privilege.

In this process, the saloonkeeper had a natural claim to political influence. His premises were not only a neighborhood club and a place of refuge from the grimness of slum life. It was also the meeting place of those running for office, and the equivalent of the smoke-filled rooms in which the better-heeled politicians made their deals and organized their election campaigns. The saloonkeeper himself was a combination banker, marriage counselor, adviser, and arbiter. He ran an employment agency for those looking for work and looked after the economic welfare of those who ran out of money between paydays or when there were no jobs to be found. A reserved man, his dignity enhanced by the curled mustache of his profession, Patrick J. Kennedy ran a good saloon. He was respected by those who frequented his establishment, and this respect served to make him a power in the rough-and-tumble politics of East Boston.

The formula was not original. Other Irish saloonkeepers in the cities of the Northeast were similarly basing their political fortunes on the gratitude of voters who saw little virtue in the austere practices of the ruling class about them. The exercise of the franchise was to them a gesture of no value, and if "P.J."—or his equivalent in New York's Tammany Hall or the cities of northern New Jersey— needed their votes, they gave them gladly in return for the far more tangible favor of a Christmas turkey, a bucket of coal or a helping hand when fate was unreasonable. At a later time, this implementation of political reality would fall before the reformer, who saw life in idealistic terms. Yet the politician of East or South Boston may have done more for his people than those who spoke grandiosely for *the* people. In his own way, Patrick Joseph Kennedy was laying the groundwork for a vastly augmented welfarism in which the White House replaced the corner saloon. Another Kennedy would be the benefactor of this system, but it would be the cream of all jests that no one would ponder its genesis.

Patrick Joseph Kennedy, standing behind his bar, did not philosophize on the uses of patronage and power. By that inadvertence which is the father of decision, he simply profited from what had come naturally to him. More than comfortable majorities reaffirmed him, and he was elected to the state House of Representatives, to the state Senate, and to the inner group which manipulated Boston by dictating how the Irish vote would go. The power of political appointment, of contracts granted or withheld, of jobs and petty graft —all these were in the hands of "P.J." and his associates. What they took from Boston, they gave to their own. By the time Patrick Joseph Kennedy married his Irish bride, he was well on the way to holding prime political power in his hands.

But power is never enough for those who build upward from low estate. Boston could elect an Irish mayor, could surrender its Yankee traditions and its boast of Athenian intellectuality. Irish laborers could challenge the business leaders who had once conducted their affairs with the same high-minded chicanery as their British cousins. But looming over this babble of Irish success were Harvard Yard, the quiet streets of Cambridge, and a whole world of social esteem that found its expression in the least pretentious of Boston's philosophers. Even brash cities like New York, never claiming the intellectual eminence of Boston, continued to look down their noses at the "micks"—a word that still echoes where prejudice resides. No matter how high the Irish swung, they could not escape a stereotype that ranged from Clancy the Cop to the Jimmy Cagney gangster. All the symbols of big-city corruption were inextricably associated with the Irish, even when the last dramatic leader of Tammany Hall was a man named Carmine De Sapio.

This is the backdrop against which the tragicomedy of the Kennedy clan must be played. This Irish heritage affected every protagonist in a story that is bound to become an American epic, from Patrick Joseph to Robert Francis. It explains why Bobby Kennedy leans so heavily on the stereotypes of Irish pugnacity, and why John Fitzgerald Kennedy molded himself into the perfect image of the Boston-cum-Harvard product, right down to the ironic manner, the detached approach, and the delicately concealed arrogance. It is the key to the Kennedy love of money and the Kennedy willingness to spend it to achieve the acceptance in American society that only a President can know.

Joseph Patrick Kennedy, first-born of P.J., grew up in an atmosphere of steadily increasing affluence. Minor civic offices came to the one-time saloonkeeper and ward politician, and his son was always aware that elections were won by a combination of political muscle and polling-place fraud. Joe Kennedy would much later recall the visit of two ward-heelers who boasted: "Pat, we voted one hundred twenty-eight times today." P.J., then an election commissioner, frankly showed his pleasure. For him, competition was the soul of virtue—competition for its own sake. His friends worked and struggled to escape the clutch of necessity. Joe challenged them from the start in their money-making endeavors because that was his nature. At every turn of his life, zest for acquiring and accumulating the coin of the realm was Joe Kennedy's distinguishing characteristic. The finer ethical points of why and how never entered his mind.

But it is a tribute both to Joe Kennedy and to his father that other values were respected. "The measure of a man's success in life is not the money he's made," Joe Kennedy has said. "It's the kind of family he has raised." This copybook maxim had deeper meaning than its hearts-and-flowers overtones might indicate. The family was the core of the Kennedy life, and wherever the family's sons and daughters ventured—Boston Latin School, Harvard, or the Democratic party— that, too, was invested with the same sense of loyalty. The desire to "arrive" socially was personal, but it never overlooked the major objective of pulling up by main force the entire Kennedy family—a lesson never lost to Bobby.

The importance of family to the Kennedys must be set in the context of Joseph P. Kennedy's idea of its organization. From childhood on, he had conceived of the Kennedys as living in a fortified city, holding off the rest of the world. The government of this entrenched unit was authoritarian and hierarchical, military in its chain of command, and brooking no dissension. In the years to come, Jack Kennedy might mutter a feeble defiance—as he did when the pressures from outside called for an open break with Senator Joe McCarthy. But in the main, the rebellions were few and of little consequence. The hierarchical principle was rigidly enforced. After Joe's marriage to Rose Fitzgerald had produced four sons, the male pecking order was clearly established. Joe Jr. was the focus of his father's ambition, with the American Presidency openly earmarked for him. After Joe's tragic death in World War II, the succession was established in Jack, with Bobby and Ted forced back into the wings until the stage of Kennedy history had been cleared. The Kennedy daughters formed a kind of female enclave of secondary note.

Joe Kennedy's decision to marry Rose Fitzgerald was, in itself, corroboration of his determination always to reach high. For all his increasing affluence and the mark he made on Boston businessmen by becoming at twenty-five the city's youngest bank president, Joe still had to erase the saloonkeeping past of his father from his social-climbing escutcheon. Rose, however, was the daughter of Mayor John Fitzgerald, the "Honey Fitz" of Boston's political legend. Given to dancing jigs on table tops and singing "Sweet Adeline" at public functions, he had the affection of Boston's mixed Yankee and Irish population. Even after Congress had refused to seat him because of irregularities in his election, Honey Fitz considered himself a good many cuts above the Kennedys. In keeping with his position, Fitzgerald had sent his daughter abroad for the kind of "finishing" which Joe Kennedy never got from Harvard. That the marriage was performed by William Cardinal O'Connell is testimony of the status enjoyed by the Fitzgeralds.

For all his talk about family, it was not Joe Kennedy who brought up the children. He was busily at work making the fortune which allowed him to settle something like $10,000,000 on each of his children. Rose Kennedy, on the other hand, attended to all the details of her children's lives—down to keeping a card file on each one. She did not consider it any kind of sacrifice to devote most of her time to their upbringing. The impact of her personality was seen most on Jack, but there is no doubt that the domineering characteristics of Joe Jr. and the abrasive personality of Bobby were modified by her attention. "I made it a point each day to take them into church for a visit," she would later tell an interviewer. "I wanted them to form a habit of making God and religion a part of their daily lives, not something to be reserved for Sundays."

In determining the course of their lives, however, Rose Kennedy was not the dominant influence. She could not even have her way about the schools they attended. In the patriarchal system that Joe Kennedy imposed, it was well and good that the daughters should attend Catholic schools. But Kennedy wanted his sons to have the kind of background which would open to them the doors that were closed to him when he attended Harvard. The family lived in Protestant Brookline and the boys attended Dexter School, which had till then admitted few if any Catholics.

Upbringing was by example. "If you bring up the older children so they do things in a good way, and give them a lot of attention, the younger ones are great imitators and will follow the older ones' example," Rose once said. Though she was by nature gentle, she could be strict. "I think when children are little, physical punishment is a good thing. I used to paddle them with a ruler occasionally because at that age that's all they understand. As they get older, you can reason with them and tell them why you ask them to do what they should do." If discipline was her responsibility, so too was making sure that they understood the value of money. The allowances they received were minuscule, and this left its mark on Bobby, who has always been tight-fisted. But early in life, Bobby discovered that his father was a "soft touch"—at least to his young son—and when the well ran dry, Joe Sr. refilled it.

In the upbringing of the Kennedy children, another important influence was Joe Jr. "He was patient and gentle with the small ones," Richard Whalen wrote in *The Founding Father*, "a good athlete who became their hero as he taught them to throw a ball, ride a bicycle, and sail a boat. But with the slight, willowy Jack, the only rival for his throne, he was a severe taskmaster and a taunting bully. They fought frequently, the young children cowering in terror upstairs as their brothers wrestled on the first floor. The fights usually ended with Jack pinned and humiliated." This may be another explanation for the tremendous differences between Jack and Bobby. In his boyhood, certainly, Bobby's hero was Joe Jr., not Jack. And he patterned his way of life on his brother Joe's, seeking in athletics and in personal competition to duplicate a record on field and in classroom which none of the other Kennedy children was able to match.

In Robert Francis Kennedy's early life and times—from the moment he was born, on November 20, 1925, in the moderately rich environs of Brookline, Massachusetts, to his entrance into the world of affairs—temper and compulsion marked his existence. The compulsion of a physically small boy to be what he was not, of a child of moderate intellectual powers to excel in the classroom, and the temper born of frustration that manifests itself in violence and withdrawal—these were all clearly in his character. To the insecurity that these engendered in him was added the instability of an academic life with no roots and no continuity. He moved in and out of twelve schools in getting his education, and in none of them did he make a real mark as student, athlete, or leader of his fellows.

Dark, irascible, and secretive in his early years, with those flashes of warmth and deprecation which today endear him to some, Bobby lived always in the shadow of his self-confident and successful oldest brother and the ironic, almost cynical, charm of Jack. Until he was superseded by the birth of Teddy, Bobby held center stage with his mother. From her, he learned to find his close associates among those less privileged. She had preached this to all her children. "I wanted them to know all groups of children so that they would see that a chauffeur's son or a mechanic's son is sometimes smarter than they are," Rose Kennedy once said. But for Bobby, the lesson was not in democracy. The effect of this training was, perhaps, just the opposite, but it satisfied a need and furnished an outlet. With the less privileged, he did not need to compensate for his diminutive size and his lack of polish.

The single constant in Bobby's unfocused life was the family interest in politics. Introducing a collection of his public speeches as Attorney General, Bobby would write, "As far back as I can remember, politics was taken with special favor and relish in our house." His first recollection of his family's "intense interest in public affairs" goes back to the 1936 Presidential election, just before he turned eleven. Franklin Roosevelt was running for a second term against Governor Alf Landon of Kansas, one of the few survivors of the 1932 Democratic landslide. Some of the President's earlier supporters, like James Warburg, wrote books to express their complete disenchantment with the President and with his 180-degree turn from free enterprise to Keynesian statism. Joe Kennedy, who had been of great help in fund-raising for the first Roosevelt campaign, steadfastly remained a New Dealer. A broadside he wrote, *I'm for Roosevelt,* has the bittersweet taste of irony for those who saw Joe Kennedy gravitate toward the right and cultivate the friendship of conservatives such as Herbert Hoover, the target of so much New Deal vituperation.

"I have no political ambitions for myself or for my children," Joe Kennedy said in that germinal year, "and I put down these few thoughts about our President, conscious only of my concern as a father for the future of his family and my anxiety as a citizen that the facts about the President's philosophy not be lost in a fog of unworthy emotion." What that unworthy emotion might have been, it is hard to say. What he stood for corroborates John F. Kennedy's assertion that his father considered businessmen "sons of bitches." "You can't tell the public to go to hell any more," Joe Sr. said in an interview when his book appeared. "Fifty men have run America, and that's a high figure. The rest of America is demanding its share of the game and they'll get it." The similarity between these sentiments and those expressed by Bobby to cheering groups of leftist students is striking.

Whatever some may have said about him, Joe Sr. was never a real part of that conservative group which broke with Roosevelt over the New Deal's more radical actions. His political thought—a significant influence on Bobby—tended toward the Populist, and emotionally he never overcame his deep resentment at America's ruling class or forgot that as an Irish Catholic at Harvard he was not invited to join the clubs which young men of less wealth and position found open to them. Even in the matter of his isolationism, interpreted by a hostile press as a manifestation of anti-Semitism and/or pro-Nazism, it could be said that, like other Irish-Americans, rather than loving the Germans, he hated the British. His opposition to American intervention in the war, and the reasoning behind it, was as tortured as Bobby's rationalization in approving the shipment of blood to the Communist Vietcong at a time when Americans were dying in Vietnam.

Joe Kennedy contributed to the myth of his conservatism by describing himself in the 1932 report of the Harvard class of 1912 as a "capitalist"—a dig of questionable humor at his Alma Mater in the terrible Depression years, when to claim employment was distinction enough in certain circles. But this can be balanced by his permament contribution to the ideological thinking of his sons—and there-fore of the country: a summer's study each for Joe Jr. and Jack under the socialist, and then determinedly fellow-traveling, Professor Har-old Laski at the left-leaning London School of Economics. A persua-sive exponent of all that runs counter to classical political and eco-nomic thinking, Laski was responsible for planting in Jack those ideas which later flowered in the New Frontier. And since Bobby came so strongly under his brother's intellectual influence, Joe Sr.'s seemingly quixotic gesture—justified by him as nothing more than giving his sons a chance to "learn about the world"—had sorry con-sequences for the United States.

Laski's socialism was the background music which echoed in the subconscious thinking of the Kennedy sons. The developing theme was more traditional. Moving onward and upward from upper-mid-dle-class Brookline, Joe Sr., already a very rich man, decided that his family would do better in New York than in Boston. "Boston," he said, "is a good city to come from, not a good city to go to. If you want to make money, go where the money is." [1] And if you want political influence, the same applies. In both instances, the place for him was New York, the world's greatest money market, the New York which can buy and sell political favor with the dollars that Wall Street produces. There were other reasons for the move. Joe Sr. wanted his children to grow up without the self-consciousness attached to the Boston Irish. He was determined that they should adopt the man-ners of the Protestant world. With the flamboyance that was almost a trademark, he packed the Kennedys into a private railroad car and shifted his base to the greener pastures of Riverdale, then a placid New York suburb of expensive homes, even more expensive schools, and open space for the rich and the privileged. There, for a time, the Kennedys settled.

Nick Thimmesch and William Johnson, writers for *Time*, have described in *Robert Kennedy at 40* what his life was like in its super-ficial aspects then: "He was a Cub Scout, a knob-kneed terror at sports, an undistinguished scholar, a reasonably profitable breeder of white rabbits in a tool shed (he opened his first bank account with the proceeds) , and the owner of a beloved pig named Porky. He once broke a toe when it was crushed beneath an old radiator that he had been forbidden to play with and he hopped about in silent agony for an hour before he dared to tell his parents of the incident. He

[1] Speaking in South Africa, Bobby told an audience of students: "My father left Boston, Massachusetts, because of the signs on the wall that said, 'No Irish Need Apply.' "

gashed his head against a heavy table when he made a blind, furious charge at his sister Eunice. He had a brief siege of pneumonia that was more irritating than critical because it came at the height of the swimming season."

This Penrodish once-over-lightly sketch could apply to almost any boy brought up in the America of that time. But it does not take into account his preoccupation with religion; his mother thought for a while that he had a "vocation" and that he would become a priest. So rigorous was his Catholicism that, in 1944, he fought strongly within the family conclave against the marriage of his sister Kathleen to the Protestant Marquess of Huntington. Like many of the older Irish, he showed from a very early age a Puritanical streak and an intolerance of human frailty, particularly in sexual conduct. Surrounded by five sisters—he was the youngest son until the birth of Teddy—Bobby had to fight hard against petticoat influence. To prove that he was not a sissy, he had to demonstrate his toughness, to prove his physical courage at every turn.

Much later in Bobby's life, Joe Sr. could say, "Bobby has always had a lot of moxie and guts. I doubt if Jack ever makes any enemies. But Bobby might make some. He's tough. Not that Jack isn't just as courageous, but Bobby feels more strongly for or against people than Jack does—just as I do." A sympathetic biographer was able to note as well that young Bobby tried the hardest and accomplished the least. "Both parents are convinced that Robert's personality was influenced by the gap of years dividing him from his older brothers and the fact that he had a difficult time keeping up with them. . . . Among the four Kennedy boys, Robert was the smallest, the one with the poorest physical coordination and the one who, until he reached adulthood, showed the least interest in intellectual pursuits." He himself has said: "I dropped everything. I always fell down. I always bumped my nose or my head." Unlike his brothers, who made it a point to conform sartorially, he registered his protest by sloppiness. "Bobby never had much concern about his clothes," his mother said. "He would appear on dress-up occasions wearing a coat of one color and trousers of another."

That sloppiness continued into his adult years, when he was Attorney General of the United States. At all but the most formal occasions, he roamed the corridors of the Justice Department in his shirtsleeves, his necktie loose, his sleeves rolled up, his trousers wrinkled—as if he had just been aroused from a heavy postprandial nap. In those years of the Kennedy Era, when the Brooks Brothers buttoned-down oxford shirt ceased to be worn by the White House "in" group, Bobby persisted in the Ivy League style, to the ironic disdain of his brother. "Bobby doesn't know any better," Jack said.

Even as a child, Bobby had the capacity for hatred that his father found so endearing. With bulldog determination, he insisted on proving a point at no matter what cost. He chose to learn to swim at the age of four by throwing himself repeatedly into the cold water of Nantucket Sound from the family sailboat, *Tenovus*, spluttering angrily each time Joe Jr. fished him out. When Joe Sr. took him out to teach him how to sail, Bobby went at it grimly, as if his life depended on it. Yet he could easily drop a project with no thought to cost or consequence. His essay into the American boy's traditional world of magazine salesmanship is a case in point. Like millions of his contemporaries, he was intrigued by the premiums which the Curtis Publishing Company dangled before small boys, and he set out each day from his Bronxville house—a successor to the Riverdale place—pedaling from home to home and pleading for subscriptions or individual sales of *The Saturday Evening Post* and the *Ladies' Home Journal*. His persuasive powers were small, and sales were not sufficient to sustain his interest. Putting aside the bicycle, Bobby took to delivering his magazines in the family Rolls-Royce, driven in splendor by a uniformed chauffeur. But when this, too, became onerous, he sent the chauffeur out alone to make the deliveries. In time, Bobby simply allowed the magazines to pile up in his room, undelivered. There is no record of what was done with them or who footed the bill for this unsuccessful venture in individual enterprise.

Very little has been said or written about Robert Kennedy's residence in New York's more fashionable suburbs. Joe Sr. was away a good deal of the time, amassing the family fortune. These were the years when Joe Kennedy was spending most of his time in Hollywood, making movies and millions. In New York, he was busy in the stock market, wheeling and dealing in stock options and drawing more in weekly salary from his various enterprises than many Americans made in a year. Bobby's up-bringing was very much in Rose Kennedy's hands, and though she made it a point to have her meals with him and to spank him, which she did frequently, he was usually in the charge of governesses and maids. The move from Riverdale to Bronxville was one more uprooting in an already uprooted life. It gave the Kennedys more room and more status. But the $250,000 mansion on Pondville Road, with its five acres of manicured lawn and garden, was more impersonal than homelike. "Hell," said Joe Sr.'s right-hand man, Eddie Moore, when he picked it out, "Kennedy doesn't want a residence; he wants a hotel."

The first real home for Bobby—and the only one until he moved into Hickory Hill in Virginia after his marriage—was "Happy Holiday," a fifteen-room white frame house in Hyannis Port which his father bought in 1928. Two and a half acres of lawn falling gently to beach and ocean, it was *the* place that all the Kennedys returned to. In time, Jack and Bobby would have houses of their own in what came to be known as the "Kennedy compound," and the family practice of strenuous sports and roughhouse touch football began there. Some years later, Joe Sr. bought still another house in Palm Beach, paying $1,000,000 for it, but for Bobby it never had the appeal of Hyannis Port.

Bobby's early years, in fact, do not lend themselves to biographical treatment. They were quiet and in-turned years in which his activities and his personality were merely adjuncts to the social life and times of Jack and Joe Jr., then attending the Riverdale School. Bobby went to parochial schools, marking time and making an undistinguished record. He was linked to a burgeoning social consciousness, which may be more hindsight than anything else. The upheavals of the Thirties and the economic chaos which resulted from them, he once noted, "contrasted with our experiences. We lived in the suburbs of New York and attended school there until we went to England. We spent our summers in Cape Cod. But it was impossible for even a child of my years not to see the contrast between the good fortune of my family and the problems and difficulties which befell other families through no fault of their own." He would return to this theme when discussing a brief term of employment with the Columbia Trust Company, a Boston bank owned by his father. It was his job to collect rents from slum tenants in East Boston, his first look at this side of life—the overcrowded rooms, the dirt, the squalor—and it further propelled him toward the statism which today dominates his political philosophy.

In 1938, Bobby's world of Cape Cod, Boston, and Bronxville suddenly expanded to include an ocean and a foreign country. In that year, his father was appointed President Roosevelt's Ambassador to the Court of St. James's, the highest diplomatic post that the United States could then bestow. Joe Kennedy's experience in government had been confined to such important but domestically oriented positions as chairman of the newly created Securities and Exchange Commission and the Maritime Commission. But he had raised substantial sums in the 1936 campaign and had helped break down at least some of the opposition to the New Deal in the financial and business community. Though one so Irish in thinking and background as Joe Kennedy seemed an odd ambassador to send to England, Roosevelt had his reasons—the most important being that he hoped to shake the British loose from their supercilious acceptance of the United States by giving them a tough antagonist. Or perhaps, as some suggested then, it was just one more of the President's pixieish gestures. In reality, there was no need for this whimsical gesture. Insecure and groping for a solution to the problem of Nazi aggression, the British were anxiously seeking America's friendship. Another factor entered into the new official cordiality: Neville Chamberlain was Prime Minister, and his views on preserving the peace coincided with Kennedy's: Don't fight.

From the start, Joseph P. Kennedy made news. He welcomed the informal visits of newspapermen to the thirty-six-room mansion which housed the United States embassy. Like the parody of an American tycoon, he propped his feet up on the desk and sounded off on America and the world. He refused to wear knee breeches when presented to the Court, and made more headlines. His report to the press on his first audience with King George VI violated all protocol, since these royal meetings are never publicized, but there were no unpleasant repercussions. When seven of the nine children arrived with Rose Kennedy, the press went on another splurge of stories, cartoons, and friendly jokes about the family. "There were pictures other than those of the Kennedys," the Associated Press reported, "but for sheer photographic space they beat the field ten to one." This honeymoon lost some of its ardor when Joe Kennedy began expressing his own opinion on United States participation in the war that was just around the corner. He proclaimed a belief in nonintervention as the wisest course for America. When he joined the get-togethers of Lady Astor, he was tagged immediately as a member of the Cliveden Set, Britain's label for the appeasers.

What suffered most, however, was Joe Kennedy's popularity at home. The interventionists, wanting him removed, by direct charge and by imputation accused him of being a fascist, an anti-Semite, and a Hitler-lover. Nothing was done by the Roosevelt Administration to defend Kennedy; in fact, certain Cabinet members joined in the campaign to tar and feather the ambassador to Britain. This smear, based on half-truths, conjecture, and a scattering of fact, attached it-

self to the Kennedy boys, who worked that much harder in their ma-
turer years to "prove" their freedom from Joe Sr.'s presumed ideological taint.

For the first time in their lives, the Kennedy boys were plunged
into world history. They fully shared Joe Kennedy's suspicions of
Britain and his conviction that the United States should remain out
of what he saw as Europe's private war. Following his bent, Jack
wrote *Why England Slept*—a "typical undergraduate effort," according to John MacGregor Burns, and a best-seller by virtue of Joe
Sr.'s influence and the help of powerful friends such as Henry Luce,
the publisher of *Time*—urging that the best way to fight Hitler was
to "make our democracy work." (This supine attitude toward the
struggle against tyranny has since been paraphrased by Bobby Kennedy in his justification of an appeasement line in Vietnam.) Joe Jr.
made his break with Franklin Roosevelt's foreign policy by voting at
the 1940 Democratic National Convention for the nomination of
James A. Farley. Bobby's affirmation of the family consensus was
more direct: in fist fights with his British classmates, he defended
America's role, as against England's, in winning the First World War.
The dinner-table monologues of Joe Sr., to which Bobby could contribute little, continued to furnish the family with its ideological
bread and salt.

Bobby's intransigence and the unbending nature of his Catholic
faith continued in those London years. In his biography of John F.
Kennedy, Victor Lasky wrote: "It is part of the family legend that
when Joseph Sr. was Ambassador, Bob was sent to a Protestant school
where chapel was compulsory. For several weeks, Bobby was ordered
to attend. Knowing the tenets of his church forbade it, Bobby refused to go. Finally, of his own accord, he packed up and left the
school." Other biographers simply state that he and Ted attended
the Gibbs School. Nevertheless, when Rose Kennedy returned from
London with the children, in advance of Joe Sr., she removed Bobby
from the school in which he had been enrolled. St. Paul's, in the
windy little town of Concord, New Hampshire, was, as Bobby informed her almost immediately, Anglican, not Catholic. He was enrolled forthwith at Portsmouth Priory, a school in Rhode Island run
by Benedictines. But his stay there was not long. Joseph Sr., in his
belief that his sons should be educated outside of Catholic schools,
intervened. There was also a matter of pulling up Bobby's sagging
academic record, so he was packed off to Milton Academy, a first-rate
preparatory school in Massachusetts.

"Whether he learned much at Milton is questionable," says Biographer Robert Thompson. "But he did make a friendship there that is still the closest he has outside his family. It is with David Hackett, who recalls that while Kennedy was not the best natural athlete at Milton, he 'made up for it in other ways.' The other ways were perseverance and toughness." His grades at Milton were average, but he pressed hard in sports, playing what has been described as "a grim, hard game of tennis" and quarterbacking the football team. There was something pathetic, yet indicative of his tenacity, in his efforts to make the glee club. He is a monotone, to begin with, and has never shown any interest in even the lighter side of cultural pursuits. He may have gone out for the glee club to temper some of the unpopularity he had won for himself by pointedly refusing to smoke or drink beer, or to relax however slightly the standards of Puritanical austerity which have been his moral trademarks. (For not allowing liquor or tobacco to touch his lips, he received $1,000 from his father when he reached the age of twenty-one. At this time, too, he was presented with his share of Joe Kennedy's multimillions.)

A preoccupied nation could hardly be concerned then with Bobby's resistance to nicotine and alcohol. The world was at war. Thousands of young Americans were fighting or dying, and millions of others had interrupted careers and parted with wives or parents to take their place in the vast military bureaucracy. Between Bobby's graduation from Milton Academy and his eighteenth birthday, there was a five-month lag. At the insistence of Joe Sr., Bobby marked time during this period. In November of 1943, when he was eighteen, Bobby volunteered for V-5 pilot training at Bates College. The war had already placed a cruel finger on Jack, a PT-boat skipper in the South Pacific. In fog-bound waters off the Solomon Islands, he had inadvertently maneuvered his PT-109 into the path of a Japanese destroyer, which sliced it in two. It hardly speaks well of his seamanship, but does not detract from his heroism in towing one wounded sailor and guiding the rest of the crew to safety in the long swim to an uninhabited island and eventual rescue, in spite of the agonizing pain of the back injury he sustained in the crash. This kind of feat appealed deeply to Bobby's urge to sustain physical punishment—the kind he had courted on the football field.

He had transferred to Harvard for naval officers' training when, in July of 1944, he received the blindingly tragic news that his brother, Joe Jr., had been killed while on a volunteer bombing mission over occupied Europe. Like all young men safely distant from the line of fire, Bobby carried a load of guilt. In the case of Joe Jr.'s death, he was thrust into a very particular anguish. For Joe Jr. had been in line for rotation, after flying his required number of missions, and could have legitimately refused the special mission which brought him death. To all the Kennedys, this loss was doubly a burden, for Joe Jr.—gregarious, brilliant, fearless—had stood *in loco parentis* to a brood of brothers and sisters during their formative years. They knew the details of his death—a secret air assault on the Nazi V-2 installations, the takeoff in a PBY-4 Liberator loaded with high explosives, the plane guided by remote control, and the premature explosion over the English Channel before the crew could parachute to safety. Bobby's reaction was a natural one. He looked about the Harvard campus and decided that he could not now sit out the waning months of the war. Violating regulations, Bobby went to Washington and asked Secretary of the Navy James Forrestal, a friend of Joseph Sr. in his Wall Street days, to assign him to more active duty. Forrestal was willing, and Bobby found himself a second-class seaman on board a new destroyer, the *Joseph P. Kennedy Jr.*, named after his dead brother. But the combat he sought, in emulation of his brothers, was not to be his. Bobby spent the rest of the war in the somnolent Caribbean chipping paint and hoping for a more glorious fate.

Presumably Bobby was aware of Joe Sr.'s activities during the war. He had plunged into the highly lucrative real-estate business in New York. One deal involved the old Siegal-Cooper building at 18th Street and Sixth Avenue. Joe Sr. bought it for $200,000, doubled the rent, demanded long leases and security payments. Complaints from the tenants reached Governor Thomas E. Dewey, who reportedly said: "That's just like the New Dealers. They're always yelling about how they're for the little people. But give them the chance and they'll gouge the little people to death." In all, Joe Sr. made an estimated $100,000,000—part of the fortune Bobby has shared—from his wartime real-estate deals.

In 1946, a demobilized Robert Kennedy accepted the inevitable and entered Harvard, following in the steps of Joe Sr., Joe Jr., and Jack. But his collegiate career bore little resemblance to theirs. He was "invited" to the same clubs—Hasty Pudding, Spee, and Varsity —but his friends for the most part were the socially unacceptable and the students who struggled financially to make their way through college. He also avoided parties and what he considered rah-rah gatherings. "Nobody who ever went to them made any real contribution," he argued. "What's the good of going to those things and drinking? I'd rather do something else." What contributions he made in other areas have yet to be recorded. "I didn't go to class very much. To tell the truth, I used to talk and argue a lot, mostly about sports and politics. I began thinking about issues about the time I went to college." Kenneth O'Donnell, captain of the Harvard football team and a close friend of Bobby, summed up the discussions of the Kennedy cronies: "We were the dozen most know-it-all in the history of the world." O'Donnell also contributed this picture of Bobby's college period: "In college in those years most of the guys were older than Bob and he was less sure of himself. Bob didn't go to social affairs or dances. He went with the common herd. His friends were persons who couldn't scrape twenty-five cents together. Bob was like the rest of us—finding himself."

If Bobby found himself at all, it was on the football field. Too light to be a likely candidate for the team, he drove himself with fanatic zeal. Obviously, he was out to prove that his lusterless days in the Navy would not be the gauge of his life. He did not *play* football; he worked at it obsessively. Ken O'Donnell, later to become one of the White House "in" group, did all he could to help a friend who was slow and awkward. All Bobby had going for him was that implacable desire to show that he was as fit for athletic kudoes as his two older brothers. This was not enough for Coach Richard Harlow. He wanted solid players, not demons possessed. And this, in effect, was the only way to describe Bobby. A myth has grown up about Bobby's football days at Harvard, untrue but never denied by its hero. Bobby was scrimmaging with the team on a cold day in 1947, repeatedly missing a block on the opposing tackle. Coach Harlow angrily berated him—until Bobby collapsed. According to the much-publicized account, Bobby's leg had been broken but he had continued to work out. This myth, never denied by Bobby, has been frequently cited as an indication of his grit. There was, however, no need for replacing the facts—Bobby *was* badly injured—with a medically impossible account. Bobby's compulsive refusal to quit in the face of pain were amply demonstrated without further exaggeration.

But all this terrible compulsion was rewarded in the last game of the season, when Harvard played Yale. To get his letter, it was necessary for Bobby to play in that game. He sat on the bench forlornly, his leg taped, certain that, like his brothers, he would not get the prestigious "H." With Yale leading thirty-one to twenty-one, and little chance for a Harvard victory in the last play of the game, Bobby was called in. Harvard kicked off and the Yale receiver made straight for the limping Bobby. Fortunately, there were others to make the first tackle, although Bobby was in the pile-up, and he hobbled off the field with his letter insured—perhaps the only success he could claim where his brothers had failed.

After graduating from college in 1948, Bobby picked himself a journalistic assignment with the Boston *Post*, a newspaper then deeply indebted to Joe Kennedy. That assignment, a plum which any reporter would have given almost anything to get, was in the Middle East, to cover the war between the Israelis and the Arabs. There was some hazard to it, as Bobby discovered. Preparing to get a lift from Tel Aviv in a convoy to Jerusalem, he ran into a tank captain who offered him alternate accommodations. He chose the tank. When he arrived in Jerusalem, he learned that the convoy had been wiped out by Arabs. His stories of the conflict, however, lacked any spark of journalistic genius. But Bobby did report that the Jews, though fantastically outnumbered by the Arabs, would win, a prediction in which his intuition proved far more accurate than the "expert" view of the State Department that an Israeli state could be established only with massive American military intervention. In one of his stories, Bobby wrote that the Jews had "much more spirit and discipline and determination" than the Arabs, that "they were tougher inwardly and outwardly."

From the Middle East, Bobby proceeded to West Berlin to observe the Berlin airlift. An attempt to get behind the Iron Curtain failed when the Hungarian government charged him with being an agent of Cardinal Spellman with a message to the imprisoned prelate, Cardinal Mindszenty. But playing at journalism was little more than a brief interlude. He had already been accepted by the University of Virginia Law School, and this seemed as good a way as any to pass the time. "I had led a pretty relaxed life," he remarked later. "I thought I was completely unprepared and ill-equipped, so I decided to go to law school." When he graduated, fifty-sixth in a class of 125, he had yet to show the promise that Rose Kennedy had seen in him when she said, "We never had any worries about Bobby."

It was at law school, however, that he began to emerge from the shadows of his pugnacious shyness. The Law School Forum had been moribund when Bobby arrived on the campus. With others, he worked to revive it, and by calling on his father's friends to speak, he was able to bring national publicity to the school. Among those he succeeded in corralling were Supreme Court Justice William O. Douglas, a close friend of Joe Kennedy and one of the more doctrinaire liberals on the high court; the New Deal trust-buster and ideologue, Thurmond Arnold; Senator Joseph R. McCarthy; his brother, Representative John F. Kennedy; and Ralph Bunche, the Negro diplomat. The invitation to Bunche caused a commotion at the university, and it was vehemently argued that no Negro had ever been permitted to speak there. But Bobby fought hard and won. Bunche spoke. This controversy brought Bobby his first taste of national publicity. When he invited his father to speak, however, the criticisms Bobby received were of a different sort. For Joe Kennedy still held to his isolationism. The common enemy was now Soviet Communism, rather than Nazism, but Joe Sr. still failed to see the danger. His speech, therefore, was quoted in full by Pravda. His argument is significant, for by changing a few words it could be mistaken for Bobby's remarks about Vietnam.

As president of the Law School Forum, Bobby introduced his father. There is no record of his words, but it is inconceivable that he had no idea of the tenor of Joseph Kennedy's refrain. The year was 1950 and the United States was caught up in a Korean police action which might have changed the course of history in Asia by delivering a costly defeat to the Chinese Communists, then struggling to establish a viable government. The senior Kennedy, however, struck out at the policy of President Truman and declared that we were fighting in Korea to "accomplish some unknown objective." But this was not all. It was vital for the United States "to get out of Korea—indeed to get out of every point in Asia which we do not plan realistically to hold in our own defense." Europe, too, should be abandoned, Kennedy senior argued. "Today it is idle to talk of being able to hold the line of the Elbe or the line of the Rhine. . . . What have we gained by staying in Berlin? Everyone knows we can be pushed out the moment the Russians choose to push us out. Isn't it better to get out now and use the resources that otherwise would be sacrificed at a point that counts?"

In 1966, Bobby would use the words and ideas that followed to call for retreat in Asia. For by a curiously shared logic, father and son, at different points of time, would counsel that the only way of defeating Communism was to surrender territory to the Communists. "The truth is," Joe Sr. said, "that our only real hope is to keep Russia, if she chooses to march, on the other side of the Atlantic, and make Communism much too costly for her to try and cross the seas. It may be that Europe for a decade or a generation or more will turn Communistic. But in so doing, it may break itself as a united force. . . . The more people that are under its yoke, the greater are its possibilities of revolt." In 1938, the word for what Joe Kennedy proposed was "appeasement." In 1950, Bobby's father had no fear of the word. "Is it appeasement to withdraw from unwise commitments, to arm ourselves to the teeth and make it clear just exactly how and for what we will fight? If . . . this is appeasement, then I am for appeasement." Recalling Prime Minister Chamberlain's "purchase" of "peace in our time," he stated flatly, "I would applaud it today. Today, while we have avoided a Munich we are coming perilously close to another Dunkirk."

By one of those ironies that plague the Kennedys, Arthur Schlesinger Jr. took up the cudgels against the Kennedy viewpoint. "Even in America, the capitalist fatherland, the deathwish of the business community apppears to go beyond the normal limits of political incompetence," Schlesinger rebutted. "The foreign policy of the business community is characteristically one of cowardice rationalized in terms of high morality. . . . That doyen of American capitalists, Joseph P. Kennedy, recently argued that the United States should . . . 'permit Communism to have its trial outside the Soviet Union if that shall be its fate. . . .' " Schlesinger missed the point. And, of course, he had no way of knowing that he would be allied in White House conferences with the two sons of the man he was attacking.

In 1955, after a highly sanitized trip with Justice Douglas through the central Asian "peoples' republics" of the Soviet Union, Robert Kennedy spoke in the ritual terms of disapprobation which are the stock in trade of so much current political discourse. Asked by *U.S. News & World Report* if he thought the Soviets were worse off than the people of America, he answered: "I think anybody who doesn't think so should take a trip there." He then went on: "I am hopeful, like everybody in the world, that what happened at the Geneva conference and what will happen at the meetings of the foreign ministers will mean peace for us all. However, on the basis of what I saw and learned in Russia, I am very distrustful that we will get anything other than smiles. We are dealing with a government to whom God, the family or the individual means nothing, and whose practice in the past it has been to make promises and treaties to serve their purposes and to break them when it has been to their advantage. It can only be suicidal for us during this period, on the basis of smiles, to strengthen Russia and to weaken ourselves."

Ten years later, Bobby Kennedy would forget these words and opt for the smiles, the promises, and the broken treaties.

3

Bobby Goes A-Politicking

WHEN Bobby Kennedy played football for Harvard, he weighed 154 pounds soaking wet. In 1946, fresh out of the Navy, his political weight was far less than that. His intellectual horizons were narrow, his range of experience limited to the modulated conflicts of the playing field, and his knowledge of people and events circumscribed by what he had heard at his father's table. He knew enough to realize that politics is muscle, and that in the game there is only one rule—that there are no rules. He was aware instinctively of what his opponents over the years never learned. Politics is war, and the victory is to the audacious, the ruthless, and the untiring. From the start, he was misjudged by those who applied the traditional standards of popularity. They could not understand why so unpleasant a young man could have any effect on voters accustomed to being wooed and flattered.

Bobby had his first taste of politics in 1946, when Jack decided to run for the House of Representatives. According to the myth, Bobby's political know-how sprang full grown from his temple in that campaign. In fact, however, his role was almost negligible, but the experience was invaluable to him. For, revising John Dewey's dictum that one must learn by doing, he learned by watching. In the primary battle for the Democratic nomination there were eight other candidates, rooted in Boston's murderous school of politics and familiar with the people and the mores of a Congressional district—the Eleventh—in which Italian and Irish factions jockeyed for power over its bursting slums. Jack Kennedy, moreover, was a weak candidate—sallow from an attack of malaria, hardly looking his twenty-eight years, an indifferent speaker, and every inch the "poor little rich kid," as his opponents called him.

But he had Joe Kennedy—wily in the ways of Boston politics, ready to spend whatever money was necessary, and clutching a fat handful of IOUs from people whom he had helped and who were now expected to return the favor. Among these were editors of Boston newspapers, and they quickly made Jack a local figure. More important was the campaign staff assembled and paid for by Joe Sr. Every aspect of the campaign was supervised by him. Nothing was left to chance. Joe Kennedy could brush this aside with a casual remark, "I just called people." But it was Joe who devised the strategy of presenting Jack as an earnest amateur, while he pulled all the strings from behind the scenes. A Kennedy cousin, Joe Kane, a veteran of a half-century of political warfare, was called in to coach Jack. Mark Dalton became his campaign manager, but no decisions were made without clearing them with the senior Kennedy. Organization was the watchword.

All the Kennedys were sent into the battle. Bobby was given an East Cambridge district to handle. The experts said that Jack would get one in five votes there, and it was Bobby's assignment to reduce the ratio to one in four. While Jack made speeches, shook hands, and flattered the right people, and while Joe Sr. sat at the telephone calling in political paper, Bobby rang doorbells, ate innumerable spaghetti dinners, and took to the streets to play softball with the kids. The technique was effective. The sight of a young multimillionaire plunging into the life of a neighborhood so oppressed by poverty won Bobby affectionate acclaim, and when the votes were counted, East Cambridge had given half its tally to John Fitzgerald Kennedy. Jack would have been a shoo-in without this bonus, but Bobby's small achievement was not lost on his brother or his father.

This was Bobby's baptism of fire in political warfare, but he never forgot it. At the time, it seemed like something of a lark, and once the nomination had been nailed down, Bobby took off on a tour of Latin America. No one gave the Republicans a chance in the district, and nomination was tantamount to election. Bobby and LeMoyne Billings, a close friend, set out to "do" the Latin American countries, and they returned with the usual pat judgments and easy clichés. "It was obvious to us then that Latin America was ripe for Communism," Billings has since recalled. They discovered that the countries south of the border had no middle class, that there were vast and bitter inequities in the political and economic organization of those countries. They saw poverty in the raw and politics at its crudest. Bobby was "extremely interested" in Juan Perón, the Argentine dictator, and in his relationship with Evita, a call girl turned *grande dame* who had married a client and become a full partner in running the country. Beyond these observations, available in any college text, the trip did nothing more for Bobby than provide him with a small geographic background in an area he had never seen. Back in the States, Bobby put this aside and plunged into his studies at the University of Virginia Law School.

His motivation was hardly urgent. "I just didn't know anything when I got out of college," he said. "I wanted to do graduate work, but I didn't know whether to go to law school or business school. I had no attraction to business, so I entered law school." With his law degree suitably framed, Bobby could have turned to more lucrative fields, leaning on his father's friends and their influence on Wall Street. But, in the same lackadaisical way he had decided on law as a means to flesh out the bare bones of an uninspired baccalaureate education, he sought an appointment in the Justice Department "because I wanted to go into the government." A baker's dozen of years later, he would put a somewhat different interpretation on this choice. "Our father repeatedly impressed upon us that nowhere but in the United States could he have achieved what he did; that we owed our blessings to the American system of government and therefore had an obligation to participate in public life. But I don't think any of us thought of public service as a sacrifice or as a means strictly of repaying a beneficent country. We looked to it as an opportunity for an exciting and fulfilling way of life . . . really an extension of family life." Nothing else then "seemed to hold the promise of a true career—the chance for responsibility at a young age or the opportunity for achievement—as did working for the government."

The Justice Department in 1951 was indeed an exciting place, though it offered more frustration than fulfillment. Communist espionage was, for the first time, getting the sustained examination in the Executive Branch that it merited. The conviction of Alger Hiss, technically for perjury but substantively for his part in a Soviet apparatus plundering the United States of precious military, diplomatic, and economic secrets, had stirred the country. The casual guardians of the nation's security were very much on the griddle, seeking to justify their former laxity and at the same time demonstrate their new zeal. Keeping the internal-security caldron bubbling was an unguarded statement by Assistant Secretary of State John Peurifoy, admitting the firing of ninety-one homosexuals from the department, a condition suspected by Congress but never before so openly advertised by a State Department official. If ninety-one had been fired, the question was asked, how many more lingered in the dusk of official secrecy? All these were questions and problems thrown at the Internal Security Division of the Justice Department when Bobby Kennedy began his government service there.

His tenure in that division was not particularly distinguished. As low man on the totem pole, earning $4,200 a year, he plowed through a steadily mounting pile of dossiers and briefs on spies and subversives. He had no more than a nodding acquaintance with the highly publicized Justice Department attorney, Roy M. Cohn, known for the successful prosecution of Soviet atomic spies Julius and Ethel Rosenberg and for his unsuccessful work on the perjury indictment of Professor Owen Lattimore. The Lattimore case had been sparked by the accusation of Senator Joseph R. McCarthy that the Johns Hopkins professor was "*the* top Soviet agent" in the United States, a charge subsequently softened to "*a* top Soviet agent." Long and careful hearings by the Senate Internal Security subcommittee under the painstaking direction of its counsel, Robert Morris, had led to the formal finding of the subcommittee that "Owen Lattimore was, for some time beginning in the 1930s, a conscious articulate instrument of the Soviet conspiracy," and that he had "testified falsely before the subcommittee with reference to at least five separate matters that were relevant to the inquiry and substantial in import." The courts, however, found the indictment faulty and dismissed the case.

Robert Kennedy, for reasons undisclosed, was moved from the Internal Security Division to the Criminal Division, where he was entrusted with cases that were at the time more explosive but generated far less political fallout. Assigned to the U.S. Attorney's office in New York, he fell heir to the Truman scandals and helped inconspicuously to build the evidence that would bring Joseph D. Nunan and Daniel P. Bolich before a Brooklyn grand jury. Nunan, Commissioner of Internal Revenue in the Roosevelt and Truman Administrations, was convicted of evading some $100,000 in taxes between 1946 and 1950. Bolich, once an assistant commissioner of Internal Revenue, was convicted of conspiring to fix a tax case. Bobby's role in these litigations was not a major one, but it gave him a taste for investigative work and for the knock-down aspects of dealing with felons, polite and otherwise. "It was a real education," he has said—and it was, in more ways than one. For Bobby chafed under the restraints that rules of evidence and court procedures imposed on him. He could never quite understand, as his later actions in congressional investigations demonstrated, the difference between an indictment and a conviction, accusation and proof.

On June 17, 1950, Bobby married Ethel Skakel at the St. Mary Roman Catholic Church in Greenwich, Connecticut, the bride's home town. The church was heavy with lilies and dogwood blossoms, Jack Kennedy was best man, and all the pomp and circumstance of the ritual were solemnly observed. Ethel's background made her a perfect mate for Bobby: educated at the Convent of the Sacred Heart and at the Manhattanville College of the Sacred Heart in New York, great wealth, addiction to the more strenuous sports, and a thorough commitment to the Kennedy clan. (In college, Ethel had roomed with Bobby's younger sister Jean. When Jack Kennedy ran for the House of Representatives, Ethel was a volunteer campaigner. And her senior thesis was on Jack's book, *Why England Slept*.) But it was not exactly a romantic marriage. Bobby had met Ethel six years earlier, at a ski lodge at Mont Tremblant in Canada. But he had dated her sister for two years before returning to Ethel. He married her a year after she was graduated from Manhattanville.

In 1952, two years after Bobby's marriage, the Jack & Bobby team was born. Bobby resigned from the Justice Department to manage Jack's campaign for Henry Cabot Lodge's Senate seat. It was a campaign fraught with dangers and ironies. For Jack, as a two-term Congressman, had hardly set Washington on fire. He was articulate and charming, and he could boast of many romantic successes. However, had he lacked the Kennedy name and fortune—and the in-built controversy that always accompanied his father—he would have been but one more of those promising young men who are pushed into semianonymity by the elbowing and headline-happy hordes of Washington. He was challenging an incumbent bearing a famous Massachusetts name and surrounded by the glow of a great victory in stage-managing the nomination by the Republican National Convention of General Dwight D. Eisenhower.

The Boston press, moreover, had already well rehearsed an earlier time when Henry Cabot Lodge Sr. had thoroughly trounced Jack's maternal grandfather, the legendary "Honey Fitz," in a Senatorial contest and gone on to the fame (or notoriety) of defeating President Wilson on the issue of United States participation in the League of

Nations. It seemed, to all but Jack and Bobby, that it was a fool-hardy time to make a try for the Senate. General Eisenhower was universally favored, and with a Republican sweep in the making, there seemed almost no chance for a young Democrat to buck the tide. There were, however, some hidden forces at work for Jack Kennedy. Conservative Republicans were still bitter over the tactics used by Senator Lodge to destroy Senator Robert A. Taft's chances for the Presidental nomination. Lodge's tactics at the Chicago convention had included the impugning of Taft's integrity and political morality, and this was hard to forgive. The Irish Catholic vote in Massachusetts, of overwhelming importance in any election, had been alienated by Democratic attempts to cover up Communist infiltration of the federal government and to discredit those who exposed it. The man who could most effectively encourage the Irish Catholic defection from Democratic ranks was Senator Joe McCarthy. But McCarthy wanted no part of Lodge. Like other Taft Republicans, McCarthy was not ready to go out of his way for the architect of Taft's defeat. He had not forgotten, moreover, how reluctant Lodge had been to fight for his party when Senator Millard Tydings and a subcommittee of the Senate Foreign Relations Committee had set out to "investigate" McCarthy's charges of Communism in the State Department.

It was enough to give the Kennedys hope, but none of the pundits would have gone beyond this. Joe Kennedy made certain that Joe McCarthy would stay out of the state—a signal to the pro-Eisenhower Boston Irish that support of Jack was sanctioned by their even greater hero. The strongly Republican Boston *Post,* in financial difficulties, endorsed Jack, and by a coincidence which surprised no one immediately received a $500,000 loan from Joe Sr. Rose Kennedy was an immensely effective campaigner. An important factor was the appeal Jack made to women, winning them over with shyness, charm, and a show of wealth. ("What is it about Jack Kennedy that makes every Catholic girl in Boston between the ages of eighteen and twenty-eight think it's a holy crusade to get him elected?" one observer asked.) There was one unexpected contribution from Bobby and his young wife, Ethel, who gave birth to their first child. "When Archbishop Cushing baptized that baby in a special ceremony just before the election," a Lodge campaigner said, "that cut the heart right out from us." These contributed mightily to the victory, as did the money Joe Kennedy poured into the campaign—officially reported as $350,000 but estimated at well over $500,000.

Certainly Bobby's direct appeal to the voters was hardly an ingredient in Jack's victory. He delivered few speeches, and these were halting and dull. Sent out to address a small group when the more vocal Kennedys could not be present, Bobby looked at them coldly and said: "My brother Jack couldn't be here. My sister Eunice couldn't be here. My mother couldn't be here. My sister Jean couldn't be here." He paused for a moment. "But if my brother Jack were here, he'd tell you that Lodge has a very bad voting record. Thank you."

Hard work and organization won for Jack Kennedy; there is no record to show that the brand of politicking developed by Bobby compared in effectiveness with the soft sell of Mrs. Rose Kennedy or the organizing genius of Joe Sr. Organization has always been the hallmark of a Kennedy campaign, and it is clear that Bobby learned much of what his father had to teach. That he took the credit while Joe Sr. worked behind the scenes merely gave him confidence. Organization gave Bobby 262,325 signatures on Jack's nominating petition, where he needed only 2,500. Organization was responsible for a network of local cells—286 in all—each one headed by a Kennedy cadreman. Committees were created to appeal to the needs and prejudices of every ethnic group, every profession, every religion. "We tried to organize every town of over six hundred voters," Bobby recalls. One innovation may have been Bobby's. Lists of registered voters were compared to police address lists, and large Democratic areas were discovered which had not a single registered Democratic voter. The troops moved into these, adding 100,000 names to the registration rolls—a significant number, since Jack's margin of victory in the election was 70,000.

Throughout the campaign, Bobby moved restlessly up and down the state, gaining the reputation for ruthlessness and surliness that became national in 1960. Democratic leaders who came in to help, but who did not measure up to Bobby's standards, were ignored or treated with disdain. Those who took umbrage were advised to lick stamps and address envelopes. Bobby took it upon himself to lecture Paul Dever, the Democratic governor of Massachusetts, on political strategy and to caution him not to make any mistakes. Dever ordered Bobby out of the room, picked up the phone, and called Joe Kennedy. "I know you're an important man around here, but I'm telling you this and I mean it," he said angrily. "Keep that fresh kid of yours out of my sight from here on in."

There is reason to believe, however, that Bobby's twenty-six-year-old brashness was welcomed by Jack. Bobby would knock heads together when that was necessary. Then an apologetic Jack would soothe feelings. But he was ready to defend Bobby's rudeness. "You can't make an omelet without breaking eggs," Jack argued. "I don't pay any attention to the beefs. Every politician was mad at Bobby after 1952, but we had the best organization in history. And what friend who was really worthwhile has he lost? I can't recall." Bobby had his own answer: "It doesn't matter if they like me or not. Jack can be nice to them. I don't try to antagonize people. But if they aren't getting off their asses, how do you say that nicely?" He was out to get results, no matter how. The means to the ends he sought were of no consequence. His job was to win elections, and if he had to tread on people to do it, to cut corners, then those who stood in his way were to blame.

The cynicism of this approach was best exemplified by one episode in the Kennedy campaign of 1952. Joe McCarthy was anathema to the liberals who professed horror at his "methods" but nearly always ended up by attacking his aims. On the other hand, without McCarthy's neutrality, Jack Kennedy did not stand a chance of defeating Senator Lodge. It was therefore a question of trying to assure both the McCarthyites and the anti-McCarthyites that Jack was on their side. To the former, he had said that "I rather respect Joe McCarthy"—and added that there may have been "something" in the charges of Communist infiltration of the federal government. To the latter, Jack would point out that McCarthy was a good friend of Joe Sr. and that he could hardly attack a man with whom he had dined at his father's house in Hyannis Port.

The McCarthyites were satisfied if Jack Kennedy refrained from open attack on the controversial Senator. But the liberals were determined to force him to take sides, certain that he would join them rather than what they considered the "Know-Nothings" on the McCarthy team. They did not, however, count on the moral flexibility of both Jack and Bobby, or the determination of Joe Sr. to avoid anything that would hurt his son's chances of election. The man chosen by the liberals to bell the cat was Gardner (Pat) Jackson, a gentle but dedicated socialist who had won his liberal spurs in the Sacco-Vanzetti agitation and later in the CIO.

Pat Jackson approached Jack Kennedy and suggested that he give serious consideration to an anti-McCarthy statement.[1] Jack agreed —if Representative John McCormack, a powerful figure in Massa-

---

[1] There have been a number of conflicting accounts of the episode. This is how it was told to the author by Gardner Jackson, and repeated in the author's presence on several occasions to friends at the National Press Club. Jackson did not want to publish the story, but others have given currency to somewhat different versions.

chusetts politics, would join him. When McCormack gave his assent, Jackson offered to draft a statement. He was invited to present it the following morning. When Jackson arrived at the Bowdoin Street apartment where Jack holed up during the campaign, he was surprised to find Joseph Kennedy present and ready to do battle. Pat Jackson was not intimidated. He began reading the statement but was interrupted almost immediately.

"You and your sheeny friends are trying to ruin my son's career," Joe Sr. shouted, trying to tear the paper out of Jackson's hand. In the loud and acrimonious argument that followed, Jack Kennedy said not a word. Then, slipping out of the apartment, he left Jackson to fend for himself. The next time Jack Kennedy met Jackson, he neither explained nor apologized. "Why does he do it?" Pat Jackson asked.

"There isn't a motive in him which I respect except love of family, and sometimes I think that's just pride," Jack Kennedy answered flatly. He might have added that it was more than that. To Joseph Kennedy, and to all the Kennedys, there has always been one overriding motive: victory. And victory was the payoff. When the votes were counted, General Eisenhower had swept Massachusetts, bringing in Christian Herter as governor against the incumbent Dever, who may have been punished by fate for referring to Bobby as a "fresh kid." The only Democrat to make it in any contest for major office was John Fitzgerald Kennedy. Jack's success, as Joe Kennedy remarked at the time, "leaves Bobby unemployed."

There was no deep worry that he would not be able to find work. The question was: What would be best for him? He had not been too happy in the Justice Department as a cog in a machine that ground out briefs and dumped them into the laps of U.S. prosecuting attorneys. Going into private practice still had no appeal. The obvious choice was a job on Capitol Hill that would give him the kind of publicity necessary to make him something just a little more than "Jack's kid brother." With this as the aim, the choice of jobs settled itself. Major press attention was being focused on Senator McCarthy, making him a formidable force in national politics. In addition, Joseph Sr. had contributed both money and the prestige of his name to Joe McCarthy's campaign for reelection. The approach to McCarthy was made by a former Assistant Attorney General, James McInerney, who recommended Bobby. But it was no secret that the Kennedy clan was behind the McInerney recommendation, and McCarthy could not—and had no desire to—reject it.

Much has been written since 1960 about the relationship between the Kennedy sons and Joe McCarthy. Most of it has been designed to prove that neither Jack nor Bobby really had any feelings of friendship for McCarthy, and that in this association with him, their sins had been of omission rather than commission. The record speaks otherwise. Defending himself for not having been a premature anti-McCarthyite and for having held his tongue until McCarthy was safely guillotined by his enemies, Jack Kennedy always cited extenuating circumstances. "The McCarthy thing?" he told an interviewer. "I was caught in a bad situation. My brother was working for Joe. I was against it. I didn't want him to work for Joe, but he wanted to." But in 1954, at the height of the agitation to censure McCarthy, Senator Kennedy was still temporizing, willing to attack "neither the motives nor the integrity of the junior Senator from Wisconsin." And he was still ready to make a qualified defense of McCarthy, in a speech he wrote to explain his position to the Senate, but never delivered:

"The hostility showed to Senator McCarthy by those outside the United States is not, in my opinion, altogether the result of his own actions, however serious they may be, but rather because he offers an easy mark to those who wish to attack the prestige and power of the United States. Even if Senator McCarthy were removed from public life, those same forces would speedily fill the void left by his passing. . . . It is because we are the leaders of the Free World that we receive this ceaseless hostility, rather than because of any single man or single action." Senator Kennedy said he could not agree that McCarthy had split the country. "Indeed, I think the [censure] action we are about to take, precipitated as it has been by the Senator from Vermont [Ralph Flanders], will have serious repercussions upon the social fabric of this country and must be recognized." His only quarrel with McCarthy, it developed, was the abusive language and tactics of Senator McCarthy's chief counsel, Roy Cohn.

This is important in assessing Robert Kennedy's attitudes when he joined the legal staff of the Senate Government Operations Committee and its Permanent Investigations Subcommittee, both of which were headed by Joe McCarthy. Bobby did not begin to seek qualifiers for his service with Joe McCarthy or the personal support he offered until he decided to run for office. "[McCarthy] said he wanted to reconstruct the committee, to go into all kinds of investigations—Communism and elsewhere," Bobby explained. "He wanted to find people who could help him do a good job." At another point, however, he said: "I went to the committee because I felt the

investigation of Communism was an important domestic issue."
While still Attorney General, he was able to say:

"[McCarthy] got so involved with all that publicity—and after
that it was the number one thing in his life. He was on a toboggan.
It was so exciting and exhilarating as he went downhill that it didn't
matter to him if he hit a tree at the bottom. Cohn and Schine took
him up to the mountain and showed him all those wonderful
things. He destroyed himself for that—for publicity. He had to get
his name in the paper. I felt sorry for him, particularly in the last
year, when he was such a beaten, destroyed person—particularly
since so many of his so-called friends, realizing he was finished, ran
away from him and left him virtually no one.

"I liked him and yet at times he was terribly heavy-handed. He
was a very complicated character. His whole method of operation
was complicated because he would get a guilty feeling and get hurt
after he had blasted somebody. He wanted so desperately to be liked.
He was so thoughtful and yet so unthoughtful in what he did to
others. He was sensitive and yet unsensitive. He didn't anticipate
the results of what he was doing. He was very thoughtful of
his friends and yet he could be so cruel to them."

If this is an accurate picture of Joe McCarthy, it was known to
Bobby when he accepted a position with the Senate Permanent Investigations subcommittee. Bobby had seen enough of McCarthy
both as a man and as a figure in the contemporary scene to evaluate
him. The qualities in the man that he would in time deplore were visible then to any naked eye. His objections came later and centered
largely on the manner in which Roy Cohn treated witnesses or the
methodology of committee procedures. When Bobby held a post
analogous to Cohn's—chief counsel to the Senate Labor Rackets Committee—his treatment of witnesses made anything done by the
McCarthy subcommittee seem pale by comparison. The simple fact
was that Bobby went to work for Senator McCarthy fully cognizant
of what he was getting into, but seeing his association with what the
liberals agonizingly believed the "most powerful man in America"
as an asset.

As the assistant counsel to the subcommittee, Bobby was first assigned to work under Francis Flanagan, a veteran of the legislative
wars who saw his job as a career rather than a crusade. Flanagan was
respected, easy-going, and cut from a pattern that Bobby recognized.
His first important duty was to do reasearch into Allied trade with
Communist nations during the Korean War. This was an issue which

brought the first break between the McCarthy committee and the Eisenhower Administration. The State Department, fearful of any disclosure which might "embarrass" foreign countries, resented the investigation. The White House felt that McCarthy was moving into areas that were its own prerogative, a contention fostered by enemies of congressional investigation.

Bobby, however, shared the limelight of this phase of the sub-committee's work. During two days on the stand, called there to present the results of his investigations, he laid bare a sordid record of Allied relations with the Communist enemy at a time when the United States was offering men and money to fight aggression in Korea. The final subcommittee report, based largely on Robert Kennedy's research, charged that:

Allied nations (mostly West European) had engaged in $2,000,-000,000 worth of trade with the Communist bloc since the outbreak of the Korean fighting.

A total of 450 ships flying Allied flags had made 2,000 trips to Red China, the major aggressor in the war. One British-owned vessel had actually transported Red Chinese troops.

Allied nations and West European ship owners cried foul and false, denouncing the spread of "McCarthyism" to other countries. The State Department raised an equivocal voice in their support. But they were drowned out by the flood of statistics the McCarthy subcommittee had amassed. One British line, based in Hong Kong, called the committee's charges a "horrible lie." It flatly denied carrying Red Chinese troops, but when the evidence proved to be indisputable, argued that the ship was commandeered. The report got short shrift from most editorial writers and pundits, but it was described by Arthur Krock, the New York *Times* columnist, as "an example of congressional investigation at its highest."

Only the subcommittee's four Republican members signed the report when it appeared in mid-July. Earlier that month, the three Democrats on the subcommittee—Senators Stuart Symington of Missouri, John McClellan of Arkansas, and Henry Jackson of Washington—had resigned, presumably because they resented Chairman McCarthy's "one-man rule" and the power, given to him by a vote of the subcommittee, to hire and fire staff employees. There was more than ample precedent in this—it is the rule rather than the exception on both sides of the Capitol—but it made a good issue in the war against "McCarthyism." The Democratic walkout was, however, but one in a series of well-orchestrated and well-amplified outcries against Joe McCarthy. These had included attacks on his staff, many of them based on press allegations and uninvestigated charges.

Bobby Kennedy resigned just three weeks after the Democratic Senators had departed, and he did so without explanation. In announcing his move, Bobby told the New York *Times* on August 1, 1953, that he would "enter the private practice of law"—a frequent threat that he has never carried out. Senator McCarthy graciously wrote Bobby a letter saying that he had been "a great credit to the committee and [done] a tremendous job." No one knows just what reasons Bobby gave McCarthy privately, but in later years he charged that the work of the committee staff was "bad, inefficient, inaccurate, and untrustworthy." Precisely what investigations and what procedures Bobby was characterizing, he has not specified to this day. And his own record, when he became chief counsel of the committee, after the 1954 elections had given control of the Senate to the Democrats and the committee to Senator John McClellan, would indicate that on major points Bobby was in full agreement with what Senator McCarthy and Roy Cohn had been pressing. It is puzzling, however, that by the time Bobby wrote *The Enemy Within* in 1959, he had conveniently forgotten one crucial month of service with the McCarthy committee.

"When Cohn took complete charge of the staff in June, 1953, I left," Bobby states in his book, forgetting the August 1 resignation date. "I told McCarthy I disagreed with the way the committee was being run, except for the work that Flanagan [the subcommittee man Bobby first worked for] had done, and that the way that they were proceeding I thought it was headed for disaster. . . . Cohn and Schine [the subcommittee consultant who became a subsidiary factor in the Army-McCarthy squabble] claimed they knew from the outset what was wrong; and they were not going to allow the facts to interfere. Therefore, no real spadework that might have destroyed some of their pet theories was ever undertaken." This can be read as rationalization, *ex post facto*. It can be sustained only if Bobby is ready to assert that he knew nothing of the substance and character of what the McCarthy committee was doing during the period that he was on the staff, particularly during his last days as a subordinate to Roy Cohn.

But here the record speaks eloquently. Those instances in which the Kennedys, both Jack and Bobby, were most critical of the McCarthy committee and Roy Cohn—the Annie Lee Moss case, to cite but one—occurred *after* Bobby had resigned. He was still active on the committee when it was conducting the investigation for the hearings on the subversive penetration of Camp Kilmer, Fort Monmouth and other Signal Corps installations. These investigations were to end in the Army-McCarthy confrontation over the promotion of Captain Irving Peress despite seriously derogatory information in his file. It was the Peress case, and the incantatory "Who Promoted Peress?", which led to the final choosing up of sides between the pro- and anti-McCarthyites. It was this investigation, too, which made Roy Cohn a major issue.

Bobby, it is true, sat behind Senator McClellan and the Democratic members, preparing lists of questions for them to ask and eventually drawing up the charges which were the basis for the censure of Joe McCarthy. But once the Democrats had taken over, it was Bobby who presented the case against the Army in lengthy hearings on the Peress affair. And his opening statement might have come from the mouth of Roy Cohn, so closely did it parallel the position which Bobby's antagonist had taken. In a chart unveiled at the first hearing, Bobby showed that G-2 had recommended that Peress be discharged from the service, that he had nevertheless been promoted, that under questioning about Communist ties he had claimed the Constitutional privilege against self-incrimination, and that he had nevertheless been honorably discharged. Pointing to the chart, Bobby then outlined the case:

MR. KENNEDY: Senator, this traces chronologically the derogatory information that came to the Army starting on October 28, 1952, when Irving Peress first executed this form. These forms have to do with security. This is not the first time that the Army had information regarding Peress, because he had registered for the Draft Act in January of 1952. . . .

These forms were made available to the Army and were submitted to the Army between October 28 and November 14 of 1954. This chart then traces the course taken by the Army, after Irving Peress had taken the Fifth Amendment on these forms, and it traces what occurred in the Army through 1953, until he was finally honorably discharged upon February 2, 1954. . . . G-2, in the Intelligence branch here, gave information to the medical section and to the reserve section that they were instituting an investigation of Irving Peress. . . .

THE CHAIRMAN: You have another chart here and would you explain that?

MR. KENNEDY: . . . This has to do with the promotion of Peress from a captain to a major. We have here the events dealing with Irving Peress's request for a promotion up here, at Camp Kilmer, and what occurred.

The G-2 officer, for instance, stated that Peress should not receive a promotion, and what divisions or sections it went through, and how it was forwarded down here to the First Army, and forwarded here down to the Department of the Army with a recommendation that he should receive the promotion.

If it was not the work of the committee, what then caused Bobby to leave McCarthy when he did?

A survey of reporters who covered the McCarthy committee and who saw Bobby in this context shows that at no time did he raise the issue of inefficiency or untrustworthiness with them. There is general agreement that he went about his business morosely, almost sullenly. In the late afternoon, when the staff would gather in Joe McCarthy's office, waiting for him to return from the Senate floor or from some appointment, Roy Cohn would sprawl out on his boss's chair, feet propped up on the desk. There would be a certain amount of horseplay, of loud humor, but Bobby would sit by himself, aloof and uncommunicative. No one paid very much attention to him, and this undoubtedly rankled. What may have bothered him even more was that Joe Kennedy's son played such a minor role in the life of the committee. Cohn, the only child of a highly influential New York judge, ran the show—though there is reason to believe that when McCarthy hired Bobby, there had been promises of great things ahead for him. Brash, blustery, and shrewd, Roy Cohn knew the uses of power and he mobilized behind him the powerful friends who supported McCarthy. Both he and Bobby enjoyed controversy and the roar of the crowd. Both were thrilled by the TV camera's glowing red eye when it was turned in their direction. ("It's like a Notre Dame game," Bobby said.) As those who covered the hearings remarked almost with unanimity, Bobby and Roy, despite superficial differences, had much in common. Roy, however, had the muscle.

"We all knew that Bobby and Roy hated each other's guts," a veteran Washington correspondent recalls. "They were intensely jealous of each other. But Bobby sulked when he saw the spotlight focused on Roy. There was never any dramatic outburst or violent exchange between them. I can't think of a single incident. But we knew what was going on. Bobby wanted to be top man, and he couldn't be while Roy was there. I think he hoped that he could cut

Roy down with Joe McCarthy—but Roy's no slouch at in-fighting.
And if Roy had been demoted, there would have been hell to pay
from people Joe needed—columnists like George Sokolsky, publishers, some of the people out West who were contributing to
Joe's anti-Communist campaign. If there were any big battles between them, only Roy or Bobby know about it—and they aren't talking."

Another correspondent, futilely wracking his brains for instances
of open warfare between Roy and Bobby, said: "The feud was there
all right. But it showed itself in petty, niggling matters, in a kind of
chronic irritation apparent in Bobby. I don't deny this. But I've always had a feeling that if Joe McCarthy's star had continued to be
on the ascendant that summer, Bobby would never have quit. Just
read the headlines and the news stories in the anti-McCarthy press
and even in those columns which still stood behind Joe." He opened
a file drawer bulging with clips, pulling one out. "Look at this. It's
dated March 26, 1953—'McCarthy Heading for Downfall? Straws in
Wind Noted.' And it wasn't just wishful thinking by a reporter who
hated Joe. Read the story. President Eisenhower was beginning to
stir a little, however feebly—and only a Senator with a strong machine in Congress, which Joe never had, can stand up against the
President. Here's Senator John Butler, who owed his seat to Joe, taking him on in the fight over confirming Chip Bohlen as Ambassador
to Russia—a fight, by the way, which Joe lost. Don't attribute this to
me, but I've always felt that Bobby quit because he was smart
enough to know that the McCarthy committee was a dead end and
would be a political liability. He switched sides at just the right time
—and to make sure that he could come back if Joe weathered the
storm, he put his resignation on a personal, rather than a
principled, basis."

When Bobby left the committee, he had no intention of going
into the private practice of law, a career which has never interested
him. Quiet participation in the long and necessary apprenticeship
with a big law firm was a boring prospect. He turned once more to
his father, a member of the prestigious Hoover Commission then
making its second monumental study of the federal government and
its bureaucracy. Joe Kennedy got Bobby a staff job, where he marked
time obscurely. The work of the Hoover Commission was vastly important, but there was no excitement—and no headlines—in its activities. When, in February 1954, six months after having joined the
staff, Bobby decided to resign, Herbert Hoover wrote him a gently
chiding letter. "I am sorry to hear that you are leaving us," he said.

"I realize, however, that there is little to do until the task forces have reported and that a restless soul like you wants to work."

During that period, the McCarthy committee had begun what could have been its most important and fruitful investigation: lax security in the Army Signal Corps, and the strong links between the Rosenberg spy apparatus and certain civilian employees. The significance of a McCarthy success at this time was not lost on his opponents who had accused him of never having exposed "a single Alger Hiss." The Democratic leadership of the Senate, realizing the effect of McCarthy headlines on the November congressional elections, urged the three minority members to return to the committee. If the investigation succeeded, they could then claim partial credit; if it failed they could join the chorus of anguish over "McCarthyism." Led by the ranking Democratic member, Senator John McClellan, the three returned, first exacting a promise from Joe McCarthy that they would be allowed to bring in a counsel of their own. That counsel was Bobby, and his real assignment was to be a gadfly to the committee staff, to prepare the questions that the Democratic members would ask, to do their homework for them, and—as Capitol Hill veterans immediately realized—to be as obstructionist as possible. Everything that went on, if it could be used against McCarthy or Cohn, was leaked to a press corps eagerly awating the kill. In public, Bobby, usually sitting dourly behind Senator McClellan during televised hearings, was not above emerging from that obscurity to challenge Roy as he questioned witnesses.

A typical clash occurred over Mrs. Annie Lee Moss, then holding the minor but sensitive job of file clerk with the Army Signal Corps. Earlier witnesses had identified Mrs. Moss as a member of the Communist party. On the stand, however, she flatly denied membership. Before she had stepped down, Mrs. Moss emerged as the heroine of the anti-McCarthy forces and the core of a controversy which included the color of her skin—she was Negro—misrepresentations of a page in the telephone directory, and other matters extraneous to the central charge that the Army Signal Corps had been remiss in enforcing security regulations. In the course of the hearing, Mrs. Moss admitted that she subscribed to the *Daily Worker,* the organ of the Communist party, and that her copies were delivered to her at home by one Rob Hall. This Rob Hall, she said, was a Negro. At this point a reporter slipped Bobby a note claiming that Rob Hall, a well-known Communist party organizer, was white. Bobby had no more to go on than this. He immediately whispered something to Cohn, and there was a brief but angry exchange. When Cohn tried to proceed with the examination of the witness, Bobby broke in. This is how the record reads:

> MR. KENNEDY: Was Mr. Hall a colored gentleman, or—
> MRS. MOSS: Yes, sir.
> MR. KENNEDY: There is some confusion about it, is there not, Mr. Cohn? Is the Rob Hall we are talking about, the union organizer [sic], was he a white man or a colored man?
> MR. COHN: I never inquired into his race. I am not sure. We can check that, though.
> MR. KENNEDY: I thought I just spoke to you about it.
> MR. COHN: My assumption has been that he is a white man, but we can check that.
> SENATOR SYMINGTON: Let us ask this: The Bob Hall [sic] that you knew, was he a white man?
> MRS. MOSS: He was colored, the one I knew of.
> SENATOR SYMINGTON: Let's decide which Robert Hall we want to talk about.
> MR. KENNEDY: When you spoke about the union organizer, you spoke about Rob Hall and I think we all felt that was the colored gentleman?
> MR. COHN: I was not talking about a union organizer, Bob. I was talking about a Communist organizer who at the time, according to public record, was in charge of subscriptions for the *Daily Worker* in the District of Columbia area.
> MR. KENNEDY: Evidently it is a different Rob Hall.
> MR. COHN: I don't know that it is. Our information is that it was the same Rob Hall.
> SENATOR MCCLELLAN: If one is black and the other is white, there is a difference.
> MR. COHN: I think that might better be something we should go into and get more exact information on.
> MR. KENNEDY: I think so.

But the headline had been made, the diversionary tactic was successful. From that point on, the question of Mrs. Moss's membership in the Communist party and the fact that the *Daily Worker*, a *must* for party members and hardly light reading for a low-echelon Army employee, became secondary to a long debate over the possibility that there were two Rob Halls both delivering *Daily Workers* in Washington. On the basis of these and similar maneuvers, an important investigation bogged down in trivia, though it was later carried forward by Bobby when he became chief counsel of the committee in the Democratic-controlled Congress of 1955. Few noted, for instance, that Bobby, to make Mrs. Moss look better, persisted in describing Rob Hall as a "union organizer"—which he was not— rather than a Communist party functionary—which he was. Nitpicking became the order of the day.

Everything, however, ground to a halt as the question of Communist infiltration and espionage was brushed aside for protracted argument over Senator McCarthy's rudeness to General Ralph Zwicker, involved in the promotion of Peress, or to Roy Cohn's attempts to get preferential treatment for G. David Schine, chief consultant of the McCarthy committee, who had recently been drafted. Also at issue were proposals made by Schine and submitted to the committee as a possible program to combat Communism. These proposals were hardly world-shaking, but neither were they malign. Senator Henry Jackson, one of the returned Democrats, found the Schine suggestion for a "Deminform," to carry the propaganda war against the Cominform, hilarious and he elaborated on his objections with great sarcasm. When the hearing had ended, Cohn, in great anger, walked over to Bobby. The colloquy, as told to reporters by Bobby but denied by Cohn, was brief:

"Tell your friend Scoop Jackson that we're going to get him on Monday," he said.[2]

"Get lost," Bobby answered.

"You have a personal hatred for one of the principals," Cohn said.

"If I have, it's justified," Bobby said. Then he told Cohn to shut up or take his story elsewhere. He was not impressed, he said, by Cohn's threat to put in the record something Jackson had written that was "favorably inclined toward Communism."

"Do you want to fight now?" Cohn is supposed to have said.

Bobby walked away, with Cohn calling out after him, "Do you think you're qualified to sit here? Do you think you're qualified?"

By this time, the reporters realized that a quarrel had been taking place. They asked Cohn what had happened. He said, "Oh, we've got a real cute kid there." When the two next met, a fist fight seemed to be in the making, but they stood glaring at each other without striking a blow. When Bobby's version of the earlier quarrel appeared in print, it was accepted as gospel truth. Senator Karl Mundt deplored the entire business and said, "I don't know and I don't care what happened." Senator Jackson, however, rushed to

[2] This may be compared to Bobby's angry shout at Senator Hubert Humphrey at the Democratic convention of 1960 for supporting Adlai Stevenson rather than John F. Kennedy: "I'm going to get you!"

Bobby's defense. "I have no doubt that what happened was what Robert Kennedy said happened."

It was to this low state that the important business of a Senate committee had fallen. In a less supercharged atmosphere, the two participants would have been reprimanded; and if they could not get along any better than that in the future, one or both would have been dropped from the staff. But by this time, the controversy between McCarthy and the Eisenhower Administration in general, and certain individuals at the Pentagon specifically, had become a major war. In a New York *Times* story on the Cohn-Kennedy skirmish, written by veteran reporter William Lawrence, the reasons for Cohn's anger at Bobby became apparent. It was Bobby, Lawrence wrote, who had prepared the questions that ridiculed the Schine "Deminform" plan and its proposals for conducting a psychological-warfare program. Reading Bobby's questions, Jackson professed bewilderment over the suggestion that civic groups would be a prime audience for anti-Communist indoctrination. What worried him, an elaborately tongue-in-cheek Jackson said, was whether Pakistan had a Lion's Club or an Order of Eagles. He was also worried, or professed to be as he followed the line of questioning Bobby had prepared for him, by Schine's use of "democratic" and "anti-Communist" as if they were synonymous. Couldn't "democratic" be turned to their own use by the Communists? Didn't it have a double meaning the enemy could steal? Finally Joe McCarthy got fed up.

"My God, man," he said sharply, "you run for office under that label."

Had Bobby Kennedy and the Democratic members so chosen, the investigation of Communism in the Signal Corps could have made a major contribution to the exposure of infiltration and foot-dragging enforcement of security regulations. It was all forgotten in the passion and boredom of the Army-McCarthy hearings, which were seen day after day by a dwindling number of TV viewers, though it was played as a combination spectacle and soap opera by all parties. In 1955, the Democrats regained control of Congress, and therefore of the Senate Permanent Investigations subcommittee. On April 25 of that year, the majority, without affirming or denying, issued its deadpan report, prepared by Bobby, entitled *Army Signal Corps—Subversion and Espionage*. It reads in part:

Early in 1953 the subcommittee received detailed information concerning infiltration of the Army Signal Corps by individuals with subversive backgrounds. The chairman was furnished with a condensation of a report containing the names of 34 individuals. It revealed that subversion and possible espionage existed at the secret radar laboratories at Fort Monmouth, N.J. The subcommittee also learned that as early as 1949 and through April 1953, the Federal Bureau of Investigation had repeatedly called to the attention of Army Intelligence information concerning subversives in the Army Signal Corps. These repeated warnings were neglected and, as a result, individuals with subversive background . . . were permitted to remain as employees in highly sensitive installations doing work of a classified nature. . . .

Every consideration was given to the fact that the Army Signal Corps was engaged in highly secret research and development and in the production of critical materials and equipment, the nature of which could not be disclosed. . . . It was only after our investigation had commenced that 35 individuals were suspended on security grounds from Fort Monmouth. It is significant that of these 35, 8 have been discharged and 3 resigned. . . . A total of 126 witnesses were heard in executive hearings. Forty-one of these invoked the protection of the Fifth Amendment when interrogated about subversive activities. Over 200 staff interviews were conducted. . . .

In the course of the executive hearings, Major General Kirke B. Lawton, commanding general, Army Signal Corps, Fort Monmouth, testified to the state of affairs at his post prior to the beginning of the McCarthy committee investigation:

THE CHAIRMAN: Would you say that since you have taken over, and especially over the past six months, you have been working to get rid of the accumulation of security risks in the Signal Corps and that you have suspended a sizable number, and you are working toward getting rid of all of those that you now consider loyalty or security risks?

GENERAL LAWTON: That is a question I will answer "yes," but don't go back six months. Let us go back—effective results have been in the offing in the last two weeks. I have been working for the last 21 months trying to accomplish what is being accomplished in the last two weeks.

THE CHAIRMAN: I think that covers it. So that you would say that in the past several weeks you are getting some effective results?

GENERAL LAWTON: Absolutely, that we have not gotten in the last four years. . . .

THE CHAIRMAN: Could you tell us why it is only in the last two or three weeks that you are getting these effective results?

GENERAL LAWTON: Yes, but I had better not. . . .

Among the committee's findings, in an investigation ridiculed by many in the press for not accomplishing anything and persecuting the innocent, were these:

> The Rosenberg spy ring[3] successfully penetrated the Army Signal Corps and related private commercial establishments [doing classified work for the Army]. This espionage ring took and obtained secrets from the Army Signal Corps and transmitted them to the Soviet Union. . . . The Rosenberg ring . . . may, on the basis of available evidence, still be operating.
>
> A secret Communist Party cell operated at the Federal Telecommunications Laboratories for a considerable number of years. One of its members had been associated with the Rosenberg spy ring. Some of its members were employed at the laboratories when subpoenaed. An employee and cell member actually had a top-secret clearance when subpoenaed. Several other members of the cell had obtained employment at equally sensitive private commercial establishments. . . .
>
> The responsible officials in charge of security matters were grossly negligent and incompetent in failing to take proper action in the cases of individuals where there was information that they were loyalty or security risks. The subcommittee was unable to ascertain from the Army at which echelon the removal of security risks was disapproved.
>
> There was a lack of proper physical security at Fort Monmouth which enabled employees to remove freely classified documents and information from the laboratories. . . .

By the time the report of the subcommittee had been issued, it had become the McClellan committee, with Bobby Kennedy as its chief counsel. The country had suffered through the Army-McCarthy hearings and the Watkins committee proceedings to censure Joe McCarthy for his "disrespect" of the Senate—a condemnation which, to the public watching Senatorial antics on television, had seemed applicable to most of that august body. Bobby worked hard for the condemnation, though he continued to avow his friendship to Joe McCarthy. And when the returns were in, he let it be known to

[3] Julius and Ethel Rosenberg, convicted of stealing atomic-bomb secrets, were electrocuted for their crime. They had, however, been involved in other espionage work, including the theft of the proximity fuse, during World War II.

friends that he favored the Senate's action, but disapproved of the very narrow grounds on which it was based: refusal to appear before the Senate Privileges and Elections Committee and the remarks McCarthy had made during the censure hearings about other Senators. "I thought he had brought the Senate and the United States into disrepute by his operation of the committee. The whole operation of Cohn and Schine was the core of it."

In 1955, however, Bobby was still tangling and untangling his loyalty to Senator McCarthy. Picked by the Junior Chamber of Commerce as one of the country's ten outstanding young men, he attended the Jaycee's banquet in Louisville. Featured speaker was Edward R. Murrow, the voice-of-doom broadcaster who had been all of the Eumenides rolled into one in his pursuit of Joe McCarthy. When Murrow rose to deliver his speech, Bobby Kennedy rose, too —leaving the ballroom and remaining in the wings until Murrow had finished. Bobby Kennedy had sat comfortably with the inquisitors during the series of investigations of McCarthy. In the months during which McCarthy, now the ranking member of the Permanent Investigations Subcommittee rather than its powerful chairman, was slowly dying, Bobby was able to use him as a buffer against Senator Mundt, a less forgiving man than the junior Senator from Wisconsin. It was not difficult to maneuver the pathetically eager McCarthy into a position where he would fight Bobby's battles with the Republican members of the committee. Certain that Mundt and others in his own party had sold him down the river, McCarthy thought he was getting back at them.

The Army-McCarthy hearings, which had been designed to destroy Joe McCarthy and the anti-Communist movement in America, killed still a third bird with its single stone: it discredited congressional investigation. This had been an aim of the left-wingers in and out of government ever since the House Un-American Activities Committee had begun its extended probes. Prior to this, they had hailed the work of the LaFollette committee, which looked into violations of civil liberties, and the Nye committee, of which Alger Hiss was counsel. Since investigators must, by the very nature of their work, delve into the workings of the Establishment, they had a habit of turning up skeletons better left buried. When the McCarthy operation had ended, by virtue of the change in the control of Congress from Republican to Democratic, it was of some satisfaction to the Democrats that they could call a halt to congressional probings. The public was tired of them, and tired of seeing shadows when substance was called for.

The first to lose by this was Bobby Kennedy. As chief counsel, he had a reputation to make. The Eisenhower Administration, with its faulty public relations and its inability to win over the press, was nevertheless not exactly a pushover—but far more vulnerable than its tough-minded predecessors. If Bobby and the committee wanted headlines, they could find a few inept politicians who might change the public's mind by offering another spectacle. When the committee set out after the Foreign Operations Administration, it found its patsy, Harold Stassen, head of the FOA. Though aging, he still clung to his former title of "boy wonder," which had come to him in the early 1940s when he was elected Governor of Minnesota. His gilt had worn off during his forlorn quadrennial efforts to snatch the Republican Presidential nomination. By then, something of a joke in G.O.P. ranks, he still clung to his hope and acted accordingly.

Bobby felt that he could make his break by getting Stassen to testify and then toasting him thoroughly on both sides. Stassen, however, was not so foolish that he would venture into the committee's parlor. At preliminary hearings, he sent as his surrogate an FOA lawyer to answer fully the committee's questions about a dubious sale of grain elevators to Pakistan. But Bobby was after publicity, not information. He decided to violate precedent by forcing Stassen to testify. He therefore made out a subpoena and sent a process server to haul in Stassen. Only under extreme circumstances are agency heads subpoenaed, but Bobby felt it would make a dramatic story. Robert McElroy, the process server, picked a bad time for his mission—April Fool's Day. At the FOA office, McElroy encountered Stassen, who indignantly refused service. The process server thereupon jammed the subpoena into Stassen's pocket, only to see it thrown contemptuously on the floor. McElroy sheepishly picked it up and left it with Stassen's secretary.

This was a battle of titans, clearly. For Stassen told the press that the subpoena was neither legal nor relevant. Bobby Kennedy argued vehemently that the service had been executed since McElroy had "touched" Stassen with the paper, a neat bit of law school lore. "The man who served it," Kennedy said, "has had a lot of experience. So whether Stassen threw it on the floor, or on his desk, or wherever, it makes no difference." The controversy might have raged indefinitely had it not become known that prior to the service, Stassen had arranged with Chairman McClellan for a time and a date, on which he eventually appeared.

But what of the committee's real work under the chief counseling of Robert Kennedy? Announcing the newly constituted Permanent

Investigations subcommittee's plans on New Year's Day, 1955, Chairman McClellan had said it would continue to probe Communist activities as "an even greater menace" to the country than the governmental waste, inefficiency, and corruption that also fell under its investigative mandate.

In mid-July, it seemed to be moving in that direction when it issued a report on the old McCarthy *cause célèbre,* the Peress case. Senator McCarthy had accused the Army of bungling and secrecy in the promotion of Major Irving Peress. He had also assailed security practices at Fort Monmouth and charged that Peress had been promoted from captain to major at a time when his Communist affiliations were being studied. To make matters even worse, the Army had honorably discharged Peress one day after it had received a letter from McCarthy indicating that the subcommittee intended to go into the case. The Peress case had led to harsh words from McCarthy in his questioning of an evasive General Ralph Zwicker, the post commander. In the course of the colloquy, McCarthy had said that Zwicker was "not fit to wear the uniform"—a slur which had created a considerable furor in the press and had been cited as an example of McCarthy's irresponsibility and his penchant for smearing people.

The subcommittee's report cited forty-eight instances of error "of more than minor importance" on the part of the Army in its handling of the Peress case. It noted instances in which the Army was "deceptive," practiced "gross impositions" on those handling the investigation, and showed disrespect for the subcommittee. The bill of particulars against the Army ran to almost six pages of the report, prepared by Bobby and his assistants. Though there was no mention of subversion, it was a damning indictment—and one which Bobby Kennedy and the Democratic Senators he was advising during the Army-McCarthy hearings had denied or studiously avoided. Joe McCarthy pronounced himself satisfied and praised Bobby by calling the report "a great tribute to the staff of the committee." But it had come a little late, and with no apologies. One section of the report, moreover, threw an interesting light on Senator McCarthy's treatment of General Zwicker:

> Files of the subcommittee contain a memorandum prepared by C. George Anastos, former assistant counsel, wherein it is reflected that on January 22, 1954, General Zwicker furnished Mr. Anastos certain specific information of a security nature relating to Irving Peress including the fact that Peress was a card-carrying Communist

from 1948 to 1952; that in 1951 he was a Communist Party organizer; that . . . his wife Ethel was a member of the Communist Party and that she attended Communist Party meetings and held such meetings in her home. . . . Accordingly, when he appeared before the subcommittee on March 23, 1955, General Zwicker was interrogated on the security information purportedly furnished Mr. Anastos, as reflected in the latter's memorandum of January 22. General Zwicker categorically denied giving security information of any kind to Mr. Anastos. . . . Mr. Anastos was called before this subcommittee on March 31, 1955. He stated that General Zwicker furnished by phone all the specific security information which was attributed to him in the memorandum. . . . He further testified that his telephone conversation with General Zwicker was monitored by Miss Mary Morrill, a former subcommittee stenographer, and that both he and Miss Morrill took notes of the conversation. Thereafter, he dictated the memorandum of January 22 from his notes as well as those of Miss Morrill, which she had typed. Miss Morrill recalled monitoring the Anastos-Zwicker telephone conversation of January 22 and Mr. Anastos dictating to her the results thereof.

Congress and the nation paid little mind to all this. The Fort Monmouth investigation was ancient history, and the McClellan committee had moved on to bigger and better cases, politically speaking. One of them involved President Eisenhower's Secretary for Air, Harold E. Talbott, in a "conflict of interest." The Kennedy-directed staff had worked for three months assembling evidence, and on July 14, it peremptorily summoned the Secretary from a military conference at Quantico, Virginia, for an "informal" talk with Bobby. The Democrats on the committee hammered away at charges that Talbott, in a "special partnership" with an engineering firm, had both solicited and profited from business with defense contractors, using his influence as Air Force Secretary. Talbott insisted that the profits he had made came from nondefense business. Such casual contacts he may have made on the firm's behalf, he argued, did not constitute a use of his official position for his personal advantage. It was a touchy point and a quibble on Talbott's part, but to most people he appeared to be the victim of his own naïveté. There the case would have died but for the "leak" to the New York *Times* of letters he had written to contractors on Air Force stationery. A Republican subcommittee member, Senator George Bender, immediately accused Bobby of giving the damaging documents to the newspaper.

Bobby flatly denied it, though he admitted that "there was only one person who handled the letters and it was me." This, he argued, was no proof that he was guilty as charged. "I don't think you should say it if you don't know, Senator," he said. "I resent it." Senator McCarthy defended Bobby against the Bender accusation, but this was unnecessary. Though the letters were not conclusive evidence of improper activity, they cast enough doubt on Talbott's probity to free the Democrats from precisely the same comment that Bobby had made to Bender—that they should not have made the accusation of "conflict of interest" if they didn't know. By late July, Talbott had submitted his resignation, still pleading his innocence. And Bobby had demonstrated once more that he was dedicated to the Kennedy precept: The important thing is to win.

But controversy lay about him. Before the Talbott case had broken across the nation's front pages, Bobby had led the subcommittee into the investigation of a tangle of double-dealing in military uniform procurement. The inquiry helped produce six fraud convictions. But Bobby had little pleasure handling a Chicago capmaker, Harry Lev. Committee investigators suspected him of having shortchanged the government to the tune of 577,000 garrison caps by altering contract specifications, then of having bribed the right people to prevent discovery of his crime. But on the stand, Lev was hard to pin down, and after a day of attempting it, Bobby, according to one newspaper account, "dissolved in despair . . . moaning, 'For crying out loud.' "

A former military purchasing agent, who had presumably accepted a $2,000 kickback from Lev, was a more fruitful witness, but she brought Kennedy little joy. Tripped time and again by contradictions between her executive and public testimony, she finally burst out that Bobby and his senior aide, Carmine Bellino, had put her in a "hot room" and "browbeaten, badgered, and kicked me around." Pointing a finger at the chief counsel, she summed up what others who ran into Bobby's prosecution methods had felt: "He can be as sweet as sugar and then the next moment—bam!"

This pursuit of the picayune though necessary work of a watchdog committee was interrupted by Bobby's trip to Soviet Asia with Supreme Court Justice William O. Douglas. Back at his McClellan committee stand, he again picked up the East-West trade issue that he had investigated three years earlier as his first major assignment with the McCarthy committee. The position he took contrasts interestingly with his present views on the subject. At the time, however, he called the extent of Western trade with Red China "astonishing" and criticized the Eisenhower Administration for yielding to Allied demands by relaxing restrictions on the shipment of strategic goods. (He was later to approve of the late President Kennedy's efforts to increase trade between East and West, and even urge it under President Johnson.)

A major target of his inquiry was the reported approval by the United States of the principle that Britain should consider "economic value to the exporter" as well as the strategic character of the goods traded with Red China in determining the propriety of the deal. "Almost unbelievable," said the Robert Kennedy of that day, was the American agreement allowing Britain to sell 200,000,-000 pounds of copper wire to the Soviet Union. In a letter to the New York *Times* of April 10, 1956, Bobby attacked the Administration's refusal to divulge what items still were embargoed as strategic and what ones had been taken off the revised list of proscribed articles. The information held secret here, Kennedy said, was freely published in England. In another letter to the *Times*, he likened current East-West trade "for profit" to what this country pursued with Japan in the 1930s. "This should have taught our allies and ourselves a lesson," he asserted. "It apparently has not."[4]

From a purely personal point of view, the most important of Bobby's investigations involved Murray Chotiner, a Republican political strategist whose name was inextricably linked with that of Vice President Richard Nixon. Chotiner had returned to private law practice, though it was anticipated that he would be back in harness when and if Nixon ran for the Presidency. As a national figure, Chotiner was of small consequence. Like most campaign managers, he shunned publicity for himself, seeking instead to focus attention on his candidate. To the professionals, however, he was known as perhaps the most astute worker in his field. If Murray Chotiner could be thoroughly discredited, the Democrats would profit in three ways: (1) Nixon would be deprived of a tremendously important asset in his bid for the Presidency, (2) the Eisenhower Administration would be soiled, and (3) Nixon's association with Chotiner could be parlayed into further "proof" of the Vice President's alleged venality.

The mythology of Nixon's horrendous conduct during the 1946

---

[4] Not all of Bobby Kennedy's 1956 views contrast with his 1966 opinions. For example, speaking to a Catholic convocation in New York in March 1956, he advanced the already tired argument that military Communism can be fought only with welfare-state weapons. "If we are going to win the present conflict with the Soviet Union, we can no longer support the exploitation of native peoples by Western nations," he said. "We supported France in Indochina for too long and the same thing is happening now in Cyprus."

campaign which won him a seat in the House of Representatives and the 1950 Senate race against Helen Gahagan Douglas had been so frequently replowed by the Democrats that it had lost its effectiveness. Nixon's public posture in the Vice Presidency and the restraint with which he had conducted himself during President Eisenhower's period of incapacity after his heart attack was fresher in the public mind, and to keep reiterating that he called Mrs. Douglas a Communist, which he had not, no longer sent the citizenry scurrying for the storm cellars. Something new had to be added. If it were, the major beneficiary would be Senator John F. Kennedy, already planning the steps which would lead him triumphantly to the White House.

The excuse used by Bobby to haul Chotiner before the McClellan committee was tenuous enough. He had made several calls to clients from the White House, thereby impressing them with his important connections. This was hardly an example of unbridled "influence peddling," nor would Bobby normally have hung his case on so slim a branch. Committee investigators, at Bobby's behest, searched the Chotiner record for some evidence of wrongdoing, some improper act involving government contracts which brought him within the jurisdiction of the investigating Senators. But they could find nothing. This, however, did not deter Bobby. Chotiner was the kind of person he could hate—fat, wearing clothes of a cut that would not be fashionable on an Ivy League campus, and not given to the upper-class niceties.

If Murray Chotiner could not be charged with any misdeeds, Bobby discovered, there was still the matter of his clients. Among them were men who had run afoul of the federal government. It was Bobby's feeling that lawyers who represented unsavory clients were themselves somehow involved and should be made accountable.[5] On this basis, Murray Chotiner was called as a witness. Chotiner's crimes, as they were developed, simply became those of his clients. There were, left over from a House investigation, two letters written to him by Sherman Adams, Eisenhower's White House chief of staff, discussing a case pending before the Civil Aeronautics Board. With Adams on the griddle for having received a vicuna overcoat from Bernard Goldfine, this seemed like pretty incriminating stuff.

Even more incriminating, as it was presented to the committee, was Chotiner's "admission" that he had received a $6,000 fee for defending Herman Kravitz, a New Jersey clothing manufacturer,

[5] As Attorney General, Bobby lectured bar associations for not taking steps against lawyers who represented clients who took refuge behind the Fifth Amendment.

who was subsequently convicted of embezzling government property. Senator McClellan, in summing up the case against Kravitz, announced that he had "obtained improper favors from the Quartermaster Corps, delivered substandard garments and made unconscionable profits at the expense of the taxpayer." Another client was Marco Reginelli, a military uniform contractor, who was described rather fancifully by Bobby as "the top hoodlum in the Philadelphia and New Jersey area." [6] And Bobby volunteered to a listening world, "Reginelli is in a Baltimore hospital—delirious." No evidence against Chotiner was adduced by the committee; but in the presentation of the case against him, his conduct was made to appear somewhat unethical, as if the Anglo-Saxon tradition limited a lawyer exclusively to the defense of the innocent and high-minded.

Chotiner pleaded in vain to be allowed to present his own case, and Bobby and the committee solemnly promised that he would be given an opportunity to return for a full rebuttal. This promise was never kept, and Chotiner never recovered from that semi-lynching. From that moment on, by further association, Nixon was belabored for what Chotiner was presumed to have done. "Nixon," Earl Mazo wrote in his biography of the Vice President, "was in no way implicated. But every news story tied Chotiner to him. This delighted those anxious to bypass Nixon's nomination and caused the Vice President to sever his political relationship with his ingenious campaign technician." In 1960, when Nixon ran against Jack Kennedy for the Presidency, Chotiner was not permitted to direct the campaign, depriving the Vice President of the precision organization and the devotion to detail that was the Chotiner trademark. Instead, there was confusion and overlapping of functions. Nixon lost by a margin of 100,000 votes—which Chotiner might well have delivered.

In politics, the blindfolded goddess of justice sometimes takes a quick peek at the participants. If Richard Nixon never learned this, Robert Kennedy did. He was destined to move to greener pastures, to the sensational investigation of racketeering in one carefully delimited area of labor, to put aside with other childish things the investigation of Communist subversion in the federal Establishment and the indiscretions of Republicans. A brief note in one of the reports prepared by Bobby for the Senate Permanent Investigations Subcommittee touches on the trail of unfinished business that he left behind:

[6] The late Robert Humphreys, former *Newsweek* editor, political publicist, and adviser to the Senate Republican leadership, once remarked to Chotiner: "You've got to admit that those were pretty bad clients." "That's right," Chotiner answered. "But do you know who sent them to me? Tom Dewey."

"The work of the subcommittee, during the past year, was unnecessarily diverted for approximately four months due to charges and countercharges involving officials of the United States Army. . . . Investigation and testimony established that the Communist Party has successfully infiltrated national defense industries and is in a position to acquire vital information concerning our military secrets and our military effectiveness. The employment of Communists in defense facilities is a clear and present danger to the national security. Many investigations conducted by the staff in connection with this subject have never been made part of executive or public hearings, and a great deal of additional investigation is contemplated in this regard."

The contemplation must have been brief. Except for a few minor exceptions, Robert Kennedy never pursued the "clear and present danger to the national security." When Senator Joe McCarthy died, he was buried in Appleton, Wisconsin, his home town, on May 7, 1957. Buried with him was the McCarthy Era. Among the mourners who flew from Washington for the ceremony was Robert Kennedy.

4

The Taste of Power

IN 1957, when the investigation of labor racketeering exploded across the nation's front pages, a Washington correspondent for *Newsweek*, telephoned Senator Irving Ives, the quietly liberal New York Republican. The reporter was attempting to check a sensational story to be broken by the Select Committee of the Senate set up to investigate corruption in labor-management relations.

"You better check that with Bobby Kennedy," said Senator Ives.

The reporter explained that he had gotten the story from Bobby in the first place. "The last story he gave me was completely untrue," the reporter added. "If it had run, I probably would have lost my job."

"I don't know anything about it," Ives insisted. "The only time Bobby talks to me is to yell at me."

"But you're a United States Senator and vice chairman of the committee," the reporter said. "How can Bobby—an employee of the committee—treat you that way?"

"There's nothing I can do about it," Ives answered. "Every time I try to, Bobby hides behind his brother Jack's skirts."

Senator Ives was a long-suffering man, and the chances are that his efforts to curb Bobby Kennedy were not very strenuous. Had he tried to make an issue of it, he would have found much more opposition from Senator John McClellan, the chairman, than from Senator John F. Kennedy. In those years of decision and indecision, McClellan enjoyed Bobby's brashness, his capacity for work, and his determination to treat every difference of opinion as a cowboys-and-

Indians conflict in which, as almost every writer since then has noted, the good guys were pitted against the bad guys. As a strong Southern conservative, McClellan also liked the contrast between the stern but ironic decorum he maintained at all times and Bobby's frequent outbursts of anger and unlawyerly unconcern for the proprieties of a hearing room. The senior Senator from Arkansas was also more than a little aware that Bobby's undisguised liberalism would serve as a rod to draw labor's lightning in an inquiry so fraught with political peril.

In hearings dealing with life and death, with the gangster penetration of unions presumably set up to protect rather than prey upon the working man, with millions of dollars spent in fraud and corruption, Bobby could also offer a certain amount of comic relief to the millions who watched in fascination as the sordid story played itself out on their television screens. Perhaps the most famous episode of this nature occurred when Bobby Kennedy, as chief counsel of the Senate Labor Rackets Committee, was questioning a woman described by him as a "madam." As he read an affidavit describing in technical detail certain fine points of the business of prostitution, Bobby's voice began to waver and a flush of Puritanical embarrassment began to color his face.

"A call house is distinguished from a regular house of ill fame," the chief counsel read, "which is sometimes known as a walk-in, by the fact that the clientele is a select one. By that I mean that unless a person is known or is referred, he cannot gain access to the house. It may fairly be termed an 'exclusive clientele' operation. A house of ill fame, or a walk-in, will accept anyone who comes to the premises. Another . . . another feature . . . another feature of . . . of the call house is . . ." and Bobby could read no longer. He let out an embarrassed whoop of laughter and buried his face in his hands.

Cabell Phillips, writing in the March 17, 1957, New York *Times Magazine,* completed the scene: "The chairman regarded him impassively for a moment, then the merest flicker of a smile creasing the corners of his mouth, he asked with sepulchral dignity: 'Does counsel desire that the chair take over the reading of the affidavit?' The meeting came to order again after a few rollicking minutes and counsel waded through his assignment without further interruption. But the incident had highlighted once again one of the most remarkable June-December relationships [Washington] has witnessed in many years, and one that is destined to hold the center of the investigating stage for a number of months to come.

"The McClellan-Kennedy team—its senior member is 61, its

junior member 31—has been working in harness since 1953. It is a strangely assorted pair. McClellan has the astringent, disapproving manner of a stern man of the cloth. His mere glance can convey a chilling sense of barely controlled outrage. His flat, deep-pitched voice and carefully articulated words are never raised above a conversational level, but they pack all the authority of a drill sergeant's command.

"Kennedy reminds you vaguely of those modest, well-bred young upperclassmen in their sedate Brooks Brothers' suits whom you would be likely to meet at a faculty tea at Harvard or Dartmouth," Phillips noted. He argued then what many in the legal profession have since found hardly accurate—that the labor rackets investigation was outstanding "for its thoroughness and for its adherence to fair and dignified rules of procedure." *Time* magazine reported that "in the hearing room, Kennedy took a terrier grip on recalcitrant witnesses, accusing, badgering and interrupting in his high-pitched bean-and-cod-accented voice." The record of the committee, moreover, is a chaotic account of serious matters in which the rules of evidence were violated probably more than in any other hearings before or since. Those antagonistic to both Senator McCarthy and Robert Kennedy insist that the latter learned from the former, and then carried those teachings on to new depths of investigative license. The difference in public reaction, of course, is that the McCarthy committee was dealing with the respectable and the mighty, called before a Senate body looking into Communist and fellow-traveling subversion, whereas the McClellan committee dealt with men whose backgrounds were frequently criminal and whose lives were seedy. Law and principle, obviously, made social distinctions.

This, of course, creates a problem. In one of its reports, the McClellan committee could note with full justification that "well-nigh incalculable power over our economy is wielded by [the Teamsters'] union. . . . Whoever controls the Teamsters controls much more than the immediate destinies of 1,500,000 union members; he and his lieutenants reach into every household in the land." James Riddle Hoffa was the man singled out, and the report found that his leadership "is tragic for the Teamsters Union and dangerous for the country." This is a value judgment that the millions of words of testimony may bear out, but it is not evidence and was, in fact, extraneous to the legislative purpose of the investigation.

It is the function of congressional committees to educate as well as to find a basis for legislation—a view held by Woodrow Wilson but alternately asserted and denied by the pundits, depending on whose ox was being gored. In assessing the value of the educational process, the aims and methods of the committee in question are of importance. But any analysis of the McClellan committee and of the course it took under chief counsel Robert Francis Kennedy can be made to appear as an attempted rebuttal of the thesis quoted above. That all labor unions, the Teamsters not uniquely, should be held to stringent rules which protect the rights of the individual member and the health of the body politic is not the major issue. Pertinent here are other questions which boil down to the probity of Bobby Kennedy, to his character, and to his fitness for high executive office. It is in no wise a defense of James Hoffa or his surrogates in the Teamsters Union to note what many observers regard as a flagrant violation of legal rights and legal prerogatives in Bobby's drive toward good aims. High-handedness is the father of tyranny, no matter by whom practiced, and it is the tyranny of the Teamsters and of Walter Reuther's United Auto Workers which should be the concern of all citizens.

It should be noted first that the investigative agency managed by Bobby Kennedy was carefully named the Senate's Select Committee on Improper Activities in the Labor and Management Field. Yet in its *jehad* against the Teamsters, the committee's first success was to bring to book David Beck, president prior to Hoffa's ascendancy, for his personal income-tax evasions, a matter of little direct relevance. The first legal action against Hoffa was for wiretapping, a litigation in which the government's prime weapon was its wiretaps of the defendant. Its case against Hoffa for attempting to "fix" a jury was based on a government violation of the lawyer-client relationship. And potentially its most successful case against Hoffa to date has been an indictment charging him with using union funds for his own defense, when that defense was a function of the Select Committee's continuous assault on him. All these litigations would not have been relevant had Bobby Kennedy succeeded in translating into admissible evidence his long catalog of charges against Hoffa.

The story is a long and detailed one, and it has been given extended treatment only in Kennedy's unblushing account, *The Enemy Within*. Researchers for that book consisted of the largest investigative staff on Capitol Hill—a corps of forty-five lawyers, accountants, and trained investigators—as well as the services of the Internal Revenue Service, the Bureau of Narcotics, the General Accounting Office, and the Federal Bureau of Investigation. Contributing time and effort for specific inquiries were local police departments and state and city investigative agencies. The bill for all of this was $350,000 of the taxpayer's money. Did this array of talent labor so mightily merely to bring forth a mouse? The present level of corruption in the trade-union field does not seem to be appreciably lower, and the unions are actively at work seeking congressional sanction for the watering down of the Landrum-Griffin Act, the result of the public indignation over some disclosures of the McClellan committee.

It all began on a quiet day in 1956, when Bobby Kennedy, restless as always, could find no agency of the government kind enough to offer itself up to the Senate Permanent Investigations Subcommittee as a sacrificial lamb in the cause of congressional excitement. In this frame of mind, he was chatting with Clark Mollenhoff, an investigative reporter for the Cowles newspapers and one of the most indefatigable diggers after fact on the Washington scene.

"There's corruption in the Teamsters," Mollenhoff told Bobby. "Why don't you investigate them?" The chief counsel demurred. Other efforts by congressional committees had led to nothing, he said. And, he added, a subcommittee of the Government Operations Committee would have no jurisdiction in this field. Mollenhoff suggested that political pressure may have been responsible for past failures to strike pay dirt. "And you do have jurisdiction," he said. "Unions are tax-exempt, they are required to file financial statements with the Secretary of Labor, and this brings them within the scope of your committee." These financial statements, moreover, were never checked by either the Labor Department or by Internal Revenue for accuracy or honesty. Certainly there was enough visible corruption in the International Brotherhood of Teamsters, the Operating Engineers, and the Bakery Workers to justify a tentative look, Mollenhoff argued.

Armed with the researches of two House investigations and leads from Teamster factions seeking the overthrow of President Dave Beck, Bobby decided to do some detective work on the West Coast. He had, of course, a mandate from Senator McClellan to embark on a "nationwide survey of the labor scene," a broad enough description to open *some* door to the Government Operations Committee's jurisdiction. At every turn in his preliminary survey, he ran across cases that any police reporter could have recited to him—unsolved labor murders, garbage collection rackets, goons in the garment districts of New York and Los Angeles, collusion between unions and employers which cheated workers of their bargaining rights through "sweetheart" contracts. He had but to turn over any stone to find teeming life.

"Some cases cried out for investigation," Bobby wrote in *The Enemy Within*. "There was the union organizer from Los Angeles who had traveled to San Diego to organize juke-box operators"— a notoriously rackets-ridden business. "He was told to stay out of San Diego or he would be killed. But he returned to San Diego. He was knocked unconscious. When he regained consciousness the next morning he was covered with blood and had terrible pains in his stomach. The pains were so intense that he . . . stopped at a hospital. There was an emergency operation. The doctors removed from his backside a large cucumber. Later he was told that if he ever returned to San Diego it would be a watermelon. He never went back."

Plentiful though the leads were, they hardly merited the interest of the United States Senate and its powerful investigations arm. Bobby had been pointed by an anti-Beck Teamster lawyer in the direction of Frank Brewster, head of the union's Western Conference. But when Brewster ducked out of town, Kennedy and his assistant detective, Carmine Bellino, were ready to call it a day. Coincidence and chance intervened. Visiting a "friend of a friend," Bobby was given a lead which, for him, broke open the Teamsters investigation. For "Mr. X," to use Bobby's designation, informed him that the real evil genius in the union was not Brewster, but its president, Dave Beck. Mr. X also supplied Bobby with a key name. In Chicago, he said, there was a labor "consultant" who made purchases for Beck through the companies he represented. From this consultant, Bobby could get the story of Beck's $163,000 house, built for him by the Teamsters, then sold to them by Beck, who in turn received it as a present from his grateful members. Other suggestions and rumors came from Mr. X.

Bobby and Bellino flew to Seattle to begin what grew into their mammoth probe. They registered in a hotel under the cloak-and-dagger names of "Rogers" and "Basilio." The hunt was on. At all times, it was stamped with Bobby Kennedy's snob reactions to people. When he finally caught up with Brewster, who had been plundering the Western Conference for years, Bobby could say of him that "I never felt [he] was an evil man, that he was a gangster or a hoodlum or wanted such people under him in the Teamsters Union." Brewster's saving grace was that he dressed well and abjured toilet water. On the other hand, John English, the I.B.T. secretary-treasurer, who did not play up to Kennedy, received considerably different treatment. Bobby conceded that English was a man of integrity, but he could not resist adding this psychoanalytical note:

"Although he appeared to hate corruption and dishonesty, it was primarily a hatred of Dave Beck. He liked and accepted Jimmy Hoffa."

In describing Dave Beck, Bobby Kennedy would write: "What struck me about Beck on [my] first visit, and subsequently when he testified, were his eyes. At first they appeared to be lost in his large oval face; but soon you noticed it was Dave Beck's eyes more than anything else that attracted your attention."

Eyes seem to obsess Bobby, perhaps because, beneath his slightly downturned look, the blue of his own can be so disconcertingly and and detachedly opaque. In his almost rhapsodically anguished accounts of his relations with Jimmy Hoffa, the eyes are again the locus of his interest. "In the most remarkable of all my exchanges with Jimmy Hoffa not a word was said," he wrote in *The Enemy Within*. "I called it 'the look.' . . . The first time I observed it was in the last days of the 1957 hearings. During the afternoon I noticed that he was staring at me across the counsel table with a deep, strange, penetrating expression. . . . It was the look of a man obsessed by his enmity, and it came particularly from his eyes. There were times when his face seemed completely transfixed with this stare of absolute evilness. . . . Sometimes he seemed to be concentrating so hard that I had to smile . . . but his expression would not change by a flicker.

"During the 1958 hearings, from time to time, he directed the same shrivelling look at my brother. And now and then, after a protracted, particularly evil glower, he did a most peculiar thing; he would wink at me. I can't explain it. Maybe a psychiatrist would recognize the symptoms."

Whatever it was, whether eyes or manner, Bobby developed a living hatred of his witnesses. "They are sleek, often bilious and fat, or lean and cold and hard. They have the smooth faces and cruel eyes of gangsters; they wear the same rich clothes, the diamond ring, the jeweled watch, the strong, sickly-sweet-smelling perfume." Reporters who covered the hearings might have some difficulty in recognizing them from those words. For, whatever evil the men who took the stand may have done, they looked awkward, bumbling, and sometimes frightened in the awesome surroundings as they faced the television lights, the distant disapproval of Senator McClellan, and the drumfire of questions from Bobby and the Senators. Of all the Teamster witnesses, only Harold Gibbons, the union's St. Louis czar, an intimate of Jimmy Hoffa and the Teamster "intellectual" and ADA liberal, could feel relatively at ease. He may not have gone to the best schools, but he had gone to school. He spoke grammatically and was therefore liberated from the intense discomfort of the semiliterate when plunged into a context where words are subtle and destructive weapons.

The time for these observations was still in the uncertain future when Bobby Kennedy and Carmine Bellino flew to Chicago on a slushy winter's day to talk to Nathan Shefferman, the mysterious labor consultant. He was affable but vague. He denied knowledge of improper dealings with Beck or the Teamsters. His records, however, were more explicit. Subpoenaed by the Kennedy-Bellino team, they were taken to a Chicago hotel where for the five days before Christmas the two men studied them. They were far from decisive in themselves, but they furnished leads on which Kennedy's case against Beck was ultimately based. "As we left Chicago," Bobby wrote, "we knew that Dave Beck was through as a labor leader and as a national figure. It was just a matter of time. The documents we had just been reading provided the evidence that would finish him." This is dramatic but it is hardly the case. Of the $370,000 Beck took in a balance of $120,000 had been repaid in 1954, long before the investigation began. Still another $50,000 had been repaid, leaving a balance of $120,000, which Beck put back in the Teamster treasury when his troubles with the Senate investigation began. There was evidence in the Shefferman papers and in what other investigators discovered to show Beck in a bad light. The manner of the "borrowing" and the repayment, as well as kindred other matters, proved that he was a crook—but not an indictable one. He was brought down for tax evasion, and Internal Revenue had been on the trail before Bobby Kennedy even considered looking into the Teamsters Union.

The contrast between Shefferman's benign lectures on the principles of decent labor-management relations and the contents of his financial records gave Bobby and the committee investigators a sense of treasure trove. But it was to be short-lived. Bobby had counted on an examination of the Western Conference's records to nail down what Shefferman's papers indicated. But a Teamster West Coast attorney, Sam Bassett, went into the state courts and won an injunction barring the Senate Permanent Investigations subcommittee from access. The court held precisely what Bobby had argued to Clark Mollenhoff when a labor rackets investigation was proposed: that this was straying too far from the subcommittee's mandate. This point had already been raised on and off the floor of Congress by those who saw the McClellan committee action as a dangerous precedent which might lead to investigations of other, less frowned upon, labor unions such as the United Auto Workers or the International Union of Electricians, both of which are sacrosanct among liberals and profess utter purity. Bobby, however, was in orbit.

"It seemed unlikely to me that a state court judge would determine that a committee of Congress in Washington, D.C., did not have jurisdiction in such a matter," he stated angrily. "But this judge granted the Teamsters the injunction they wanted. We were barred from the records while we appealed."

A lawyer trained in courtroom practice and having the experience of many litigations would have been less puzzled at the lèse-majesté and bumptious pretension of a state judge. But attorneys for the Teamsters did not fail to understand the significance of the ruling. High Teamster officials descended on Bobby's small and crowded office in the basement of the Senate Office Building to protest that he was conducting a "fishing expedition" by delving into the bank accounts and records of the Teamsters Union. In a heated session, Bobby countered that financial records filed by the union were false and that the government was doing nothing about it. This made it a matter in keeping with the Senate's overseer function. Whatever the legal status of the McClellan committee may have been, Bobby had the facts on his side. A check at the National Labor Relations Board, a body with important watchdog functions, showed that only on rare occasions were these financial statements even read. "They were considered secret information," Bobby wrote, "and were not available to the public or to the press." The NLRB, moreover, casually argued that the Supreme Court had ruled that "these reports did not have to be true. It was necessary only that they be filed each year, regardless of their accuracy." The U.S. Treasury did not examine these records because the unions were tax exempt—a practice it does not follow in other instances.

There was a simple answer to the question of jurisdiction: setting up a select committee specifically chartered by the Senate to look into matters involving the corruption in labor-management relations. Support came from those who feared that the Democratic margin of control in the Senate—one vote—could be lost by one Senatorial death, returning the chairmanship of the Investigations subcommittee to Senator McCarthy. Others wanted some representation from the Senate Labor Committee. When the Senate Labor Rackets Committee was created, it included John McClellan as chairman, Irving Ives as vice chairman (courtesy of Joe McCarthy, who realized that, his seniority notwithstanding, his own appointment to the second spot would plunge the group into controversy before it got off the ground) , Pat McNamara, John F. Kennedy, Sam Ervin, Joseph R. McCarthy, Karl Mundt, and Barry Goldwater. When Joe McCarthy died, Carl Curtis took his place.

In March of 1957, Teamster president Dave Beck, who had been evading the service of the subcommittee, conceded that the new body had jurisdiction over matters of labor-management corruption. For almost a whole day Beck held forth (to Bobby Kennedy's obvious annoyance) , answering the questions of Senators who were simply exercising their prerogative. Bobby's annoyance turned to anger, and increased an old antipathy when Senator Mundt's questioning provided Beck with an opening to advise the committee to "write into congressional law absolute compulsion for accounting of funds, if possible by certified public accountants." Bobby had entered the hearing room feeling sorry for "a major public figure about to be utterly and completely destroyed before our eyes." Now he saw that figure lecturing the committee. When, late in the afternoon it was his turn to ask questions, he went straight for the jugular. "Did you," he asked, "take some $320,000 of union funds?" Beck promptly invoked the Fifth Amendment.

> MR. KENNEDY: "Do you feel that if you gave a truthful answer to this committee on your taking of $320,000 of union funds that that might tend to incriminate you?"
> MR. BECK: "It might."
> MR. KENNEDY: "You feel that yourself?"
> MR. BECK: "It might."
> MR. KENNEDY: "I feel the same way."
> THE CHAIRMAN: "We will have order, please."

To the less enthusiastic observers, exchanges such as this only deepened their suspicion that thirty-one-year-old Bobby Kennedy was hopelessly naïve. His tendency to assail a witness whose response did not suit him detracted from an admittedly skillful staff operation. Others saw in these reactions a clear indication of Bobby's moral absolutism. He felt that the Teamster president was guilty, and therefore he could not understand the difficulty of getting an outright confession. This further confirmed his belief in the witness's guilt and relieved Bobby of the need to comply with rules of common courtesy or legal decorum. In these first encounters with evasive or recalcitrant witnesses, Bobby developed the technique which served him throughout the inquiry. He simply dumped allegation, conjecture, and fact into the record, making no differentiation. If necessary, he incorrectly and improperly summarized this patchwork of fact and hearsay, carrying his conclusions much further than his dubious premises warranted. *The Nation,* an extreme-liberal publication, was later to characterize this methodology in scathing terms. By 1962 letters to the New York *Times* would make their protest, and members of the Senate would add their criticisms to the *Congressional Record.* By 1964, a committee of the House of Representatives would vote for an inquiry of its own into Bobby's manner of conducting prosecutions, only to see itself thwarted by Representative Emanuel Celler, an undeviating Kennedy adherent.

With Dave Beck out of the way, later to be convicted of income-tax fraud, Bobby Kennedy moved on to the man everyone conceded would be the successor to the Teamster presidency, Jimmy Hoffa. From that point on, a tangled web of conspiracy and counterconspiracy obscures the record. The observer may say that he *thinks,* that he is *convinced,* that James Riddle Hoffa is guilty as charged in the voluminous Select Committee records and its privileged reports. But between the assumption and the proof demanded by Anglo-Saxon jurisprudence, there is a chasm which the accuser must bridge. To the major charge that Hoffa violated the law in his governance of the Teamsters Union, there is only the damning Scotch Verdict: Not Proven. The responsibility for failure to nail down what has been described as an open-and-shut case must fall to Bobby Kennedy. And he must bear the blame for putting personal vendetta above the public weal, of attempting to leap over barriers set by the experience in law of generations, and by his failure to put first things first. Or, it may be that the charitable explanation is fairest: That Edward Bennett Williams, Hoffa's lawyer, was smarter and better than Bobby Kennedy or the platoon of U.S. attorneys who went into battle since the hearings began. A *prima facie* case of blunders and overconfidence can certainly be made, in which the public has not gotten the protection which this era's tax bill entitles it to receive.

The errors and attempted legal shortcuts of Bobby Kennedy and his aides in their pursuit of Jimmy Hoffa forms the heart of this account. They gave the slum-born, slum-raised, and up-from-the-depths union leader the status of a hero to his rank-and-file Teamsters and continue to make him a legal *cause célèbre.* Exhibit A, then, is the story of John Cye Cheasty, perhaps the first victim of the Kennedy method. Six days before Bobby was to have his first meeting with Jimmy Hoffa, he was visited in his cluttered Senate office by the

lawyer-investigator, who had phoned earlier with a promise to tell
a story that would make the committee's collective hair stand on end.
On the face of it, Cye Cheasty had everything to lose and nothing to
gain by speaking up. Financially and professionally, he could suffer
from reporting to Bobby Kennedy that he had been approached by
Hoffa, that he had been paid $1,000, plus a $2,000 monthly retainer,
to plant himself in the McClellan committee as a Teamster spy. He
was to report on all anti-Hoffa activity in the committee staff and
copy such documents as might be of help to the Teamsters in their
continuing battle.

Predictably enough, Bobby turned Cheasty into a double agent in
order to trap Hoffa. This had been the purpose of Cheasty's visit and
it made sense in the context of the coming Hoffa-Kennedy confrontation. The FBI was informed and worked with the McClellan
committee to develop the evidence for charges that Hoffa had attempted to subvert a committee investigator. The $1,000 he had ini-
tially received—minus minor expenses—was carefully marked and
filed for future use. Subsequent payments were delivered by
Cheasty and handled in the same way. At the same time, Hoffa was
fed through his "agent" enough information to keep him happy.
A month later, minutes after a meeting with Cheasty at which committee documents were passed to him, Jimmy Hoffa was arrested. In
his moment of triumph, Bobby said exultantly, "If Jimmy Hoffa isn't
convicted, I'll jump off the Capitol dome."

But Hoffa was not convicted, and when the jury brought in its
verdict of innocent, Ed Williams jauntily told the press he was
offering Bobby Kennedy a parachute. That part of it the chief counsel took fairly well, although he showed some pique that his original
remark had been quoted by the press. His real indignation was at
the acquittal itself, but he consoled himself by finding scapegoats.
To those who would listen, he explained this setback:

1. Williams had been too clever, and there was an implication
that there was something slightly reprehensible about this. As counsel for Hoffa, he had made judicious use of his challenges in picking
a jury, making sure that he had eight Negroes in the box. Then he
had chosen as associate counsel Martha Jefferson, a Negro imported
from the Midwest. During the course of the trial, Williams had invited Joe Louis to visit the courtroom and, in the presence of the
jury, to demonstrate his friendship for the defendant.

2. The government prosecution had been inept and asleep at the
switch when it allowed a drunkard, a dope peddler, and a suspected homosexual to slip onto the jury without challenge. "Such

people," Bobby said, "are not prohibited from jury service. But they certainly are persons the government might find antagonistic to the aims of law enforcement in a criminal court."

3. Williams had completely surprised the prosecution by putting Hoffa on the stand. It jolted Bobby's ethical sensibilities. As he saw it, Williams knew that Hoffa was guilty and therefore should have ordered his client to stand mute—a bit of reasoning that brought smiles to experienced trial lawyers. In point of fact, had Hoffa not testified, there would have been criticism from those who stubbornly believed that once under oath he would destroy himself. The prosecution was ill prepared for this maneuver, Bobby noted. "As a result, while Hoffa testified with vigor and force, the cross-examination was unimpressive. It lasted only twenty minutes." Again, a trial lawyer could have explained to Bobby that pounding away at a witness who stands firm only impresses his testimony on the jury.

There was one small postscript to the trial. Because of Joe Louis' presence in the courtroom, Bobby Kennedy and the Select Committee decided to investigate him. What this had to do with labor racketeering, and how it could be justified, except as the punitive use of a Senate committee, is a question for others to ask. Bobby nevertheless set out in pursuit. "The former fighter was a lonely figure," Bobby wrote in *The Enemy Within*. "We found him [in Chicago] in a third floor apartment, sitting in a chair and reading a newspaper, with both the radio and the television going." After some questioning, Louis left the room and Bobby blandly asked one of his assistants to get a Louis autograph for one of the young Kennedys. When the request was made, Joe Louis said, "I'll give it to you for his son, but not for him. Tell him to go take a jump off the Empire State Building." Pity for Louis is the reason Bobby gives for never calling him as a witness before the Labor Rackets Committee. The outcry which would have attended this kind of intimidation may have been a more practical consideration.

But the road ahead continued to be mined with this type of device. The fall of 1957 was fat for Hoffa, lean for the Senate Labor Rackets Committee. The Teamster rank and file had seen the bribery trial as the persecution of one of their own.With Beck out of the way, the new notoriety opened the door for Hoffa's election to the presidency of the Teamsters. It was not, however, to be that simple. Every possible pressure and instrumentality to bring about Hoffa's defeat was employed by Bobby Kennedy. Late in September, with Hoffa in Miami preparing his campaign, new hearings were called.

Jim Clay, in a frankly glowing biography of Hoffa, gives the chronology:

"On Tuesday committee chairman McClellan announced his intention to call Hoffa to the stand again on Saturday. On Wednesday a New York grand jury indicted him for perjury in connection with an old wiretapping charge. Hoffa's lawyers appealed to Senator McClellan who agreed to wait until after the convention." The committee issued an interim report listing some thirty-three "improper activities," which accused Hoffa as unfit and unworthy of any position of trust in the labor movement. Senator McClellan put further pressure on the convention by wiring the Teamster leaders gathering in Miami that most of the delegates assembled there might have been illegally chosen. Secretary of Labor James P. Mitchell was pressed into service, and he called on the delegates to weigh carefully the committee's unproved charges against Hoffa. Simultaneously, thirteen Teamster members took the anti-Hoffa case to court in Washington, claiming with McClellan that the convention delegates had been improperly selected. A temporary injunction to postpone the election was granted by the federal district court, then set aside the following day. An appeal was made to the Supreme Court to restore the injunction, but this was denied by Chief Justice Earl Warren.

The refusal of the Supreme Court to intervene was based on the lack of any substantial evidence to back the claims of the thirteen dissident Teamsters. Yet Bobby continued to contend that his investigators had "proved" that 56.2 percent of the delegates were illegally selected and another 39 percent had questionable credentials. To Bobby, though not to Chief Justice Warren, it was possible to "establish" that only 4.8 percent of the delegates who elected Hoffa had any "clearly legal right" to vote.

"These events," Jim Clay wrote "served to solidify Jimmy's support rather than destroy it. . . . He was not a shoo-in. Had the outsiders stayed out of it, it is barely possible that his opponents might have mounted a successful coalition against him. But with so much unsolicited advice the Teamsters' convention was like a teen-age love affair. Try to break them up and they run off and get married." And the marriage lasted longer than most teen-age elopements. The wiretap trial resulted in a hung jury, with the vote eleven to one for conviction. The point to be litigated was whether or not Jimmy Hoffa had hired an electronics expert to place "bugs" on the phones of some of his Detroit Teamster subordinates. Allegedly, Johnny Dio, a notorious New York hoodlum, had arranged for the bugs. This second setback rankled, particularly since victory had been snatched from Bobby by one vote. But perhaps the juror had heard Hoffa's words to the convention which elected him president: "I have no fight with the McClellan committee. . . . But when a congressional committee concentrates on a personal attack or misuses its power, it can be dangerous for all of us. Something is wrong when a man may be judged guilty in a court of public opinion because some enemy or some ambitious person accuses him of wrongdoing by hearsay or inference." Tough-talking and ungrammatical Jimmy Hoffa had not written those words, but his ghost-writer knew whereof he spoke.

In 1958, after a second trial on the wiretapping charge, Hoffa was acquitted. In the course of the proceedings, it was discovered that the prosecution had built its own case on wiretap evidence. There was talk of jury tampering from Bobby, but nothing came of it. There was a fleeting victory when the AFL-CIO, panicked by the mounting criticism of labor engendered by the McClellan committee hearings and fearful that this might lead to a thorough and dispassionate investigation of other practices of the trade union movement, booted the Teamsters out of the federation. Though this saved Jimmy Hoffa the large sums of money he had been paying the AFL-CIO in per capita dues, the expulsion bothered him. It hurt to be consigned to outer darkness by fellow unionists. However, this achievement of the labor rackets hearings became a liability when Hoffa set out to raid those unions which stood in his way. Without the AFL-CIO on his back, he felt, his plans for holding the nation's economy in his hands by a threat of tying up its transport began to look less grandiose and more feasible.

A second "achievement" was longer lived. Prompted by McClellan committee charges that the convention had been rigged and encouraged by a wave of anti-Hoffa sentiment, dissident Teamsters again went to court to prevent Hoffa from taking office as president. A stern judge appointed a three-man Board of Monitors to hold the International Brotherhood of Teamsters in receivership until it had cleaned house. In 1959, Bobby was predicting that the monitors would gather enough evidence during their stewardship to remove Hoffa from office. More than one convicted criminal, he asserted, was drawing the pay and allowance of his union office while in jail—a practice he found not at all reprehensible when Walter Reuther and the United Auto Workers acknowledged that it was not foreign to them. But the Kennedy satisfaction was shattered by a court decision that resulted in the dismissal of two of the monitors for conflict of interest. On Capitol Hill, slow-talking but indefatigable Sidney Zagri, the Teamsters' legislative counsel, was able to convince influential Congressmen of all political beliefs that the Board of Monitors was seeking to perpetuate itself beyond its one-year tenure, and had, all along, been milking the union for exorbitant administrative fees. In July 1960, a federal judge dissolved the board and restored Hoffa.

Once again, Robert Kennedy had an explanation—the perfidy of an "apparently honest" milk-wagon driver named John Cunningham who had headed the anti-Hoffa "dissident thirteen." "By mid-1958," Bobby wrote, "I began hearing rumors that John Cunningham had switched, that he was now siding with Hoffa. . . . I couldn't believe that right under our very noses Hoffa could take over the head of the '13' insurgents. . . . But there had been inducements. Since the middle of 1958, Jimmy Hoffa and his union had been paying some of John Cunningham's bills." Again it was a case of the good guys versus the bad guys. The allegation may have been true, but Bobby never proved it. Much more relevant to Cunningham's defection was the mounting dissatisfaction with monitor rule among the rank and file and the leadership hierarchy. Significantly, Chief Counsel Kennedy's "explanation" made no mention of the "perpetuation in office" charge or of the claim that the "reformers" were making a fat living out of their principled duty.

The battle was not over. But before Robert Francis Kennedy became Attorney General of the United States, what had he done to break the power of the witnesses he had placed in the limelight of the Senate Caucus Room? Had he adduced evidence to rid the Teamsters of the Hoffa machine? Writing for *The Progressive* in 1963, Sidney Lens noted that Attorney General William P. Rogers, a liberal Republican with an excellent record of Senatorial investigation during the Truman scandals, considered most of Bobby Kennedy's work too amateurish to be useful in court.[1] And Harold Gibbons, a member of the Teamster General Executive Board and therefore suspect of motive, presented a bill of particulars which to date remains unchallenged:

It is interesting to see that in three years of investigation in connection with our union, reputed to be completely dominated by

[1] The unkindest cut of all came from Hoffa: "I sat down and put on paper everything I could think of they might ask questions about. Then I got with my lawyers and we went over every item. We'd rehearse what we thought Kennedy would do and we got it right damn near every time. He's not the brightest fellow in the world, you know."

racketeers and hoodlums, one hundred and six names were mentioned.

We searched high and low for sixteen of these names and never found them among our union files or in any respect as being officials or in any way connected with the Teamsters.

Nine of these names we found to be members of the union who had never held any position other than as members. And, you well understand that if an employer hires a person we are obligated under the law to accept him into membership. . . .

We found that thirty-four of those mentioned were former officers or employees but who were no longer associated with the Teamsters in any capacity.

We submitted the names of eight others who were officers or employees of the Teamsters who had been arrested but never convicted of a crime.

We submitted the names of twenty-six people who were officers, agents, or employees who were convicted of misdemeanors or felonies before employment by the Teamsters or election to office. Some of these [convictions] went back twenty years before the men became active in anything connected with the Teamsters.

We had thirteen who were convicted while officers or representatives of the union and were still so engaged. Among these thirteen were arrest records consisting of pleas of guilty to city ordinances relating to disorderly conduct or traffic violations. . . .

There were thirteen, as a total, who could be said to be law breakers who were at the time we filed this report still members of the Teamsters and holding office. Out of a membership of more than 1,700,000, that's not a bad record. It seems to me that in a three-year investigation as widespread as it was, that to be able to come up with only thirteen violators was a case of the mountain having labored and brought forth a mouse.

Gibbons might have added that Teamsters are, by and large, pretty tough people, as tough as longshoremen and as prone to violence. The habits of work and behavior carry over to union affairs. Gibbons' summary, of course, begs the question of gangster control. But it is a startling commentary on the results of an investigation which convulsed the labor movement and the nation. The cost in money was high, but the cost in damages to the investigative process and to the rights of witnesses was incalculable, as another bill of particulars may show.

Let it be noted here that what follows involves the Kennedy method rather than content.

In March 1959, the newspapers carried sensational stories about an insurance company which handled union welfare funds. The company was charged with exacting "excessive payments," but there was little more in these accounts than what Bobby Kennedy had said. The verbatim transcript of the hearing on which the stories were based is interesting.

MR. KENNEDY: Do we find that the brokerage fees that were paid were excessive?

MARTIN S. UHLMANN [a committee investigator]: Yes, we found them to be excessive.

MR. KENNEDY: Excessive in comparison to what standards?

MR. UHLMANN: With the Code of Ethical Practices that has been adopted and accepted by virtually all state insurance departments. . . . I am testifying here only on the relationship between the commissions that have been paid by the [company] under this policy, as opposed to what it should have been under the Code of Ethical Practices. . . .

SENATOR CAPEHART: Are you saying that the Code of Ethical Practices, then, is less than the 10 percent down that you just related?

MR. UHLMANN: Without a question. It has been pointed out earlier how much less it is. . . .

SENATOR CAPEHART: Did you check the records of any other insurance companies or just take the so-called Code of Ethics figures?

MR. UHLMANN: I took the Code of Ethics figures, but . . . I have also discussed it with top officials of at least six insurance companies in several states.

SENATOR CAPEHART: And they told you they pay a lower rate?

MR. UHLMANN: By and large, yes, sir. . . . Of course since the code was adopted in 1957, they have all inserted that in their contracts, so that the code—

SENATOR CAPEHART: Was this insurance written prior to the adoption of the code in 1957?

MR. UHLMANN: Yes, it started, some of it, in 1950 and 1951.

SENATOR CAPEHART: Then the next question is: what relationship does this have to the code if the code was not adopted until 1957?

MR. UHLMANN: . . . I am not in a position to testify on that. . . . I would be getting into an area where I just don't belong."

In a somewhat different category is Bobby's own special manner of arriving at a predetermined conclusion. He had insisted that a close relationship existed between Hoffa and one Joseph Holtzman, although Hoffa flatly stated that Holtzman "wasn't any particular friend of mine." In subsequent testimony, it was established that a trade association of Detroit laundries had been involved in negotiations with a Teamster local. A trade association of the laundries advised its members that the dispute could be settled for $17,500 in cash through a middleman who would pass the money on to a "higher up" in the Teamsters Union. The money was paid and the contract signed. The only connection between this payoff and Jimmy Hoffa was that he had appeared at one of the negotiation sessions. Bobby held that the money had gone to Jimmy Hoffa. The transcript tells the story:

> SENATOR MUNDT: Do you know to whom [the money] was paid?
> MR. MILLER [a laundry worker]: Well, I paid it to John Meissner.

Three other witnesses, all laundry owners in Detroit, testified that they had given their part of the payoff to John Meissner and Howard Balkwill. One of the witnesses added that he "was told" the money would be "given to Mr. Holtzman who was engaged as a labor relations man."

> MR. KENNEDY: Did you believe . . . that the payment that you had been making to Mr. Holtzman, at least part of that went to Mr. Hoffa?
> MR. BALKWILL: Well, we wouldn't have any right to say that it did.
> MR. KENNEDY: Where did you believe the money was going?
> MR. BALKILL: Well, we knew it went to Mr. Holtzman. . . .
> MR. KENNEDY: You believed that it was to go to Mr. Hoffa?
> MR. BALKWILL: Well, I wouldn't make that statement either.

For more than a day, Bobby Kennedy tried to get one witness to say that Hoffa had received the money. Since Joseph Holtzman was dead, he could be of no help, and this prompted one Senator to say, "I am looking for a live witness who knows something about this." On the stand, Hoffa faced the question.

> MR. KENNEDY: There is a situation in this case where, according to the testimony, no hearsay whatsoever but the sworn testimony of yesterday, there was a payment made of $17,500, a payoff, in order to get an intervention from a higher-up in the Teamsters Union. Then you intervened. Can you give us—
> MR. HOFFA: What does that mean?
> MR. KENNEDY: Can you give us any more explanation of that?

MR. HOFFA: What does that mean? That I got the $17,500? Is that what you are insinuating? If you do, I did not get it.

MR. KENNEDY: You did not get that money?

MR. HOFFA: And I deny under oath that I got it.

MR. KENNEDY: You did not get any of the money?

MR. HOFFA: I did not.

As reported in a Washington *Post* headline, these categorical denials added up to: "Witnesses Link Hoffa To Payoff." Bobby made his point.

The treatment of witnesses engaged the attention of Alexander Bickel, a Yale law professor, who published his findings in the *New Republic*. The McClellan committee, he wrote, "with Mr. Kennedy in the lead . . . embarked on a number of purely punitive expeditions" characterized by "relentless, vindictive battering" of witnesses. Exhibit A was Joseph F. Glimco, head of a Chicago Teamster local. A sordid character who reminded Bobby of a "madam" because of his use of toilet water, Glimco was hardly one of nature's noblemen. His police record was not distinguished but neither was it reassuring. And he persistently clung to the protection of the Fifth Amendment.

MR. KENNEDY: And you defraud the union?

MR. GLIMCO: I respectfully decline to answer because I honestly believe my answer might tend to incriminate me.

MR. KENNEDY: I would agree with you.

THE CHAIRMAN: I believe it would.

MR. KENNEDY: You haven't got the guts to answer, have you, Mr. Glimco?

MR. GLIMCO: I respectfully decline to answer. . . .

THE CHAIRMAN: Morally you are kind of yellow inside, are you not?

That Kennedy badgered witnesses was conceded by Joseph Rauh, a former chairman of Americans for Democratic Action. "Any abuses were not due to 'vindictiveness,'" Rauh argued, "but to his lack of experience. If it sometimes led to abuse of witnesses, it sometimes led to witnesses like Hoffa getting away with murder. . . . Far from browbeating Hoffa, it was more a case of Hoffa browbeating him." In fairness to Bobby Kennedy, he must have suffered from chronic frustration as he attempted to elicit answers that his witnesses did not intend to give. Some were shrewd enough to offer a soft answer where indignation was indicated. A giant of a man named Barney Baker had the press laughing with him and against Bobby by bland admissions of his acquaintance with underworld characters whose very names seemed to offend the chief counsel:

> MR. KENNEDY: Did you know Cockeye Dunne?
> MR. BAKER: I didn't know him as Cockeye Dunne. I knew him as John Dunne.
> MR. KENNEDY: Where is he now?
> MR. BAKER: He has met his Maker.
> MR. KENNEDY: How did he do that?
> MR. BAKER: I believe through electrocution in the city of New York of the state of New York.
> MR. KENNEDY: What about Squinty Sheridan? Did you know him?
> MR. BAKER: Andrew Sheridan, sir?
> MR. KENNEDY: Yes.
> MR. BAKER: He has also met his Maker.
> MR. KENNEDY: How did he die?
> MR. BAKER: With Mr. John Dunne.

It could not have been pleasant for Robert Kennedy to be played with in this manner. His anger was most obvious in the famous double-talk sequence with Jimmy Hoffa over the purchase and use of pocket-sized German tape recorders called Minifons:

> MR. HOFFA: What did I do with them? Well, what did I do with them?
> MR. KENNEDY: What did you do with them?
> MR. HOFFA: I am trying to recall.
> MR. KENNEDY: You could remember that.
> MR. HOFFA: When were they delivered? Do you know? That must have been quite a while.
> MR. KENNEDY: You know what you did with the Minifons and don't ask me.
> MR. HOFFA: What did I do with them?
> MR. KENNEDY: What did you do with them?
> MR. HOFFA: Mr. Kennedy. I bought some Minifons and there is no question about it, but I cannot recall what became of them. . . . I have to stand on the answers that I have made in regards to my recollection and I cannot answer unless you give me some recollection, other than I have answered.

Repelled by Hoffa, civil-liberties advocates nevertheless held that Bobby's way of circumnavigating stubborn or unresponsive witnesses was to employ the wholesale use of "guilt by association." The chief counsel, it was repeatedly charged, would place a witness on the stand simply to allow the reading into the record of what investigators had culled, a raw file on the luckless individuals giving in full detail nuggets of sensationalism which would never have been admitted in court. Any attempt to do so would have won a prosecutor the strong rebuke of the presiding judge. Bobby could write, with no compunction since he was addressing himself to an "evil" person, that Jimmy Hoffa's chosen associates were "convicted killers, robbers, extortionists, perjurers, blackmailers, safe crackers, dope peddlers, white slavers, and sodomists"—a catalog of infamy which, true or false, carried no weight as evidence.

In *Power Unlimited,* a scholarly analysis of the McClellan committee hearings, Law Professor Sylvester Petro of New York University went to the heart of the matter:

> The principal responsibility of Congress for the conditions disclosed in the McClellan Record lies in the violation of one of the fundamental principles of a free society—the principle that every man who feels himself aggrieved by unlawful conduct has a right to a day in court and to immediate relief from the Court when irreparable damage is threatened. This right Congress has taken away from employers and employees injured by even the most vicious trade-union conduct. In doing so, Congress has also insured the weakening of employer resistance to the most anti-social and corrupt trade union demands.
>
> Upon frequent occasion during the hearings, Chief Counsel Kennedy and some members of the Committee heaped scorn as well as direct accusations of impropriety upon employers who had yielded to shakedowns or who had accepted unions before the acquired voluntary majority status among the employees. In all such instances the employers were not fundamentally to blame. The blame belonged, in any proper analysis, to the Federal government and to the Congress which made it impossible for the victims of trade-union wrongdoing to secure any help from the law.

In case after case Bobby Kennedy included millions of words of testimony showing that labor goons had used violence and intimidation against both the employer and his employees. But Kennedy showed a degree of bafflement and antagonism to those who would not knuckle under. When a truck driver, William Young, testified to his resistance, Bobby showed obvious incredulity:

> MR. KENNEDY: With the fact that you had rocks thrown through your windshield ten or twelve times and were beaten up, and these

other threats, didn't you feel that you would want to stop driving?

MR. YOUNG: No, I didn't.

MR. KENNEDY: For what reason?

MR. YOUNG: Well, I had faith in the company. I stuck with them.

MR. KENNEDY: You had faith in the company?

MR. YOUNG: Yes, and I stuck with them, with the good Lord's will.

MR. KENNEDY: The good Lord's will?

MR. YOUNG: That is right.

The chief counsel, however, was perfectly aware that the corrupt unions bought and sold whole locals, that they compelled employers to sign up with these locals before going through the seemingly unnecessary provisions of the law which required representation elections. He knew of the refusal of the National Labor Relations Board to protect individuals deprived by some unions of their civil liberties, their livelihood—and sometimes their lives. An employer in Niles, Illinois, told the story of his relations with the Bartenders and Waiters Miscellaneous Union. His refusal to accept the contract thrust under his nose led to the appearance of a group of strange pickets, none of them his employees, who blocked access to his restaurant. Then he was visited by two union officials:

"They said they wanted to talk over the matter of me joining the union for my employees, and I told them that in my opinion they were going about this all wrong, that if they would come in and say that my employees wish to represented by them that was another story, but I said, 'As far as I know, none of my employees want you to represent them,' and I said, 'For me to join for them against their will, or to force them to join in order to keep their jobs was just the same as telling them what church they had to belong to if they wanted to work for me.' "

The union's answer was to launch a war against customers and employees—with tacks spread over the parking lot, tires slashed, and cars ruined by sugar poured into gas tanks. "The Teamsters Union cooperated with them so that we were unable to get any deliveries of food. We were unable to have our garbage taken out. We were unable to have our money removed by armored express, so we had to do that ourselves. . . . We had to go to the source of food or to other restaurants," the restaurant owner testified. When dumps refused to handle the restaurant's garbage, the health authorities turned on him, not on those joining this illegal, secondary boycott. He finally had to cart his garbage to another town. "Then there was intimidation. Our employees were intimidated, they were followed home, run off the road. They drove cars, followed right to their homes. Girls going home late at night were followed and were fearful." Local and state authorities refused to do anything about it.

"I called the state police for protection of the Howard Johnson truck coming from Cleveland. . . . I had a hard time getting them. I even went down to the office, but they didn't seem to be around. Finally I got him on the telephone, and he said, 'Well, I'm sorry, but my hands are tied. I have been called off by the Governor's office, it is a local proposition and we cannot do anything. I am so mad, and our men are so mad, that they are hot under the collar. All of those hoodlums, we would like to put them in jail. But I can't do anything about it.'

"I said, 'This is interstate. They are coming through the state. They are not in the state. It is not local.'

"He said, 'I can't do anything about it now. But I will tell you now, you are getting a raw deal.' "

In the end, the restaurant owner had to give in. He allowed the names of his employees to be put on the union's membership rolls and paid dues for them to cover an entire year.

In a well-run investigation, subpoenas would have been issued for those in the Illinois governor's office who had called off the state police. Local police officials would have been compelled to justify their actions. The NLRB would have been called in, and the local union would have been ordered to show cause why its charter should not be suspended. Yet, though Chief Counsel Kennedy filled the record with similar episodes of union lawlessness and political collusion, nothing very much was done about it. Bobby's eyes were on Hoffa and the Teamsters. They were, so to speak, his reason for investigative existence. To stray from this obsessive concern would have opened up areas too touchy to contemplate. The entire labor movement would have descended on him en masse had he ventured to expose the NLRB to the country's television viewers as a passive tool of the unions, corrupt or otherwise, or to hold it to account for its failure to do what it had been set up to do. It was better to inveigh against the employers and not mess with political dynamite.

The gap between Bobby's protestations and his actions, between principle and expediency, would, however, become most clearly visible in his reluctant move to investigate a union necessary to his brother's already forming plans for capturing the Democratic Presidential nomination in 1960, and in his defense of Jack Kennedy's toothless labor bill at a time when Bobby was informing all and sundry that the only way to fight labor racketeering was through the enactment of stringent legislation rigorously enforced. For the first time, as he fought against an adequate investigation, Bobby took on the Republican members directly, reverting to the "fresh kid" approach which had so infuriated Governor Dever in 1952. The politics behind it were smart. The labor leader in question was Walter Reuther, and he could do much to make or break an aspirant for the nation's highest office.

The case against Jimmy Hoffa would remain in public abeyance while the Select Committee argued in its executive sessions over the handling of the Reuther investigation. Behind the scenes, committee investigators continued to search for the evidence which somehow eluded them but which they were certain would slam prison doors behind Jimmy Hoffa. There were reports that the committee had on its payroll, to aid in this search, a wiretapper and planter of hidden microphones.

The leads came in by the thousands, with unexpected results. The wife of a truck driver reported that he was bringing home a short pay envelope every week because he had to kick back to the union agent. Pierre Salinger, making his start with the Kennedys as a committee investigator, thought he had a good lead until the driver himself came in. He had been keeping a mistress on the side and that was where the money went.

Retrospectively, the question can be asked: Did Bobby Kennedy's experience as chief counsel of the Senate Labor Rackets Committee prove in any way educational? The question must be answered in the negative. For in spite of his repeated statements of repugnance for Teamster misdeeds and his reiterated fear of what James Hoffa was doing to the union's membership, Bobby continued to defend the kind of labor statutes which permitted the very excesses he had publicized. When he was elected to the Senate, he joined the group of unrestrictedly pro-labor legislators in his refusal to consider the need for a ban on compulsory unionism—the so-called "right to work" laws—and gave his blessings to the efforts of the AFL-CIO to weaken the prohibition against secondary boycotts by unions. The Senate Labor Rackets Committee report, however, spells out in abundant detail the consequences of compulsory unionism and the secondary boycott in pages prepared by Bobby or written with his approval.

The report devotes a considerable amount of space to the conflict between Desmond Barry, president of the small Galveston Truck Lines, and the Southern Conference of the Teamsters Union. Desmond had learned that his company was paying dues for its employees to an Oklahoma City local, even though no contract existed and no certification election had taken place. When he ordered payments discontinued, the union issued an ultimatum. Barry thereupon arranged for a meeting between Teamster officials and his employees. At the outset, the Teamster officials, according to the committee report, told the employees flatly that their desires were unimportant, that the contract was between the union and Barry, "not them."

> MR. BARRY: During that meeting, I asked any of our employees if they wished to question those members of the Teamsters Union that were making these demands. They did not seem to wish to, so I asked the specific question: "What will happen if any of my employees does not desire to belong to the Teamsters Union?"
> He said, "Then he wouldn't haul any freight for Galveston."
> I said, "Whoa, wait a minute. What about the Texas right-to-work law? . . ."
> So to the demands, we now had some very thinly veiled threats. Nevertheless, they left when they saw that our drivers were getting a little unhappy with them. I asked my employees if they wanted the union to represent them. They said, "We do not." I said, "That's all I need to know. I will not force you into a union against your will. . . ."
> THE CHAIRMAN: There was a majority present?
> MR. BARRY: Correct, sir. Following that we began to get additional demands for us to sign a contract. . . . They were accompanied by economic pressure. I had my attorney, Jim Saccamanno, send a letter [to the Teamsters] suggesting to them that they petition for a representation election, and if that election indicated that they did represent our employees I would sit down and bargain in good faith. That letter was sent to [Local] 968 in Houston [and to] Local 886 in Oklahoma City, and neither one has yet been replied to.[2]
> The secondary boycott was imposed against us [but] to me there were very peculiar circumstances to the invoking of that boycott. There was no notice officially put out by the Teamsters Union, to any of the motor carriers that were involved in that boycott.

The committee report states that "Barry explained that his company's operation called for interchange or interline of freight at Oklahoma City where it was destined for points beyond that city, but all carriers there refused to accept freight tendered by his company. . . ."

---

[2] There had been repeated testimony of employers who were compelled by threats to sign union contracts with locals which had not enrolled a single member. The employer then paid the dues for his members, or else deducted them from pay checks.

SENATOR ERVIN: These companies base the boycott of the freight handled by your company on the "hot cargo" clause in their contracts with the Teamsters?

MR. BARRY: Correct, sir.

SENATOR ERVIN: And the Teamsters apparently invoke these "hot cargo" contract provisions solely because of the fact that you had refused to compel your employees to join Teamsters. . . .

"Barry testified that the 'hot cargo' secondary boycott was in effect from April 18 to 29 before the Teamsters sent a notice to the motor carriers that Galveston Truck Lines had been declared officially unfair," the report states, although, according to Barry's testimony "not a single employee of Galveston Truck Lines was on strike, not a single one ever went on strike or on the picket line. We had no picket line." The "hot cargo" clause, as a result of court action by Barry, was declared illegal in a ruling of the Interstate Commerce Commission, but the Teamsters simply ignored the ICC. Barry also gave chapter and verse to show how compulsory unionism and secondary boycotts put the small truckers out of business. This led the chief counsel to comment:

"Certainly it has been a trend of the Teamsters Union to move against the small trucking companies in the United States. Most of the larger trucking companies are signed up. So if these smaller trucking companies go out of business, that just means more business, perhaps, for [the big ones]. At least from our investigation, we haven't found that they have been reluctant to enforce the 'hot cargo' clause."

But though he was stern in the committee room, he did not carry his disapproval of the secondary boycott or the practices of compulsory unionism beyond that point. To have done so—and to have used the instruments of law when he was Attorney General against the practices described by Desmond Barry—would have alienated Walter Reuther and the unions allied to the Democratic party.

The why and the wherefore became apparent when Reuther and his Auto Workers Union were called before the Senate Labor Rackets Committee, and when John F. Kennedy made his bid for the Democratic Presidential nomination.

5

---◄─◄─◄■▶─►─►───

Whitewash, Incorporated

THE McClellan Labor Rackets Committee was set up by
the Senate with a clear mandate: to investigate improper activities
in labor-management relations, in the use of union funds, and in the
treatment of union members by their own officials. Under Bobby
Kennedy, the racketeering aspects of some of the more obviously
corrupt or controversial unions became the prime target. Since
these unions had but small power in the Democratic party, this kept
the political life of both Bobby and his brother Jack relatively un-
complicated. The major targets of the committee's onslaught were
the Teamsters and the Carpenters, and these, as more than one newspaperman quickly noted, had frequently thrown their support to
the Republican party in national elections. The Carpenters, in fact,
had been the mavericks of the AFL-CIO, continuing their uneasy
support of Republican candidates long after the United Mine
Workers had failed to lead the labor movement out of the Democratic party in the years before World War II.

The Republicans had zealously joined in the hunt against the
Teamsters and the Carpenters. They hoped by this to reinforce
their claims of impartiality and put the Democratic majority on
the spot when the United Auto Workers was summoned before the
committee, allowing their day of reckoning to dawn on the union
most powerful in political influence, and most active in financial
and ballot-casting support of Democratic Administrations. The
Republican minority was convinced—and the record proved—that
even a cursory examination of UAW activities would disclose at

least corruption in its middle echelon and flagrant violation of labor law on all levels. But as the sensational and sensationalized hearings progressed, it became apparent that Bobby had no intention of turning a real spotlight on the UAW or on its president, Walter Reuther.

Sensing conflict within the committee, the more independent reporters pressed Bobby for a flat statement, one way or another, about his plans for the UAW. With them, he was either evasive or hostile, depending on the degree of "loyalty" that he had encountered. To the "in" group among the Capitol Hill correspondents, he professed himself satisfied that there was no need to investigate this particular house of labor's many mansions. The UAW was honest, he argued, and so was Walter Reuther. The union had been previously investigated, he said. Why plow that ground once more? The answer, of course, was twofold. First, previous investigations had shown serious legal lapses by the UAW—organized violence, corruption, and a disregard for members' rights. In fact, when Reuther had taken control of the union a decade before, he had openly created a blacklist of his enemies in its official family and seen to it that they were forced out. Secondly, the Teamsters, too, had been repeatedly investigated, but this had not restrained Bobby from devoting full time to a new inquiry. His views on the subject of the UAW were later formalized in *The Enemy Within*.

"Before these stories [of his refusal to investigate the UAW] began to circulate," Bobby wrote, "I had sent Vern Johnson, one of our staff investigators, to look into the UAW-Kohler fight and to see if he could unearth any information that would warrant our making a full investigation and holding hearings. On May 27, he reported back. *There were charges and counter-charges by both sides, he said, but he had found nothing new that would add to the millions of words taken by the National Labor Relations Board, or make another probe worth while.*" (Emphasis added.)

This was an interesting approach. In its investigations of other unions, the Labor Rackets Committee had retraced the steps of previous congressional groups, thereby turning up leads for new material. It had held 104 days of hearings, called 486 witnesses, produced 17,489 pages of testimony, and issued a 462-page interim report in 1957. In 1958, the committee had held another 103 days of hearings, called 547 new witnesses, and filled another 17,919 pages of testimony. An exhaustive search of the books of "enemy" unions had occupied months of staff time, and every lead had been tracked down. Ninety-one staff employees had participated, 158 people were borrowed from the General Accounting Office, and members of local police departments gave their help. At the same time, the FBI, the Internal Revenue Service, the Justice Department, the Immigration and Naturalization Service, the Federal Bureau of Narcotics, the Department of Labor, the General Services Administration, and the Treasury Department were called upon for additional services. In contrast to this, one investigator and two justifications were sufficient to clear the UAW in Bobby's mind.

A number of reporters, assigned by their publications to cover the Senate, were not satisfied. Day after day, they brought back reports of a growing split between Democrats and Republicans on the committee. Samuel Shaffer of *Newsweek,* who had over the years won the confidence of Senator Karl Mundt and other Republicans by his impartiality, followed this phase of the committee's internal struggle. An item he wrote for *Newsweek* brought the trouble to a head. "Counsel Robert Kennedy," the magazine reported, "has ignored continued demands for investigation of Walter Reuther, GOP members say privately, and they further emphasize the coincidence that the labor leaders subjected to the committee's sharpest attacks are the ones who have stood in the way of Reuther's domination of American labor." Republican anger was compounded by the knowledge that a Kennedy-Reuther alliance was in the making. This alliance was necessary if Jack Kennedy was to get the support of Reuther at the 1960 convention, support that was vital for any candidate seeking the Democratic Presidential nomination.

Jack's labor record in the past had hardly been pro-labor. When the unions were battling to kill the Taft-Hartley bill, calling it a "slave labor law," Jack, then a Congressman, had written a separate minority report calling for the inclusion of a labor "Bill of Rights" which would make the measure even tougher. But this had been before the Presidency loomed as a real possibility, and throughout the Rackets Committee hearings, he had shown his eagerness to make amends for his past foolhardiness. Eventually, he became one of the leading champions of the UAW in the United States Senate, and Bobby accompanied him every step of the way. The conflict over the UAW within the Senate committee was the curtain raiser for the ambitions of Jack and Bobby.

The *Newsweek* story, therefore, was laid before the committee by an irate Senator Kennedy, who stated with a straight face: "I don't have any information that would accord with that and I think that if that is the opinion of the members they should come out and say if they believe the counsel has ignored demands for an investigation of Walter Reuther." In a manner typical of Senate committees, the argument quickly shifted to the irrelevant question of responsibility for the *Newsweek* item, and the Republican members denied that they were the "reliable" sources mentioned. Nevertheless, the charge had been aired, and it became apparent to Bobby that it could build into a damaging issue against his brother and the committee. There were hurried consultations between the chief counsel and Chairman McClellan, resulting in a shrewd decision. A recognizably Republican member of the investigative staff would be assigned the investigation of the UAW. If he came up with nothing, the Republican minority would be gagged. If he struck pay dirt, the Democratic majority could piously take credit for its lack of bias. This show of magnanimity failed to impress the Republican Senators, but they accepted it as the best they could get from Bobby.

Jack McGovern was the Republican staffer assigned to make a preliminary study of the UAW. But Bobby assigned him only one other investigator to help in this tremendous task. The committee's vast manpower resources that had been turned loose on the Teamsters and on other unions were withheld, and so was the aid of those executive arms which had cooperated with Bobby in the investigation of unions that he had singled out for the full treatment. At the same time, Bobby quietly sent Carmine Bellino, his most trusted aide, and a team of assistants to prepare a countercase more favorable to Reuther and the UAW. When, in October 1957, McGovern submitted a report substantiating serious charges of UAW irregularities, Bobby attempted to discredit it by claiming that it was all old stuff, a regurgitation of anti-UAW testimony from the NLRB files. Simultaneously, he plunged the committee into another internal controversy by charging that McGovern was withholding evidence from him and turning it over directly to the Republican members. He also accused McGovern of supplying false and inflammatory information to the press.

But Bobby's smoke screen failed. He might charge, as he did, that the stories of a Reuther whitewash were planted by the Republicans with labor-hating pundits. But the fact remained that no real investigation had been undertaken. Even press comment unfavorable to the Republicans and favorable to Bobby had to state the terms of the conflict within the committee, which began to feel a loss in public esteem. To quiet this, Bobby decided to visit Sheboygan, Wisconsin, the scene of the long and violent Kohler strike, taking with him a pair of investigators, in a show of preparation for the UAW hearings which, in view of Republican pressure, could no longer be postponed or prevented. His description of this visit to the scene of prolonged violence, in which the United Auto Workers had clashed continuously with the Kohler Company and with non-strikers, is replete with errors of fact, gaping omissions, and a frank hostility to management. His account in *The Enemy Within* is in striking contrast to the evidence which the committee reluctantly took once the log-jam of Bobby's opposition had been broken. For example, he stated categorically that in the Kohler Company's enamel shop "temperatures *ordinarily* range from 100 to 200 degrees" and that the men there were compelled to sustain this kind of heat for eight hours at a time. Under such barbarous conditions, one would have expected the Kohler workers to walk out as one man when the UAW moved in to organize them—which, of course, never happened. More revealing are Bobby's characterizations of management, labor officials, and their physical surroundings:

"Conger [Lyman Conger, the company attorney], thin-faced, with a hawk nose, has a high-pitched voice and a cleft in his chin, which he kept pulling throughout our interview. His face, his manner and his whole body seemed to tighten up at the mention of the UAW. He made no secret of his deep and abiding hate for the union. It was an all-consuming hate—a thing unpleasant to see. Conger made no bones about this: He was in charge and he was running the company as the company had been run when he was a boy. . . . It was Mr. Kohler's company and Mr. Kohler or his delegate was going to run it—not Walter Reuther or the UAW. Before giving in on this principle, Conger made it clear, the company would close down. . . .

"Even the office where we talked was stage-designed to perfection. It had pasty yellow walls and on one of them hung a picture in a cheap frame. It looked as if it had been bought in a five-and-ten-cent store. We sat on stiff wooden chairs which, like the desk, must have been there for at least thirty years."

As against this, there was Bobby's treatment of the labor side: "That afternoon, we interviewed the UAW leaders . . . in their office on the second floor of a rambling Sheboygan building. . . . The office, with its long wooden desks and rows of benches, its walls marked with posters and slogans, looked like the campaign headquarters of some lesser political candidate who knows he couldn't lick city hall. They were not happy to see us. . . . These men felt hatred, too. But it was hatred born of anger and frustration—not the insatiable hatred that Conger seemed to feel."

"Kohler's labor problems date back to 1897," Bobby would write, "when the company cut the salaries of all its workers by 50 percent."

He might just as easily have quoted a 1934 story from the Cincinnati *Times-Star*: "During the depression the Kohler Co. has maintained an outstandingly generous policy towards its employees. Although its business fell off like that of all other manufacturers, there were no cuts in pay until 1931, when hours were reduced ten per cent. Later, rates were moderately reduced. Not until August, 1933, was a man laid off for reasons of economy." It is true that there was a residue of bitterness over a 1934 strike—Bobby's account simply states the union side with no mention that it had been disputed—and over the paternalism of the Kohler Company, which, though economically beneficial to the employees, may have irritated them.

The account of the controversy between the Kohler Company and the UAW, however, is long and complicated. Among the salient points are these: Roughly one-third of Kohler's 3,334 employees voted to strike in 1954. Though the excuse for the union's reign of terror against nonstrikers and the company was that it was "provoked" by Kohler, the first acts of violence were admittedly committed by union people. More than 800 acts of violence by the union were reported. Goons were imported by the UAW to organize the illegal mass picketing which prevented nonstrikers from entering the plant, though the exact number of these goons varies from the UAW's assertion of "ten or twelve" to eyewitness estimates of at least 100. The UAW spent well over $10,000,000, an amount that was vastly disproportionate to the economic stake of the local union. The UAW, by its own admission, hoped to make an example of Kohler, by smashing the company so thoroughly that others opposed to compulsory unionism would get the hint and capitulate.

For Bobby, very little of this mattered. He found the local UAW leaders to his liking, as he recounted in *The Enemy Within*: "I was impressed with the difference between these officials of the UAW and the men Jimmy Hoffa and Dave Beck surrounded themselves with in the Teamsters Union. . . . These men wore simple clothes, not silk suits and hand-painted ties. . . . There was no smell of the heavy perfume frequently wafted by the men around Hoffa." This kind of guilt—or innocence—by inhalation was, however, not covered by the Rules of the Senate or the United States Code. It was therefore vitally important that the Republican investigation, though it was not equipped to scan the many acres of UAW records, be discredited. There were "leaks" to friendly reporters that the Republicans were out to "get" Reuther, that Senator Goldwater and his colleagues were looking for a face-saving way to call off the investigation because it had turned up so few good leads, that the

Republican staff was hopelessly inept and thoroughly dishonest. These charges were later detailed and retailed in *The Enemy Within.*[1]

But how true were these charges? To begin with, Bobby and the majority staff looked into the Kohler case and its cousin, the Perfect Circle strike—two instances of union terror and brutality involving the UAW—but found nothing wrong. Secondly, gross instances of UAW corruption were uncovered by the Republican staff and made part of the record despite the obduracy of Bobby and the Democrats. Thirdly, in such instances, there was no followup by the majority staff.

Bobby's answer was always the same: "Why didn't you do to Reuther what you did to Beck and Hoffa, I have been asked. The reason is very simple and is the answer to this whole question. Reuther and the UAW have made mistakes, as I have pointed out, but as a general proposition the UAW is an honest union and Walter Reuther is an honest union official who attempts to run an honest union. For some people that is unfortunate but nevertheless it is true. Any attempt to equate the UAW with the Teamsters or Reuther with Hoffa will fail—and in fact, did fail. The sooner this fact of life is accepted in the country, the better off we shall all be." The conclusion was *a priori* and *a posteriori,* the former because of ignorance and the latter because of a determinedly closed mind. The report of the Democratic majority, which Bobby wrote, cited several instances of UAW corruption, as well as violations of law and civil liberties, but none of these are mentioned in *The Enemy Within.* The McClellan committee record shows, moreover, that when facts cut too close to the quick of Bobby's preconceptions, he either attacked the witness or set up an altercation which obscured the point. In one instance, for example, he charged that an anti-UAW witness was "out of his mind," which was demonstrably untrue. In another, he berated Senator Curtis in a manner never heard before in a Senate hearing, and then retired strategically behind the broad back of Senator McClellan.

It should be noted here that once UAW witnesses were on the stand, Bobby questioned them on the acts of violence which they or their colleagues had committed at the Kohler and Perfect Circle plants. (They were subsequently given the brush of a humming-

---

[1] Robert Kennedy made $125,000 from sales and movie rights to the book. Joseph Kennedy Sr. insisted on reviewing the contract. When he objected to certain clauses, he was told, "But Bobby said they were all right." "What does he know about it?" Joe Kennedy said brusquely.

bird's wing in his book.) And he occasionally tried to cut short Walter Reuther's dissertations on trade union "philosophy" by demanding categorical answers. But like his brother, Bobby always found good and sufficient reason for the acts of the UAW in the iniquities of management. When Herbert Kohler testified, Bobby questioned him on the company's policy on maternity leave. Could a woman get back her job after having the baby? He found this exchange to be an instance of Kohler callousness:

> MR. KENNEDY: Can the girl always get her job back within two years? Is that written in the contract?
>
> MR. KOHLER: No, we don't guarantee her job. We try to take her back.
>
> MR. KENNEDY: There is no guarantee of that?
>
> MR. KOHLER: No, sir.

But he applauded the stand taken by his brother, Senator Kennedy, when a UAW employee told the committee that he had been forced to pay $5 a week in kickbacks to the union for a compulsory "flower fund" to which some had been forced to "contribute" as much as $43 a week. "It seems that if you are going to partake of the loaves and the fishes that you have to contribute something to maintain the organization," Jack Kennedy said, as if union dues were not enough. "It seems to me that if you did not like it you should have worked someplace else." This, of course, was Jimmy Hoffa's view, though neither of the Kennedys could see the similarity. But these are generalities. An analysis of the McClellan committee record supplies the specifics.

On UAW-condoned and/or -directed violence:

In discussing the Kohler and Perfect Circle strikes, Sylvester Petro, a professor of law at New York University, underscores one point which has eluded students of the subject. "No racketeering unions were involved here," he wrote in *Power Unlimited*. "If there were thugs and ruffians, they were attached to a traditional union. And the union officials were not preoccupied with fattening their own bank accounts or embezzling union funds. The officials of the United Automobile Workers are, so far as an outsider can tell, as dedicated to trade unionism as they say they are. If their conduct raises a problem for society, therefore, it cannot be dismissed as the old problem of how to keep racketeering down—it must be faced, instead, as a genuine trade union and labor-relations problem." This, perhaps, was in the mind of Chief Counsel Kennedy when he said to one UAW official:

"You spent thirty minutes telling the committee about what a terrible thing the company was doing in all of this. If the company did not want to sign with the union or felt that the demands of the union were too great, they had a right to take that position.

"Ultimately, when the strike came along, the first illegal act was done by the union, and that remained for fifty-seven days until the court intervened. . . . It was done by the international officers of which you were one, and of which there were at least a dozen out there."

The issue at question was picket-line violence—justified by the union because it reflected the "will of the majority"—and the union's contention that the only rough tactics observed were committed by management and nonstrikers. The union conceded that there was mass picketing, but argued that it was orderly and legal. According to Allan Grasskamp, president of the UAW Kohler local, the union had issued strict orders against violence. The only instances of improper conduct that he admitted, at least early in his testimony, involved vandalism to his home and damage to the cars of strikers. It took Bobby Kennedy some time to get a forthright answer from Grasskamp about the union's intention to keep nonstrikers out of the plant by force. "The pickets were walking so closely together or with their arms through one another that it was impossible to get into the plant," the chief counsel pointed out.

> MR. KENNEDY: It is a fact that you kept people out of the plant, did you not, when they wanted to come into the plant?
> MR. GRASSKAMP: [finally] Yes.

Another witness, Harold N. Jacobs, a Kohler employee, testified to his inability to get into the plant. "I asked the chief of police of the town of Kohler, Mr. Capelle, if he would try [to get me in] and he made the attempt. But they would not open the line." Senator Irving Ives, ever the advocate of labor, asked Jacobs if he had been "personally" threatened. Jacobs' reply went right to the point. "They told me," he said, "that if I drove my car in they would tip it over, and I had phone calls, and I recognized the man's voice, and he told me I was going to get beat up if I drove across the line. He said, 'We are not a bunch of kids. If you think you are going to get in, you are not going to get in today or any other day.'" A request for help from the sheriff of Sheboygan, friendly to the strikers, did not help. "He went across and talked to some of the people . . ." Jacobs testified. "He came back and told me that if I attempted to get in,

there would be bloodshed." A UAW official, Jesse Ferrazza, identified repeatedly by other witnesses as a member of the imported
goon squad, kicked Jacobs when he tried to get in on foot. Jacobs
had also seen Ferrazza "kick one man in the groin with his knee."

Mrs. Alice M. Tracey, a widow with four children, also attempted
to get in. She told the committee that Ferrazza, identified now as an
administrative assistant to Emil Mazey, vice president and second in
command of the UAW, had "tromped" on her "with something besides soft-soled shoes." When a woman on the picket line struck Mrs.
Tracey, she struck back with her hand. The pickets thereupon
charged her with carrying a concealed weapon, but a search made on
the spot proved that the only lethal thing in her possession was her
lunch. The sheriff's office proved to be of no help in restraining illegal
activity. When Mrs. Tracey called to ask when they were opening
up the line, she was told, "What do you want us to do, go out there
and get our heads bashed in?"

Dale Oostdyk, a nonstriker, gave the committee a sample of the
UAW's methods of recruiting new members. Trying to get into the
plant at night, he was chased by union pickets. "It was quite muddy
. . . and it slowed me down, and I noticed some more pickets in
front of me, and I turned and I almost ran into them. One of them
jumped on my back and about that time there [were] at least three
or four more there and some of them kicked me in the back and on
the side and two of them picked me up by the arms. One picket
. . . hit me on the left temple while the other two were holding me,
and . . . they swore at me and called me names and said that I
ought to be killed for trying to go to work."

Oostdyk was then dragged to a UAW soup kitchen where he
was ordered to join the union and walk the picket line. Ferrazza, the
representative of the UAW's top leadership at Kohler, "told me that
it was a good thing I was not in Detroit, because I would have been
killed in Detroit during a strike." But Oostdyk was lucky. Willard
Van Ouwerkerk, 125 pounds and five feet six inches in height, was
approached by a woman in a Sheboygan tavern who berated him for
not going on strike. "As I got off the stool," Van Ouwerkerk testified,
"somebody hit me from behind in the back of the head." Knocked
unconscious, he was thoroughly kicked. He came to with four broken
ribs and a punctured lung, which kept him in the hospital for some
twenty days. His assailant—"about 230 pounds," according to his
own testimony, and six feet three—admitted the assault to the
McClellan committee but argued that he had been badly treated by
the courts. "My position is," he said, "I think I got a very unfair and

unjust trial on the sentence side of it." Obviously, the UAW thought so, too, because it continued to pay him his UAW salary while he was in jail. Bobby Kennedy voiced no criticism of this, though he had decried the Teamster practice of doing precisely the same thing.

John Elsesser was at home watching television with his daughter on his lap when two jars crashed through his window, splashing paint all over the house. He was kicked in the groin by UAW strikers, dynamite was planted in his car—the explosion failed to kill him but shattered his wife's eardrum. Later he was assaulted and kicked in the groin while taking his family for a drive. An attempt to unload a clay boat at the Sheboygan docks resulted in further picketline violence. Air lines on trucks were cut, abrasives placed in the engines, and rods were rammed through radiators. A contractor was kicked so severely that he was permanently scarred. Damage to his equipment ran to some $7,000.

In the face of this testimony, the UAW nevertheless persisted in its contention that it did not condone violence and would have prevented it had the facts been known to its officers. Yet Mazey, second only to Reuther in the UAW hierarchy, was present at the plant site, and was seen by the committee in films of picket-line violence. UAW officials were present every day, a fact corroborated by many witnesses and never denied. There was one dramatic confrontation between the UAW's John Guanaca and William Bersch Jr. Bersch testified that his sixty-five-year-old father was so badly beaten by Guanaca that he had to be hospitalized for eighteen days. The old man never fully recovered and died shortly thereafter. And Sheboygan Chief of Police Waldemar Capelle described the union's refusal to abide by the law:

> THE CHAIRMAN: You mentioned a number of labor leaders or representatives of the International UAW, I believe, whom you have identified as being present [at the picketing]. It that correct?
> MR. CAPELLE: Yes, sir.
> THE CHAIRMAN: I believe you said . . . that they appeared to be leading the strike or in charge of it, giving directions and so forth.
> MR. CAPELLE: Yes, sir.
> THE CHAIRMAN: Did they ever obey any orders that you gave in your official capacity as chief of police with respect to permitting the ingress and egress of those who wanted to work?
> MR. CAPELLE: No, sir.
> THE CHAIRMAN: In other words, all they gave you was opposition, obstruction, and mass picketing to prevent it?
> MR. CAPELLE: Yes, sir.

THE CHAIRMAN: So they are bound to have known mass picketing was going on to the extent that it provided resistance that denied those the right to go in who wanted to go in, and the only thing that could have been done, in your judgment, is to have used greater force in order to open the way up?

MR. CAPELLE: Yes, sir.

Bobby Kennedy dragged out of UAW vice president Emil Mazey a far more damaging set of admissions concerning the union's knowledge of the illegal acts committed during the Kohler strike. These admissions were a far cry from the public declarations of purity and ignorance issued by the UAW's highest echelon. Professor Petro states flatly that the McClellan committee record "inexorably establishes the responsibility of the International UAW in the unlawful mass picketing. It financed the whole affair; some of its principal officers and many of its agents were continuously on the scene, participating in the mass picketing; and a number of witnesses, some of them clearly disinterested, were convinced that the International officers and agents were in control." What Mazey told the committee is but a small part of the record:

MR. KENNEDY: Just answer my question, Mr. Mazey. Did you know, during the period of the strike, that [the massed pickets] were keeping nonstrikers out of the plant?

MR. MAZEY: Yes, I knew they weren't going in, and so they must have kept them out.

MR. KENNEDY: Didn't you know, as a matter of fact, that they were keeping the nonstrikers out of the plant?

MR. MAZEY: Well, I think if you would come right down to it, they probably were.

MR. KENNEDY: You knew it at the time?

MR. MAZEY: Yes, sir.

MR. KENNEDY: Did you as a representative of the International, the person second in charge of the International UAW, take any steps to prevent this illegal, or at least improper, action of keeping the employees who wanted to go to work from their jobs? Did you take any steps to insure that the picket lines were open for those who wanted to go to work?

MR. MAZEY: I did not. . . .

MR. KENNEDY: Now, is it the policy of the International to condone this kind of, at least, improper action of keeping people from their jobs when they want to go to work?

MR. MAZEY: It was my opinion that every worker out there had a right to protect his job.

MR. KENNEDY: And do you feel that they have a right to protect their job physically stopping those who want to go to their jobs?

MR. MAZEY: Well, there was a court action.

MR. KENNEDY: Just answer my question. Do you feel that that is proper?

MR. MAZEY: I do.

The UAW also resorted to threats of violence and intimidation. The text of a broadcast made to strikers and nonstrikers alike in Sheboygan tells the tale. The speech was made by Robert Burkhart, one of the principal UAW representatives at the strike. ("I was in general charge of the situation," Burkhart told the committee.) And it was as skillfully handled a piece of incitement to violence as any the committee had contemplated. "Anything that happens to them [the nonstrikers] as being accursed from now on out, if I can use such a term as that, certainly they have got to live with it," Burkhart told a rally and a radio audience.

"Now we know who they are. We have taken pictures of them. We have taken down the license plate numbers, we have made notes of what their names are, and just like anything else in life, every action has a reaction. You cannot do anything in this life but that something happens in consequence of your actions and those people should not go without those consequences. . . . I predict to you that the time is coming in Sheboygan County, after these people learn the lesson they have coming to them, that it will no longer be necessary for us to have picket lines either. They will have learned their lesson and will have learned it well. . . . Let's do everything we can to keep them away from the plant before they get to the picket line. . . ."

Burkhart was highly indignant that the Kohler Company indemnified nonstrikers whose homes were damaged by paint bombs, acid bombs, rocks, and gunshots. These payments, he said, encouraged the nonstrikers to resort to violence. It was a neat twist of logic, but Emil Mazey went even further. He saw in the $21,297.88 spent by the company to help uninsured victims of UAW depradations an "incitement to vandalism." "If we assume this to be true," Senator Carl Curtis asked, "don't you agree that the expenditure of union dues for court costs, fines, attorney fees, and sustenance for convicted felons is, to say the least, the passive condonation of violence?" [2]

---

[2] It is interesting to note that the Justice Department is seeking to put Jimmy Hoffa in prison for using union dues to pay legal fees in his defense against government court action. Bobby Kennedy had sharply assailed this "evil" in the Teamsters but saw no cause for indignation when it was practiced by the UAW.

Mazey could not see this. "No, I don't think so, sir," he said. ". . . The president of our union has been the victim of violence" —reference to the shooting of Walter Reuther years before by a racketeer-Communist combine.

Walter Reuther and other UAW witnesses contended that the Kohler Company was responsible for every single act of violence and vandalism, even when committed by UAW members and officials, because it did not shut down the plant when the strike was called. Reuther found this reprehensible and un-American, although as the courts have repeatedly ruled, a company has complete legal, social, and moral rights to continue operating during a strike. These rights, in fact, are as basic as the right to strike.

During the Perfect Circle strike, in the summer and fall of 1955, there were more than 200 acts of violence, including arson, in New Castle, Indiana. These acts included a concerted assault on the plant by thousands of strikers and imported goons—as well as UAW representatives and agents armed with rifles, shotguns, and rocks. Although the union denied any complicity, it did offer to call off these assaults if the company shut down. In fact, E. J. Kucela, an assistant regional director of the UAW, was quoted in testimony as having said that "the union would be willing to go back to peaceful picketing if the management and the city and state police would co-operate and stop protecting nonunion workers." A UAW representative warned state officials that "if the plant operated there would be more violence of the same kind. . . ."

Could this, perhaps, have been what Bobby had in mind when he said, "It was not possible then or during the hearing to show that the union had ordered or condoned [violence]. In my estimation, though union officials protested to the contrary, there was no great evidence that they took major steps to stop it. In addition, the union, though it did not import gangs of goons as the company charged, did permit some ten or twelve organizers to come in and lend a hand. Of itself, there was nothing wrong with this. However, two or three of these were big hulking men, and the testimony revealed they were under no direct instructions and were permitted by the UAW to do exactly what they wished. The result was that two of them caused considerable trouble and got into serious trouble." Here Bobby ignored all the testimony of observers and accepted as gospel truth the challenged statement of the UAW.

And Bobby makes no mention of the fact that the UAW's second in command, Emil Mazey, was on the scene and directing operations. To Bobby illegal mass picketing—and hundreds of acts of vandalism, beatings, and intimidation—ceased to be illegal when perpetrated by the UAW. Without belaboring the point, it may be noted that the National Labor Relations Board report, which Bobby boasts that he studied, carefully noted that the UAW was responsible for the assaults on nonstriker homes. "None of the International representatives in charge of the violent tactics," Professor Petro writes, "none even of those who were guilty of violent assaults, were either punished or dismissed from the UAW, although its top officers admittedly knew about them." To the Messers Reuther, Mazey, *et alia*, nonstrikers were "traitors" to be dealt with summarily, and Bobby concurred. In effect, both Reuther and Bobby were ready, in their defense of the right to strike, to declare null and void the right not to strike.

By the time *The Enemy Within* was being written, Bobby's brother was strenuously preparing for the 1960 campaign and engaged in negotiations with the AFL-CIO for its endorsement. But when Walter Reuther was on the stand, Bobby's pugnacity, and his need to appear impartial, triumphed over his diplomacy. He asked questions about matters he later squeamishly avoided in his book. For example:

> MR. KENNEDY: If the International representatives find that the local people are performing some illegal or improper activity, certainly they can take steps to put a stop to that. . . . They are responsible to the International union, are they not?
>
> MR. REUTHER: They are.
>
> MR. KENNEDY: And finally and ultimately responsible to you personally, as the president of the union?
>
> MR. REUTHER: That is correct. . . .
>
> MR. KENNEDY: Do you have any explanation as to why the International did not take steps to end the mass picketing when it began?
>
> MR. REUTHER: Let me tell you what my understanding of the situation was. First of all, Mr. Kennedy, we don't argue with the point of view that says—
>
> MR. KENNEDY: Will you just answer the question? . . .
>
> MR. REUTHER: As soon as it was brought to my attention, as soon as we had a clear definition that the activities up there were improper, we ceased them.
>
> MR. KENNEDY: What did you mean? You did not know that on the fifth of April, for instance, that the strikers were keeping the people who wanted to go to work outside? . . .
>
> MR. REUTHER: I personally was not familiar with the situation

on the Kohler picket line, but other people in the International union were, because I was later advised.

MR. KENNEDY: Why didn't they take steps at that time?

MR. REUTHER: All right. Because in the judgment of the people who were handling it at the time, and this involved a number of lawyers who were working on this thing, they felt there was a doubtful area there. . . .

MR. KENNEDY: I am not talking about that. I am talking about the fact that these people were preventing other people who wanted to go to work from going into the plant. . . .

MR. REUTHER: On the question of whether they should have kept people out, we have no argument. I think that was an improper activity. . . ."

But Reuther had no answer to Chief Counsel Kennedy's next question: "Did you criticize [publicly] the mass picketing or any of those things that were going on, or the home demonstrations?"

("Home demonstrations" sounds innocuous. But in *The Enemy Within*, Bobby felt called upon to be gently reproving of them. His description: "A group of strikers would gather in front of the house of a nonstriker, chanting and yelling catcalls. These demonstrations were, of course, frightening, particularly to the man's family. . . . Often UAW officials were present, proof that the union was not discouraging these activities." Not mentioned in this carefully deodorized description: the stones and paint bombs, and the shouted threats of further violence, which accompanied the catcalls.)

The UAW, however, was not too concerned by the damage that might be done to its public image by disclosures of labor violence. The press, for one thing, was interested primarily in evidence of financial skulduggery which it hoped to compare with the Teamster disclosures. UAW witnesses, moreover, did not squirm but stood their ground, defending illegal violence as if it were a constitutional right of the labor movement. The union, in fact, had grown and prospered by using violent tactics since the sit-down strikes of 1937, imported from Europe by the young Reuther and condoned by Michigan state authorities. Reuther himself had boasted of the use of force in the first strike to project him into the ranks of UAW leaders. Financial scandal, however, would have done the UAW president irreparable harm and deprived him of his dual role as spokesman for the liberal-left and pillar of the Democratic party. The UAW had, so to speak, dined out on its reputation for "clean" unionism. It was therefore essential for Reuther to prove that he was as clean as a hound's tooth. The country was growing increasingly suspicious of the great sums of money in union treasuries and of the uses to which it was put. The Teamsters investigation had cast a long shadow over the integrity of the entire labor movement, and Reuther was determined to use the Senate Labor Rackets Committee as a forum to end this disquieting situation.

With Bobby's help it was all stage-managed very neatly. Though few had ever suggested that Reuther was personally dishonest, the question was projected as a major "issue" for the committee's inquiry. Two months before he took the stand, Reuther had asked Bobby to investigate thoroughly his use of union funds and his own finances. This was a waste of committee time, but Bobby readily agreed, sending Carmine Bellino to do a meticulously detailed study of Reuther's bank account. With something of a flourish, therefore, Bellino testified that Reuther kept excellent records, that he lived within his salary as UAW president, that he did not destroy checkbooks, and that he almost never dealt in cash. He also indicated that the books of the UAW seemed to be in good order, though he admitted that his look at them had been cursory. The publicized exchange between Bobby and Bellino put the icing on the cake and allowed Reuther to claim that the UAW had been given a clean bill of health.[3]

> MR. KENNEDY: So the procedure that we have found in some people that have appeared before the committee, of dealing completely in cash and keeping the money in cash in a little box at home, that procedure was not followed?
> MR. BELLINO: In this particular case with Mr. Reuther, and also his union, the procedure is entirely vastly different from the other union leaders that we have had before us and which we have investigated.

And later:

> MR. KENNEDY: What about the expenses from the union, Mr. Bellino? What occurred as far as the expenses are concerned?
> MR. BELLINO: Mr. Reuther's expenses invariably—he would submit expense accounts to his union at the per diem. . . . It ranged from $7.50 to $12 a day. I found in instances when he was traveling

[3] No favorable or adverse report was possible without a careful audit by General Accounting Office officials, the kind of audit that the Teamster records had received. Nor was there any attempt to look into contributions by the UAW, from general funds, to such nonunion organizations as Americans for Democratic Action.

or was on business for the AFL, during that period of time he did accept the check from the AFL, he would not submit a bill to the "UAW"—the AFL-CIO per diem was $35—later on he found, at least his procedure was to turn in his check from the AFL to the union and receive the lesser per diem from the union.

Though Bellino was well informed in these matters, he failed to notice the existence of regular kickbacks by some UAW officials, lightly disguised as contributions to a "flower fund." This fund, according to the McClellan committee report, was controlled by Reuther, the six vice presidents of the UAW, and the secretary-treasurer. There was also a "flower fund" for each regional head-quarters of the UAW. (The name derives from the time when members passed the hat to buy flowers for a departed member's funeral.) There was no accounting of the money in the fund, and at the end of the year, all records were destroyed. In the final report of the Labor Rackets Committee, the Democratic majority would casually admit the existence of this fund, but Bobby ignored it in his later defense of Walter Reuther.

To Bobby, Reuther was by definition honest, and therefore the UAW was honest. Anyone who questioned this pat deduction was anti-union, a crook, or anti-Kennedy—if not all three. No matter what evidence was adduced, Bobby continued to insist that no further investigation was necessary, dropping the entire business into the laps of the harassed two-man minority staff. The majority report, signed by Senator McClellan, makes no bones of this, particularly where the Kennedy apathy touches on the case of Richard Gosser, a vice preisdent of the "honest" UAW and an "insider" in the leadership since 1946, when he had thrown his weight behind Reuther's drive for the UAW presidency. "As Chairman of the Committee," McClellan wrote, "I think it proper for me here to state that the foregoing UAW-Gosser investigation was conducted by the Republican members of the Committee and their counsel; also that the subsequent executive and public hearings were held at the request of Senator Curtis[4]. . . . The witnesses, however, were not examined by the regular members of the Committee staff, nor were the Democratic members of the Committee made acquainted by Senator Curtis, or other Republican members of the Committee, with the nature of the testimony that was to be represented. . . . Thus, this particular investigation was conducted by the Republi-

[4] Carl Curtis, a Nebraska Republican, who was named to the Committee on the death of Senator Joe McCarthy. The Gosser disclosures receive extended treatment later in this account.

cans and the hearings thereon were held for their accommodation. Therefore, they are entitled to all credit and chargeable with all blame for the adequacy or inadequacy and for the character of the record made, which record now speaks for itself."

But did it? Senator McClellan has always been given to ironic thrusts, and it was not clear then to those who discussed his words with him whether he was criticizing the Republican minority or making a record of his own. He knew, of course, that Senator Curtis and the minority staff had been hamstrung at every turn, that any information they passed on to Bobby had a way of reaching the subjects under investigation. If he read the newspapers or talked with the reporters who covered the investigation, he was aware that Bobby also "briefed" those friendly to him, playing down the importance of what the minority planned to develop at future hearings. Procedure rather than substance became the significant factor in this byplay, and Bobby makes much in *The Enemy Within* of the fact that witnesses called by the Republicans were put on the stand in open hearings without prior executive session questioning at which their testimony could be weighed and sifted. According to his account, he considered this improper. But he did not explain why the minority was driven to follow that course. The minority report, when the hearings were concluded, spelled it out:

"Through this period, Reuther and his UAW attorneys, joined by Senators Kennedy and [Frank] Church, contended that closed hearings were unfair to the UAW and demanded that they be made open. Consequently, the Committee voted to hear the remaining nine witnesses in open session. . . . Once Reuther's demands for open hearings were granted, however, the proponents of open hearings, now joined by the chief counsel, insisted that open hearings were also unfair to the UAW and demanded that any further hearings into the UAW, public or private, be suspended." But the minority report goes further:

"Thus, these hearings were conducted under the most trying conditions. Due to repeated delays and continuances of the Committee, many witnesses, in order to testify, were required to make four round trips from their jobs in Toledo and Detroit to Washington, D.C., and, in addition, suffered the losses of many weeks of needed pay as a result of being absent from work. Moreover, the actions of the chief counsel were designed to obstruct any really effective hearings into the issue of corruption in the UAW. The record demonstrates to any impartial reader that he openly acted as defense counsel for those under investigation, although the UAW was already repre-

sented by an impressive array of three able lawyers, and assumed
the role of avenging angel toward witnesses who, under subpoena,
were cooperating with the Committee to expose corruption in the
UAW. Authorized to take no part in the proceedings, he, nonetheless, officiously praised pro-UAW evidence and belittled that which
tended to prove investigative charges. And, when it was proved that
Gosser's corruption had been whitewashed by Reuther and the entire top leadership in the entire UAW International, he, with an
eye to the press tables, denounced the hearings as a 'fraud.'

"We can safely say that never in all our combined experiences with
committees of Congress have we witnessed such a display of obstruction, impertinence, and disrespect by an employee of the Senate."

This might be dismissed as a partisan rebuttal. But a reading of
the record sustains the charges. Beyond the record, however, is the
cool cynicism of a chief counsel who gave a clean bill of health to a
union whose leadership was in trouble with the Internal Revenue
Service for nonpayment of income taxes to the amount of some
3,000,000 dollars falsely collected as "expenses." This is what the
Treasury demanded of Reuther, Mazey, and other high officers,
though they only paid approximately five percent to settle the suit
out of court. This is in itself a possible indication that the UAW's
books were not so scrupulously kept as Bobby and Carmine Bellino
represented them to be. As Attorney General, Bobby would prosecute Hoffa for using Teamster funds to finance his defense in the
marathon litigations initiated by the Justice Department. But
Bobby saw no parallel, nor did one present itself to him as the
1960 Presidential campaign moved closer.

Significantly, the bill of particulars that should have been drawn
up, as a starting point for investigation, by Bobby during the UAW
hearings was produced in 1961 by Randolph Gray, a former executive board member and financial secretary of Local 12-UAW, and
Harold Bilheimer, a member of Local 773. Their complaint
against Reuther and Mazey, as summarized by the Detroit *Times,*
follows:

> The spending of millions of dollars falsely described as "expenses"
> when in fact it is used as salary.
> The spending of thousands of dollars camouflaged as expenses
> when in fact it is spent for political purposes.
> The use of union funds for illegal purposes.
> Expenditure of union funds for political purposes.
> False recording of expenditures of union money.

The defendants . . . charge that any person critical of Reuther or Mazey is not only "disregarded" but in some instances has been "punished."

Gray and Bilheimer charge also that union members are taken from their jobs in various parts of the country at election time and forced to work on behalf of candidates chosen by Reuther and Mazey.

These workers are paid from the union treasury and the money involved is earmarked as "expenses." . . .

Collections for the [flower]fund are "under duress and coercion," the suit says, and employers who do not contribute are "punished by the defendants." The suit claims that no accounting of the flower fund has ever been made. . . .

Had there been the slightest disposition by Bobby Kennedy to pursue these leads, the Gosser case would have been his great opportunity. For here were all the elements which had evoked his righteous indignation in the Teamster proceedings. Richard Gosser, alias Richard McMullen, alias Richard Goffer and Richard Goofer, had "a police record of arrests and indictments for burglary, auto theft and receiving stolen property," according to committee records. "He was convicted of armed robbery and sentenced to 2½ to 15 years." His highest salary at the UAW, as head of the Toledo local, was $12,000 a year, yet he was able to afford a house in Toledo and another in Hollywood, Florida. He had numerous bank accounts, a ranching firm holding 1,184 acres in Michigan, and 1,829 acres in Florida. As senior vice president of a union priding itself on its honesty, he should have been compelled by Reuther to explain these holdings and his ability to acquire the money to buy them. True, he had a sizable income from slot machines, but this was hardly something to commend him to a committee which had taken such a dim view over the involvement of Teamster officials in this kind of enterprise.

The majority report is surprisingly replete with the details Bobby found unimportant or irrelevant. Among the activities of Gosser's local, there was, to begin with, the strange relationship between John D. Dale, a management consultant, and Peter Zvara, an international representative of Gosser's Toledo local. Dale testified that he was paying Zvara a fifteen percent "finder's fee" for steering union business to Dale's company. In this improper, if not illegal, way, Zvara made $63,000, which was paid to him through dummy corporations. Other witnesses testified to similar arrangements which

Gosser had permitted between union officers and management. Zvara, when questioned, took the Fifth Amendment. Other UAW officials did the same, and despite Bobby's frequently expressed repugnance for others who hid behind the skirts of the Constitution, there was no outcry from him.

"About 1945, Melvin Schultz and Richard Gosser invested $4,000 each in a business . . . called Colonial Hardware Co. About 1949 or 1950, Gosser bought out Schultz for the amount of money Schultz had invested," the committee report stated. "Later still, Gosser sold the hardware store to Local 12 [his local] for . . . $44,720.64, plus fixtures, $5,500. Gosser did not deny . . . receiving income from Colonial"—to the tune of $39,645. He admitted that there was a "flower fund" to which all officers and international representatives were compelled to contribute. Records of this "fund" were retained "only until the end of the year and then destroyed."

"Lloyd Speidell testified that he became recording secretary of Local 12 in Toledo in 1944 and quit in 1948. Speidell said there was an arrangement peculiar to the Willys-Overland unit whereby, even though there was a checkoff for union dues payments, members were required to go to the local and get a card punched; no other receipt was accepted as a requirement for voting [in union elections]. Speidell said that during the war, the Willys-Overland unit made up about 15,000 of a total membership [in Gosser's local] of 45,000. At election time, Speidell said, cars under Gosser's direction came out to the Willys-Overland plant and transported the members who were favorable to Gosser down to the local to vote during working hours. Others came on their own, if at all. He said the votes cast usually ran about 500 to 800 for an election. . . ."

The majority report continues: "Speidell gave hearsay testimony that men were taken off the local payroll and put on the International payroll, which carried a higher salary, but they continued to function in the local and were required to kick back the difference in salary to Gosser. One instance of this involved Frank Molik, who was on the International payroll. . . .

"Jess F. Motsinger, of Detroit . . . has held numerous offices in Kaiser-Frazer Local 142, including the presidency, which he held in 1950-51. He was appointed International representative by Walter Reuther and assigned to Gosser. At the outset of his assignment to Gosser, he was called in by [the] administrative assistant to Gosser, and was told he would start paying $5 each week to the flower fund in cash. He was warned not to have to be asked for it.

On one occasion he failed to pay because his paycheck was mis-routed and subsequently [pay] checks were held up.

"In 1953, Emil Mazey sent around cards to be signed, authorizing $2 per week payroll deductions for the UAW-CIO Political Action Group. Motsinger felt he had to do it to keep his job. This contribution is separate from the flower fund. . . . Motsinger . . . was expected by [International representative Russell] White to report more pledge cards [in a Philadelphia representation drive] than he actually had. Motsinger was eventually discharged by UAW after his altercation with Russell White."

This committee statement of facts had been drawn up on the basis of voluminous testimony. The Bolman case, however, is particularly interesting because of Bobby Kennedy's reaction. John E. Bolman's testimony concerned a farm at Sand Lake, Michigan, purchased by the Will-O-Land Sportsmen's Club, an organization headed by Gosser and made up of a number of UAW members. The Sand Lake property was purchased for $9,500 and improved by UAW members who were ordered to work there. If they were late or did not go there at all, they were fined—a fact thoroughly attested by many witnesses, by the partial admissions of Gosser himself, and by letters he had written. Two parcels of the Sand Lake property were later sold to a Mr. Davis for $12,500. Still another parcel was sold for $12,500. Finally the remainder of the farm was bought by a subsidiary of Gosser's local, the Automotive Workers Building Corporation, for $20,000. In short, Gosser and his friends had made a profit of $35,500 on an investment of $9,500—not as gaudy as some of the Teamster deals, but pleasant. In addition, supplies for the farm were purchased from Gosser's Colonial Hardware Company.

At a meeting of Gosser's local, Bolman introduced a motion calling for an accounting of the Automotive Workers Building Corporation. As he was speaking, a UAW member, Walter Murphy, walked from the front of the meeting hall and hit him hard enough to break a bone in Bolman's face. Others joined in the assault.[5] Bolman testified that he had introduced the motion because he was certain that the Automotive Workers Building Corporation was being run for Gosser's profit. By examining bills from Colonial

---

[5] Bobby's later summation of this episode is interesting. Justifying his lack of interest in pursuing an investigation of the attack on Bolman and the reasons behind it, he brushed the matter aside as nothing more, "in my estimation, than two individuals who have had some drinks getting into a fight in a plant, and one of them hitting the other with a Coke bottle or a bottle of pop."

Hardware, Bolman had also discovered that Gosser was selling supplies to the Sand Lake farm at inflated prices. Unable to get an accounting via orderly union procedures, Bolman filed suit to gain access to the books and to enjoin a UAW gift of a lifetime lease on a cabin at the farm for Gosser. When he refused to withdraw his suit, Walter Reuther expelled him from the Union—which meant that he could no longer work at any unionized automotive plant.

In the course of the suit, a firm of auditors was called in to examine the books, but as in Teamster cases, the records were, in the words of the Democratic majority report, "insufficient to permit an audit." The case eventually was settled out of court, with the UAW paying court costs. The Bolman story was supported to a degree by Randolph Gray, later to file suit against Reuther and Mazey, who was then recording secretary. Gray corroborated Bolman's account of the fracas, introduced letters to show that Gosser's office penalized UAW members who did not work on the farm, and added that UAW employees were occasionally required to work at Gosser's hardware store. And he recalled one $810.40 bill from Colonial Hardware to Automotive Workers in which there was an overcharge of $382.10. As a result of his protest in that single instance, $120.00 was rebated. He further testified that when Bolman filed his suit, Gray was ordered by the UAW attorneys to keep the records out of sight. He had, Gray said, hauled them around in the trunk of his car. Eventually, according to his account, a UAW lawyer had destroyed some of the records in Gray's presence.

This pile-up of evidence against the "honest" UAW enraged Bobby. He sent investigators to Toledo to dig up what, if anything, could be used against Bolman and Gray. The counterattack, as launched before the McClellan committee, consisted of charges that Gray was biased because he had been feuding with Gosser; that Bolman was a stooge of the Committee to Save Toledo Payrolls, a group organized to fight a pension plan then being proposed by Gosser; that Bolman was a jailbird and crazy.

The record of the hearing at which Bobby openly allied himself with the UAW against his own Senatorial employers is an interesting one. He had seen the evidence of financial irregularities piling up against Gosser. Witnesses had testified to John Bolman's beating at a UAW meeting, for standing in opposition to the leadership and for seeking, by parliamentary means, to get an accounting of union funds. The obvious question of any objective observer would be: If the pathetically undermanned Republican minority could unearth this much, what would a full-fledged investigation have brought to light? Only by discrediting Bolman could Bobby salvage the carefully constructed picture of UAW virtue. Wise in the ways of the press, he knew that if Bolman were merely accused of being a management stooge, it would make good headlines.

Gosser had proposed a pension plan for Toledo, Ohio, companies under union contract with the UAW. This had been opposed by the Committee to Save Toledo Payrolls, presumably a management group. The need, therefore, was to link Bolman with the Toledo committee, and to make it seem that his perfectly proper demand for an accounting by Bolman was malignly and corruptly motivated. Breaking into Bolman's testimony, Bobby took over the questioning.

> Mr. Kennedy: At that time, Mr. Bolman, had you taken a stand on this pension—
> Mr. Bolman: You need not finish. I had not, and I didn't even know anything about this pension plan.
> Mr. Kennedy: Do you know why they raised that question?
> Mr. Bolman: Sure I know why they raised it. It was the old red herring, as I explained before.
> Mr. Kennedy: Did you ever take a stand on the pension?
> Mr. Bolman: I never did.

Bobby repeated the question in a variety of forms, getting the same categorical denial that Bolman's opposition to Gosser was connected with the fight over the pension plan. In the movies, this tactic works wonderfully, with the witness finally breaking down and confessing. Its purpose is to convey the impression that the cross-examiner knows the witness is lying and hopes to wear him down. But, as every experienced lawyer knows, badgering a witness frequently has the effect of reinforcing his story and making him seem the underdog in an unequal contest. Failing to break down Bolman, Bobby tried finally to link him with the antipension committee.

> Mr. Kennedy: Evidently, this committee, the Committee to Save Toledo Payrolls—
> Mr. Bolman: I think that is what they referred to . . .
> Mr. Kennedy: As I understand, too, I believe it was Mr. Gosser's idea, and the officials from the union, who were trying to put the pension into operation, and it was being opposed by the Committee

to Save Toledo Payrolls. Did you ever have anything to do with the Committee to Save Toledo Payrolls?

MR. BOLMAN: None whatever.

Bobby worried that for a while, attempting to imply that Bolman's legal bills in a suit against Gosser and the UAW had been paid by the antipension-plan committee. It was already in the record, and from a reputable witness, that Paul Block, publisher of the Toledo *Blade,* had engaged the attorney for Bolman and paid the fees. Realizing that he was losing his audience, Bobby shifted abruptly to a personal attack on Bolman in which he made use of the researches of his investigators.

MR. KENNEDY: How many times have you been arrested, Mr. Bolman?

MR. BOLMAN: I would say two or three times.

MR. KENNEDY: How many times have you been convicted?

MR. BOLMAN: Twice.

MR. KENNEDY: Three times, would it be?

MR. BOLMAN: All right, let us say three. You have the record, and put it in evidence.

Bobby preferred to state as fact that Bolman had been arrested "many more times than three times." Bolman refused to take this lying down.

"I understand the object in checking the credibility of a witness," he said sharply, "but I would like to point out something else, too. I recall statements [by Bobby] made to the effect that because these cases were approximately ten years old, they had no real value. Now it seems as though something that happened thirty years ago seems mighty important."

Under questioning by Senator Curtis, Bolman was able to amplify this testimony.

Q. Mr. Bolman, this serious trouble that you were in and you say you served time for, about how long ago did that take place?

A. I say approximately thirty years ago. . . .

Q. Have you been in serious trouble since?

A. No, sir.

Q. And approximately how old were you when you got in trouble?

A. The last time, twenty-one.

Q. And how old are you now?
A. Forty-eight.

But Bobby did not intend to let it go at that. He found it highly
suspicious that a newspaper publisher should supply Bolman with
counsel. In an explosive speech to the witness, to the committee,
and to the television cameras, he said:

"Here are the attorneys under very unusual circumstances. You
don't contact them. They contact you, and you go and visit with
them, and they tell you that you don't have to pay them, somebody
else pays them. During this same period of time the employers were
getting together and were opposing Richard Gosser.

"I would like to say, Mr. Chairman, this is the very thing we went
out and investigated. Our two investigators went out there and
talked to these attorneys and they admitted that these charges
were all a fraud, they couldn't sustain the charges, and that they
went to this man, and the charges were then brought because the
employers wanted to ruin the pension plan in Toledo. Mr. Block
the publisher admits it at this time and so did the attorneys admit
it."

This was a shocking statement. If the attorneys had, in fact,
spoken as Bobby charged, then they were guilty of highly unethical
conduct both in betraying a client and, at the time they had handled
his case, in violating their oaths as officers of the court. The following day, in the presence of the committee, Robert Manuel, as assistant counsel, insisted on making a statement.

"Mr. Chairman," he said, "would you indulge me for one moment? There is something in this record that should be set clear
because it reflects on my integrity and the integrity of Senator Curtis. . . . This is in regard to a statement by the chief counsel yesterday." Here Manuel picked up the record and pointed to Bobby's
outburst. "He is stating that Mr. Ells, the attorney for the *Toledo
Blade*, had admitted to our investigators that [the charges made by
Bolman] were a fraud. I called Mr. Ells last night and he said that
he had made no such statement. . . . He asked me to state for the
record that he had made no such statement."

Bobby, however, did not falter. Never one to admit error, he responded with righteous indignation when he was brought to book
—as if the minority members had somehow transgressed by pointing out his irresponsible behavior. At such times, he would cry out:
"I am telling the truth, and I don't care who else says it. I am telling

the truth." Not once did he retreat from a statement made earlier at the hearings, an attack on the committee such as no other counsel could have survived, or at least no other counsel who was not the son of a powerful friend of the chairman and the brother of a member already being discussed as the next Democratic candidate for the Presidency.

"I think it is the worst situation I have ever seen since I have been with congressional committees," he said. "I want to make it clear that myself and the people under my direction have . . . had nothing to do with this [UAW] investigation. I think it is a completely intolerable situation and should not be allowed to go on, but this is the decision of the committee."

"It is a bad situation," said the chairman solemnly. It was not improved by his subsequent rulings. At Bobby's request, during an executive session, McClellan sent Senator Curtis' administrative assistant out of the room, barring him from the hearing although he had prepared the material on which the minority member's questions were to be based.

For Bobby, the answer to all the evidence and the charges against Gosser and the Toledo local of the UAW—the slot machines, the violence, the real-estate deals, the purchases at inflated prices from a store owned by a union official—was provided by Walter Reuther's defense. "I happen to know Dick Gosser and I know he has made a great contribution to this union," Reuther said on the stand. "He is a decent, honorable citizen, and I know he would not take a dishonorable penny from any one or any source."

"But you would agree that the practice of someone buying and selling to themselves with other people's money is not a good practice, not ethical, would you say?" Senator Curtis asked.

"That is precisely why we asked Mr. Gosser to sell his interest in the hardware store," Reuther answered.

There are two other curious episodes which are revealing of Bobby's method and the workings of his mind. During one of the pitched battles, early in the committee's series of hearings on the Auto Workers, in executive session attended by the Republican minority and the steamrolling Democrats, Senator Goldwater protested that unless the committee applied the same standard of investigatory zeal to the UAW that it had to the Teamsters, the Carpenters, and other unions, no purpose would be served by calling Walter Reuther to testify. It was clear to him that the UAW president would simply be given a forum and the free publicity of a televised hearing. But, he added, should the committee decide to invite Reuther, he would have some questions to ask him. In *The Enemy Within*, Bobby summed up Goldwater's statement in a manner which gave a totally erroneous impression and seemed to sustain his own view that there was no need to investigate the UAW.

"On March 5 [1959]," Bobby wrote, "Senator Goldwater suddenly announced at a committee meeting that he saw no reason to call Walter Reuther; he did not believe Reuther could add anything, although if he did come he would have some questions to ask him. I thought Senator McClellan was going to faint at this. After all the charges of cover-up, whitewash and shielding, after months of investigation [*sic*] and weeks of hearings, Reuther's chief antagonist, Senator Goldwater, was suggesting that there was no reason to call him. When the Chairman recovered from his surprise, he said he would not be a party to denying Reuther an opportunity to testify."

The second episode concerns a letter presumably written by Victor Reuther and jointly signed by him and Walter when they were working in the Soviet Union in 1933. It was a loud hosanna for Communism, for the Soviet system. "You know Wal and I were always strong for the Soviet Union. You know we were always ready to defend it against the lies of the reactionaries," it said. "Here are no bosses to drive fear into the workers"—this at the time of the Stalin terror. "No one to drive them in mad speedup. Here the workers are in control. . . . In our factory, which is the largest and the most modern in Europe, and we have seen them all, there are no pictures of Fords and Rockefellers and Mellon. No such parasites, but rather huge pictures of Lenin. . . . In all my life, Mel, I have never seen anything so inspiring. Mel, once a fellow has seen what is possible, where the workers gain power, he no longer fights for an ideal, he fights for something which is real, something tangible. . . . Carry on the fight for a Soviet America."

It was the kind of letter many young men in the early Thirties might have written, particularly those who, like the Reuthers, had been working closely with the Communist party at the time. What made it interesting was the Reuther refusal to admit the letter was genuine, without ever calling it a forgery. It had appeared several times in the *Congressional Record*. The *Labor Digest* had published it in 1937. And it had been published by the *Saturday Evening Post* in August 1948, with an explanatory note: "*Both the Reuthers concede that Victor wrote a personal letter to Mel Bishop, describing with approval the strivings of the Russian workers for economic improvement*," the magazine stated. "Walter says it was

a burst of adolescent enthusiasm' and adds that whoever gave
currency to the circulated version distorted the original and made
additions to it, including the closing phrase. Victor agrees with
this. . . . *He did not, as requested, indicate on the forwarded copy
where distortions or additions had been made."* (Emphasis added.)

In *The Enemy Within*, Bobby mentions the "famous letter the
Reuther brothers allegedly wrote to one Mel Bishop, a friend in
America, praising the Communist system. We located Mel Bishop.
He had left the UAW in the late 1940s after becoming closely associated with some of the gangster element in Detroit. . . . In
our interview, he said that letter had been written by Victor
Reuther, not Walter, and that around 1933 he had given it to his
then schoolteacher for safekeeping. . . . [The schoolteacher] said
she had never seen such a letter. . . . Because of Mel Bishop's un-
reliability, no one ever raised the question of the letter at the
hearing." And then, with startling frankness: "So even this maneuver
was unsuccessful."

The Democratic bill of particulars as published in the committee report offered a *prima facie* case against the UAW which
can nowhere be found in the signed works of Bobby Kennedy. But
before this document was to be laid before the nation, there were
several flurries to cap the history of the investigation. In October
1959, when the hearings had finally been concluded, Bobby told
an audience of California students that he and the Labor Rackets
Committee "couldn't find a single thing out of line" with Walter
Reuther and the United Auto Workers." Senator Goldwater rebutted by telling reporters that he could "not believe that Bobby
Kennedy would make such a statement." More acerbically he
added: "I hope that in the future Bobby will adhere more closely
to the facts." Another off-the-cuff remark by Bobby had greater
repercussions. Again with no thought of the morrow, he told reporters that several management and labor witnesses had offered
to support Jack Kennedy for the Democratic Presidential nomination if only Bobby would go easy on them. Tampering with a Senate committee is a felony, and by not reporting these attempted
bribes, if they had in fact been offered, Bobby had made himself an
accessory after the fact. Senator Mundt immediately asked why
Bobby had remained mute. The chief counsel had no explanation to
offer, nor would he name the culprits. At this point, McClellan,
who ran his committee—except Bobby—with an iron hand, called
Mundt off, and the two Senators told the press that too much had
been made of what was apparently a "casual" remark.

In 1960, as both parties began to gird for the coming Presidential contest, the Republicans leaked the text of their minority report on the UAW hearings. There was an outcry on Capitol Hill with Senator Philip Hart, a Michigan Democrat elected with UAW support, making a unique contribution to the rules of parliamentary courtesy. These rules forbid personal attacks by one Senator against another. Hart, however, charged that the report had violated the rules by "slandering" his state.

The minority report was not one to leave Democratic tempers unruffled. It found that the Gosser investigation had demonstrated "corruption, misappropriation of funds, bribery, extortion, and collusion." Though it praised Bobby's overall role in the Teamster inquiry, it added with a certain restraint that the Republican minority was "dismayed that the chief counsel . . . was not only reluctant, but actually refused, in more than one instance to probe into areas which would have fixed the responsibility for the clear pattern of crime and violence which has characterized and has generally been associated with UAW strikes."

In "answer," Bobby released a chapter of his forthcoming *The Enemy Within* to the press, together with a statement: "The report of the Republican members of the Senate Rackets Committee is false. That I, as an employee of the committee, could overrule the will of the members of the committee is patently ridiculous." That he had refused to probe touchy areas was a matter of record. It was, however, "patently ridiculous" to think that he could have got away with this behavior but for the intervention of the chairman and of another Senator named Kennedy. To Bobby, the Republican criticism had resulted from their blind "across-the-board hatred for organized labor—which fails to differentiate between honest and corrupt labor officials." He also accused them of having "consistently tried to blacken the name of labor"—interesting remarks to make in an election year.

The real battle over labor racketeering, violence, and disregard of members' rights was joined when Senate and House began moving toward the legislative purpose for which the hearings had been designed—a new labor-management bill which would close the loopholes in the Taft-Hartley Act and prevent the kind of abuses that the hearings disclosed. At this point, both Jack and Bobby Kennedy set out to prove their affection for organized labor, at least for that portion of the AFL-CIO which could throw its weight into the balance at the Democratic convention. Senator John McClellan and other members of the Senate Labor Committee wanted as strong a bill as possible. Senator Kennedy, with Bobby pulling the strings, fought tooth and nail to prevent passage of a new law which would offend Walter Reuther and the UAW. When McClellan attempted to include in the bill a "Bill of Rights" such as Jack had unsuccessfully proposed in 1947 as an amendment to Taft-Hartley, the Kennedys were vehemently against it. (The provisions of this labor "Bill of Rights" were drawn up, interestingly enough, by the American Civil Liberties Union.) Forgetting his preachments on "democratic unionism," Reuther joined forces with the Kennedys.

The House's Landrum-Griffin bill had teeth which Reuther and the UAW could not pull. On the Senate side, Jack Kennedy joined with Senator Sam Ervin to introduce the much softer Kennedy-Ervin bill. From the sidelines, Bobby inveighed against the House measure, describing it with his usual hyperbole as a bill that would "outlaw all union contract provisions designed to protect the working man and woman from sweatshop competition"—a hysterically inaccurate characterization. Jack Kennedy was chairman of the conference committee entrusted with reconciling the weak Kennedy-Ervin bill and the strong Landrum-Griffin. Though he succeeded in watering down the House bill through a series of compromises, Jack Kennedy was still dissatisfied and requested that his name be removed from the final draft of the measure.

Bobby, too, found much to criticize in the Landrum-Griffin Act. "It falls," he said, as if the law should play favorites, "with equal weight on all unions." And it did not, as he would have wanted, give preferential treatment to those unions which use their power in a "socially responsible manner." At the 1959 UAW convention, Jack Kennedy demonstrated that his heart belonged to Walter, even though he himself had reluctantly voted for Landrum-Griffin. "I realize that the Labor-Management Act of 1959 is not the bill you wanted or I wanted," he said. "It contains many features inserted by the enemies of labor."

The brotherly performance was so much at variance with previously stated positions of the Kennedys that the St. Louis *Post-Dispatch* was constrained to editorialize: "Senator Kennedy . . . presented himself to the public as a vigorous champion of legislation to curb the excesses of certain union leaders. Yet, when the chips were down, Senator Kennedy was found fighting for a weaker bill. . . . Although there was no occasion for a Senator to mix into the labor controversy in the House, Kennedy took it upon himself to warn that branch against adopting a bill which contained effective curbs on secondary boycotts and blackmail picketing.

"His brother . . . took the same line. The Kennedys, in short, were strong for a labor bill, but not for a labor bill that offended the union leaders too much. . . . Fighting for the union leaders' position while posing as the author of labor law reform does not recommend him."

A postcript can be found in Victor Lasky's *JFK, The Man and the Myth*: "On June 8, 1960, the Washington *Star* reported that at a news conference in Grand Rapids, Michigan, 'Senator Kennedy said he was hopeful of getting backing from United Auto Workers' President Walter P. Reuther before the Democratic convention opens July 11.'

"Senator Kennedy already had that backing."

6

The One-Man Firing Squad

POLITICS is the daughter of history, unkempt and illegit-
imate but with a wanton attraction that few men can resist. For all
their professed reluctance to accept the political road, Jack and Bobby
Kennedy were political men. For Jack it was always a game, an affront
to the sensibilities of the class into which his father's millions had
projected him. He could remain slightly aloof, slightly sardonic, like
the man who takes an overdressed and over-brash doxy to the Junior
League Ball. To Bobby it was the equivalent of war, to be fought to
the hilt with no holds barred and no quarter given. For one, the
great issues that wracked the world in the Fifties and Sixties were
an intellectual exercise, ploys in the kind of personal one-upmanship
which hardly considered the ethical imperatives of greatness. To the
other, they were nothing more than the psychological guides with
which to influence and condition the responses of the electorate.

It was this concept of politics which led to the description of
Bobby Kennedy as "a one-man firing squad for Jack." As such, he saw
no need for finesse, no need to consider the feelings of those whose
help he solicited or whose objections he was sent to quiet. During the
1960 Democratic convention—as all Los Angeles seethed with one of
the bitterest contests for the Presidential nomination since 1924,
when after prolonged balloting the exhausted delegates cast the prize
at the feet of John W. Davis, the least objectionable nonentity—
Bobby could stand before an undecided state caucus and tell them
bluntly: "We are a young group and we're going to take over
America." He meant it then as he does today. Ideology was a matter

of choice, subject to later revision, like an airline schedule, but the grasp of power was the real and the true. From the start of his political career, in the shade of an older brother who had hierarchical preference in the Kennedy pantheon, this is what always mattered to Robert Francis Kennedy. In later time, he would become the vehicle, but the passion of his effort changed not at all. In the battle, he offered the kind of unquestioning loyalty which combat requires— and this is to his credit. Eunice Kennedy Shriver instinctively realized this when she said:

"All this business about Jack and Bobby being blood brothers has been exaggerated. First there is a big difference in years. They had different tastes in men, different tastes in women. They didn't become really close until 1952, and it was politics that brought them together. That's a business full of knives. Jack needed someone he could trust, someone who had loyalty to him. Jack knew he had a person like that with Bobby around." It was primitive loyalty, a loyalty which sometimes failed to grasp precisely what his brother was about. Speaking before the Foreign Student Service Council in Washington after President Kennedy's inauguration, Bobby could falter on simple ideas. "You people," he told the students, "are exemplifying what my brother meant when he said in his Inauguration address: 'Ask what you can do for—uh—uh—do not ask what you can do—ask not what you can do for your country but—uh—' Well, anyhow, you remember the words. That's why my brother is President."

The important thing for Bobby was that Jack was President. The whys and hows of that stark fact would occupy his attention as Attorney General and later, in the context of personal tragedy, as the heir to his brother's role in history. Until then, the focus of his energies was in the act of winning, of taking over the reins of government from older and less determined men. It was this singlemindedness which made Bobby the ferocious campaigner in a series of onslaughts on the public consciousness unparalleled even in a time when politics had reverted to the hammer-and-tongs manner, if not the techniques, of the Jacksonian era.

In any study of Bobby's development as the 1960 kingmaker, the earlier campaigns assume importance mainly for what they taught him of the logistics of elections. It is doubtful that he learned much of what makes people tick, for even when people are most important to him, he sees them simply as objects which can advance or retard his progress. In the glow of hindsight, the President would say in 1961, "My 1952 campaign was terribly disorganized. Then Bobby came in. And there was a tremendous change in two or three weeks. We had a lot of fights on our hands, but he got things organized and moving. He got people working in all of the counties." From the manner of Bobby's accession to the job of managing Jack's Senatorial campaign, and from other evidence, it is clear that another hand was pulling the strings: Joe Sr. got Bobby the job. Walking into campaign headquarters one day, Joe Sr. turned on Mark Dalton, the Boston lawyer who had managed the previous Kennedy campaigns without pay. The old man demanded the books, spread them out before him, then, according to an eyewitness, "shoved his finger in Dalton's face and yelled: 'Dalton, you've spent ten thousand dollars of my money and you haven't accomplished a damn thing.' The next day Dalton was gone."

Others who worked with the Kennedy team corroborated this. "When Bobby came in," said one aide, "we knew it was the old man taking over. What had Bobby done up to that time politically? Nothing. Not a damn thing and all of a sudden he was there as campaign manager, waving the banners." Bobby himself has conceded that "I didn't see the strategic part of it. I was more concerned with organization. I didn't become involved in what words should go in a speech, what should be said on a poster or a billboard, what should be done in television." But Bobby is very vague about who shaped the strategy and made the decisions. No one person really, he said, and certainly not Joseph Kennedy. "I don't think he actually told us what to do or gave us ideas. Most of these things just evolved."

Simple fact remains that it was Joe Sr. who pushed a reluctant Jack into the battle for Henry Cabot Lodge's Senate seat, that he handled the older politicians, that he raised the money ("We concede you that role," Jack had said) and mapped out all the major strategy. The details were left to Jack Kennedy's aides, with organization Bobby's particular task. A Boston attorney summed it up this way: "The father was a tremendous factor in the campaign. He remained out of public view. He didn't run things, but they happened according to his plans. He cast the die." Where decision making was left to others, it was Jack and not Bobby who made them. This is not to detract from his natural ability to set an organization in motion and, far more important, to keep it moving. This is perhaps the most difficult job in a campaign, but as Bobby described it years later, he instinctively knew how.

"Our object," he told reporters Ralph Martin and Ed Plaut, "was to get a little work out of as many people as possible, instead of a lot of work out of a few. In addition to the secretaries, there were other groups organized. . . . The idea was to keep the groups small, make everyone feel he was contributing something important. We didn't want each group to be too aware of what the others were doing. It was organized on a statewide basis, but we emphasized the local groups.

"It would cause too much jealousy if the statewide organization were too prominent. We might have the chairman of the dentists' committee, who was an Italian in Boston, and an Irish secretary who was a dentist in Worcester, and a chairman of a Frenchmen's committee in Fall River, who was a dentist, and this could turn into a three-way fight. So we tried to keep them all separate until the end and pull them all together . . . in the last ten days for a final coordinated drive, the last telephone campaign . . . and all that."

The early Kennedy campaigns for House and Senate, however, had been conducted in the family fiefdom where Joe Sr.'s money and muscle could be effectively exercised. No show of force was really necessary, for the order of battle was known to the politicians. The patriarch of the clan could pick up a phone or write a check and what he wanted done was done. Moving into the national arena was a different matter. Money still retained its eloquence, but it could not be the sole voice. The Kennedy name was no longer the open sesame to the secret councils of powerful politicians. In some states, it was a handicap. And at every turn, the shadow of Eleanor Roosevelt fell across Jack Kennedy's political fortunes. Neither forgetting nor forgiving the ambiguity of the role he played during the McCarthy troubles, Mrs. Roosevelt was vocal in her opposition to him. No amount of Jack's abundant charm or chill could alter her views on his Presidential potential.

The Kennedys had learned that a difference existed between their Massachusetts enclave and the broad reaches of the United States. It had taken a defeat in the 1956 Vice-Presidential battle to convince Jack and Bobby that more money, more effort, and above all more planning would have to go into the 1960 bid for the Presidency. Joe Sr. became aware, too, that he would have to mobilize and husband his influence if he was to contribute more than his checkbook to the obsession that had governed his life—the making of a President. Jack Kennedy had little to offer in the way of a political record. Youth, the "reverse English" of his Catholicism, and what the New York *Times* called "the most videogenic personality of our times" were his main stock in trade. The professional politicians considered him neither a threat nor a promise in the jungle of Massachusetts politics.

The 1956 Vice-Presidential attempt taught Jack Kennedy and his brother Bobby, as usual doing his part for the Kennedy dynasty, the cardinal error of politics: taking success for granted. The Kennedys were sure that Adlai Stevenson would, when the chips were down, select Jack as his running mate. He had as much promised it, and the logic of bloc voting seemed to dictate the choice. Catholics had been defecting from the Democratic party in substantial numbers ever since the Hiss case and the McCarthy disclosures. A young, attractive candidate with the name of Kennedy, who had very carefully not antagonized the South, yet remained on good terms with Northern Democrats, would be an asset as a running mate to any candidate. The brother act before television cameras had brought them valuable exposure. The liberals were disgruntled at Jack's refusal to stand up and be counted during the fracas over McCarthy, but this gave him added strength among Irish Catholics who saw the gang-up on McCarthy as somehow linked to the social pretensions of the white, Anglo-Saxon Protestants.

Behind the scenes, Bobby had weighed these assets. And he could add two more. Jack Kennedy, as the point of the Kennedy patrol, had reconnoitered the Massachusetts political scene and then done battle with the professionals. In the bitter guerrilla war, he had shown that he was a knife fighter of no mean talent. By taking risks, and with the kind of luck that goes with enterprise, he had defeated the anti-Stevenson forces and emerged the leader of the state's delegation to the 1956 convention in Chicago. More important was the realization by Bobby and the other campaign strategists that the press could be used to tremendous advantage if old ways were put aside and reporters were treated like king-makers rather than sideline observers.

In *JFK, The Man and the Myth,* Victor Lasky skirts the full significance of this discovery. "Hardly had Kennedy gotten back to work [after his series of drastic operations] before items began to appear that he was being increasingly discussed in high places as a possible running mate for Adlai Stevenson. One of the first was published in the 'Periscope' column of *Newsweek,* which is devoted to political and global gossip. Typically, Kennedy telephoned Periscope editor Debs Myers to ask who was doing all the discussing. 'Me,' replied Myers."

For those who knew how "Periscope" operates, this sounded like a humorously accurate comment. But Myers was a former Stevenson speechwriter with his roots deep in Democratic soil. That a page he edited carried such an item was, presumably, an index to Stevenson's thinking. And the 1952 Democratic standard-bearer was thereby "compromised" without his knowledge or consent. Whether or not Debs Myers was ever the source for some of his prognostications, in this instance the inspiration came from elsewhere. For the Kennedy brothers were working diligently, and in tandem with Joe Sr., to convince the nation's mass media that, like Abou ben Adhem, Kennedy led all the rest of Stevenson's possible choices for the Vice-Presidential nomination. But all the wishful thinking and the almost (but not quite) commitment of Stevenson failed the Kennedys. When Stevenson was nominated by the convention, he announced that in violation of all tradition he would not choose his running mate. It was up to the convention to decide. The confident Kennedys suddenly learned that in politics the fix must be unequivocal. Jack was angry and Bobby was furious.

The Stevenson ploy should not have come as a total surprise to the Kennedy brothers. In the spring of 1956, Stevenson had hinted to R. Sargent Shriver, a Kennedy brother-in-law, that he might allow the convention to pick the Vice-Presidential nominee in order to give some color to proceedings that seemed doomed to the dullness that lack of contention imposes. This intelligence had been passed on to Joseph Kennedy, who used it as an excuse to warn Jack that a try for the Vice Presidency would be ill advised and ill timed. Eisenhower, said Joe Sr., had the election sewed up. A bad Democratic defeat would be blamed on the presence of a Catholic on the ticket. Jack and Bobby had seen it differently. Jack's administrative assistant and alter ego, Theodore Sorenson, had explored the possibility of a second-place spot on the Democratic ticket and was convinced that it would do no harm. Working with Governor Abe Ribicoff of Connecticut, he had rounded up a solid bloc of New England delegates. The South, matching Jack's half-hearted commitment to civil rights to that of other Democrats, felt that it had found in him the eloquent "moderate" who could talk the liberals' language but remain aloof from the liberals' battles. Carmine De Sapio, Tammany Hall's soft-spoken boss, showed some willingness to commit himself when it was risky to do so—a gesture for the Kennedys which was unrewarded when years later he needed help from the White House to survive the attack of his political enemies in New York.

When the convention's hoopla began filling Chicago, Jack and Bobby set out to sew up the necessary delegates. They had by this time so committed themselves that Joe Sr. joined in the effort, if only to save Jack from too bad a defeat. Vacationing in the French Riviera, he took to the transatlantic phone to call in what political paper he could. Peter Lawford, another one of Jack's brothers-in-law and a member of Frank Sinatra's Rat Pack, traded on his Las Vegas friendships to win over the Nevada delegation. New York had promised its second-ballot votes to Kennedy. The would-be candidate, moreover, had marked up points by his appearances at state caucuses. When he delivered the nominating speech for Stevenson, he marked up some more through his ritualistic attack on Richard Nixon. There was one setback—the opposition of Eleanor Roosevelt, implacable as she would be to the end, because of the Kennedys' refusal to turn on Joe McCarthy. In a brief and icy interview, she told Jack that his explanation "simply was not satisfactory." But Stevenson had not stampeded the Vice-Presidential candidates by throwing the choice to the convention, and the Kennedy brothers were still fairly certain that they had it.

The bombshell struck twenty-four hours before the balloting was to take place. In that moment of confusion, the four Senators really vying for the Vice-Presidential nomination—Kennedy, Hubert Humphrey of Minnesota, Albert Gore of Tennessee, and Estes Kefauver of Tennessee—scoured the corridors and the caucuses in the scramble to pick up delegations and delegates. Neophytes in the convention ritual, the Kennedy brothers had no time to placate the various wings of their party. Bobby had failed to give the Midwestern agrarian liberals proper reassurances, and they stood up against Jack for his stand with Republican Secretary of Agriculture Ezra Taft Benson on flexible price supports. The South was ready to go with him, but other sections of the country had to be convinced. During those last hours of jockeying for place, Bobby doggedly roamed the floor of the convention, certain that his last-minute pleading would bring in the votes he needed.

"Bobby Kennedy was supposed to be floor manager for Jack at that convention," a member of the Kennedy team has said, "but that's a lot of crap. There was no floor manager. There was just nobody in control. Everybody was out on his own, talking to anybody and everybody he could, and there was a hell of a lot of overlapping."

The lesson for Bobby was there: Last-minute planning doesn't work. The night before, according to Sorenson, "Bob Kennedy and John Bailey held a hectic meeting of family and friends in our suite. Assignments were handed out. Efforts were made to reach key leaders. But we acted largely in a state of confusion and ignorance. We had no plans, no facilities, no communications, no organization, little know-how and very few contacts." Nevertheless, the press had already begun to talk of the excellent organization in the Kennedy camp, perhaps because, as one Humphrey supporter complained, "Those Kennedys had printed signs. You should have seen our hand-lettered things." That much was Bobby's doing. He had found a printer able to do a fast overnight job.

Minutes before Jack Kennedy was nominated, Bobby could be seen on the convention floor trying to persuade House Democratic leader John McCormack of Massachusetts to make the seconding speech. When McCormack, who had been pushed out by the Kennedys as kingpin in his state's Democratic machine, demurred, Bobby said to him with heavy-handed sarcasm, "Thanks a lot, Congressman." At the last moment, McCormack reluctantly agreed and he was almost physically dragged to the platform by Bobby. The speech, however, consisted of generalities and political bromides which only in its closing lines alluded to the candidate. Senator Quentin Burdick of North Dakota would recall the anguish of those hours. "I'll never forget Bobby Kennedy during the balloting, standing in front of our delegation with tears in his eyes, pleading for our support," he said. "It didn't do any good. Jack had voted for sliding-scale supports and they don't like that in our part of the country. He stood there trying to explain his brother's voting position but we said we were sorry and the delegation wouldn't listen to him."

For a brief time, the tide seemed to be running in Jack's favor. Lagging behind Kefauver on the first ballot, he had pulled ahead in the second when New York switched to him and Senator Lyndon Johnson threw the Texas delegation behind "the fighting sailor who wears the scars of battle." This was Jack's high point, with the nomination just thirty-eight and a half votes out of his grasp. Bobby moved about the floor, prematurely thanking delegates and making a V-for-Victory sign when the TV cameras picked him up. At the Stock Yard Inn, Jack was sprawled on his bed, inelegantly stripped down to his shorts. He saw Bobby's signal and jumped under the shower. He had changed and was waiting for the summons of the convention when the third and final ballot gave the nomination to Estes Kefauver.

At the convention hall, however, he appeared smiling and self-possessed to offer his congratulations to the winner. Then, back at his suite, he telephoned his father in France. "We did our best," he said. "I had a lot of fun and I didn't make a fool of myself." Bobby's reaction was typical. "We'll show them," he said in a fury. "We should have won. Somebody pulled something fishy on us and I'll find out who it is." In time, his recollection of that moment would change. "I was terribly disappointed to be in a battle and lose," he told an interviewer years later, "but when that roll call was over, I walked over to Jack and I said to him that it was the luckiest thing that ever happened to him."

The bitterness was not Bobby's alone. Jack Kennedy too was hurt. Back in the privacy of his suite, he sat glumly rehearsing past events and looking for a scapegoat. Bobby, however vindictive his original reaction, looked for something more practical—techniques that would bring victory in the next national try. "It really struck me that it wasn't the issues which matter," Bobby would recall. "It was the friendships. So many people said to me they would rather vote for Jack, but that they were going to vote for Estes Kefauver because he had sent them a card or gone to their home. I said right there that we should forget the issues and send Christmas cards and go to their homes next time."

Bitter as the taste of defeat may have been to Bobby, and sinister as the suspected conspiracy against his brother may have seemed, he was ready to accept it and to turn it into a lesson in convention-handling. According to political etiquette a candidate for the Presidency must disclaim interest until he formally declares, several months before the convention. This practice imposes a frequently unwanted coyness on a Presidential aspirant, but it also gives him maneuverability. He can advance or withdraw, depending on the state of his political fortunes; and only the press, the politicians, and the voters are ever able to see through his stratagems. Though Bobby and Jack consistently denied that the White House was their goal, no one was fooled. Jack confessed it in 1956, before the abortive Vice-Presidential coup, to Arthur Schlesinger Jr., Harvard professor, ideologue of Americans for Democratic Action, and the *enfant presque terrible* of the New Left. Jack had just come through a "private crisis of identity," to quote Schlesinger, a nontheological dark night of the soul which strikes the more senstive of the rich young men who find life purposeless because there is nothing they really must strive for. The Presidency, which many would have thought an impossible goal, replaced the pot of gold that lies at the end of other men's rainbows. But Schlesinger was not the only one to whom Jack passed the implicit word. To Bob Considine, veteran newspaperman and driving reporter, Jack remarked:

"Joe was the star of our family. He did everything better than the rest of us. If he had lived he would have gone on in politics and he would have been elected to the House and Senate as I was. And like me, he would have gone for the Vice-Presidential nomination at the 1956 convention, but unlike me, he wouldn't have been beaten.

Joe would have won the nomination. And then he and Stevenson would have been beaten by Eisenhower and today Joe's political career would have been in a shambles and he would be trying to pick up the pieces." On second thought, obviously, both Jack and Bobby saw that the events in Chicago could be turned to their personal use.

Bobby asked for and got a sinecure appointment as "special assistant" to Adlai Stevenson's campaign director, James Finnegan. Little was expected of him and even less than he wanted to do. His purpose during the seven weeks he spent accompanying the candidate was to learn the ropes of Presidential campaigning. From an assessment of Stevenson's weaknesses and strong points, his errors of omission and commission, Bobby hoped to evolve his own plan of action when Jack made the big try in 1960. Stevenson's style of slicing fine distinctions even finer did not appeal to Bobby, who appreciated a more combative approach. The staff work, he observed, was poor and relations with the press minimal, though reporters with the Democratic candidate were more than eager to help. Stevenson, Bobby felt, tried to do too much, working and reworking routine speeches until it was almost air time, avoiding contact with the crowds, and selecting as his prime issues those with little sex appeal and much sophistical complexity. These qualities, Bobby felt, indicated weakness to him. He decided then that Jack's campaign would have to be one in which audacity and frontal attack were accompanied by flanking movements and the guerrilla night-riding of his assistants.

Jack Kennedy, as part of the plan for 1960, set out to increase the public awareness of him gained by the tautly dramatic balloting for the Vice-Presidential nomination. To this end, he made 150 major speeches in 26 states, ostensibly in behalf of Adlai Stevenson and Senator Kefauver. Everywhere he went, he had been preceded by advance men who got out the crowds, arranged for the television cameras, and stirred up high-school girls always ready to give an Elvis Presley welcome to the casually handsome young Senator from Massachusetts. There were mutterings in Democratic circles that Jack was more interested in building himself up than in getting votes for the ticket, and this suspicion was translated into hostile questions from reporters. But neither Jack nor Bobby were disturbed. In their journeyings, they had sensed a revulsion to politics in the country. The Truman scandals, the Army-McCarthy televised circus—contrasted to the benign and "above the battle" character of President Eisenhower's public manner—set the tone for 1956. Jack therefore turned an almost nonpartisan look at his audiences, criticizing both parties or granting credit to the Republican opposition. In 1960, Republicans who remembered his 1956 refusal to join in the smears on Richard Nixon, almost his defense of the Vice President, were ready to accept the Kennedys as more open to reason than the typical Democratic spokesmen whose main stock in trade was a Devil tagged G.O.P. "I'm not criticizing Richard Nixon except to say that he is a conservative," Jack Kennedy said apologetically to a national audience, and won himself a reputation for statesmanship and fairness.

The 1956 elections over, the Jack & Bobby team returned to Washington. In tandem, the two men worked at impressing the Kennedy name on the public consciousness. Bobby's work with the Senate Rackets Committee gave him a reputation for being a tireless fighter against labor corruption. Jack played the "moderate" to the hilt. The South was the area most allergic, or so it was presumed, to his Catholicism. Jack made the circuit below the Mason-Dixon line, wooing segregationists like Senator Herman Talmadge of Georgia. As he had on the McCarthy issue, so he did on the civil rights question—to the point that at least one newspaper, the *Christian Science Monitor,* suggested that John F. Kennedy could be a possible standard-bearer for a 1960 Dixiecrat party. He was, moreover, more than willing, as early as 1957, to tell newspapermen that he would be a good man to bridge the gap between Northern liberals and Southern conservatives in the Democratic party. In 1958, Jack's name was mentioned with increasing frequency as a conservative contender for the President. When Governor James Coleman of Mississippi endorsed Kennedy at the 1958 Southern Governors' Conference, the Associated Press was so overcome by the reaction that it reported: "You would think that he was a Dixiecrat, a descendant of Robert Lee, and a man who eats hominy grits and corn pone three times a day."

The Kennedy campaign, however, was not definitively launched until October 28, 1959, at a morning meeting in Bobby Kennedy's house in Hyannis Port.

Earlier in the year, on April Fool's Day, the "in" group had met at Joseph Kennedy's Palm Beach home to prepare for the Hyannis Port session. Ted Sorenson's notes include state-by-state notations as well as the following: ". . . Publicize poll results to key people . . . Have Protestant staffmember go out to certain states . . . Get list of labor delegates . . . Keep the field crowded . . . Foreign policy, peace emphasis . . . Run against other candidates—not God."

Theodore H. White lovingly describes the morning gathering in *The Making of the President, 1960:*

"They met in the living room of the house of Robert Kennedy, the same living room that one year and eleven days later was to be their command post on election night. It was, as participants remember, a frosty New England day, quite clear. . . . The room in which the men met was a simple one too—furnished in yellow and green lounge chairs, several worn easy chairs, and a hassock or two; open to the sun, dominated by a big fireplace. . . . Sixteen people attended this conclave, nine at least should be starred for the record. . . . Only two of these nine—the candidate and his brother—had ever participated in Presidential politics before, but each of the nine was in his way to prove indispensable. And though the campaign had been underway for a long time, this was the first time they had all gathered together in the same room."

There were Jack and Bobby; Kenneth O'Donnell, former captain of the Harvard football team and the man who had arranged to get Bobby his letter; Lawrence O'Brien, wearing all the assurance and placidity which makes the good professional politician; Theodore Sorenson—"my intellectual blood bank," Jack had called him; Stephen Smith, Jack's brother-in-law, who had given up a lucrative post in January 1959 with Founding Father Joe Sr. to open the first campaign headquarters in Washington; Lou Harris, a pollster of parts, who brought new controversy to the science, art, or Ouija-board manipulation of this new adjunct of politics; Pierre Salinger, a recruit from Bobby's staff of the Senate Labor Rackets Committee, who often played the Court Jester; and John Bailey, boss of Connecticut, tough, cynical, sophisticated, and ruthless in a manner which Bobby would both understand and appreciate.

"These men here assembled," Theodore White noted, "were those who had survived a decade of Kennedy selection. All of them were, in their own fields, quality men. In the Kennedy lexicon, no phrase is more damning than 'He's a very common man.'" There were others in the room, but they represented the hewers of wood and the drawers of water. "These others," White wrote, "were part of the machinery, not leaders. Lastly, present on the roster, was Joseph P. Kennedy, onetime Ambassador to the Court of St. James [*sic*], father of the candidate—a force unto himself."

At this meeting, the announcement was made that Ted Sorenson would be assigned the role of national policy chief. Bobby would replace him as campaign manager. And Bobby took over that afternoon. The country was divided up among the various lieutenants, with Bobby sharing the task of holding sympathetic Southerners in line and winning over those who were dubious of Jack's ability to win the nomination. Facing the Kennedy team was a reluctant but still potentially powerful Adlai Stevenson, the voluble but shrewd Senator Hubert Horatio Humphrey, Senator Stuart Symington, and the favorite sons of important states.

The major task of this inner group was to beg, borrow, or buy every delegate vote that had not been nailed down, to win over sufficiently large masses of voters to triumph in the key primaries, and to convince the nation's opinion-makers that Jack Kennedy—a man who was even then telling interviewers that he had no "organized philosophy of life" and wanted the Presidency because "there was the opportunity"—represented their last, best hope in 1960. There were problems and difficulties along the way. Bobby and his cohorts would have to accept the bear hug of ADA without antagonizing the conservatives, to appear both liberal and anti-Communist, to opt for a radical "civil rights" program without angering the South, and above all never to do or say anything which would seem to attack the rigid Populism of Joseph P. Kennedy. In handling John F. Kennedy, they had to disguise his attitude toward people even as they attempted to paint over his disconcerting boyishness by changing his hairdo. James MacGregor Burns, writing with upsetting honesty, had described the candidate as being "as casual as a cash register." Max Lerner of the New York *Post*, setting aside his endless disquisitions on the sex urge, found JFK "metallic, sometimes cold, sometimes unbending." The *Ladies' Home Journal* saw him as "a cool, calculating machine that is constantly saying, 'What's in it for me?' "

Bobby was not so well known, but the politicians had already felt the edge of his hand and tongue. His years with the Senate Rackets Committee, though colored a roseate hue by many Washington correspondents, had nevertheless established him as a young man of explosive temper and vindictive afterthought. "Money and gall are all the Kennedys have," an exasperated Barry Goldwater once remarked. But he was wrong, at least about Jack. In the Age of Television, Jack was, as the New York *Times* had remarked, videogenic—and as the final results showed, this was more important than a program, an organized philosophy, or a genuine quality of mercy.

At the Hyannis Port conclave, a decision was made by John Bailey and Bobby Kennedy, entrusted with knocking heads together, that Jack Kennedy would have to enter two primaries, of the sixteen scheduled in 1960, in order to be able to stampede the Democratic convention. The first of these, set for April 5, 1960, was the Wisconsin primary where he knew he would be pitted against Senator Humphrey. Wisconsin would be a test of his vote-getting abilities in a Midwestern state that knew not Harvard but could see over its border to Minnesota, the ebullient Hubert's bailiwick. The importance of Jack's Catholicism would also be put to the test there, and so would the carefully evolved strategy of crying "prejudice" as a means of mobilizing the Catholic vote while shaming Protestants into declarations of broadminded support. West Virginia was the second primary of strategic importance to the Kennedys. To them, and to their supporters, this would be a real test of whether a rich and Catholic candidate could make it in a poor and Protestant state.

This is not to say that Bobby, as campaign manager, had written off the value of other states. He realized early in the game that having every delegate and every delegation locked up before the chairman's gavel had called the convention to order was insurance against last-minute emotional stampedes to other candidates. To this end, Bobby and John Bailey prepared a detailed organizational manual covering every possible contingency and outlining every step to be taken in the creation and management of local Kennedy groups. ("It's got everything," one campaign worker remarked, "from how to bring in the town big shot to how babies should be kissed.") At the same time, Bobby brought the politician's traditional little black book, the record of peccadilloes and preferences of those with whom the Kennedy machine must deal, to high efficiency. The modern substitute was a card file which the candidate could consult to find out everything there was to know about each delegate to the convention, each local leader, each influential citizen. Particular emphasis was given to those states in which a primary battle could be foreseen—Wisconsin, Oregon, Nebraska, New Hampshire, Indiana, and West Virginia.

With money no object, and the almost inexhaustible Kennedy bankroll at his disposal, Bobby was able to travel freely lining up Kennedy-for-President state and county chairmen.[1] Where other candidates had to waste precious time raising money, Bobby and

---

[1] "His [Joe Kennedy's] money has given him advantages in this campaign," James Reston wrote of Jack Kennedy for the New York *Times,* in one of the great understatements of the campaign. "His father advanced him $270,000 to buy a plane. . . . There is no doubt that this—plus a great deal more for paid assistants and television —has given him opportunities his competitors have not enjoyed." Reston might have noted that the operation of the plane cost Kennedy $15,000 a month. Estimates of the total amount spent by Joseph P. Kennedy hold at the tidy sum of $7,000,000.

Jack simply pushed ahead, their assistants charmed by the repeated litany, "Don't worry about the cost." They could also campaign in comfort, for the Kennedy plane had all of the comforts of home, from a television set to a private bedroom. Two pilots were always on standby duty. No organizational detail was considered too picayune for Bobby, no wig too big for him to knock off.

The unexpected power of the Kennedy machine left the professionals shaken and apprehensive. Its first major success was in Ohio, whose sixty-four delegates were a prize for any candidate. Governor Mike DiSalle of Ohio had hoped to bind them to him by running in the primary as a "favorite son"—a classic device for compelling the candidates to bid for his support with promises of future patronage. In past instances, candidates made no frontal assault on a favorite son; instead they tried to cajole him into agreeing to release his delegates before the first convention ballot, or at some other psychologically appropriate time. But the Kennedys wanted to demonstrate their strength early. Six months before the convention opened in Los Angeles, Bobby had delivered an ultimatum to DiSalle, threatening to destroy his political career unless he endorsed brother Jack. His language, DiSalle associates later disclosed, was hardly fit for mixed company. At a private meeting with the Ohio governor, Jack Kennedy threatened to face DiSalle in a primary fight. With polls taken by Lou Harris, he was able to convince DiSalle that in such a contest, the "favorite son" would lose, thereby undermining his position in the state. Governor DiSalle sadly capitulated. "What could I have done?" he lamented. "Those Kennedys play rough and they play for keeps."

The same kind of pressure was used on Governor Millard Tawes of Maryland. Bobby wanted his support. Tawes wanted to be free to wheel and deal at the convention. Bobby threatened to wreck the Tawes machine in the state, and to prove his point began setting up an organization in Baltimore, with Representative Torbert Macdonald of Massachusetts, a school friend of Jack, running messages from the candidate to the governor. When state and county leaders began defecting to Kennedy, Tawes hastily issued the endorsement which guaranteed Kennedy's victory over the maverick Senator Wayne Morse, running in the hope of giving the Kennedys what he thought would be an extremely damaging setback.

The Wisconsin primary, Bobby believed, would clinch the nomination for Jack Kennedy—if properly handled. Polls by Lou Harris showed Kennedy leading Hubert Humphrey by the comfortable margin of sixty-three percent to thirty-seven percent. Such a one-sided margin, however, would do little to enhance the Kennedy candidacy. It was necessary to make it look like a real contest. And Bobby, realizing that, said, "The American people like an underdog." He thereupon set out to convince the press that Jack's chances were not good, that he wanted his brother to stay out of the state. He complained bitterly that the Democratic organization was soft and useless. Reporters were shown conflicting polls to "prove" that it was a toss-up between Jack Kennedy and Hubert Humphrey. The press, of course, happily fell into the trap. Speculative stories began appearing in the newspapers, creating an atmosphere of tension and drama.

The stories, however, noted that Jack Kennedy was not backing down, that he intended to take his chances. So flagrant was this bid for sympathy that Murray Kempton was constrained to write: "The Kennedy boys are wonderfully engaging—and I keep telling myself, fundamentally decent. But I wish they'd stop saying, gee whiz, kids, we're outnumbered, but we're going to carry on. Jack Kennedy goes against Hubert Humphrey in the Wisconsin primary with most of the money, most of the charm, most of the killer instinct, and, we might assume, most of the potential votes. . . . And Bobby Kennedy goes around saying that Jimmy Hoffa will spend anything to beat Jack. This statement does not say outright that Hoffa is contributing money to poor Humphrey, but what other inference is possible? [2]

"It would be foolish to deny that among forward-looking enlightened members of the party of progress there has been for at least seven years a longing for some Democratic candidate to come forward with an instinct for the jugular. Generally speaking, by actions of this sort, the Kennedys seem to have won professinal approval. . . . Jack Kennedy's proclamations of desperation in the Wisconsin primary are a moral issue more delicate. . . . Kennedy has a pollster in whom he has every reason for confidence. He must therefore be as coolly confident in private as he is afraid in public. He is telling us something which he himself is better equipped than anyone else to think untrue, and after that, he makes gentle little speeches to college kids talking about the need to revive the national morality."

Kempton, always a maverick, has the longest journalistic needle of any man in the profession. Operating by a combination of warm-heartedness, irony, and intuition, he has the ability to cut to the

---

[2] Hoffa did campaign against Kennedy in Wisconsin but never offered any help to Humphrey, who would have violently rejected it.

quick in a way which sometimes appalls him. In several brief paragraphs, he had laid bare the Kennedy method, worked out by Bobby and his campaign aides.

There was one instance in which Bobby's "underdog" strategy—and perhaps the whole campaign—blew up in his face. In an unguarded moment, Bobby said gleefully in the presence of a reporter that Wisconsin was "in the bag." When the reporter printed this comment, Bobby went into a tremendous rage, calling him a "Stevenson Jew." It took all of Jack Kennedy's persuasive powers, exercised over a private lunch with the reporter, to mollify him. Had he reported Bobby's remark then, the old charges of anti-Semitism that had swirled around Joseph Kennedy Sr. would have been revived, and the crucial Jewish vote, which went overwhelming for Jack, would have been compromised.

The Catholic issue was played for all it was worth in a state with strong Catholic groups in almost every county. Milwaukee, crucial to any candidate, had been given the full Bobby treatment. "Anyone who doubts this," Howard Norton wrote in the Baltimore *Sun*, "may go through the Kennedy headquarters and look through the card files. The name, address, telephone number, and other pertinent data on every one of the [30,000] Kennedy adherents is listed there." And so much money was being spent that Jack Kennedy remarked at a New York dinner for Democrats, "I got a wire from my father that said, 'Dear Jack: Don't buy one vote more than necessary. I'll be damned if I'll pay for a landslide.' "

Armed with his statistical and organizational paraphernalia, Bobby underscored his "concern" for his brother at every turn. Making all the moves that a worried campaign manager would make —although they were unnecessary—he stumped the state during that cold winter, addressing church socials, political groups, and students, spinning horrendous stories about Jimmy Hoffa to workers and farmers. Humphrey could not be faulted on the issues, unless Jack and Bobby were ready to relinquish their new-found liberal pose. Smear and innuendo were necessary. As Bobby moved about the state, he invoked the specters of Jimmy Hoffa and the multimillionaires of Texas, implying that they were in the Humphrey camp. Jimmy Hoffa, he warned thrilled audiences, was planning to enter the state personally to lead his minions into battle against the racket-busting Kennedys. Humphrey could argue that "whoever is responsible" for this use of the Teamster bogey "deserves to be spanked"—and he could hang the charge on Bobby by adding, "I said spanking because it applies to juveniles." But only the press and the practitioners of mass communication could make his counterattack effective. Instead, newsmen like NBC's Sandor Vanocur, openly partisan to the Kennedy cause, made Humphrey seem like a monster for speaking out. On a *Meet the Press* telecast, Vanocur hit him with questions such as:

"Senator, for the last three weeks you have gone around the state attacking Senator Kennedy on his voting record. . . . Don't you think that if Kennedy does become the Democratic nominee this is going to hurt your party's chances in the November election?"

Or the veiled threat:

"Senator, if you don't get the nomination, you are going to campaign for a third term as Senator. Don't you think the Republicans in your state are going to pick up the charges from your lips and throw them against you, running on the same ticket with this man you have attacked? . . ."

This did not deter Humphrey from continuing the unequal battle. He still hoped that he could reach the farmers and the industrial workers on the basis of his voting record, that he could lure Jack into a television debate in which he could demonstrate his superiority as a candidate. But the Kennedy forces, taking their orders from Bobby, refused to be sucked into any face-to-face confrontation. Humphrey was also certain that the state's Catholics would put bread-and-butter considerations above pride in a candidate of their own religion. He might have been right but for an unexpected and disconcerting development in the last days of the primary campaign. Unidentified literature, viciously anti-Catholic, suddenly began flooding the state. Strangely enough, it was sent, as the liberal columnist Marquis Child reported, "largely to Catholics and often to individuals in care of the local chapter of the Knights of Columbus." Few, however, bothered to ask why anyone, no matter how twisted his mind, would try to defeat a Catholic by sending anti-Catholic literature to Catholic organizations.

Humphrey's campaign manager could demand an investigation to determine the source of the "hate" literature, or denounce it as "despicable," but the damage had been done. As primary day drew near, Bobby began to predict that the underdog was pulling ahead. Rumors that Jack Kennedy's sweep would be great enough to win all the state delegates were circulated. The road to the nomination stretched ahead with no obstacles, no booby traps. As the returns came in on April 5, Bobby and Lou Harris holed up in a suite at the Pfister Hotel in Milwaukee to study their charts and scan their projections. The communications center they had set up was connected by direct telephone wire to the room where the candidate and a few members of his family waited for the victory sign.

The Wisconsin primary gave Kennedy fifty-six percent of the vote and two-thirds of the delegates to the convention. But the victory was not decisive. Under Wisconsin's primary system, registered voters were allowed to participate in the primary of either party. Kennedy's margin of victory came from Democratic and Republican Catholics who had crossed over to register their indignation at the "hate" literature. Ironically, Jack's refusal to stand up and be counted on the McCarthy issue—on the advice, if not at the order, of Joe Sr.— and Humphrey's attacks on his rival over this refusal, helped the Kennedy campaign. The vote for him was particularly heavy where McCarthy had been strongest. Though Jack Kennedy had won in Wisconsin, he had not laid to rest the argument that a Catholic could not be elected President of the United States.

It was therefore mandatory that the Kennedys mount another primary campaign in a state whose population was not so heavily Catholic.

The next primary—just four weeks away, on May 10—would be in West Virginia. This was a stroke of luck for the Kennedys, though few in the press saw it that way. West Virginia was a solidly Protestant state, and this is what the pundits reiterated in their commentaries. But it was also one of the most tolerant in racial and religious matters that the Kennedys could have found. Negro-white relations in West Virginia had always been good. The West Virginians were also a people of great pride, and the press hullabaloo about bigotry and intolerance put them on notice that they would be judged by the rest of the country on their reactions to the Kennedy-Humphrey battle. "Once the issue could be made one of tolerance or intolerance, Hubert Humphrey was hung," Theodore White wrote. "No one could prove to his own conscience that by voting for Humphrey he was displaying tolerance. Yet any man, indecisive in mind on the Presidency, could prove that he was at least tolerant by voting for Jack Kennedy."

And the religious issue it was to be. When Bobby arrived in West Virginia, the day after the Wisconsin primary, he and Larry O'Brien studied the polls, received the reports from their men in the field, and decided to make their weakness a point of strength. They had troops in plenty for a state of that size: the entire first team of Kennedys, Franklin Delano Roosevelt Jr.—slightly unemployed since his account as public-relations man for the Trujillo regime had been shot out from under him—and an army of seventy-five volunteer field men, in comparison to Humphrey's ten. They also had available to them all the facilities that a fat exchequer could buy, while Humphrey traveled about in a bus. In a state that had been so thoroughly passed over by the national prosperity, the obvious financial bankruptcy of Humphrey's organization should have appealed. And the knowledge among the voters that while Bobby and O'Brien worked around the clock, Jack was vacationing in Montego Bay, a luxury resort in the West Indies, should also have had a negative effect.

At the Kennedy team's first meeting in Clarksburg, Bobby took command and with O'Brien made up the table of organization, mapped out strategy and tactics, and sketched out the propaganda line. The state was divided up into eight territories, each with its own headquarters and a subheadquarters. Experienced and well-heeled volunteers were to be chosen to staff these headquarters and to plan local tactics meticulously. Wiener roasts, ox roasts, door-to-door canvassing, a saturation telephone campaign—all of these were mapped out as if the Kennedys were marching to war. The most important order to the troops, however, came from O'Brien. A seasoned politician, he knew that in West Virginia Bobby's tack of riding roughshod over local politicians would put an end to Kennedy hopes. West Virginians, he pointed out, were polite and soft-spoken. They were economically downtrodden. But they would rise up as one man if they were pushed around. Therefore, O'Brien made it a flat rule that the Kennedy operative in each of the eight areas must report to local Democratic leaders—the county courthouse boys—on everything they were doing, before they did it. This seemed like wasted motion to Bobby, but he reluctantly concurred.

At every turn of the dial, Jack Kennedy showed up on television, while Humphrey traveled commercial airliners, carried his own bags, and worried over the $17,000 he still owed for the Wisconsin primary campaign. He could complain bitterly, "I can't afford to run through this state with a little black bag and a checkbook," but Bobby countered that Humphrey was playing "fast and loose with smears and innuendoes." Humphrey could lash out that "politics is a serious business, not a boy's game where you can pick up your ball and go home if things don't go according to your idea of who should win. Bobby is pushing the panic button." But when the Kennedy television commercials showed Jack as a war hero, and Franklin Roosevelt Jr. could say with impunity of Humphrey, "He's a good Democrat but I don't know where he was in World War II"—imputing that Humphrey was a slacker in a state which had given more men and suffered heavier casualties than any other in the Union—there was little that could be said or done.

But the main thrust of the campaign was religion. At every meeting, Jack argued passionately that he wanted religion kept out of the campaign. If no one raised the issue, Douglass Cater of the *Reporter* wrote at the time, Kennedy brought it up himself. So did the correspondents who covered Kennedy and Humphrey. Joseph Alsop, writing from a mountain village, stated that after interviewing eighty families, he found the "shoeless, the slatterns, and the slobs" were for Humphrey. The primary, he added, "looks like a very ugly business in which Humphrey can only win—if he does win—for very ugly reasons"—ignorance and bigotry. The more Humphrey disclaimed this, the more he was accused of emphasizing the issue, if only by indirection. To add to his frustration, Jack Kennedy interrupted the West Virginia campaign to appear in Washington before the American Society of Newspaper Editors, pleading for an end to the religious discussion which had been his daily stock in trade. But, as Harold Lavine, then *Newsweek*'s top political reporter, quietly noted, "Anti-Catholic sentiment did not prevent Alfred E. Smith from carrying West Virginia in 1928."

In West Virginia as in Wisconsin, Bobby could not resist bringing up one of his favorite themes, Jimmy Hoffa. The Teamsters were hardly an issue in the state, but Bobby warned that Hoffa had ordered his union to give their all for Hubert Humphrey. In the Kilkenny Alley that West Virginia had become, Humphrey shot back, "Bobby said if they had to spend half a million to win here, they would do it." This came closer to the truth than he realized. For when the shooting was over, the Baltimore *Sun* put its finger on what was probably the secret of the Kennedy victory: contributions to candidates for local office who beat the drums for their benefactor—religion or not—and to the courthouse politicians. "Long tradition has built up a system of filling the county campaign chests by almost openly 'auctioning off' the support of the county machine to the highest bidder among the candidates for national office," Howard Norton wrote in the *Sun*. "This is a completely honest procedure. . . . And, in appreciation of the contribution, the county machine throws its support to the successful bidder. Once the bidding is completed, the party leaders . . . print up on little slips of paper the official 'slate' of candidates whom they urge the voters to accept. . . . These 'slates' generally are kept under wraps until the morning of election day. Then, when the organization's automobiles go into the hills and start hauling the voters to the polls, copies of the official slate are pressed into the hands of the party faithful. Only at this point does the average faithful member of the Democratic party in West Virginia suddenly come to know who he is going to vote for." (For a while, both the Republicans and the Johnson adherents pressed for an investigation of Kennedy spending in West Virginia. Nothing came of it. After Kennedy's death, Sorenson admitted that it was "customary in West Virginia" to buy votes for local candidates and slates, and that Kennedy money "may well have been" spent for this purpose. But he denied that the Kennedys had bought any votes directly for Jack.)

It was because of those "official slates" that Bobby and Jack could make predictions of doom and gloom, present their direful polls to the thousands of party workers they had enrolled in the battle against bigotry, yet be confident once the polls had closed that they had won. Only the magnitude of that victory came as a surprise: Kennedy, 220,000; Humphrey, 142,000. Nevertheless, in the hours of waiting before the tally had been announced, Bobby paced the floor of the converted barbershop in Charleston which was the Kennedy headquarters. Two hours after the polls had closed, Bobby was all a-grin. "I couldn't have done it without my brother," he said.

The postlude to the West Virginia campaign was presented later that night. Humphrey had not yet conceded defeat and was still in his hotel room when *finis* was written to the drama. In Arthur Schlesinger's colorful account, "Word came from the hotel switchboard that 'Mr. Kennedy' was below and was coming up to the Humphrey suite. The room froze; everyone supposed that Jack Kennedy was back from Washington where he had gone earlier in the day. In a minute the door slowly opened. It was Robert Kennedy, slight and youthful in a raincoat. He walked the length of the silent room to Muriel Humphrey, kissed her, almost to her consternation, then shook Hubert's hand. The two men left the suite together and walked through the gusts of spring rain to Humphrey's campaign headquarters. There Humphrey read his statement of withdrawal [from the Presidential race] before the television cameras. Soon they went out in the night to greet the victor, at last flying in from Washington."

The Wisconsin and West Virginia campaigns, however, left deep scars and some of them have never healed. Before the Democratic convention, in a hot and smog-ridden Los Angeles, had given the nomination to Jack Kennedy, other wounds would be inflicted. And reporters not too dazzled by the Kennedy effulgence would remember, with a soon-forgotten twinge of apprehension, that the Kennedys had not been exactly candid with them. Comparing notes, they discovered that two polls prepared by the same organization, one shown to them during the Wisconsin contest and the other during the West Virginia confrontation, had recorded drastically different results. The first poll had given Kennedy a seventy-to-thirty lead over Humphrey. The second showed Humphrey ahead of Jack by a sixty-to-forty margin. Yet both polls had borne the same date. ("I wonder," said pollster Elmo Roper, "if these polls are not being used to frighten people out of running for office or into getting aboard someone else's bandwagon.")

The Kennedy bandwagon was picking up momentum and the politicians noted it. The "bandwagon psychology" became epidemic in Democratic circles, and it was encouraged by a memorandum which Ted Sorenson had prepared late in 1955. Ten years later Sorenson would write that it "made no pretense at being a comprehensive and objective study. It was a political answer to the sweeping assertions made against nominating a Catholic for Vice President." It had helped Jack Kennedy in 1956, but it was of vastly more value as the time for the 1960 convention approached. For it argued with some energy that "there is, or can be, such a thing as a 'Catholic vote' whereby a high proportion of Catholics of all ages, residences, occupations, and economic status vote for a well-known Catholic candidate or a ticket with special Catholic appeal." Though Catholics accounted for only one-quarter of the nation's vote, their concentration in large cities gave them great weight in the electoral college. And the report, circulated under John Bailey's name, added that there were fourteen "pivotal Catholic states" whose proportions of adult Catholics ranged from Rhode Island's sixty percent to Ohio's twenty percent. In 1952, none of these states had gone Democratic and their 261 electoral votes had swung the election to Dwight D. Eisenhower.

In short, while Kennedy protested that the religious issue made him an underdog, his campaign aides were telling politicians, less interested in religion than in winning, that Kennedy's Catholicism made him the candidate most likely to win. It was not on issues, however, that Bobby counted but on organization, pressure of any kind, propaganda, and singlemindedness. He had learned in 1956 what it meant to stand in the glare of the lights with hand outstretched. He had known the panic that strikes when a floor manager does not know exactly what forces he has at his disposal, when he can only hope rather than manipulate. It would be different this time. He would make certain that everything worked perfectly at

Los Angeles, even the coffee machines at Kennedy headquarters. (They ran out of coffee once, for three and one half minutes.)

The preparations were necessary and would have been made even if Jack Kennedy had been pledged all the convention votes. The Kennedy forces, in fact, sometimes acted as if that were the case. "You can't beat somebody with nobody," they said, quoting the old political adage. And as the bandwagon rolled, they seemed to have a point. Adlai Stevenson, with two defeats behind him, could have mobilized a considerable army had he chosen to; liberal Democrats still idolized him and the party's Old Guard would have rallied to his cause had he asked them in time. Lyndon Johnson, the most able and the shrewdest of those whose names were being suggested in any day's edition of any newspaper, was biding his time, certain in the gross miscalculation that he could outwit Kennedy when the time came. The other contenders, Senator Stuart Symington of Missouri and the dark horses waiting for the baby spots to illumine them, were no threat. They watched and prayed that one of their number would take on Kennedy, but they were too timid to try it themselves. Only a bad slip by Jack or Bobby could slow the Kennedy progress toward the nomination.

A slip did occur. The May 1960 summit conference between Nikita Khrushchev and President Eisenhower had broken down when a U-2 reconnaissance plane was shot down over the Soviet Union. The State Department had bobbled in its explanations. Facing Eisenhower in Paris, the Soviet dictator had launched a vitriolic attack, phrased in gutter language, and demanded that the President "apologize" to him for the incident. The President had, of course, refused. The Democrats, however, might have made political capital of the breakdown of the conference—the handling by the Eisenhower Administration had been inept—except for Jack Kennedy. Campaigning in Eugene, Oregon, he was asked whether he would have apologized had he been President. To this, Kennedy answered: "I certainly would express regret at the timing and give assurances that it would not happen again. I would express regret that the flight did take place." Senator Johnson seized the opportunity. "I am not prepared to apologize to Mr. Khrushchev—are you?" he thundered to audiences. "I am not prepared to send regrets to Mr. Khrushchev—are you?" "No," the audiences roared. And that roar reverberated throughout the country. Efforts to take back the Kennedy statements or to obscure it in contradictory statements failed, and the bandwagon's momentum was imperceptibly slowed.

Backing and filling about the South, Kennedy also ran into trouble. On the one hand, he told Northern liberals that he would win the nomination without Southern help and, when Lyndon Johnson declared himself a candidate, added that he did not intend to seek that help. Then, when the Southern delegates Bobby had wooed so assiduously reacted, Jack wrote them personally to show that his heart still yearned to be on the nether side of the Mason-Dixon line. At the same time, former President Truman had declared war on Jack with a stinging rhetorical question: "Senator, are you certain that the country is ready for you?" Liberal newspapermen like James Reston of the New York *Times* considered this a low blow and said so. Few delegates were lost to Kennedy by the Truman attack, but at that point no one could accurately predict this.

Despite these setbacks, Bobby did not slacken, did not despair. Working through National Committee Chairman Paul Butler, he was putting the screws on those who did not see the light. Convention space was denied to Adlai Stevenson. Delegations not in the Kennedy camp were assigned to hotels miles away from the convention headquarters at the Hotel Biltmore in Los Angeles. Some found themselves in Pasadena, and it was not uncommon for compatible but anti-Kennedy delegations to be separated by a $10 to $15 cab ride in the sprawling city. This prevented the formation of a coalition which could withhold the nomination from Kennedy through enough ballots to put him out of business. And the old Hoffa charge, now amended to link the Teamster leader and Senator Johnson, was trotted out. The campaign would have lacked the Bobby touch without it.

When the delegates began to arrive in Los Angeles, they found the lobbies of the Biltmore blocked by bevies of Kennedy dancing girls performing their routines where space was most needed. They were also met with rumors of the mushrooming Stevenson movement. The Sports Arena was besieged by Stevenson pickets, led by activists from Harry Bridges' left-wing union. Their chanting, once the convention had opened, sounded like the old Madison Square Garden demonstrations of the Popular Front days, but they were impressive enough to inspire "Kennedy Bandwagon Falters" headlines in the local press. In this mad jumble, Bobby stormed from delegation to delegation, cajoling and threatening. On crowded elevators, he stared dourly at newspapermen who favored candidates other than his brother and cut them dead. Jack Kennedy looked about him gloomily and suggested that if the convention turned against him, he would "put Bobby into the Massachusetts picture to run for governor" where his "nerve" would be an asset.

Bobby's nerve, however, had already led him into making the prediction that Jack would be nominated on the second ballot. His estimate was modest, but it led Johnson to make an angry comment. "There are countries in the world where such pure arrogance is customary in politics," he said. "This is not that kind of country."

The entry of Lyndon Johnson into the lists gave Bobby a chance to break loose from the Southern delegates he had been attempting to woo. Typically, once he decided he had no use for them, he jettisoned them, as if he had never wanted them in the first place. And with considerable foresight, he made use of his liberation. In the eighth-floor suite occupied by the Kennedys and their favored associates, Bobby made the break official, certain that in the long run it would do Jack Kennedy good with the Northern politicians who really wielded power. Coatless and tieless, and standing on a chair, he laid down the line on the platform.

"I want to say a few words about civil rights," he said. "We have the best civil rights plank the Democratic party has ever had. I want you fellows to make it clear to your delegations that the Kennedy forces are unequivocally in favor of this plank and that we want it passed in the convention. Those of you who are dealing with Southern delegations make it absolutely clear how we stand on civil rights. Don't fuzz it up. Tell the Southern states that we hope they will see other reasons why we are united as Democrats and why they should support Kennedy, but don't let there be doubt anywhere as to how the Kennedy people stand on this."

Bobby's grasp of other ideological matters was not so great. On a television program, he was questioned on the Connally Reservation, an amendment to legislation accepting United States participation in international bodies, which reiterated the supremacy of the Constitution. Bobby said he had never heard of it. This was a shocker, coming from a man already being mentioned by the press as the next Attorney General, should Jack win nomination and election. He was told that his brother favored repeal of the Connally Reservation. "In that case, I presume it should be repealed," said Bobby. "But frankly, that's not my province. I'm just on the team and Jack's the captain." But if he failed that test, he was getting high marks in more practical matters.

All candidates keep a file index of the delegates to a convention. The cards contain background information that the candidate's staff has been able to gather about the delegates' political background, preferences, weaknesses, and other pertinent matters. The file system set up by Bobby was far more flexible. Men were assigned to cover specific groups of delegates. Their every fluctuation of support for the candidates was recorded as faithfully as if they were keeping a fever chart. And the changes were made immediately. A secret telephone to Kennedy headquarters, manned twenty-four hours a day, was the vehicle for this information. As rapidly as changes occurred, they were phoned in and noted down. Bobby was determined not to repeat his failures of 1956. Communications were the key. "From the Kennedy command post on the eighth floor of the Biltmore," Sorenson wrote, "a vast telephone network linked all offices with all the residences, a cottage behind the Sports Arena Convention Hall, and the seats of the Kennedy leaders on the convention floor. Kennedy floor workers had their own walkie-talkies. . . . A wide assortment of volunteers—Massachusetts delegates, unoccupied spectators, old Kennedy friends was assigned to eat, drink, and live with each of the 54 delegations, to report regularly on their moods, questions, and trends, and, above all, to keep track of their votes."

Those working for Kennedy were signing on for the duration, with no coffee breaks, no socializing, nothing but work. When there were signs of battle fatigue, Bobby turned on them like a junior General Patton and barked: "We're not out here to go to Disneyland. We're not out here to go to night clubs. We're out here to work. If you're not out here to work, you can turn in your staff badges right now. There are plenty of people who would like to have them." Members of the staff complained that he treated them like dirt, but they remained. Bobby snapped and snarled at men twice his age, with no realization that there was anything wrong with this. It was this manner, brought to a point of abrasive perfection at the convention, which led one columnist to describe him, after Jack had been nominated, as "Nixon's secret weapon." And Jim Bishop wrote that Bobby was "the spinning dervish with the tight halo. He condemns and praises men as though all of us were serfs in some big Kennedy estate. . . . When he concludes a short, confidential chat with a political leader, the man is left with the feeling that . . . if he doesn't do exactly as Robert tells him, God will strike him dead. I would not like to see the young man appointed to a high office."

Perhaps it has been this quality in Bobby, appealing as it does to the latent masochism in the human animal, which may account for his success. In a situation like the 1960 convention, it effectively cut through the fuzzy thinking of the liberals who dominated. "We can't miss a trick in the next twelve hours," Bobby said on the morning of the day of balloting. "If we don't win tonight, we're dead." Then he called in his fishermen to tell him what delegates they had in their nets. "I don't want generalities or guesses," he said coldly. "There's no point in fooling ourselves. I want the hard facts. I want to know only the votes we are absolutely guaranteed on the first ballot." Then he questioned each man as if he had him on the witness stand. The tally was 740, just twenty-one short of the number needed for nominating Jack. This, he knew, was enough to send non-Kennedy delegations rushing for microphones to change their votes while there was still time to claim allegiance to the patronage that a winning candidate can dispense. One of the professionals suggested that his well-disciplined delegation could withhold some of its votes so that on the second ballot Kennedy's total would increase—an old convention gambit. Bobby vetoed it. He was going for broke.

That night, the Democratic convention went through a ritual almost as old as American political parties—the torture of nominating speeches, multiple seconding speeches, and demonstrations for each nominee. Bobby had failed in his effort to get Stevenson to present Kennedy's name to the convention, and Orville Freeman was accorded the honor. Speaker Sam Rayburn, tough and stolid, nominated Lyndon Johnson. Then Eugene McCarthy, in perhaps the only eloquent speech of the convention, spoke up for Adlai Stevenson, the sad and confused leader of the assembled liberals. The Sports Arena surrendered itself to pandemonium which nothing could still, and the Kennedy floor leaders, Bobby and Governor Ribicoff of Connecticut, looked about apprehensively. Could this be the 1960 version of the demonstration with which, twenty years earlier in Philadelphia, Wendell Willkie had seized the nomination from the sure winner? Even turning out the lights could not still the clamor. But Bobby had done his work well. In the balloting, the Kennedy delegates held firm. When the roll call reached Washington, Kennedy had 710 votes and the stampede was on. This time, there was no need for Bobby's V-for-Victory sign. John Fitzgerald Kennedy was on his way.

What happened in the next few days has been reported in as many variations as there were principals in the drama. Jack Kennedy's reasons for choosing Lyndon Johnson for his running mate were always murky. And since those still alive may have an interest in not disclosing all they know, it is likely to remain so. This much is fact: During the course of the convention, it was known that Bobby had, with varying degrees of commitment, promised the nomination to

Senator Henry Jackson of Washington, Governor Orville Freeman of Minnesota, and Senator Stuart Symington. During the day that followed the Kennedy nomination, rumor and conjecture filled the halls that ringed the Sports Arena. At the Biltmore, the same rumors and conjectures were being repeated. But by the following morning, the reporters with the best sources and the keenest noses were certain that the Vice-Presidential nominee would be Symington. There were many reasons why this made sense, but only one counted: Kennedy wanted him and Bobby concurred.

At 10:00 o'clock that day, few in the press corps disputed this, and some reporters were already writing their stories on the choice. Then, in a flurry and a scurry, the news broke. Kennedy's choice was Lyndon Johnson, the man who had cut him up most severely in the fight for the Presidential nomination. Among the liberals, there was a loud and agonized wail. It couldn't be true, they shouted. If they had known of this, they never would have voted for Kennedy. In all the turmoil, few had any facts, any explanations. Before the morning was up, John S. Knight, publisher of a chain of newspapers, and the author of this account had received reports from different but trustworthy sources that the Kennedy choice had not been a free one. According to these reports, Jack and Bobby, with the general assent of the "in" group, had decided on Symington. But Jack had been visited by Speaker Sam Rayburn, still smarting over the defeat of his friend and fellow Texan, Lyndon Johnson. Rayburn had first suggested and then demanded that Johnson be given the second spot on the ticket. When Kennedy demurred, Rayburn announced that if Johnson were not offered the Vice-Presidential nomination, he, Rayburn, would personally tear the convention apart with a floor fight against Symington. Jack Kennedy bowed to *force majeur* and agreed to the Johnson candidacy.

This story was denied. But since none of the principals has been able to agree on any alternative, the presumption must be that someone is hiding something. Three elaborate accounts exist—one by Arthur Schlesinger (based on the long memorandum of Philip Graham, publisher of the Washington *Post*) , one by Ted Sorenson, and a third by Philip Potter, a Baltimore *Sun* correspondent (and now Washington bureau chief) . Brief accounts have appeared before, and since all of them are contradictory, they do nothing to bring concordance to the tale. Schlesinger states flatly that Kennedy offered the nomination to placate the South, confident that Johnson would refuse. Both Potter and Sorenson deny this and insist that Kennedy really wanted Johnson. Schlesinger believes that Bobby did his best to sabotage the negotiations between the two principals. Johnson, in the Potter account, exonerates Bobby. Schlesinger quotes Bobby as having said, after the deal had been consummated: "My God, this wouldn't have happened except that we were all so tired last night" —hardly the outburst of someone who had been aware of and favoring the Kennedy-Johnson compact as described by some of the participants. In evidence, also, is Bobby's attempt, when sent by his brother to make final a deal already agreed upon, to offer Johnson the chairmanship of the Democratic National Committee, a rather sophisticated insult which could have terminated further conversation had not Speaker Rayburn, to whom the offer was tendered, responded with a monosyllabic and scatological expletive. This incident somewhat dims Bobby's denial, in 1965, of the charge that he had acted on his own during those critical hours. "Anyone who knows the relationship between President Kennedy and myself would know that doesn't make a great deal of sense," he said. "The idea that I would go behind my brother's back doesn't make sense."

The record would indicate that, at least in this instance, it did make sense. Bobby *had* flatly promised liberal leaders just before the balloting that Johnson would not get the nomination. That the promise was necessary in the anti-Johnson atmosphere of the Kennedy camp indicates that something was in the wind, and inner-circle liberals had sniffed it. There is no doubt that Sam Rayburn, who had rudely opposed any Kennedy-Johnson ticket, changed his mind abruptly, that the first time it was proposed to Johnson he showed a receptivity surprising to his aides and associates, and that the "negotiations" described in the Graham memo smack of the lady who doth protest too much. It is also a probability, based on the evidence, that Jack Kennedy, having thought through the question of a running mate before the balloting, was compelled to give himself an "out" for the assurances he and Bobby had given the liberal-labor bloc in order to win himself the nomination. Did he withhold the facts of the situation from Bobby, letting him move ahead on his own without consulting his brother?

Whatever the facts and the motives, the convention which, in William S. White's words, had "gathered, all in one piece, every possible modern tactic of pressure and persuasion, gentle and otherwise," reached a point at which delegates like ADA's Joseph Rauh would wrestle in view of the television cameras to prevent their states' standards from being paraded in the pro-forma "demonstration" for a Vice-Presidential nominee.

The reactions to the Johnson switch were bitter:

James Blair of Missouri: "We've just been run over by a steam-roller."

James A. Farley of New York, who had been assured it would be Symington: "Why, that's impossible."

Economist Robert Nathan of Washington, D.C., who early in the primary drive had been threatened with the loss of clients if he did not support Kennedy: "This is a complete violation of an under-standing."

A now-forgotten wit in the press room: "This puts Kennedy just one heartbeat away from the Vice Presidency."

Only Mrs. Cyrus Eaton, wife of the industrialist who had flown to Paris to shake Khrushchev's hand after he had insulted President Eisenhower, dissented. In her wheel chair on the convention floor, she made a comment that proved she was shrewder than most of those about her. "This guarantees Jack Kennedy's election," she said.

So ended the 1960 Democratic convention—as H. L. Mencken wrote in another context of the "traditional Democratic method"—with "howls, bellowings, and charges of fraud." The Republican convention, always a calmer performance, had its own disappoint-ments as Richard Nixon knuckled under to Governor Nelson Rocke-feller and then chose as his running mate United Nations Ambassa-dor Henry Cabot Lodge, perhaps the laziest campaigner the Repub-lic had seen in living memory.

Both Democrats and Republicans, as they assessed the impact on the public of their conventions, their platforms, and their candi-dates, were agreed that the months ahead would see the bitterest political campaign in many decades. They were also agreed, though they said it only in private, that they had presented the voters with a big ideological muddle. The labels and the shibboleths were con-fused, with bitterness and unity at work in both parties.

The labor side of the campaign alone presented its contradictions and its off-beat aspects. Since 1936, labor had moved into a vacuum in the Democratic party created by the Roosevelt-Truman policies. In the most recent elections it had furnished large sums of money and, far more important, the trained manpower to get out the Demo-cratic vote. The driving force behind this had been United Auto Workers president Walter Reuther and some of his colleagues of the old CIO.

Labor, in fact, was one of the mainstays of the organization which Senator John F. Kennedy built in the three years before the conven-tion. During the last hours before the balloting in Los Angeles, when young Bobby Kennedy panicked, fearing he lacked the votes to send his brother over the top, labor delegates and lobbyists scurried about the convention floor promising, cajoling, and pressuring. The selection of Majority Leader Lyndon Johnson to fill the second spot on the Democratic ticket sent labor into a tailspin.

The result of labor's anguish could be noted in a quiet but significant meeting during the G.O.P. convention in Chicago between thirty-five labor leaders and a group of important Republicans. None of these unionists, it is true, came from the highest echelons of the AFL-CIO. They represented the local unions or state bodies. The head of a mechanics local said that he would campaign for a Nixon-Lodge ticket because he was "double-crossed" by Senator Kennedy.

These dissidents were whipped into line before the campaign got under way. But they reflected the feelings of much of their membership. And, in the final analysis, their feelings were unimportant. Other factors loomed larger. Reporters and observers agreed that Bobby Kennedy could make or break Senator Kennedy in the campaign ahead. Bobby had emerged, some insiders felt, as the dominant member of the Kennedy team, if only because the convention password had so frequently been, "Clear it with Bobby." When a prominent Washington newspaperman said of Bobby with an affectionate wryness, "He has all the patience of a vulture, without any of the dripping sentimentality," he was expressing another consensus. Those who had already developed a fanatical devotion to Jack were fearful lest Bobby's disregard for others, and his lack of that instinct which warns a politician that he is treading on toes, would do damage to the personality that Senator Kennedy was trying to impress on the public as his own.

In the days immediately following the convention, Bobby threatened to do just that. Moving into a touchy political situation in vote-heavy New York, Bobby succeeded in widening the split between the regular Tammany organization, headed by faithful Kennedy supporter Carmine De Sapio, and the so-called "reform group," of which Mrs. Roosevelt and former Air Force Secretary Thomas Finletter were the leaders. In a "pep" talk to the reform group, Bobby laid down the line: "I don't give a damn if the state and county organizations survive after November, and I don't care if *you* survive. I want to elect John F. Kennedy." Neither the Tammany organization nor the reform group enjoyed the harangue, and as a result, an impartial chairman was called in and Bobby was ordered to remain out of New York. Aware of the predictions that, if elected, Jack would make Bobby his assistant President, a disgruntled New York

Democrat remarked that this would "make Sherman Adams look like Caspar Milquetoast."

The role of Bobby Kennedy in the campaign, however, was hardly one that Sherman Adams would have countenanced. For Bobby was aware that most of the working press covering Kennedy was solidly liberal and almost pathologically anti-Nixon. It was therefore possible to take a leaf from Lenin—"to use any ruse, cunning . . . evasion, concealment of truth"—without any worry that it would get more than a flicker of attention on the front pages. The record of the campaign, when examined dispassionately at this remove, explains why friendly biographers of the younger Kennedy pass over it so rapidly—a little more than one page in the major effort. The method evolved by Bobby was to hit and run, hoping that no one would notice the license plate of the fleeing car. If there was discovery, the matter could be brushed aside as inconsequential or irrelevant. When Nixon was in the hospital, for example, Kennedy was asked to comment on one of Harry S. Truman's more blatant diatribes which associated the Republican standard-bearer with "racial, religious, and anti-union bigotry." Kennedy refused to repudiate the attack on the ground that he did "not plan to comment on Vice President *Nixon or any of his actions* until he is out of the hospital" —a neat way of letting the Truman record stand without openly endorsing it.

The gentle glow of Theodore White's prose style washes over this approach to candor, even as it adds a rosy hue to Bobby's actions by descriptions of the warm and exciting meetings at Hyannis Port at which strategy was discussed. Reams of copy were written which, unconsciously or otherwise, obscured the facts by stressing the organizational brilliance of Bobby's mind or the details of his strategic thinking. Given his resources in volunteer and labor-financed manpower, he worked excellently. His insistence that the major drives be in the nine large states which held 237 of the 269 electoral votes needed to win made sense. So, too, did the plan to concentrate the candidate's campaigning time in the industrial Northeast. But it was not a particularly revolutionary idea. Neither was the much-publicized registration drive. Bobby was aware that of the more than 100,000,000 Americans eligible to vote, 40,000,000 would not register unless the Democrats and their labor allies drove them to it. His "prediction" that seventy percent of these habitual nonvoters would vote Democratic was a guess that could never be proved or disproved. When a *Newsweek* reporter asked him where these estimates came from, Bobby could snap: "These are not estimates. They are facts and figures." But he had no real way of knowing. A team of fifty state chairmen, a paid staff of eight "leaders," two hundred county registration chairmen, and thousands of others on a part-time basis were able to hike national registration figures, but whether the 6,800,000 voters were added to the rolls because of the drive has yet to be determined. Campaign scheduling was the domain of Kenny O'Donnell. Organization, *per se,* was handled at the Democratic National Committee level by the experienced Larry O'Brien, on the Kennedy-Johnson Volunteers level by Byron (Whizzer) White. In New York, the most critical state of all, Bobby was forced to withdraw, sending in his stead William Walton, a one-time reporter for the leftist *PM* and for *Time.*

Bobby could state, as he did before the campaign began, "We're trying to get an organization going that is bigger than U.S. Steel, and we're trying to do it in three months. It's a fantastic job." And he could add: "It's a day-to-day operation. You can't leave it alone. That's what happened to Stevenson. You have to keep up the pace all the time. Some little thing may happen that is totally insignificant by itself, but after twenty-four hours it may be a full-blown problem." But the painstaking effort that this required was sometimes too much for Bobby. Theodore White in *The Making of the President, 1960* tells of an afternoon when the door of Bobby's office at the National Committee headquarters opened and he "exploded" into a group of his own people. "What are you doing?" he shouted. "What are we all doing? Let's get on the road. Let's get on the road tomorrow. I want us all on the road tomorrow." Having spoken, he slammed the door shut.

His prime virtue was that he saw the election as he saw everything else—a struggle for life and death in a jungle world. Victory was all that counted in those harrowing days. If it required that he be all things to all men, that he be the propagandist *par excellence,* that was all right with him. In mid-August, for example, while he was publicly excoriating the Republicans for dragging their heels on civil rights and verbally assaulting Southern Democrats in Northern newspapers, he could meet secretly with Governor John Patterson of Alabama. Patterson pleaded with Bobby to ease up in order to make it a little easier for politicians below the Mason-Dixon line.

"All Negro agitation began in the South under the Eisenhower Administration," Patterson said, "and specifically under Republican Attorney General Rogers. The South had no opportunity to air its grievances and civil rights became a matter of coercion. Senator Kennedy has said that integration is a moral issue. If a Kennedy Administration takes office, the pressure will be eased. At least we will get a hearing instead of having the federal government insist on ram-rodding civil rights down our throats." He was not contradicted by Bobby and could return to Alabama with a report that the Kennedys would be "sympathetic" to his position.

In the huddles of the Kennedy first team, it was Bobby who urged that his brother resort to "low-road" campaign oratory. Bobby's reasons for this were highly practical, but hardly ethical. Nixon, he argued, was a prisoner of his reputation as a rocking, socking campaigner. Therefore, he would key his oratory to the "statesmanlike" and "high-road" pattern. Jack Kennedy could therefore bite and gouge with no fear of retaliation from an inhibited Nixon.

Among Bobby's innovations was a "People Machine" for which the Democratic Advisory Committee paid $65,000. This computer was fed information on people's attitudes, arriving at an evaluation of what public reaction to specific political stimuli would be. (Use of this machine was later denied, then admitted when it was pointed out that its findings were sent directly to Bobby, who had also contributed $20,000 to its purchase.) The People Machine served one purpose for Bobby: it strengthened his argument that pounding away at Kennedy's Catholicism would help rather than hurt. "It makes no sense to brush the religious issue under the rug," he said repeatedly. And though the Kennedy brothers had asserted after the West Virginia primary that the issue was dead for all time, they revived it and used it throughout the campaign. As Victor Lasky noted, Kennedy "repeatedly urged American voters to forget his religion by reminding them of it." According to Lasky, moreover, Bobby "was placed in charge of making sure that the voters would be constantly reminded of the necessity of forgetting the religious issue."

"Did they ask my brother Joe whether he was a Catholic before he was shot down?" Bobby asked at the opening of a Cincinnati headquarters. "It is not important as to what church a candidate attends on Sunday, but whether or not the prestige of the United States, as leader of the free world, can be restored," he said to groups in New York's Catskill Mountains. He charged the Republicans with spending $1,000,000 on anti-Catholic literature, and it was not until after the election was over that the Fair Campaign Practices Committee disclosed that a thorough investigation failed to substantiate any part of the damaging allegation. When Dr. Norman Vincent Peale and a group of Protestant clergymen issued a statement expressing concern over the possibility of having a Catholic in the White House, the glee among the Kennedy people was unrestrained. Jack Kennedy was despatched to Texas to address the Houston Ministers' Conference. Drawing its information from Bobby, *Time* stated, "Hard-boiled Kennedyites run a continual poll on the Catholic vote, know that Jack's confrontation by the Houston Protestant ministers helped them with Nixon-minded Northern Catholics—and know that a fall-off of interest in religion will weaken them in the same area. Bobby plans to show a film of Jack Kennedy's session with the Houston clergy in every state."

This was precisely what he did. In every city with a large Catholic population, the film was shown on prime television time. Liberal Catholic publications like *Commonweal*, perturbed over the possible consequences of this political use of a sensitive issue, protested, as did the Republicans. Columnists found it ironic that the same people who extravagantly praised such anti-Catholic publications as Paul Blanshard's *American Freedom and Catholic Power*, which saw a Papist conspiracy to take over America, were now the loudest in their outcry against the "bigotry" of Republicans who were doing their frustrated best to ignore the issue entirely. "Repeated observation, examination, and study has convinced this committee that the Republicans—with only rare and short-lived exceptions—were scrupulously careful to avoid abuse of the religious issue," the Fair Campaign Practices Committee asserted—but that was after Kennedy was elected.

Bobby, however, did not restrict himself to the religious issue. Late in the campaign, he charged that a "secret transcript" of the so-called Kitchen Debate between Nixon and Khrushchev had been classified "top secret" by the Eisenhower Administration. Since the debate had taken place in the presence of some sixty American reporters and a great crowd, this was a *reductio ad absurdam* of charge-throwing. There had, moreover, been no transcript, and Nixon himself had compiled all the quotes from news stories, printing them up in a pamphlet along with the speeches he delivered on his 1959 trip to the Soviet Union. The voters could not be expected to know the facts, however, and Bobby succeeded in creating doubts about a Nixon exploit which had delighted most Americans.

Perhaps the most astonishing demonstration of the Bobby Kennedy technique was the Jackie Robinson episode. Like other well-informed Negroes, Robinson knew that Nixon had worked hard and quietly to break down barriers to Negro employment in a number of fields. He knew Nixon and respected him. He had therefore endorsed the Nixon candidacy, a gesture of some consequence coming as it did from the first man to break the color barrier in major-league baseball. To rebut Robinson, and to minimize his influence among Negro voters, Bobby appeared on the Barry Gray show, a radio "talk" program, with a series of charges against Robinson. The trump cards were allegations that Robinson worked for a company with bad labor relations whose head was a Republican. The implications were obvious.

Robinson, whose self-possession is as great off as on the baseball diamond, answered calmly that his employer was a registered member of New York's Liberal party, that he had contributed $5,000 to Hubert Humphrey's primary campaigns, and that the labor relations allegations "were brought up by the head of a union who has since been indicted for alleged illegal activities"—the kind of unionist Bobby had railed against in his Senate Labor Rackets Committee days. "I don't see where my company has anything to do with his brother's having had breakfast with the head of the White Citizens Council and the racist Governor of Alabama," Robinson added, alluding to one of the criticisms he had made of Jack. "To me, the most revealing part of the whole attack was Robert Kennedy's reference to eighteen million Negro Americans as 'his Negroes'—meaning Jackie Robinson's. Apparently young Bobby hasn't heard that the Emancipation Proclamation was signed ninety-seven years ago. I don't run any plantation and I suggest to Kennedy that he stop acting as if he did."

The effect of Bobby's activities began to worry the men around Jack Kennedy. They were also having a bad effect among Democrats who expected a modicum of courtesy during the campaign period, however rapidly that might end once a new President was installed. They protested to Kennedy that Bobby's treatment of his fellow partisans left much to be desired, particularly where the South was concerned. When South Carolina and Florida leaders complained to the candidate of a particularly virulent Bobby outburst against them, Jack said Bobby was "young and very hotheaded." In his apology, there was an implication that he and Bobby had quarrelled over this. The Southerners were somewhat mollified, but like their New York colleagues, they extracted an agreement from Jack that Bobby would be kept out of their states and that he would stop berating state political leaders just because they did not agree with him on all matters.

Given this background, Bobby nevertheless set himself up as a one-man "truth squad," trailing Richard Nixon from city to city. Rolling into a town the Republican candidate had just left, Bobby would call a press conference to steal a headline or water down the effect of Nixon's words. When Nixon called on Jack Kennedy to retract his assertion that "seventeen million Americans go to bed hungry every night"—a "statistic" based on a study showing that too many people diet in this country—Bobby answered, "Mr. Nixon should spend more time in the country," and cited instances of poverty, undoubtedly true but not germane. In the South, Bobby would give as an example of his brother's independence the choice of Lyndon Johnson for running mate.

No one has faulted Bobby on his ability to seize any opportunity. The Reverend Martin Luther King was arrested, along with fifty-two others, for invading an Atlanta department store and staging a "sit-in." King was sentenced to four months of hard labor at the Georgia Reidsville State Prison, and his wife announced that she was afraid he would never get out alive. This was late in October, with little more than a week left to the campaign. Jack immediately called her to express his sympathy. Bobby went further than that. He phoned the sentencing judge to call for King's release. Within twenty-four hours, Martin Luther King was out on bail, and his father was expressing gratitude to Jack Kennedy. "Because this man was willing to wipe the tears from my daughter's eyes"—his daughter-in-law, really—"I've got a suitcase of votes, and I'm going to take them to Mr. Kennedy and dump them in his lap."

When the election tally had been made, Jack Kennedy had won, with a plurality of 119,450 votes over Nixon and no majority. Had Bobby helped or hurt? "If there was a net victim of religious prejudice," Elmo Roper wrote, "it was Nixon more than Kennedy." The Sorenson report, which under John Bailey's name was so carefully studied, gave Bobby his idea of victimizing his fellow Catholics by convincing them that they were fighting religious bigotry. The Catholic states went for Kennedy, and there is enough evidence to warrant the conviction that "Protestant" states like Texas and Missouri were stolen from Nixon. Nothing was done about this, though the Republicans urged Nixon to challenge the election. Behind the scenes, others prevailed on him, particularly President Eisenhower, whose first spontaneous indignation was dissipated by a reading of the daily papers.

In the making of one President, Bobby, therefore, could claim considerable credit. Hugh Sidey, a *Life* correspondent, found that the circumstances were propitious for the candidate's brother: "Bobby had one immense advantage in his national political dealings. He could be tough because he was the candidate's brother, a peculiar position for politics, indeed. Nobody was jealous of his position since it was one of birth. He sought no special job nor was he under outside influence. He was in the strongest possible position from which to say no."

He did suffer one devastating defeat. His five-year-old son David was for Nixon.

7

The Not-So-Blind Goddess—I

IN October 1963, *Life* magazine, in an unusual burst of temper, devoted half of its editorial page to an essay entitled, "Hold Your Nose at Bobby's Pork." The slightly ambiguous title referred to the political practice of dipping into the Treasury's pork barrel for costly items of value only to the dominant Establishment's patronage rolls.

"Eighteen months ago the Kennedys urged Congress and the regulatory agencies to overhaul the transportation industry that employs one out of six U.S. workers and accounts for one out of five dollars of the gross national product," the *Life* editorialist wrote. " 'Greater reliance on the forces of competition and less reliance on the restraints of regulation' was what the Kennedys said they wanted. . . . But when it comes to decisions that affect transportation, the Kennedys want More for Massachusetts, the family's political base, and an odor of pork arises."

Specifically, *Life* cited the case of Northeast Airlines, which "employs 1,237 Bay Staters, including a lot of ingenious lobbyists. . . . Senator Ted, as any Senator might do for his constituents, devoted his maiden speech to denouncing the Civil Aeronautics Board decision to cut off Northeast's temporary certification for the New York-Miami run. But then the Attorney General, Brother Bob, got his Justice Department to petition for reargument of the whole thing even though the case had been argued for two years, ruled on and disposed of. The pressures focused on one man—CAB Chairman Allan Boyd, a Florida Democrat. . . . Poor Boyd even had to put up with rumors that a relative was getting a payoff from Eastern and National airlines, that Boyd was hoping to run for governor of Florida with big airline money support, etc. . . ."

Life held its nose over a railroad merger case. None, the magazine found, had greater need to cut costs than the Pennsylvania and the New York Central. "The ICC had already approved mergers for many major railroads, had even allowed the Chesapeake & Ohio to take control of the Baltimore & Ohio despite labor opposition. But last fortnight the Attorney General intervened before the ICC to stop the Pennsylvania-Central merger plan. Apart from the fact that labor did not like it, why? Because, says the Attorney General, the Pennsy and the Central should stand apart to merge with other, smaller carriers. What carriers? The New Haven Railroad and the Boston & Maine, for example, which are in such appalling financial trouble that nobody wants to merge with them unless forced to. These are railroads that serve Massachusetts.

"Poor railroad industry! . . . [It] must now suffer the Kennedys in a political mood, *i.e.* at their worst."

There were others, still faithful to President Kennedy, whose lamentations and apprehensions were inspired by the Attorney General, the second youngest in American history and the most politically motivated since Harry Daugherty ruled over the Justice Department in President Harding's day. Reporters, in the endless bull sessions which occupy their hours of waiting, could trade tales of varying horror when they discussed Bobby Kennedy. Earl Mazo, then of the New York *Herald-Tribune,* earned some unwanted attention when his experiences became public property. Mazo, a hardworking, painfully honest reporter, had been writing at some length of the Billie Sol Estes scandal, a case which involved the plundering of Agriculture Department funds, financial highjinks, the suspected murder of investigators, and an attempted Kennedy Administration cover-up. (Estes had joined the antibigotry crusade in Texas during the 1960 campaign, then reverted to type by sponsoring attacks on the "menace of Communism and Catholicism.")

The case was embarrassing to the Administration, for the gist of newspaper exposure had been the fact that the Justice Department had done nothing to stop Estes' predatory activities until they had been spread over the nation's front pages. A furious Bobby summoned Mazo to his impressive office—four times the size of the President's—to reason with him. "Bobby's so-called 'lecture,' as it has been described, was in reality a childish outburst," Mazo has said. "He was so enraged over our coverage of the Billie Sol Estes scandal that I expected at any moment he would throw himself to the floor, screaming and bawling for his way. Instead, he paced back and forth, storming and arguing. It was something to see." Not so childish was the file he waved in Mazo's face. In earlier accounts, Mazo implied that these were his income-tax returns—a favorite weapon to bring the recalcitrant to heel—although later, when the incident had become public property, he suggested that it "might have been" the Estes case file. Columns on the same case by the battling Allen-Scott columnist team, detailing White House strong-arm tactics in support of Edward Kennedy during his primary battle with Edward McCormack for the Massachusetts Senatorial nomination, inspired vituperative telephone calls to Robert S. Allen questioning his facts and his motives. Even Roscoe Drummond, the quiet-speaking New York *Herald-Tribune* columnist, was berated for his comments on the Estes case.

These extracurricular vendettas of the Attorney General had inspired the apocryphal story of a sign at the Justice Department: WATCH OUT: LITTLE BROTHER IS WATCHING YOU. But they had not been entirely unexpected. When President Kennedy, in December 1960, appointed Bobby to the touchiest, most politically powerful post in the Cabinet, the response was incredulous dismay from liberals and conservatives alike. Robert D. Novak, then a reporter for the *Wall Street Journal* though himself politically left of center, wrote that as Attorney General Bobby might well be an "unqualified disaster," not only because of the implications of nepotism or the brotherly link with the President but for his "aggressive, sometimes abrasive personality" and his "policy of speaking loudly and carrying a big stick."

"Moreover," Novak wrote, "lawyers both inside and outside the government question Mr. Kennedy's legal qualifications for the job. Since receiving his law degree at the University of Virginia— one of his classmates recalls Bobby as 'something less than a whiz in the classroom'—he has picked up only the sketchiest of orthodox legal experience: No private practice at all; a brief stint [seven months] as a low-level Justice Department lawyer during the Truman Administration, Capitol Hill jobs first aiding and then fighting against the late Senator Joe McCarthy, and finally his big chance as chief counsel of the Senate Labor Rackets investigating committee. What's more Mr. Kennedy's highly publicized three years of running the rackets committee won few plaudits from fellow lawyers.

" 'Bobby was awfully quick to draw sweeping inferences from

awfully thin pieces of evidence,' comments a government lawyer who is not particularly unfriendly to the next Attorney General. An avowed foe, a criminal lawyer who clashed with Mr. Kennedy during the rackets probe, contends: 'Time and again before the Mc-Clellan Committee, I saw him march a witness right up to the brink of what looked like a really hot disclosure—only to fluff it. I attribute this to one thing: Inexperience. . . . His low point came perhaps when he tried to discredit Harold Gibbons, Teamsters vice president and self-educated 'egg-head' of the union; the verdict of most who looked on was that Mr. Gibbons, no lawyer, tied Mr. Kennedy in knots."

There was no doubt that as chief counsel, Bobby's legal lacks were balanced by an ability to juggle several investigations at once and to handle his large staff in a gargantuan job. But as Novak and others were aware, he had shown little patience "with the cumbersome apparatus of Anglo-Saxon jurisprudence in his zeal to put Mr. Hoffa . . . behind bars." Civil liberties proponents were deeply concerned over his "badgering of witnesses, his use of hearsay testimony by police officers, his frequent practice of making a case against a witness without giving him a chance to reply the same day." His single standard, political expediency, troubled many who felt that he could learn a little law in time. "A liberal Democratic Senator," Novak reported, "found this out when he tried to convince Bobby of the wisdom of reducing the oil depletion allowance, bringing out an array of economic, social, and moral arguments. 'But,' Mr. Kennedy asked when the Senator had finished, 'what does it mean in votes?' "

What was known of Bobby's political views tended to show that he had little concern for internal security and that, once in the Justice Department, he intended to use the Federal Bureau of Investigation in a manner that opened the door to making it a national police force—something FBI director J. Edgar Hoover, the Congress, and the American people opposed. Bobby advocated turning over secret FBI files to United States Attorneys prosecuting labor racketeers and other "evil-doers." But Bobby's idea of evil was always conditioned by the particular political feuds then engaging his attention. Businessmen, conservatives, Republicans, and those who fell under the cloud of Administration displeasure might at any time find themselves included in that category. A determined Attorney General like Bobby would feel no compunction about using those highly explosive "raw" files, filled with unsifted material not yet evaluated by conscientious experts, and capable of destroying lives and reputations in the Gestapo manner. Although Bobby Kennedy had immediately announced that he would divest himself of all political responsibilities, leaving this to Democratic National Chairman John Bailey, a cliché-ridden Washington noted that this was like expecting a leopard to change his spots.

The Republicans looked on the appointment of Bobby with equanimity. They had dusted off two statements, one by John F. Kennedy, just before the election, that "nepotism is dangerous to the public interest and to our national morality"; the other, by Bobby, that appointing him to a post in the Cabinet would be "nepotism of the worst sort." Party strategists would have preferred seeing Robert Kennedy in the State Department, whose Secretaries are suspect by definition and whose tenure is always stormy. Bobby had intimated to friends that he had his eye on that position, or on the job of Defense Secretary. This second ambition had brought a few covert smiles, for the idea of a man who had spent his military service chipping paint taking over the helm of the Army, Navy, and Air Force and the direction of the Pentagon seemed slightly more than ludicrous. But even the Justice Department presented opportunities to the opposition party, and it intended to use them.

At behind-locked-doors sessions of the Republican leadership, the strategy was developed. When Bobby came up for confirmation before the Senate Judiciary Committee, the Republican members would be thoroughly briefed on every slip, slur, and bobble in Bobby's career. They would have his law school record, the liberal criticisms which had appeared in ultraliberal weeklies like the *Nation* during his service on the rackets committee, and other such *materia medica* of his qualifications. They would question Bobby, read their material into the record, and abstain from voting either pro or con on his appointment. Then, if he acquitted himself badly, they could say, "I told you so" and make what capital they could do it. If he did well, no one would bother to recall it. But when Bobby took the stand, looking young and eager amid the walnut paneling and rich marble, Minority Leader Everett Dirksen had already decided that his personal relations with the White House were more important than the Republican party's need for building up a record.

It was, James Reston of the New York *Times* wrote, as if Bobby had arrived "expecting to do battle with Jack Dempsey and instead found himself confronted, most agreeably, by Shirley Temple." Following Senator Dirksen's lead, the Republicans pirouetted away

from anything damaging. Dirksen, acting like a man who must per-
form a distasteful duty, read from a few editorials critical of the
appointment, making it very clear that the sentiments expressed
were not his own. The Democrats were slightly more vigorous in
their questioning, but they too acted like uncomfortable Devil's
Advocates whose hearts belonged to Daddy. With no more trouble
than that, Bobby Kennedy was ensconced behind a Hollywood-size
desk—perhaps the largest in official Washington—surveying a forty-
by-twenty-two-foot office, the pious blind-goddess murals surround-
ing him, and an arched ceiling overhead.

There is no doubt that he shook up the Justice Department. It
had grown lax under President Truman's Attorneys General; too
cautious under President Eisenhower's first Attorney General, Herbert Brownell; and too soft, except in the Anti-Trust Division, under William P. Rogers. Bobby's appointments of deputies were
politically astute. Byron White and Burke Marshall, for example,
were respected in the legal profession and combined keen legal in-
sights and the unhurried, unhysterical approach which balanced
Bobby's impetuosity and devotion to action, no matter what its out-
come. In staffing subordinate positions, Bobby announced that he
would pick only those whose claim to the job for services rendered
during the campaign matched their legal talents. "You've been
recommended to us by a number of people," he would tell them.
"But I want you to know that these recommendations aren't the
reason why we're appointing you. We've investigated you ourselves,
and we're satisfied. So you don't owe your job to anybody. The
others just weren't qualified, but you were. Base your decision
on the facts, and if you make mistakes, you'll get our support just
so long as you acted with honesty and integrity."

President Kennedy had been joking when he told the Alfalfa
Club that he had made Bobby the Attorney General because "I saw
nothing wrong with giving him a little experience before he goes
out to practice law." Bobby, however, was wise enough to get himself some instant experience, much as an underequipped judge will
seek out the brightest law-school graduates to serve him as secretaries. Along with White and Marshall, the former serving as
Deputy Attorney General and the latter as head of the Civil Rights
Division, Bobby brought in men who, their politics aside, were a cut
above those generally found in the government's legal hierarchy:

Nicholas Katzenbach, Office of Legal Counsel (and later to become Attorney General), who tried to give systematic formulation
to Bobby's musclebound approach to law enforcement; Lee

Loevinger, head of the Anti-Trust Division, a former judge of the Minnesota Supreme Court; Ramsey Clark, son of Supreme Court Justice Tom Clark and a partner in a lucrative Dallas law firm, to head the Lands Division; Herbert Miller, Criminal Division; Louis Oberdorfer, the Tax Division; John Douglas, Civil Division.

Of these men, three had been Rhodes Scholars; two had been on *Law Journal* at Yale; three came from important Washington law firms. And they were all cut to the New Frontier pattern of youth and strenuous activity. A Justice Department veteran would tell Anthony Lewis of the New York *Times*: "For years our position has been to take no position unless we absolutely had to. Now I'm told that if there are two sides to an issue of substance, we're going to take one of them." Katzenbach formulated the new philosophy—to many, violative of the Anglo-Saxon principle that the law must be an arbiter and not a partisan—when he said: "One can use law creatively to achieve social and political objectives. The law doesn't have to be neutral." But what it would be partisan about remained a question in the first days of Bobby's tenure.

There were areas in plenty for Justice Department action. The nation's internal security had suffered badly as a result of the anti-McCarthy furor. Anti-trust had always been emphasized under both Democrats and Republicans, but what form would it take in the New Frontier? Civil rights was a big question mark for an Administration that had courted the Negro vote as never before but made reassuring noises to the South. There were few doubts that James R. Hoffa and the Teamsters were in for trouble. Organized crime as a target for prosecution and dissolution appealed strongly to Bobby. And there was also the pile-up of litigation in a hundred different areas to occupy the Kennedy department, enough to keep Bobby busy and away from the rest of the government—or so it was thought.

Of all the areas of law enforcement taken over by Bobby, the most explosive was civil rights. But no one quite knew where he stood. After his appointment, an old friend of the Kennedys had said to Stan Opotowsky: "Bob Kennedy has no strong feelings about civil rights. He is not for the Negroes and he is not against them. His decisions will be entirely political. But once his mind is made up, he'll stick to it. He won't be talked out of anything." The political choice was dictated by a Kennedy reading of the election results. And according to the Sorenson-Bailey theory, President Kennedy could count on reelection only by nailing down the big industrial states, all of them with large Negro populations, even if the South defected. The one Southern exception was Texas, but by pressure and fraud this had been taken once and could be again. The politically bright decision, therefore, was made rapidly. Civil rights would be the major Justice Department activity under Bobby.

This was made manifest when Justice Department Democratic party scouts were told to make their primary surveys of talent on the campuses of Negro colleges and law schools. In one year, the department raised the Negro representation among Justice lawyers from ten to fifty. Implementing a White House order on Negro hiring, Bobby told all United States marshals to give prime consideration to the hiring of Negro deputies. To criticism that he was imposing a reverse racism by giving preferential treatment to non-whites, Bobby replied that his criterion "is not that they are Negroes, but that they are qualified." Another justification was offered: The Negro had been for so long discriminated *against* that a little discrimination *for* could hardly be faulted.

Jack Kennedy had made strong promises of civil rights action. By the time he assumed the Presidency, he had seen that his standing in the House and Senate would suffer if he translated his denunciations of alleged Eisenhower Administration foot-dragging into concrete proposals. "If we drive [the moderate] Southerners to the wall with a lot of civil rights demands that can't pass anyway, then what happens to the Negro on minimum wages, housing, and the rest?" he said. The strategy therefore was to leave most of the sound and fury to Bobby while maintaining a state of relative calm in the Congress. There would be voting-rights bills and allied legislation to which Bobby could give his vigorous support while the White House contribution would be little more than token.

Having plumped for this, a politically cheap way to win over the Negro while protecting the New Frontier's congressional flank, Bobby began almost immediately to push for voting rights by enforcing statutes already in the books. Voting rights, he said, were the major hope and most expeditious route for redressing Negro grievances, a feeling that probably derived from his knowledge of what the Irish, and other immigrant stock, had been able to achieve. Testifying before a House Appropriations subcommittee in February 1961, the Attorney General cited fourteen counties in four Southern states as prime targets for Justice Department legal action. These were areas where Negroes outnumbered whites but could not be found in the registration books. By the end of April, Justice did, in fact, file its first such suit against the State of Louisiana and East Carroll Parish. In this action, it sought to overturn the parish's requirement that each new voter must be "identified" as to residence and qualifications by three already enrolled persons.

For two years, then, Bobby carried the civil rights ball for the Kennedy Administration. The President sent up to the Hill only three additions to the legislative base of his civil rights "program": In 1961, a routine extension of the life of the Civil Rights Commission created under President Eisenhower; in 1962, the poll-tax amendment, ratified by the states, which banned this requirement for voting in Federal elections; and a measure to prohibit discriminatory literacy tests, which was rejected by the Congress. The accent was on court action and on improved relations with the more moderate Negroes, then still in control of the civil rights movement. "The direct accessibility of Robert Kennedy," one Negro leader said, "through the simple act of a telephone call from a citizen in distress is no small achievement." It opened the door to what some would call Justice Department meddling in matters not within its jurisdiction and, more serious to the health of the body politic, to the encouragement of the more extreme civil rights organizations which used the availability of the Attorney General as a means of publicizing their rapidly escalating demands.

The beginning of Bobby's complete involvement in the civil rights battle came on May 6 when he delivered the Law Day speech at the University of Georgia at Athens. Painstakingly phrased, the address was in fact a frontal assault on the problems of racial discrimination, launched amidst those who, in little time, Bobby would think of as "the enemy." "I happen to believe that the 1954 decision [on school desegregation by the Supreme Court] was right. But my belief does not matter. It is the law. Some of you may believe the decision was wrong. That does not matter. It is the law. . . . You may ask, will we enforce the civil rights statutes? The answer is: 'Yes, we will.' " This was the usual formulation he addressed to Southern audiences. But then Bobby pushed ahead to the Prince Edward County school case, then roiling Virginia. Instead of submitting to a court order to integrate its public schools, Prince Edward County had closed them. Bobby's answer had been to intervene in behalf of Negro students who had filed suit to get the school reopened. The Justice Department had asked for an injunction "against any public support of any public schools in the state until public schools are reopened in this county." This was asking the court to penalize other counties for what was being done in Prince Edward, a request so broad and extreme that federal intervention was rejected out of hand. Bobby defended his action in the Law Day speech, but his more experienced aides were already aware that it had been a tactical error, and one which had left the Prince Edward schools closed or deserted of white students for four years.

The first test of Bobby's civil rights mettle came shortly thereafter in the sordid and tragic flare-up of violence in Birmingham, Alabama. The spark was ignited by a group of white and Negro "Freedom Riders" who set out to tour the South in two chartered buses, a Greyhound and a Trailways, to dramatize the Supreme Court's ruling against segregated accommodations in interstate travel. That the Freedom Riders were within their rights cannot be disputed. That their journey into the South would be considered a provocation was predictable. In fact, the FBI had reported to the Attorney General at the outset of the "ride" that it expected violence along the way. But this warning had been forgotten as the Freedom Riders drove through Virginia, the Carolinas, and Georgia. Their test of desegregation on interstate travel facilities was, to that point, uneventful, and it therefore proved nothing.

The night of May 14 brought the expected violence when the Greyhound was attacked by a mob at Anniston, Alabama. A fire bomb thrown into the bus finished it off. The Trailways bus made it to Birmingham, but without police protection the riders were beaten by toughs and hoodlums awaiting their arrival. The Attorney General received the news of these two attacks on the Freedom Riders and issued orders that the department "make preparations." Decisive action at that time, before the mobs had gotten out of hand, would have prevented what came later. But Bobby was content to send down as an observer his administrative assistant, John Seigenthaler. He also called a political friend of Alabama's Governor John Patterson to ask that police protection be provided for the riders. It was his thought that it would be best to let them continue on to New Orleans. "If they don't make it, if they are forced to return to New York, there'll be others," he said. But when no one could find Patterson, Bobby called the state's Commissioner of Public Safety, Floyd Mann, to ask for guarantees that the riders would be allowed to continue on to Montgomery without incident.

Mann agreed to the police escort but reported that no bus driver could be found willing to take the risk of driving an integrated bus. He also warned that the bus terminal was being taken over by an angry mob—"a very serious situation." The better part of valor would have been to keep the Freedom Riders under cover until

Birmingham had quieted down. But Bobby persisted in his plan to push ahead. In a stormy conversation with the Greyhound representative, Bobby refused to accept the explanation that no bus drivers could be found. "Well, hell," he said, "you can look for one, can't you? These people have tickets and are entitled to continue the trip to Montgomery. We have gone to a lot of trouble to see that they get on this trip and I am most concerned to see that it is accomplished."

Southern newspapers took this to be obvious proof that the Freedom Riders had been sent—or encouraged in their venture—by the Attorney General. Bobby denied it vehemently, but his use of the "we" further inflamed the situation and angered Governor Patterson. Eventually, although Bobby continued to press the Greyhound officials—"I am— the government is—going to be very upset if the Freedom Riders do not continue their trip"—the riders were finally flown to New Orleans, where the police put them in protective custody. But four days later, a new batch of Freedom Riders showed up in Birmingham. Escorted back to the state border by police, they returned the following day. Throughout the state feeling was running high over the "invasion," and there were reports that Negro and white college students were being recruited to follow the first two in waves.

Now worried, the Attorney General put twenty United States marshals on an alert status in Washington and waited for developments. The President, however, insisted that nothing was to be done until he was certain that a "maximum effort" had been made to get Alabama authorities to take control. To this end, John Seigenthaler, still on watch duty for Bobby, was designated the President's representative and authorized to consult with Patterson. Seigenthaler reported that the governor had the situation under control. He also told Bobby that Patterson had flatly stated that "all people" in Alabama would be protected. The Freedom Riders mounted their bus and rolled out of Birmingham without incident. There was, moreover, no trouble on the ninety-mile trip to Montgomery. But once at the bus terminal, another and more terrible riot broke out. The Riders, both black and white, were badly beaten and Seigenthaler was knocked unconscious when he tried to help a girl. Deputy Attorney General White decided that the time had come for intervention. It was a Saturday, however, and Bobby was horseback riding. Given the news on his return, he called the White House to get permission to send in the marshals, and ordered White to "get those guys moving."

Then, changing to business clothes, he rushed from his McLean, Virginia, estate to the Justice Department, taking time out to throw the first ball at an FBI ball game.

At the Justice Department, and with the President's authority to take what steps he thought necessary, Bobby despatched his twenty United States marshals, now reinforced by 83 guards from the Bureau of Prisons, 100 Alcohol Tax Unit police, and 100 deputized marshals. At the same time, the FBI was sent in to "intensify its investigation of the incident." A federal judge granted the department an injunction against the Ku Klux Klan, the National States Rights party, and other groups which might interfere with "peaceful interstate travel." Other trouble, however, was brewing. In the Attorney General's office, Bobby was "using the telephone as a chain smoker uses cigarettes," as one observer put it. He talked with the President, with Byron White, with Negro leaders, with Southerners, with others in the government.

Among those he spoke to was the Reverend Martin Luther King. The madness at Montgomery, King thought, was a perfect backdrop for his crusade of "nonviolence." He informed the Attorney General that he was on his way. The city was now calm and Bobby wanted no further trouble. But King would not be overcome. Ignoring Bobby's pleas, he set out for Montgomery, where he assembled the Freedom Riders at the First Baptist Church. Learning of his presence there, the dispersed mob began to gather at the scene. With only 150 marshals, all that could be mustered at the time, there was an ominous possibility that the day would end in bloodshed. The National Guard was required and Bobby convinced Governor Patterson to call it out in the defense of the Reverend King. When King, barricaded in the church, called Bobby, he was greeted with a quip:

"Well, Reverend, are you praying for us?"

King was not amused. Nor was he pleased with the Attorney General's performance, and said so. "Now, Reverend," Bobby answered him, "you know that without those federal marshals all of you would be as dead as doornails." Somewhat mollified, King subsided, and the besieged group was safely evacuated. With a corps-sized escort, the riders departed for Mississippi, where they were promptly clapped into jail. This was what Bobby wanted. "It should be settled by the courts and not forcibly by a howling mob, National Guard troops or federal marshals," he said.

With the Freedom Riders out of harm's way, Mississippi's Governor Ross Barnett called Bobby to inform him that they would be released immediately if they gave assurances that there would be no more bus riding. When Bobby called King to give him the news, the Negro leader would have no part of the arrangement. He wanted the Freedom Riders in jail where they could publicize "the brutality of the South" and bring new demonstrators into the fray. Bobby's irritation was natural, and he told the Reverend King that this kind of reasoning would "not have the slightest effect on what the government is going to do in this field or any other." At this point, King threatened to send 100,000 students into Alabama. "It is creative, moral, and nonviolent," he said righteously. This time, Bobby was not amused.

The Birmingham episode, filling the news columns for days, was the opening gun in the "nonviolent" war on the South. It won an Interstate Commerce Commission regulation carefully spelling out its ban against segregation on interstate travel facilities. It prompted the White House to threaten that Federal aviation funds would be withheld unless air terminals were desegregated. In all of this, Bobby held, action was taken under the power of law, express or implied. The use of marshals in Alabama had its sanction in law, he argued, though Governor Patterson and others claimed that it had all been illegal and unconstitutional. Yet, in a speech for overseas broadcast by the Voice of America, Bobby returned to the "gradualism" which in 1964 the Democrats would charge, in their anti-Goldwater polemics, was an evasion of responsibility.

"We are not going to gain ground against prejudice by just laws," said Bobby. "Because prejudice exists with people throughout the world, not just people of this country. . . . But we have tried to make progress and we are making progress. That is what is so important. . . . My grandfather came to this country many years ago. He was brought up in Boston and when he went out to look for a job there were signs on many stores that no Irish were wanted. Now . . . an Irish Catholic is President of the United States. And we feel that the same kind of progress will be made by the Negroes. There is no question about it. In the foreseeable future a Negro can achieve the same position my brother has."

His idea of progress in that speech made the Supreme Court's "all deliberate speed" seem like a toboggan. And he was particularly moderate where the politically touchy issue of racial discrimination in housing was concerned. On the campaign trail in 1960, Jack had been sharply critical of President Eisenhower for not solving the problem "with the stroke of a pen." "A simple executive order," he had said, could put an end to discrimination in the sale or transfer of any residential construction relying on government loans or guarantees—the Federal Housing Authority and the Veterans Administration (GI Bill of Rights mortgages) being two examples. The executive order, Kennedy claimed, could even be extended to housing financed by conventional loans, since most banks were insured by the federal government. Once in the White House, neither the President nor Bobby spoke of that simple "pen stroke." When the subject was brought up, they had a series of explanations in which the blame was hung around the necks of the minority Republicans in Congress, the Southern Democrats, or both. In 1961-62, the Kennedys had held their fire ostensibly to win Senate confirmation of a Negro, Robert Weaver, as administrator of the Housing and Home Finance Agency. Then the Kennedys said that they were waiting for passage of the 1961 housing bill, so that opposition to the putative executive order would not damage the measure in transit.

Through most of 1962, the matter of timing was invoked when mention was made of a housing order. Now, the Administration had set its mind on creating a Department of Urban Affairs. This required congressional approval, which might be denied if an executive order on housing reconstituted the Republican-Southern Democratic coalition. Then the President let it be known that he would appoint Robert Weaver to the new Cabinet post, clearly not worried about its impact on Congress, and the new department died a-borning. Not until late in 1962, when the riots at the University of Mississippi were over, did the Kennedys feel that it was safe to act. And even then, the executive order as drafted fell far short of its advance publicity. Handed down on November 20— Bobby's thirty-seventh birthday—its restrictions exempted residential structures already built and those conventionally financed by commercial lending institutions.

Early in 1962, Bobby's report on the Administration's "tremendous success" in making civil rights breakthroughs lent added credence to the analysis of policy made by Rowland Evans in the New York *Herald-Tribune*: "The Administration's central civil rights strategy—don't risk the loss of Southern votes on other issues by pressing civil rights legislation—is the Attorney General's brainchild." For the points made by Bobby hardly seemed a matter that even the most moderate Negro civil rights leader could really rejoice over. The Commission on Equal Employment Opportunity, headed by Vice President Lyndon Johnson, got more publicity than its predecessor, Richard Nixon's Committee on Government Contracts, but did far less. Credit was claimed by Bobby for the deseg-

regation of schools in various Southern cities, but the original spadework had been done by the outgoing Republicans. And as the National Association for the Advancement of Colored People did not
fail to remark, the Civil Rights Commission had officially taken
exception to the Administration's central civil rights strategy. To
Bobby's prideful announcement that the Justice Department had
filed fourteen new voting suits and registration procedures in sixty-
one counties, the commission had answered that "there can be no
single approach which will bring an end to discrimination."

("Indeed," Arthur Schlesinger would write in 1965, "the Commission became so fearful of the conception of voting as the panacea
that, in Burke Marshall's view, 'it went out of its way' in its 1961 report to point to twenty-one Southern Counties where Negroes
voted freely with no effect on segregation.")

Bobby, however, continued to stress the voting side and the personal side as the best answers. For himself, he could point to his
resignation from the exclusive Metropolitan Club of Washington
over its refusal to admit Negroes to membership. He entertained
nonwhites in his house in McLean. And on one occasion, he arranged a White House audience for an elderly Negro retiring from
the Justice Department. None of this added very much to the well-
being, political or economic, of the Negro, but it did make headlines and generate the kind of controversy which never hurts a politician.

In that "goodwill" period before Bobby had decided to go all out
against Southern predilections, there was to be one more outburst of
the sound and fury which accomplishes little for major principals
and even less for the country as a whole. The point in contention
was the registration of James Meredith, a twenty-nine-year-old Air
Force veteran who had applied for transfer from Jackson State
College to the University of Mississippi. He achieved it after the
disruption of state and federal relations, the use of armed forces,
the railroading of a retired general to a mental institution without
due process, and the death of two people. Very few gained anything
by it, and in time the farcical nature of the negotiations between
Mississippi's Governor Barnett, Bobby Kennedy, and the President
would reflect no credit on any of them. Bobby, however, saw it as
a great victory.

The Meredith case began when the NAACP petitioned the federal courts for redress. It was rebuffed but carried the battle to the
Fifth Circuit Court of Appeals, which reversed the district court
and ordered Meredith enrolled at "Ole Miss." After some legal

jockeying, Supreme Court Justice Hugo Black sustained the appeals-court verdict. At this point, Governor Barnett relieved the "Ole Miss" registrars of their responsibilities and liabilities by having himself appointed a "special registrar." When Meredith tried to register, he was personally turned away by Barnett, who had told Bobby: "I consider the Mississippi courts as high as any other court and a lot more capable. . . . I am going to obey the laws of Mississippi." (He was basing his stand on the doctrine of "interposition," an issue settled by *force majeur* in the War between the States.) Though the courts threatened Governor Barnett with contempt actions, and finally did cite him, there was little that could be done without bringing in large forces of United States marshals and eventually a federalized National Guard and United States Army paratroop units. One of the attempts to enroll Meredith was thwarted by Lieutenant Governor Paul Johnson. Another attempt was called off when Meredith and a posse of twenty-five unarmed United States marshals learned that an "unruly" crowd of 2,500 people and 500 Mississippi state police were blocking the way on the "Ole Miss" campus.

During this tugging and hauling, Governor Barnett and the Attorney General were frequently on the phone. In one conversation, Barnett said of Meredith, "It's best for him not to go to 'Ole Miss,' " and Bobby replied, "But he likes 'Ole Miss.' " While Governor Barnett dramatically proclaimed the sovereignty of Mississippi and Bobby announced, "We'll use whatever is necessary to do the job," the two men were busy trying to work out a face-saving formula, unknown to the rioting students, the troops who had been flown down to a Southern camp for emergency action, or the embattled liberals in the North who demanded Barnett's scalp. The transcript of their telephone conversation makes interesting reading today:

> ROBERT KENNEDY: I will send the marshals that I have available up there in Memphis and I expect there will be about twenty-five or thirty of them and they will come with Mr. Meredith and they will arrive wherever the gate is and I will have the rest of them have their hands on their guns and their holsters. And then, as I understand it, he will go through and get in and you will make sure that law and order is preserved and that no harm will be done to [Chief Marshal] McShane and Mr. Meredith.
>
> GOVERNOR BARNETT: Oh, yes. . . . General, I was under the impression that they were going to pull their guns. This could be very

embarrassing. We got a big crowd out here and if one pulls his gun and we all turn it would be very embarrassing. Wouldn't it be possible to have them all pull their guns?

KENNEDY: I hate to have them all draw their guns as I think it would create harsh feelings. . . .

BARNETT: They must all draw their guns. Then they should all point their guns at us and then we could step aside. . . .

LIEUTENANT-GOVERNOR PAUL JOHNSON: It is absolutely necessary that they all draw their guns.

Barnett was still afraid that his constituents might suspect him of "cooperating with the Federal government."

BARNETT: You understand we have had no agreement.

KENNEDY: That's correct.

BARNETT: I am just telling you—everybody thinks we are compromising.

KENNEDY: I am just telling you that we are arriving and that we are arriving with force.

The "constitutional confrontation" had descended to this, and Bobby was aware of it. "I think it is silly going through the whole façade [*sic*] . . . of your standing there, our people drawing guns, your stepping aside. . . ." Publicly, he was comparing Mississippi to Hitler Germany and expressing his dismay because "everyone is accepting what that fellow [Barnett] is doing. There are no protests anywhere—from the bar or from professional men or from the professors. I wouldn't have believed it." Barnett privately continued to ask for "shows of force" and to propose other devices for appearing to have no choice in registering Meredith. One plan called for a grandstand play at the Oxford campus of "Ole Miss" while Meredith was being registered at the Jackson campus. But this, Bobby didn't buy. "Sneaking Meredith off to Jackson for registration doesn't meet the problem," he said. "It doesn't really make sense, does it?" Nor did it lend the proper aura of federal intransigence and dominance. But Barnett's final plan for spiriting Meredith into the dormitory while the crowds were elsewhere occupied was finally bought by the President and Bobby, no longer repelled by the silly "façade."

But sneaking Meredith into the dormitory so that he could be registered the next day neither saved face for the Kennedys nor prevented the outbreak of violence. The "façade" was indeed silly.

Crowds of students, boisterous from the football game they had just attended, returned to the campus and congregated at the university administration building, the Lyceum. On the telephone, Bobby pleaded with "Ole Miss" officials, with the football coach, with anyone who would listen, in a most un-Attorney Generalism manner, to find some way of distracting the students, but nothing came of it. The band of steel-helmeted United States marshals and their deputies, 550 strong and armed with tear-gas guns, set themselves up as a defense perimeter around the Lyceum. When Barnett's 200 state troopers developed a habit of melting away if trouble approached, Bobby angrily called the governor to demand their return. But as dusk became darkness, taunting campus mobs exchanged expletives for stones and bottles, which they hurled at the marshals. Sniper fire killed one state trooper and a French news-agency reporter. Tear gas made the air unbreathably acrid. At the pleading of Nicholas Katzenbach, the federalized National Guard made its appearance, inspiring further violence from the students. Finally, in the tiny hours of morning, the Army arrived from its nearby base.

The enrollment of James Meredith on October 1, 1962, seemed almost like an anticlimax. Until his graduation in the following August, he was protected either by troops or by civilian law officers. He, perhaps, was the first casualty of the political tug-of-war between Bobby Kennedy and Governor Barnett. There was another, and collateral, victim, former Major General Edwin Walker. His distinguished military career had been cut short by the group of Senators, led by J. William Fulbright, who deplored the anti-Communist nature of the information-education program under Walker's command overseas. Appearing before the Fulbright committee, he had been treated like a pariah, and in the period that followed he was hounded and insulted by the press and by any member of the Congress who wanted to make a headline. He had been compelled to resign, rather than to retire, and lived in bitterness in Dallas where, prior to President Kennedy's assassination, Lee Harvey Oswald took a shot at him one dark night. Under the circumstances, no one could expect General Walker to have the most balanced and calm view of the Kennedy Administration.

When the "Ole Miss" agitation had come to the boil, General Walker, the commander of the troops that had been called to enforce integration in Little Rock, took to the radio to announce: "This time I am out of uniform and I am on the right side and I will be there." At Oxford, he mingled with the crowd, gave pro-

Barnett and anti-Kennedy statements to the press, and comported himself sadly and badly. A wire-service reporter, however, could not limit himself to describing this pathetic display. He gilded the lily by a false description of Walker inciting the mob to storm the Lyceum and leading it in charges against the marshals. This was enough for Bobby. At his orders, Walker was arrested for "inciting a rebellion" and, without psychiatric examination, he was spirited away to the mental ward of the federal penitentiary in Springfield, Missouri, where he was held incommunicado. It took five days of legal action by Robert Morris, one-time counsel to the Senate Internal Security subcommittee and a former judge, to bring about the release of General Walker. Without evidence and without witnesses, the government could only sweep the Walker case under the carpet. Eventually, he sued the wire service for libel and won substantial damages.

The Meredith case settled nothing. One Negro had been admitted to the University of Mississippi at great cost to the Treasury and to American prestige abroad. For Attorney General Kennedy, however, it marked the beginning of a new phase in his thinking. Heretofore, he had pushed for the Negro cause out of a conviction that it was politically smart. Now he felt personally affronted by the refusal of Governor Barnett and the state of Mississippi to accept his word as law. He looked on the battle as part of a personal vendetta against the South. He would still say, "It's voting rights that count." But he was determined to impose a tough policy on the South, and ready to embrace extreme measures and even more extreme solutions to the Negro problem. The President's talk of "voluntary compliance" might soothe some, but not Robert Kennedy. The bit was in his teeth.

It was sometimes hard to hold it there. Bobby's actions and reactions are visceral. He feels first, then thinks, and complexities upset him. As the nation's outstanding civil rights activist, he could not understand why the Negro world did not offer accolades and devotion. And he never realized that the extremist Negro agitation had little to do with past or future legislation, with improvement of the human condition for Negroes, with public accommodations, or even with equality. The Negro extremists were, in fact, as viscerally motivated as he, striking out in retaliation for real and imagined wrongs, for revenge on a world they had never made. James Baldwin, epicene and passionate in his diatribes, had pitched his pipe accurately in a book which drew its title from the Negro spiritual's couplet:

God gave the rainbow sign
No more water, the fire next time

Bobby was therefore chagrined and bewildered when, following a brief meeting of his own instigating with Baldwin, he gathered together with a group of Negro intellectuals and entertainers in his New York apartment, hoping to bring them into the Kennedy ranks and to demonstrate his personal goodwill. Present were Baldwin, Lena Horne, Harry Belafonte, playwright Lorraine Hansberry, Professor Kenneth Clark of the psychology department at New York's City College, Assistant Attorney General Burke Marshall, and others. The meeting was opened by Jerome Smith, a Freedom Rider who had been badly beaten in the South. Smith began by saying: "Being in the same room with you makes me feel like vomiting." Bobby responded with justfiable anger, and his indignation increased when the group sided with Smith. What had started inauspiciously degenerated into a squabble.

As long as Negroes were treated badly in this country, Smith said, he felt that his people had no moral obligation to fight for the United States. He was applauded. There was talk of shipping arms to the South. Bobby's use of federal troops in Alabama was derided as an attempt to protect the white population. When Burke Marshall broke in to state that he had consulted with Martin Luther King before the troops were sent in, he was laughed at. Bobby, in turn, laughed at Baldwin for suggesting that the President personally escort Negro students into the University of Alabama. ("He didn't get the point at all," Baldwin said later.) Attempts by the Attorney General to discuss specific legislation or to argue that the urban-renewal program would help break down segregation in housing evoked no interest from the Negro group. Bobby asked them for suggestions, for any plans or ideas they might have for improving the Negro condition, but they avoided this as if it really wasn't relevant. Then he pointed to the record of his administration in civil rights.

"If this is the best you can do," one of the participants said, "the best is not enough."

"The record of the Justice Department is totally inadequate," Baldwin added.

"They didn't know anything," Bobby said later to Arthur Schlesinger. "They don't know what the laws are. They don't know what the facts are. They don't know what we've been doing or what we've been trying to do. You couldn't talk to them as you can to Roy Wilkins [head of the NAACP] or Martin Luther King. They didn't want to talk that way. It was all emotion, hysteria. They stood up and orated. They cursed. Some of them wept and walked out of the room."

When the meeting had broken up after three hours of futility, Dr. Clarence Jones, representing King, said privately to Bobby: "I just want to say that Dr. King deeply appreciates the way you handled the Birmingham affair."

"You watched those people attack me over Birmingham for forty minutes, and you didn't say a word," Bobby answered bitterly. "There's no point in your saying this to me now."

Another participant who had visited the Kennedys' home in Mc-Lean on many occasions also had private words of consolation. "Of course you have done more for civil rights than any other Attorney General," he said.

"Why do you say this to me?" Bobby replied. "Why didn't you say this to the others?"

The answer was frank: "I couldn't say this to the others. It would hurt my relationship with them. If I were to defend you, they would conclude I had gone over to the other side."

The "secret" meeting and what had happened there became known almost immediately. And to inquiring newspapermen, Baldwin reported that Bobby was shocked at the passion displayed by so many "disparate Negroes." He spoke of the "mutual shock" but suggested that the Attorney General "now knows more about the Negro situation than he did before. I am not prepared to say that the discussion was a failure. No one can afford to look on it as a failure. It has got to be looked at as the beginning of a dialogue." In retrospect, he may have been right. "The fact that Bobby Kennedy sat through such an ordeal for three hours proves he is among the best the white power structure can offer," said Professor Clark. "There were no villains in that room—only the past of our society."

The "mutual shock" did nothing to cool Negro passions, particularly among the affluent. But it proved that Bobby's compulsion to strike back could be curbed. The pounding he had received did not deter him from moving ahead with his legislative program. Having put his hand to the plow of policies which would ensure his brother's reelection in 1964, he was not ready to take it off. When on June 19, 1963, the President sent a new civil rights act to Congress, Bobby was ready and willing to defend it even though his prinicpal antagonist on the Senate Judiciary Committee was Senator Sam Ervin Jr., a North Carolina lawyer known for his knowledge of constitutional law. The bill included provisions forbidding discrimination in public accommodations and new authority for the Attorney General to initiate school-desegregation suits. It also called for the withholding of funds from any project, directly or indirectly financed by the federal government, that practiced racial discrimination.

Senator Ervin strongly attacked the public-accommodations clauses of the Kennedy bill on the ground that it was "condemned by its manifest unconstitutionality. Neither the commerce clause of the Constitution nor the Fourteenth Amendment can save it." In defense, the Attorney General argued that no part of the bill was "of more vital and immediate significance" than the public-accommodations provisions, although he was willing to exempt swimming pools, barber shops, and beauty parlors, if they did not cater to interstate travelers—a concession that would impose impossible conditions of enforcement. The public-accommodations section of the bill, he told the Senate committee, was nothing new. Thirty-two states had similar laws that were "far more encompassing and far more stringent than the legislation we have suggested." In August, however, he watered down the section prohibiting the use of federal funds on discriminatory projects and offered a substitute which allowed the disbursing departments and agencies to write their own enforcement regulations. The new provision also ordered that "all efforts" must be employed to bring about "voluntary compliance" before funds were cut off. And state agencies would have the right to demand judicial review of any federal order holding back funds.

"With its emphasis on ending discrimination, rather than terminating assistance, and its provision for judicial review," an uncomfortable Bobby Kennedy said, hoping this doubletalk would placate opponents of the bill without arousing Negro leaders, "the revised [provision] constitutes an improvement on the original proposal." Nevertheless, as *U.S. News & World Report* commented: "All in all, the President's Civil Rights bill puts in one package sweeping powers to end all forms of segregation. Most of these powers would rest in the Attorney General's hands. . . . It is a vast grant of power that the President is seeking for his brother, Robert Kennedy. That point of the Civil Rights bill is stirring up a furor. Federal authorities, notably the Attorney General, would police stores, hotels, restaurants, lodging houses, theaters. There would be new threats, new powers over employers, schools, voting—nearly everything."

Kennedy efforts to bring about enactment of this radical change in American jurisprudence were a kind of backdrop for other significant acts covering the 1963 period.

On January 17, he made his first appearance in court as an attorney to argue against Georgia's unit system of voting for state office. It was, in a way, Kennedy Day at the Supreme Court. At the opening of the session, Bobby moved the admission of his brother, Senator Edward Kennedy, to the Supreme Court bar. Among the spectators were Bobby's wife Ethel, Mrs. John F. Kennedy, two Kennedy sisters, Mrs. Sargent Shriver and Mrs. Stephen Smith, and a large group of friends. The litigation concerned Georgia's methods of electing state officials by making each county a unit, somewhat like the electoral college. Urban counties with large populations, therefore, could be outvoted by rural counties with considerably fewer numbers of voters. In his opening argument, Bobby alluded to voting practices which, ironically, had been immortalized by both his grandfathers.

"We used to have a saying in my home town of Boston: 'Vote early and vote often,' " the Attorney General said. "In Georgia, if you lived in a rural area and voted early you accomplished the same result. . . . The ideal is one man, one vote." Justice Arthur Goldberg noted that the logic of the Attorney General's argument struck at any state in which the rural areas, though numerically smaller, dominated the state legislature. And he asked Bobby, anticipating a later reapportionment decision of the high court, why he did "not have the courage of your convictions." "We have the courage," said Bobby, "but we do not think it is necessary."

"Do you think it is rational to give a rural voter seven and one-half times the voting power of the urban voter?" Goldberg asked the counsel for the state of Georgia. The answer was lost on the court. "Yes," said E. Freeman Leverette, "speaking constitutionally and not in terms of political science." The court overruled both Georgia and the United States Constitution, which leaves all matters of apportionment to the states.

On May 3, Martin Luther King's demonstrators clashed with Birmingham police. Bottles, rocks, and paving stones hurled at the police were met by streams from power hoses and riot-trained police dogs. The nation's chief law-enforcement officer, Robert Kennedy, saw in this clash the understandable expression of resentment from "people who have been the victims of abuse and deprivations of their most basic rights," but questioned the timing of their protest marches. Burke Marshall was sent to Alabama to seek white cooperation in redressing Negro grievances. A "settlement" was announced on May 10. Its major points called for desegregation of certain public accommodations and for increased nondiscriminatory hiring by the big employers in Birmingham.

Two days later, bombings of the house and motel room of Martin

Luther King's brother signaled the beginning of a white backlash in the city. President Kennedy, urged on by Bobby, declared his readiness to federalize the National Guard and moved Army units into bases in Montgomery and Anniston. A month later, Governor George Wallace threatened to "interpose" himself between the federal government and the registrars at the University of Alabama, to prevent the admission of two Negro students. He backed down before federal force was invoked. In June, Bobby told a Hearst team of newspapermen—William Randolph Hearst Jr., Frank Conniff, Warren Rogers, and Milton Kaplan—that he foresaw dangerous Negro rioting during the coming summer, that progress in sustaining Negro voting rights had been made, that 500 policy-making jobs were now held by Negroes, and that "seventy or so" school districts had been desegregated. The possibility of racial violence breaking out, he said, was greater in the North than in the South.

"The Negroes are concerned in Birmingham about being able to sit at a lunch counter, employment, taking the signs off drinking fountains, and taking the signs off rest rooms. Well, you can do that and release a valve. . . . But in the North, in Chicago or Los Angeles or San Francisco . . . what steps would you take to release that valve? What you have to do is really take some drastic action, so you could have a more serious situation in the Northern cities than you have in the South." And he felt that the Birmingham riots, with the pictures widely broadcast, "aroused Negroes in all parts of the United States to feel they wanted more action—not just by the federal government, but more action in their day-to-day living. I think they disturbed the conscience of the nation."

In September, after the bombing of a church in which four Negro girls were killed, Bobby Kennedy appeared on NBC's "Today" show to answer charges from the NAACP that the "hesitant and piecemeal approach of the Administration toward protecting civil rights will no longer do." Bobby's hesitant and piecemeal answer was that "this is not just a question of the President proposing legislation, then it's going to be enacted automatically. . . . Congress, I think, has a responsibility." This was not the answer demanded by the Negro leadership. Months earlier, Medgar Evers, director of Mississippi's NAACP, had been shot to death by a sniper near his house in Jackson. Robert Kennedy had attended the funeral in Arlington Cemetery. He had also given his phone number to Charles Evers, the dead man's brother, suggesting that he call at any time if there was trouble in Mississippi.

"Whenever I had the need to call him," Charles Evers has said, "I've never found it too late or too early. . . . He has done more for us personally than any other public official. Had it not been for him, there would have been many more murders and many more beatings than we have had in Mississippi in the last four years. Mr. Kennedy did more to help us get our rights as first class citizens than all the other U.S. Attorney Generals put together."

This meant much to Bobby, particularly after the treatment he had received from Negro intellectuals well removed from the firing line. It confirmed him in the feeling that the civil rights bill he had defended for months before House and Senate committees was, along with the prosecution of James Hoffa, his major "unfinished business." He said so on November 21, to a New York *Herald-Tribune* reporter. The next day, John F. Kennedy was assassinated in Dallas.

8

The Not-So-Blind Goddess—II

FROM the moment Robert Kennedy first strode into the large and imposing room that is the Attorney General's office, it was clear to all hands that something new would be added. Where the corridors of the Justice Department Building on Pennsylvania Avenue had echoed emptily, they now sounded the call of frenetic activity. The decorous atmosphere vanished as the Attorney General bustled from office to office, his shirt sleeves rolled up and his mop of hair ruffled. The leisurely pace of research and preparation, of digging for precedent and planning for litigation, became a thing of the past. Working hours were increased and swing shifts set up in key departments so that a lawyer was always on duty to receive the Attorney General's requests for information or his demands for action. President Kennedy's wishes were anticipated in order to give him what legal opinions he might need before he had requested them.

Even the veteran members of the staff were impressed, although some were somewhat dazed by the atmosphere of a revival meeting which Bobby Kennedy took with him in his peregrinations about the department. Those sudden appearances in offices which had never seen an Attorney General in person served notice that every member of the staff was expected to be on his toes at all times, to be as cyclonically at work as the head man. If Bobby's idea of togetherness was a little strenuous for some, they were mollified by seeing their immediate superiors being put through their paces by the boss. There may have been some acid remarks about Bobby's disregard of departmen-

tal regulations, but these were never repeated to inquiring newspapermen.

The most obvious violation was the Attorney General's habit of
bringing Brumus, his large, black Labrador to work with him.
Bobby's excuse was that Brumus got lonely at home when his wife
and the children were away. It was much better to bring him to work
and to have "pretty girls take him for walks"—the pretty girls being
Justice Department secretaries relieved of less important duties. Visitors might step on the dog's water dish and get a slight wetting, but
Bobby found this hardly tragic and even a little funny. His laughter
disgruntled some, however. Though federal law prohibited taking
dogs into federal buildings, Bobby was not disturbed. And sour comments from Congressmen were both climaxed and rebutted by Representative Clarence Brown, an Ohio Republican, who told his colleagues that it didn't really matter whether or not Brumus accompanied Bobby. "The country seems to be going to the dogs anyway,"
he said.

Far more disturbing was the Attorney General's attitude that he
knew best in all matters, whether of high import or lowly consequence. This attitude was best exemplified in his chilly disregard of
security regulations and the experience of others. One of his subordinates had been dropped by the Office of Strategic Services when it was
discovered that the Soviets had been blackamiling him because of a
secret (unnumbered) bank account he kept in Switzerland. He was
subsequently hired by the Central Intelligence Agency, then asked
to resign when his past history was discovered. Yet Bobby had placed
him in a post requiring high security clearance and refused to transfer him to a less sensitive spot in the Justice department.

This, of course, was consistent with Bobby Kennedy's opinion that
there was no domestic Communist threat, an opinion which he imple-
mented by reducing the size of the Internal Security Division at Justice until, to quote a Washington newspaperman, "it could meet in a
phone booth." Whatever fears of internal subversion he may have
nourished were confined to the "radical right," an amorphous group-
ing that included any and sundry whose views and political activities
disturbed the Liberal Establishment. And even this service to the prevailing trauma of the ritualistic liberals came later in his tenure. At
his first press conference, he had called the John Birch Society "ridiculous," adding that it made no contribution to the fight against Communism. Its members, he said, were, "I think, if anything, a hin-
drance." To other reporters, he stated that the Birchers were simply

"noisemakers" whose only possible threat might be that they had a "disproportionate" influence on Congress.

The policy of the Justice Department under Bobby was, however, to speak roughly of the Communists while acting gently toward them. One of Bobby's first acts as Attorney General was to lift the ban on incoming propaganda mail from Communist countries. This ban, against the free distribution of Iron Curtain country mail to Americans who had not asked for it, had been imposed by President Harry S. Truman in 1948. This put no restrictions on scholars, newspapermen, or librarians who wished to receive Communist literature for professional purposes, or on individuals who were interested for reasons that were none of the government's business. Its major achievement was to relieve the post office of the expense it incurred in doing the Kremlin's work—a favor not returned by the Soviet Union, which routinely confiscated American newspapers, magazines, and other printed matter. A check made nine months after Bobby had lifted the ban indicated that some 8,000,000 packages of propaganda materials had been sent into the United States from the Soviet Union, the captive nations, and Red China. They had been sent, at the American taxpayers' expense, to churches, schools, homes, and libraries.

Those of left-wing orientation were willing to suffer Bobby's verbal animadversions as long as they could bask in the light of such decisions. And the mixture was always as before. In June 1961, following a Supreme Court decision upholding the constitutionality of the 1950 Subversive Activities Control Act, the Attorney General sharply warned the Communist party members to register. But a full year had elapsed before he got around to asking the Subversive Activities Control Board to designate ten party members as Communists and to order their registration as a preliminary step against the Communists. Vigorous anti-Communists felt that the delay was more suggestive of Bobby's real intentions than his repeated references to the danger of Communist espionage and subversion. On April 20, 1962, the San Diego *Union* summed up critical comment by editorializing:

"The record shows that Attorney General Robert Kennedy has failed to carry out his bold, charge-ahead promises to prosecute the Communist Party and its members. It is bad enough that his failure to act vigorously allows the Communists to avoid in numbers a court decision, but the pity is that Mr. Kennedy's attitude shows no indication that he will deal in the future with the party as he should. Bobby Kennedy refuses to believe the Communist Party in the United States is strong enough to worry very much about. This lack of concern by the United States Attorney General must give the Communists great solace. . . . Bobby Kennedy should lay off the pleasures of politics and traveling and get down to business, in this case, the deadly business of Communist conspiracy."

The San Diego *Union* may have been answering Bobby Kennedy and the off-the-cuff comments he made in April 1962 to a meeting of the Advertising Council of America:

"Well, I would say that I don't think the Communists have any power in the United States. I think that it always poses a problem when you have even a small group active within a country who takes [*sic*] orders and instructions and are [*sic*] financed by a foreign power, as the Communist party of America is at the present time. They have no following. They have been thoroughly discredited throughout the United States, largely through the work of the FBI and to some extent through congressional committees and the work of newspapers. So they really have no following. The great problems and difficulties, in my judgment, are external. . . . It doesn't lie with the Communist party here in the United States, with the exception that I mentioned: The eight thousand or nine thousand people who take their orders and their instructions from the Soviet Union. . . . I think that what is almost hysteria about the activities of Communists within the United States is misplaced apprehension."

However, Bobby's failure to take the internal Communist threat seriously and to curb it by constant exposure and public disaproval contributed to the growth of the so-called New Student Left, thoroughly infiltrated and often completely dominated by Communist cadres which have operated in the privileged sanctuary of public apathy and government sloth. "It took only one man—Klaus Fuchs, a seemingly harmless research scientist—to steal the secrets of our atomic bomb in New Mexico and give them to the Soviet Union," columnist David Lawrence wrote in rebuttal of Kennedy's words. "The menace of Communist activity inside the United States can hardly be minimized."

On Bobby's part, however, there was little apprehension, misplaced or otherwise. In his capacity as Attorney General, Bobby had considerable leeway in interpreting the statutes governing the issuance of visas to aliens. The law clearly barred the admission of Communists unless, in the opinion of the Attorney General and the Secretary of State, it was in the best interest of the United States. Bobby read the statute in a manner which puzzled or angered security agencies and increased their difficulties, but delighted the extreme liberals and the left-wing pundits. Although Moise

Tshombe, president of separatist Katanga, was a friend of the West, he was barred from the United States and his mission to plead his country's cause. The Congo, from which Katanga had seceded, was in a state of chaos and overrun by Communist-financed and Communist-armed terrorist bands. Cannibalism and savagery were rife, and white men and women were being slaughtered and mutilated. In Katanga, the Tshombe regime had established a multiracial regime, law and order prevailed, and the economy was sound. But its existence was threatened by the United Nations, which had sent its troops in not to quell the rebellion within the Congo but to crush President Tshombe. The State Department has since tacitly admitted its error in supporting a United Nations military adventure of dubious legality which further aggravated the situation. But neither Bobby nor the State Department has explained why they turned their backs on a friendly Tshombe, who sought only the common courtesies of international relations from this country.

If Tshombe was barred by the Attorney General's fiat, others were not so harshly treated. Two terrorists from Angola, Holden Roberto and Mario de Andrade, had no difficulty being admitted to the United States. Both men were Communist-trained and leading a guerrilla attack against an ally of the United States. The Portuguese, having felt the edge of Roberto's knife, had amply supplied the Justice Department and the State Department with the background and the record of the terrorism which threatened Angola. Yet Bobby ruled that it was to the best interest of the United States to admit Roberto and Andrade. There were others, too, who had no difficulty in gaining admission, among them Cheddi Jagan, then the Marxist-Leninist leader of British Guiana, who at the time was using his country as a way station for the shipment of arms from Castro's Cuba to the South American interior for use against governments friendly to the United States.

This policy led a Senate committee to complain, "There is unjustifiable consistency in a policy which arbitrarily excludes friends of the United States who are not excludable under the law, while granting visas to known Communists and mass murderers, who are sworn enemies of this country, and whose exclusion is called for by law."

In *A Thousand Days* Arthur Schlesinger presented the White House view of Bobby's penchant for favoring those excluded by law as opposed to those who should have had the protection and welcome of the government. "The basic immigration law," Schlesinger wrote, "excluded politically suspect aliens from the country unless a

waiver could be obtained from the Department of Justice. The definition of political dubiety was broad and loose, and the result was
often the denial of visas to eminent writers and scholars for having
committed an offense against ideas of political propriety at some
point in the remote past. Robert Kennedy thought the system in-
jurious to the national interest, granted waivers whenever the State
Department asked for them, and if the Department hesitated, often
spurred it on to make the application."

Bobby was ready to spur on the State Department to more serious
assaults on the security system. It is the duty of the Justice Department to make certain that other agencies of the federal Establishment do not abuse or violate law or executive orders. The State Department, following the downfall of Senator Joe McCarthy, had
allowed its security procedures to fall into noxious desuetude. The
law demanded that all applicants for employment receive a security
check and clearance before they were hired. Under extraordinary
circumstances, the Secretary of State could waive this provision, hiring a needed person before investigation had been completed. In
two years of the Kennedy Administration, however, the waiver provision had been invoked 616 times, in cases where the new employee
would be working with classified materials. Investigative reports,
when derogatory, were simply filed away. To cover up this excessive
use of waivers, the investigative records of those cleared were back-
dated.

It was in this context that Otto Otepka, a ranking State Department security officer, acted. Expert in his field, efficient, and armed
with a thorough knowledge of regulations, Otepka began looking
into the consistent laxity of the department. He discovered, among
other things, that Assistant Secretary Harlan Cleveland had appointed a number of people of questionable security to a committee
whose function it was to make recommendations for appointments
to various State Department posts. He was even more upset when
Cleveland summoned him to his office to question him about the
possibility of rehiring Alger Hiss, who had served a sentence
in Lewisburg Prison for perjury involving his role as a Soviet espionage agent. From time to time, moreover, he was requested by high
officials to withdraw derogatory reports on the backgrounds of appointees suggested by the White House or the Justice Department.

Though his refusal to betray his trust won him the antagonism of
his superiors, Otepka persisted in doing his duty. Puzzled by Cleveland's requests and general attitude, Otepka began a careful study
of the file on the Assistant Secretary. "When the State Department's

daisy chain tipped off Cleveland that he was being watched,"
Robert S. Allen and Paul Scott wrote in their syndicated column,
"he retaliated swiftly by having John F. Reilly, Deputy Assistant
Secretary for Security, place Otepka under surveillance. This was
quietly arranged through the office of Attorney General Robert
Kennedy, a personal friend of Reilly." The surveillance rapidly
changed into open harassment. When the Senate Internal Security
subcommittee began investigating the department's free and easy
use of waivers to hire personnel without proper clearance, Otepka
was summoned and testified truthfully. Other State Department
officials denied his testimony. To back up his testimony, Otepka
submitted to the subcommittee documentary proof of security laxity.

Fearful that Otepka's disclosures might cause a political scandal,
Reilly, with the knowledge and consent of the Attorney General,
moved in to destroy Otto Otepka and to deprive him of further
proof which he might present to the Senate subcommittee. Otepka
was therefore shunted to a paper-shuffling job. His telephone was
tapped, his files were ransacked, and he was locked out of his office.
Simultaneously, the State Department pleaded Executive privilege
when it was asked to submit records to the subcommittee. Teams of
State Department officials denied Otepka's charges, and even Secretary Rusk came to the defense of his subordinates. This, however,
was only a beginning. Three State Department officials, including
Deputy Assistant Secretary Reilly, were summoned by the subcommittee and asked if Otepka's phone was, indeed, being tapped and
if listening devices had been placed in his office. The three categorically denied it under oath. But subsequent investigation showed that
these denials had hardly been candid, as the hearing record shows:

Testimony of John F. Reilly:

> MR. SOURWINE: Have you ever engaged in or ordered the bugging
> or tapping or otherwise compromising telephones or private conver-
> sations in the office of any employee of the State Department?
> MR. REILLY: No, sir.
> MR. SOURWINE: Specifically in the case of Mr. Otepka, you did not
> do so?
> MR. REILLY: That is correct.

Testimony of Elmer Dewey Hill, a State Department official,
"amplifying" his earlier denial of having "bugged" Otepka's office
and phone:

> MR. HILL: Mr. John F. Reilly, Deputy Assistant Secretary for
> Security, asked me to explore the possibility of arranging some way

to eavesdrop on conversations taking place in Mr. Otepka's office.
. . . That evening Mr. Schneider and I altered the existing wiring
in the telephone of Mr. Otepka's office. We then established a circuit
from Mr. Otepka's office to the Division of Technical Services
Laboratory by making additional connections in the existing wiring
system. . . ."

David I. Belisle, the third to deny knowledge of a tap on Otepka's
phone, also "amplified" his testimony by appearing before the subcommittee to state that he had testified as he did because, though he
had been informed of the "bugging," his knowledge was not "first-
hand."

The record of Reilly's testimony, as well as that of his two associates, was submitted to the Justice Department for study. No
legal action, however, was taken by the Attorney General against
either his friend or the other officials. They were allowed to resign
quietly from the State Department, and that was that. Otepka, on
the other hand, was suspended by the Secretary of State. And at
Bobby's instigation, the White House classified pertinent and damning parts of the subcommittee's record.

The Justice Department did, however, seriously explore the possibility of taking legal action against Otepka, hoping to charge him
with a breach of security for permitting the Senate Internal Security
subcommittee to examine State Department documents. But this
course of action was foreclosed by Bobby. For one thing, the law
favored Otepka. Secondly, the Senate would have protested that the
Executive branch was impinging the congressional right to investigate. And thirdly, it would have broadcast to the nation the very
facts of lax security that the Administration had tried so hard to
suppress.

On the question of security procedures, Bobby remained permissive. It all seemed silly to him. He also found it somewhat ridiculous
to restrict Americans from traveling to Communist countries like
Red China, Albania, and Red Cuba. When a group of students, in
violation of federal law, went on a propaganda mission to Castro's
Communist paradise, the Attorney General brushed aside legality
and criticism by remarking, "Why shouldn't students go to Cuba?
If I were twenty-one years old, that's what I would like to do."

On the threat of Communist infiltration and subversion, Bobby
clearly subscribed to the views of Walter Reuther and Americans
for Democratic Action. To them, any concern over the internal security of the nation should be directed at the right, not the left. Po-

litical or governmental organizations that worked to expose and eradicate Communist influence were "McCarthyite" or worse. As early as the first autumn of Bobby's tenure at the Justice Department, he had been approached by Walter Reuther and his brother, Victor, with a proposal, straight out of an Orwellian novel, for the total suppression of conservative thought and action—all, of course, in the guise of protecting the United States from the subversion of the "radical right" in America. The term, coined by such left-wing socialists as Professor Daniel Bell of Columbia University, had its own built-in hypocrisies, for it was bandied about most energetically by those who had objected to the word "radical" when applied to the left. By the time the Reuthers began employing it, the phrase was being thrown at constitutionalists, conservatives, the John Birch Society, traditionalists, libertarians—in fact, at anyone who stood to the right of the Liberal Establishment.

In the fall of 1961, Walter and Victor Reuther called on Attorney General Kennedy to urge that he use the power of the Justice Department and the FBI to destroy the growing conservative movement in America. The Democrats and their labor allies had come within 100,000 votes of being defeated in 1960, and they wanted no repetition in 1964. Only by an intense propaganda campaign and some legal bushwacking could the "extremists" be driven out of public life and the marketplace of ideas. The Reuther proposal interested Bobby. He saw immediately that it could be used to drive a wedge between the FBI and its millions of supporters throughout the country. It could also be made to sow confusion in the public mind by linking the Republican party and "extremism." Most important of all, an antiextremist drive would keep the Republican party on the defensive and compel conservatives to join in the cry against undesignated "radical rightists," thereby dividing conservative ranks. That it smacked of police-state methods and violated the basic tenets of civil liberties seemed not to upset Bobby. When Bobby asked the Reuthers to spell out their proposal in writing, the Reuthers demurred. They knew how confidential papers can fall into the wrong hands. But Bobby insisted.

On December 19, 1961, a twenty-four-page memorandum was delivered to the Attorney General, who dispatched copies to all high Administration officials and to "certain sympathetic Senators and Congressmen." In this manner, Bobby was able to give it something of a Kennedy imprimatur. On Capitol Hill, Senator J. William Fulbright, chairman of the influential and closely observed Foreign Relations Committee, adopted its premises in his famous assault on the generals and admirals who expressed anti-Communist views. His sensationalized hearings led to the effective elimination of all objective discussion of Communism as a philosophy and a conspiracy. The impact of the Reuther memorandum was heightened by Bobby's open disdain for anti-Communists and the discernible reluctance with which he uttered his few "warnings" against Communist penetration of American society. Before long, the Reuther memorandum almost became known among Justice Department insiders as the Kennedy memorandum.

It deserved the designation. Bluntly written and explicitly calling for strong measures against the "radical right," it was as much a manifesto as a plan of action: "Far more is required in the struggle against the radical right than simply calling attention to present and potential dangers. . . . Speeches without action may well only mobilize the radical right instead of mobilizing the democratic forces within our nation. . . . The radical right or extreme right-wing, or however it may be designated, includes an unknown number of millions of Americans of viewpoints bounded on the left by Senator Goldwater and on the right by Robert Welch. . . . They are growing in strength and there is no reason to expect the turning of the tide. . . . Their relationship to and infiltration of the Armed Services adds a new dimension to the seriousness with which they must be viewed."

The "radical right" was endowed with many sins, according to the memorandum. It was well financed, backed by a variety of organizations, appealing to "younger people," had the support of prominent Senators and Congressmen of both parties and of "such top 'movie makers' as Jack Warner," believed that domestic Communism was a danger to America, and called for total victory over the Communists. "What are needed are deliberate Administration policies and programs to contain the radical right from further expansion and in the long run to reduce it to its historic role of the impotent lunatic fringe."

The first step to be taken by the Administration, the memorandum recommended, was to muzzle the military, to keep conservatives off active duty, and to ban military participation in the fight against Communism. Defense Secretary Robert McNamara was urged to "start his own investigation of radical right generals and admirals. These generals and admirals . . . should be warned against political activity in any way, shape or form. This might have the effect of causing the resignation of some of these generals and admirals which would certainly be in the national interest." This "strong posture" would "answer Soviet propaganda that American foreign policy is not in responsible hands and that there is a substantial 'preventive war' group in the Pentagon." It would also strengthen the hand of "factions within the Soviet Union that strive for a more flexible position on the Soviet's part"—a line which even former Secretary of State Dean Acheson had already rejected.

Point Two in the program submitted by the Reuthers to Bobby Kennedy urged the use of the Attorney General's list of subversive organizations. "Although the radical right poses a far greater danger to the success of this country in its battle against international Communism than does the domestic Communist movement, the latter have been branded as subversive by the government and the former have not." The memorandum then deplored the fact that "no one loses his job or is subjected to public obloquy because he joins one of these radical right groups; yet these groups can use the subversive list to get at liberals and moderates who twenty years earlier had joined some Communist 'front' organization which looked patriotic and socially desirable." [1] Since some of the "radical right" groups keep their membership lists secret (the Reuther memorandum to Bobby failed to note that so do Masonic groups) and promote "outright rebellion in the Army"—no corroboration of this charge was cited—the Attorney General was told to move against them. Implicit at this point was an admission that there might not be evidence to warrant placing these groups on the list. But, the Reuthers cynically argued, just "the announcement of the investigation would have an immediate salutary effect." In other words, frighten groups displeasing to the Liberal Establishment by threat of government action and FBI investigation.

Point Three called for the cutting off of funds to "radical right" groups, particularly Dr. Fred Schwartz's Christian Anti-Communist Crusade, praised by *Time* magazine and supported by many respected Americans, through the political use of the Internal Revenue Service. "Prompt revocation [of federal tax exemption] in a few cases might scare off a substantial part of the big money now flooding into these tax exempt organizations." Businesses which sponsor anti-Communist and pro-American radio and television programs would be barred from paying for them with their advertising dollars. Objecting to the content of some of these shows, the Reuther

[1] The Attorney General may place an organization on his subversive list only after a finding, supported by hearings, that it is "totalitarian, fascist, communist, or subversive, or [has] adopted a policy of advocating or approving the commission of acts of force or violence to deny others their rights under the Constitution . . . or [seeks] to alter the form of government of the United States by unconstitutional means."

memorandum offered suggestions for suppressing or censoring them. The Federal Communications Commission could be subverted to this purpose by limiting the rights of "radical right" shows to buy commercial time.

Finally, the Reuther memorandum argued that the Communist problem be put "in proper perspective" in order to "expose the basic fallacy" of anti-Communists that "domestic Communism has succeeded in betraying America and threatens its very survival." FBI director J. Edgar Hoover "exaggerates the domestic Communist problem and thus contributes to the public's frame of mind upon which the radical right feeds. . . . Each Administration since World War II has maximized the Communist problem. . . . [The Communist party] has no capacity today to endanger our national security or defeat our national policies. . . . The need now is to rein in those who have created the unreasoned fear of the domestic Communist movement in the minds of the American people and slowly to develop a more rational attitude."

Within months after his receipt of the Reuther memorandum, Bobby Kennedy had sold its salient points to key Administration agencies. The Internal Revenue Service, always permissive in its dealings with foundations, sent its accountants and lawyers delving into the files of conservative tax-exempt organizations. All anti-Communist indoctrination in the armed forces was either terminated or so watered down that it lost its meaning. From the FCC came "doctrines" and "guidelines" which made it increasingly difficult for conservative groups to buy radio and television time. By the time the 1964 campaign had rolled around, the FCC had so broadened its concept of "radical right" that stations with conservative ownership were being threatened with loss of their licenses. With Justice Department backing, moreover, individual commentators who did not accept the premises of the Liberal Establishment were driven from their posts. And Republican candidates, hamstrung by the so-called "fairness" amendment to FCC regulations, found themselves unable to buy time unless stations were ready to donate equal and free time to the opposition.

Encouraged by the Reuthers, and by the Liberal Establishment, Bobby set out to make the FBI an instrument of his own political purposes and legal predilections. For close to four decades, J. Edgar Hoover had run the FBI with a thought only to the impartial investigation of crime and of incursions on the national security. Under his administration, law-enforcement agencies were offered the superb crime-fighting facilities of the bureau. Subversives of all stripes were kept under effective surveillance. Espionage had been thoroughly combatted, although politically motivated Attorneys General had frequently failed to make use of the FBI's researches. The security aspects of the bureau's work had, of course, brought down the wrath of the Communists and their "soft on Communism" allies. But in years of attack on the FBI, no appreciable dent had been made in its armor, and only the most picayune accusations had stuck. Hoover had succeeded in keeping it out of politics, and in so doing, remaining free of the politicians, where other civil servants were forced to think in terms of expediency and the favor of Cabinets and Presidents.

With President Kennedy standing behind him, Bobby compelled Hoover to reassign his best agents, then working on internal security matters, to other cases. Had the Attorney General not been the President's brother, Hoover might have been able to present his case to the White House. But under the circumstances, he had no choice but to obey. The FBI was sent into the South to act in civil rights cases as a "national police" rather than as an investigative agency. It was enlisted to do battle with James Hoffa and the Teamsters. Reluctantly, it took on activities repugnant to Hoover and to agents trained to respect the civil liberties of the press. Correspondents who sounded off caustically about Bobby or the President, during bull sessions at their favorite "watering places," discovered that their words were being reported.

Anti-FBI stories of dubious accuracy began to appear, and it was common knowledge among reporters on the Justice Department beat that leaks of derogatory information about Hoover and the Bureau were coming from the Attorney General's office. This "information" was accompanied by persistent rumors that Hoover was on his way out. And the attacks on Hoover at high-level meetings became so sharp that Vice President Lyndon Johnson felt called upon to intercede at the White House in the FBI director's behalf. This, and the rising note of protest from friends of the Bureau in the Senate and House, caused Bobby to speak a few kind words about J. Edgar Hoover. The President, more attuned to political crosscurrents than his brother, made an ostentatious demonstration of his respect for the FBI by inviting Hoover to lunch at the White House. But insiders knew, as *Newsweek* reported, that Bobby was merely biding his time and still determined to fire Hoover after the 1964 elections.[2]

---

[2] *Newsweek*'s information was excellent. Through Benjamin Bradlee, its Washington bureau chief, it had a direct pipeline to the Kennedys. When, after the assassination of John F. Kennedy, the magazine reported that Hoover had failed to send a letter of condolence to Bobby, the source of the story (but not the motivation) was

None of this had any immediate impact on the public. After the defeat of Senator McCarthy, the mass media had decided that Americans were no longer interested in their country's security. Communism was considered a bore, and only a few diehards, ignored by the dispensers of place and favor, fought a discouraged battle or tried to outshout the gale. It was no time for Cassandras. But as Attorney General, Bobby also operated in areas which impinged on the livelihoods and lives of many millions. The Anti-Trust Division of the Justice Department had the power to crush industrial giants and to deprive millions of executives and high-salaried employees of their wages and incomes. Since Bobby had little love for and less understanding of the American businessman, he thought and spoke in old clichés.

"The business community always has greater mistrust of any Democratic administration than of a Republican administration," he told an interviewer. "It is an ideological reflex—obsolete, in my opinion —but that's one of the facts, so I don't know that businessmen, the big ones anyway, no matter what we do, will ever be in love with us." In his Rackets Committee days, moreover, he had tried to blunt the cutting edge of his investigations by railing against business. "The corruption within management is something that should concern everybody in the United States," he said. "It is extremely serious." He could never see a distinction between the labor racketeer who takes his graft on threat of shutting down a plant and the manager who responds to this kind of blackmail. His antagonism to business convinced him that business was looking for trouble, and Bobby itched to pick the fight first.

Admittedly, he had no knowledge of economics. His attitudes on the subject were conditioned by his father's "lone wolf" suspicion of corporate togetherness. To this, Bobby added a boyish admiration for the trust-busting Teddy Roosevelt, as seen in the cartoons of the day. Combined, these formed his prejudice against "bigness" in business, as if size alone colored it black. The Eisenhower Administration, particularly during Robert Bick's tenure as head of the Anti-Trust Division, had moved ahead steadily to erase mergers which resulted in price fixing, restraint of trade, and the elimination of competition. But it had never argued that a big corporation was automatically a bad one. Nor did it hold that success in business was an indication of some hidden dishonesty or flaw of character.

---

known to members of the Washington press corps. Hoover had, in fact, written such a letter to Bobby. This was quietly made public by the FBI after the *Newsweek* story appeared, with no comment from Bobby.

At his first press conference, Bobby let his views be known. He said he would give "priority" to antitrust suits for which he would search in "every section of the country." And he said ominously: "We intend to take action not only against companies, but against those [company] officials who we find are responsible for price-fixing activities." To friends in the press he let it be "understood" that he would seek maximum penalties—one year in prison and a $50,000 fine—for *each* violation of the statutes by individuals. He also proposed that the Landrum-Griffin Act, closing loopholes in the anti-racketeering provisions of the Taft-Hartley Act, be expanded to include management as well as labor.

The business community, worried enough over President Kennedy, looked about for some reassurance that Bobby would not spend all his time looking for corporate victims. It was not reassured when the Justice Department filed a multimillion-dollar suit against General Motors, allegedly because it held a monopoly in the diesel-locomotive field. Had the Attorney General bothered to examine the history of GM's entry into the diesel field, he would have learned that the coal-burning locomotive manufacturers had rejected the possibilities of diesel power, that they had laughed when GM entered the field, and that only a vast investment and the conviction that diesel oil was more efficient for locomotives had given GM a predominance in that field. Yet, having had the foresight and taken the chances, GM was now being penalized by Bobby and the Justice Department.

The first result of this was, as Donald I. Rogers noted in the New York *Herald-Tribune*, to create panic. "Corporate executives throughout the country trembled a bit and began to ask their legal advisers where—and when—the Kennedy Administration will strike next. . . . [The Justice Department] has leaked enough information about [the Attorney General's] intentions to scare even the most scrupulously honest corporate executive, as report piles on report that Bob Kennedy . . . will look askance at price moves within any industry, even those resulting from competitive forces. Some of the talk emanating from the Justice Department is plain nonsense, some utterly absurd, but there is one clear pattern that emerges: Mr. Kennedy intends aggressively to expand the activities and the jurisdiction of his department. He has already done so.

"Not yet three months in office, and he has expanded [his] jurisdiction . . . into an area which Congress has twice forbidden the Justice Department. It came to light last week that Bob Kennedy has won virtual control over bank mergers, a control that Congress some years ago specifically refused to give to the Justice Department, and denied again in 1960, just in case there were lingering doubts."

Bobby, however, had acted far more subtly. Putting to good use his relationship with the President, he had twisted the arm of the Treasury for its reluctant approval of a deal in which bank mergers would not be approved by the Controller of Currency without the Attorney General's permission. Economists, businessmen, and the Congress saw no need for Justice Department interference. Three federal agencies were already acting as watchdogs: the Federal Reserve Board, the Federal Deposit Insurance Corporation, and the Controller of Currency, who worked under the Secretary of the Treasury. State banking authorities, moreover, had veto power over bank mergers. Bobby's grab for authority, therefore, simply complicated the picture without protecting the taxpayer or the business community. The Justice Department became embroiled in a series of litigations, taking the position that every fiscal agency in the country was out of step. So disruptive was Bobby's handling of banks that eventually Congress was compelled to pass special legislation to spare the banks from unscrambling eggs and dissolving legitimate mergers.

"What the Justice Department can add, except confusion, is not known," Don Rogers commented in 1961. "If Bob Kennedy is opposed to bigness and expansionism, he might look to his own department, for it is expanding itself mighty fast." But bigness in the federal Establishment was what Bobby wanted. Early in his first year as Attorney General, he ordered his lawyers to check up on compliance with fifty-eight major cases, settled since 1940. He had also sent up to Congress a series of bills which would have further added to the work load in his department. One would have required large companies to give advance notice of any merger negotiations. The second sought power for the Justice Department to allow inspection of business records in civil antitrust suits. Under the law as it stood then, the inspection power was limited to criminal cases. This would have given Justice Department agents the power to roam at will through oceans of corporate records in one of the greatest arbitrary fishing expeditions in history. The House, driven to it by Republican opposition, defeated this last bill by a narrow two-vote margin, substituting for it a measure confining Justice agents to searches in matters already under investigation.

Bobby's plea to the Congress that the "situation is getting worse and worse" and that he was "just not getting cooperation from the business community" got him little sympathy. It was not sympathy that he wanted but action. Challenging the Controller of Currency, who had approved the merger of two Philadelphia banks, Bobby filed suit against them, thereby establishing a new yardstick for antitrust litigations. It was acknowledged that the Philadelphia merger would not establish an entity that rivaled in size the great banks of New York and other cities. But the Justice Department contended, and won its case in court, that the combined assets of the merged banks overshadowed those of other local banks. This, Bobby held, destroyed free competition. To the chagrin of successive Controllers of Currency, Bobby Kennedy filed five suits in all to stop bank mergers, and his interpretation of the law was upheld by the Supreme Court. Bobby argued with the business community, in a speech late in November 1961, that he had taken steps against just "five out of one hundred and fifty-five" mergers. He could tell his Economics Club audience, "I look upon the antitrust laws as being probusiness," and ask for agreement on the ground that the majority of collusion and monopoly complaints came from other businessmen.

But the antibusiness label was by now firmly stuck to the Kennedy Administration. It was welded on during the steel crisis when all the power of government descended on United States Steel and the other big steel companies. It began with the lengthy negotiations between the Steelworkers Union and the major companies over a new contract. The White House had intervened by urging David J. McDonald, president of the United Steelworkers, to keep wage demands "within the limits of advances in productivity." The President had also asked the steel companies to "forego a price increase." The settlement was signed and sealed with the blessings of Labor Secretary Arthur Goldberg, former general counsel to the union. On April 10, Roger Blough, chairman of the board of United States Steel, visited President Kennedy at the White House to give him a four-page statement announcing a $6-a-ton increase in steel prices. He was acting on the assumption, perhaps a naïve one to Bobby, that without wage-price controls, this was strictly United States Steel's business.

The President, however, took it as a personal affront. "My father always told me that all businessmen were sons of bitches, but I never believed it till now," President Kennedy exploded. The remark reached the newspapers and Kennedy modified it to include only steel men. (Later, he said to Adlai Stevenson and Arthur Schlesinger, "They *are* a bunch of bastards—and I'm saying this on my own, not just because my father told it to me.") At his press conference on April 11, he stood flushed and angry, saying: "Some time ago I asked each American to consider what he would do for his country and I asked the steel companies. In the last twenty-four hours, we had their answer." At this point, the steel companies were beginning to hurt. They were accused of a "doublecross" and of violating a "gentleman's agreement." The President marked it down as a "personal affair" touching on his prestige, charging that the price increase had been "a wholly unjustifiable and irresponsible defiance of the public interest" on the part of "a tiny handful of steel executives whose pursuit of private power and profit exceeds their sense of public responsibility."

But whatever capital the President might have made of the incident was lost when the federal government massed its forces to crush Big Steel. Huddling together, the President and Bobby discussed the price increase with tight-lipped ferocity, and the decision was made to strike hard, to "make an example" of the steel companies. The Defense Department would announce that it was going to take contracts away from the offending companies and give them to those which had not raised prices. There would be leaks to the press that the Internal Revenue Service was examining the returns of steel executives and the industry. The Federal Trade Commission would make known its intention of instituting "an informal investigation" to see whether there had been collusion among the steel companies to break regulations against price fixing. Congressional committees would express their interest.

The major thrust, however, was to come from the Justice Department. A dozen lawyers were put to work by Bobby, digging into the facts and searching for legal precedents. Simultaneously, the wheels were set in motion for a grand-jury inquiry into the price rise. Several news stories had quoted alleged statements made at a Bethlehem Steel stockholders meeting which indicated that United States Steel was pressuring Bethlehem to conform with the steel price hike. Bobby thereupon ordered the FBI, after working hours, to question newspapermen who had covered the meeting. And he made it very plain that he wanted immediate answers. In his book, *The Steel Crisis,* an account sympathetic to the Kennedys, Roy Hoopes described what happened:

"At about 3 A.M. the telephone rang in a two-story duplex in Philadelphia's Burnholme Park section. It was the home of Lee Linder, a business reporter for the Associated Press. Linder had covered the Bethelehem Steel stockholders meeting in Wilmington for the A.P. on Tuesday, and it was in his story that Bethlehem's President Martin had been quoted as saying that he was opposed to a rise in the price of steel. It had been an ambiguous statement, made all the more confusing by the fact that on Wednesday a Bethlehem official had said that Martin had been misquoted.

"When Linder answered the phone, a voice on the other end said: 'This is the FBI, and we're coming right out. Attorney General Kennedy says we're to see you immediately.'

" 'Who is it?' demanded Linder's sleepy wife.

" 'The FBI,' replied Linder.

" 'They've got a nerve,' his wife shot back. 'Hang up on them.' . . .

"Two [FBI agents] arrived about an hour later. They showed their identification cards and Linder let them in. They settled down in the living room and proceeded to question Linder . . . about President Martin's statement. . . . About 4 A.M. John Lawrence, Philadelphia editor for the *Wall Street Journal,* was called by the same FBI agents. They wanted to come out to talk to him about Martin's statement, but he refused to let them come. 'I told them I had nothing to say,' said Lawrence, 'so they gave up.' "

When James T. Parks Jr., a business writer for the Wilmington *Journal,* arrived at his office at about 6:30 A.M., FBI agents were already waiting for him.

The whole episode, as distasteful to the FBI as it was to those who were questioned, made little sense but it aroused many. The New York *Times* called the antisteel campaign of the Kennedys "a personal vendetta." Others saw it as a sign of Bobby's penchant for "police state tactics." Critics of the FBI leaped to the occasion by describing the early-morning visits as "nightriding." (The Bureau's answer: "When an FBI agent is called out on an assignment, he goes out at once.") "There was one thing I found distasteful about the Administration's behavior," Max Lerner wrote in his New York *Post* column. "It was the use of FBI agents to track down aspects of the steel story by dawn interviews of reporters. This may make sense if you want to catch a spy before he vanishes, but these were reporters, not spies, and this invasion of their privacy suggested a police operation."

President Kennedy tried to laugh off the whole episode by telling his press conference that newspapermen were always waking up people, so that the FBI's midnight ride was simply poetic justice. And Bobby grinned sheepishly and said the questioning "could have waited until morning." But these comments and explanations missed the point entirely. If Bobby had wanted to know what the president of Bethlehem Steel had said, it would have made more sense to ask him first, or to question some of the officers of the company who had been present. A dramatic approach to the newspapermen, however, promised headlines which would convey to press and nation the kind of mobilization that the Administration was undertaking. Bobby had achieved the proper effect, though at some cost. United States Steel, and the other companies which had also raised their prices, capitulated within three days. Threatened by massive action to break up United States Steel into smaller companies, the nation's greatest producer of steel had no other choice. The steel industry, however, was not spared. The Justice Department hauled the major producers before grand juries which handed up seven major indictments for price-fixing conspiracies, and the companies pleaded *nolo contendere* to the charges.

To Bobby's chagrin, however, the Liberal Establishment saw no virtue in his war on Big Steel. Joseph Kraft, in the August 1963 *Harper's*, summed up the case against the Attorney General. "The key point in anti-trust actions is not simply to catch price-fixers," Kraft admonished, "or even to act on all complaints of restraint of trade. The important thing is to develop a strategy, so that anti-trust pressures are brought to bear on those areas of the economy— steel, for example, or oil—where collusive arrangements have truly important consequences. In that policy-planning job, the Justice Department has not been successful. More than half of the actions in the 1961-62 period came in the food industry—a business noted for its generally competitive conditions." A Washington correspondent who covered the Justice Department put it more succinctly: "Bobby scared the hell out of big business, but it was the pickle manufacturers who took it on the chin."

The work of an Attorney General, however, consists of more than the headline-making assaults on large corporations or the even more spectacular attempts to impose racial understanding with federal marshals and a big shillelagh. There is the grim task of fighting crime and prosecuting criminals, a guerrilla operation in which patience and persistence are the payoff. At every hand there was evidence that organized crime was growing, capturing legitimate businesses and even moving into the banks. If the power of the "syndicate" were not enough of a menace, there was a steadily rising crime rate which the FBI, in its Uniform Reports, noted with tragic regularity every six months.

It was Bobby's ambition, as expressed to a friend, "to go down in history as the Attorney General who licked the Mafia." But the leap between that ambition and its fulfillment was never negotiated by Bobby. His successes as a crime fighter certainly were not impressive. The annual cost of crime, according to FBI director Hoover, totaled $22,000,000,000. Bobby himself would warn Congress: "While there are still crimes of violence, the modern criminal has become more sophisticated in the planning and perpetration of his activities. . . . He has moved into legitimate businesses and labor unions where he embezzles the funds and loots the treasuries." This was true when he took office and even more so when he had left. For there was an in-built difficulty in eradicating crime which Bobby was not ready to face: the involvement of the same big-city machines which had contributed so much to his brother's victory.

"The Attorney General's war on crime," columnist Holmes Alexander wrote, "is an enormous undertaking which is already showing him the corruption of city, county, and state governments, where most of the officials are Democrats—and Democrats to whom he owes debts of gratitude from the 1960 Presidential primary and general elections. When Kennedy cracks down on these men, we'll know he has triumphantly confronted his moment of truth." Senator Estes Kefauver had thrown away what chances he had of getting the Democratic Presidential nomination by antagonizing the Democratic political bosses with his investigation of organized crime. Did Bobby intend to go the same route? Reporters in Washington watched to see with what "full vigor" he would act against Democratic malefactors.

The start seemed auspicious. His most famous case brought down two Democratic Congressmen, Representatives Thomas F. Johnson of Maryland and Frank W. Boykin of Alabama. On October 16, 1962, they were indicted on eight counts of conspiracy and conflict of interest. Charged with the Congressmen were J. Kenneth Edlin, an officer of a Maryland savings and loan association, and William L. Robinson, one of Edlin's associates. Bobby Kennedy announced that the four had conspired to accept money and to participate in real-estate transactions in exchange for their services in influencing the Justice Department to dismiss a prior indictment against Edlin. The Congressmen were further charged with having delivered speeches in the House of Representatives, favoring the interests that were paying them. Edlin eventually pleaded "no contest" to a mail-fraud charge and served six months in a federal jail at Tallahassee. In the course of the trial of Johnson, in Baltimore on April 17, Bobby appeared as a surprise witness for the prosecution. He was cross-examined by Johnson, who acted as his own lawyer, and ended up by weakening the government's case. From the transcript:

MR. JOHNSON: In the course of our conversation, do you remember that defendant Johnson and Congressman Boykin made it clear they were not there to ask favors or to interfere with the Department of Justice?

MR. KENNEDY: I believe that was the gist of it. I didn't think at the time that there was anything improper in your visits.

The case of the two Congressmen, moreover, came to nothing. The Supreme Court threw out the conviction, but no one could fault Bobby for not trying. His approach to the Billie Sol Estes scandal was a little different. Though he admitted candidly that every Administration had its corruption and "we're going to have [it] over the next few years," Bobby strove mightily to play down the manipulations of Billie Sol and his fraudulent cotton allotments and fertilizer storage-tank deals. The Estes case reached high into the Administration. Estes had been an enthusiastic supporter of the Kennedy Presidential candidacy. He had wide contacts in the Administration and considerable political influence. His operations began in 1959, but his major crimes were committed in 1961 and 1962, a fact which did not prevent Theodore Sorenson, John F. Kennedy's speechwriter and alter ego, from dismissing the Estes case as "manipulations under the previous Administration's cotton and grain program."

Though there had been repeated hints of Billie Sol's speculations and peculations, the Justice Department sat mute. By the spring of 1962, Estes was billing himself as the "world's largest warehouser of grain" with an income from the government, in this enterprise alone, of $5,100,000. It was known to a variety of people that many of the storage tanks against which Estes received millions of dollars in subsidies were nonexistent. Yet nothing was done until private citizens had nudged Texas authorities into breaking the case. Hearings before the McClellan committee were kept secret and the transcripts were never published. To this day they have been kept out of the hands of eager researchers seeking links between Billie Sol and the Kennedy Administration. Stories on the case in the New York *Herald-Tribune* so angered the President that he canceled his subscription to the paper. Bobby's role was to keep the press in line.

The war on crime took another turn under Bobby's leadership when a small-time hoodlum and paid assassin of the "syndicate," Joe Valachi, was spirited out of a federal prison and brought to Washington for intensive questioning. Criminologists and law-enforcement officials have given little credence to sensational accounts of a vast underworld organization, the Mafia. But Bobby was convinced that the Mafia, as described by lurid crime writers, actually existed. Joe Valachi, speaking as a confessed member of Cosa Nostra, presumably a subdivision of the Mafia, was ready to substantiate the Kennedy belief. For months he was kept in hiding while teams of Justice Department lawyers questioned him. Then, with much fanfare, Valachi was presented to the McClellan committee as a witness. Day after day, he told lurid stories of murder and violence and the "inside" of gangster life. The fascinated public listened to this witness in whom Bobby Kennedy had "full confidence." But when Valachi had finished his testimony and was returned to jail, where he was guarded night and day from gangster vengeance, there were no indictments and no great anticrime sweep. New York police officials, lawyers, and judges found little in what Valachi had to say that was new or more than hearsay, of no value to prosecutors. One police captain summed it up when he commented: "By Valachi's own testimony, he was only small potatoes in the mob at the time."

Arthur Schlesinger, in his dedicated effort to find the best in all that Bobby did, wrote of his "broad war against the crime syndicates." And Bobby tried to use the horrendous Valachi testimony as the basis for more comprehensive legislation to fight "a private government of organized crime, a government with an annual income of billions, resting on a base of human suffering and moral corrosion." The timing of the Valachi "disclosures," however, raised some eyebrows among veteran political observers. Frank Kluckhohn summed up their jaundiced views in *Lyndon's Legacy*: "Not incidentally, the three-ring circus Valachi hearings were stage-managed by Bobby Kennedy at precisely the time the Otepka case broke into [the] headlines.

"The Otepka case, of course, is of enormous significance to the well-being of our national security. . . . Staging the Valchi hearings at that precise moment was an attempt by the Kennedy Administration to distract public attention from the security risks scattered throughout [the government]—as then being enunciated by Otto Otepka."

It would be more charitable to suggest that Bobby wanted to inject a sense of urgency into his demand for legislation legalizing wiretapping by federal agencies. Local, state, and federal law-enforcement agencies had been using wiretaps with impunity against those under suspicion. But whenever the courts discovered this practice in a particular litigation, there was trouble. Wiretapping, barred by the "statute" of the Federal Communications Commission, was illegal, but this "law" had been honored more in the breach than in the observance by almost everyone in the federal Establishment. During the Roosevelt Administration, Harold Ickes had planted taps on the phone lines of his fellow Cabinet members and then used the information thus gathered to bedevil them.

Conservatives, well aware that indiscriminate wiretapping could be used to destroy political dissent, were leery of giving the Attorney General broad powers to eavesdrop on their conversations. The liberals agreed with the Washington *Post's* criticism of the legislation which Bobby sent up to the Hill:

"[The Justice Department] wants Congress, in brief, to let the Attorney General authorize wiretapping in any case which he thinks involves national security—and, for good measure, in any case involving kidnapping. He wants Congress, in addition, to authorize . . . wiretapping in connection with any 'serious' crime on the basis of a court order from any Federal judge. And on top of all this, he wants Congress to allow wiretapping by state authorities for whatever crimes the states consider 'serious' provided only that some state judge can be persuaded to issue a court order. One fallacy in this proposal is that a court order to wiretap is in some way analagous to a search warrant."

The Post returned to its criticism on a later date when it noted that "a search warrant limits a search to specified objectives in particular premises. The ambit of surveillance is narrowly circumscribed. But wiretapping, by its very nature, indiscriminately invades the privacy of anyone who happens to use the tapped telephone, whether he calls it or is called on it, whether he has any connection with the crime under investigation or not, whether the particular conversation concerns criminal conduct or business projects, social relations or private opinions. In addition it may make audible to official snoopers conversations privileged under law, such as those between lawyer and client, doctor and patient, priest and parishioner. Finally, a search warrant authorizes no more than a single search, while a telephone wiretap authorization under the Attorney General's bill would let the police tap continuously for forty-five days with renewals for twenty days."

Bobby's pleas for legislation to tap telephones might have found significant congressional support but for the prevalent view that he would use this right for means and ends other than the national security or his war on crime. William S. White, in one of his columns, laid bare these fears when he wrote that "an unpleasant odor of police-state methods—of instances of illegal wiretapping and of

Federal snoopery over the mail of private persons—is arising from
the vicnity of the U.S. Department of Justice." Among the "highly
unpopular" victims of these methods was Roy Cohn, then under indictment on federal perjury and conspiracy charges, of which he was
subsequently cleared. Bobby had carried his old feud with Cohn to
an extreme, subjecting him to thirty hours of interrogation in which
he had been asked 4,852 questions. Cohn's mail had been watched
by the post office, at the request of Bobby's Justice Department.
Agents trailed him everywhere he went, and letters were written to
banks and brokerage houses warning them against him. The Justice
Department first denied Cohn's charges, columnist White reported,
then admitted them.

But however strongly he felt about Roy Cohn, Bobby was not
ready to act in other, far more serious, areas. Juvenile delinquency
was raising the hackles of many citizens who decried the crime in
America's streets and called for strong action against the muggers,
rapists, murderers, and hold-up men who roamed New York, Washington, Chicago, Los Angeles and other major American cities. In
his shirtsleeves, Bobby took a walk—well surrounded by press and
television—in 1961 to learn what life was about in the teeming Harlem slum. His arguments and homilies were widely reported, and
one sentimental observer wrote that "he looked like a bop himself,
sitting there on the curb, with his coat slung over his shoulder." He
preached thrift and industry and respect for law to the Negro boys,
and his talks with the Viceroy gang on its own turf made colorful
reading. But once the television camera had stopped grinding and
the Viceroys had drifted away, there was little to show for his mission.

Others took a different view of his achievements. "In the Washington judgment," Arthur Schlesinger would write, Bobby Kennedy
"turned out to be the best Attorney General since Francis Biddle
twenty years earlier. But this was a lesser part of his services to the
President. When he first decided to appoint his brother to the Cabinet, I do not know how much John Kennedy expected Robert to do
besides run the Department of Justice and be available for private
advice and commiseration. The Bay of Pigs, however, changed all
that."

The Bay of Pigs—and all the many problems of running a government.

9

---◆◄◗▶◆---

Taking Liberties

A PROSECUTOR can gain fame and fortune in many ways. He can take the way of Thomas Edmund Dewey—the coldly efficient scourge of crime, methodical and ruthless—whose most sensational case led to the conviction of Lucky Luciano for the one crime he had probably never committed. There is the way of Homer Cummings, who enlisted the powers of his office to clear a man unjustly accused of murder. And there is the way of the prosecutor who seizes upon one issue and makes it his own. Robert Kennedy had no need of fortune, and fame was already his, if only as a result of the focus on his abilities which a relationship to a President of the United States gave him. Yet whatever virtues he may have had as Attorney General—and many members of the mass media were convinced that he brought a new effulgence to the office of national prosecutor—he was ready to compromise grievously to satisfy an obsessive desire to destroy James Riddle Hoffa, president of the countrys' biggest union.

It was more than crusading zeal that drove him on. His hatred of Jimmy Hoffa came from that tight-lipped Jansenist streak in his nature which seethed at all that the Teamsters Union stood for. He could phrase it in a verbal concern for the plight of rank-and-file members, saddled with union corruption and strong-arm methods. But by and large, the dues payers in Hoffa's union were not particularly bothered by Hoffa's alleged peculations. They saw in him a union boss who more often than not got them good wages and fringe benefits. If, by the way, he made himself rich in the process, they were not overly concerned. It was not that Bobby deplored the Hoffa philosophy of justifying means by ends, for this was inherent in his own. He simply saw Hoffa as an evil that must be destroyed. And to this end, he dedicated much of his time as Attorney General, and much of the taxpayers' substance.

That this would be came through loud and clear during the 1960 Presidential campaign. On three major occasions, Senator John F. Kennedy had sounded the call to battle. In Raleigh, North Carolina, he had said, "I will not be satisfied as long as Jimmy Hoffa remains at the head of the Teamsters Union. And I think it would be extremely helpful to have a Justice Department which pursued and administered present laws with vigor involving Mr. Hoffa." During his first television debate with Vice President Richard Nixon, he said, "I am not satisfied when I see men like Jimmy Hoffa, in charge of the largest union in the United States, still free." And in Salt Lake City, he charged, "In my judgment, an effective Attorney General with the present laws that we now have on the books can remove Mr. Hoffa from office. And I can assure you that both my brother and myself share a very deep conviction on the subject of Mr. Hoffa."

For the Kennedys, the guilt of the Teamster president was no longer a matter of debate. He had been pronounced guilty as charged by the extralegal device of congressional confrontation—most notably the televised and publicized three-year inquiry of labor-management corruption by the Senate Labor Rackets Committee, in which the two Kennedys shared high billing. Due process seemed not to concern them. To Bobby's disappointment, however, the Teamster rank and file had shown little respect for what had been read into the record by the chief counesl or his investigators. As Attorney General, Bobby had greater resources—and a far greater problem. He had to move from inference of guilt to proof of guilt, from accusation to legal indictment. In the hearing room, the accusation had been sufficient and Bobby's method was nowhere more ably employed than in the questioning of Joseph Glimco, president of Teamster Local 777 in Chicago. A staff investigator had read into the record a long list of Glimco's arrests, with only a few minor convictions, thereby setting the stage for what followed: another catalog of "associates" and people "who have been seen in his company." "In court, this would have been entirely improper. But it made its point and enlivened the proceedings. "There followed a goodly company fully equipped with such nicknames as 'The Waiter,' 'Little New York,' and 'Cherry Nose,'" Professor Alexander Bickel wrote. "Some were allowed to remain identified by their nicknames only. Others were further placed as 'another member of the Chicago syndicate,' or 'a close friend of Mr. Hoffa.' "

This was followed by allegations that, if provable, could have led straight to a court of law and conviction for a series of felonies: receiving kickbacks, milking the union treasury, running extortion rackets. It even became part of the hearing record, by Bobby's method of guilt by allegation, that Glimco had violated his marriage vows by having an affair with his secretary, and his labor vows by financing the liaison with union funds. Since Glimco took the Fifth Amendment, from which there was no deviating for fear of "opening the door" to the loss of his constitutional immunity, Bobby easily got his story told by making flat statements in the form of questions:

> Mr. Kennedy: Then, when you were indicted . . . you used these kinds of contacts [Cherry Nose and others] in order to intimidate witnesses and get them to change their story?
>
> Mr. Glimco: I respectfully decline—
>
> Mr. Kennedy: You got your citizenship and abused it, did you not?
>
> Mr. Glimco: I respectfully—
>
> Mr. Kennedy: Did you ever do anything to help the union membership, one thing? . . . You don't care anything about yourself and these other people who are gangsters and hoodlums, do you? . . . And you defraud the union.

Bickel's comments, written with such authority as a law professor from Yale can exact, foreshadowed what was to come when Hoffa was presented to the court. "In terms of legitimate ends he was appointed to serve, this was totally useless. Mr. Kennedy's purpose was now to condemn and to punish, to cleanse the labor movement single-handed. . . . He was not any longer laying the foundation for legislation to be enforced in court, but attempting to render it superfluous. . . . Mr. Kennedy was within the law, but just barely. He used against Glimco a good deal of innuendo, based no doubt on what Mr. Kennedy sincerely believed to be true information, but not based on any fact that could be vouchsafed to Glimco or to the public. . . . Mr. Kennedy appears to find congenial the role of prosecutor, judge, and jury, all consolidated in his one efficient person. . . . No doubt he sought to serve the public interest as he sees it."

As much as Bobby Kennedy ever understands his critics, he understood what Bickel and other critics were saying about him. So, to his Hoffa compulsion was added the need to confound them. One of his first acts as Attorney General, therefore, was to organize what later became known as the Hoffa Brigade. Its leader was an old subordinate from the Rackets Committee, Walter Sheridan. The members of the brigade had one purpose in life, to "get Hoffa." Their tactics were, from the start, more fitted for jungle warfare than for the courts and might be characterized as a form of lawyers' counter-insurgency. It was this unofficial division which organized the trials of Jimmy Hoffa, procured the witnesses, developed the strategy —though always in close consultation with Bobby—and carried out the litigation.

But there was more than one arrow in the Kennedy quiver. He still felt that he could eradicate Hoffa by use of the same publicity techniques which had proved so valuable in his day as chief counsel to the Rackets Committee. He was, however, handicapped. For once a case against a Teamster official or an unsorted labor racketeer had passed the indictment stage, circumspection became mandatory if the defendants were not going to be handed the opportunity to claim that a fair trial had been denied them by prejudicial publicity. The McClellan committee had found its pursuit of justice inhibited by the indictment of Tony "Ducks" Corallo, a New York gangster, for conspiracy to fix a federal bankruptcy proceeding. A report on underworld control of a Teamsters "dummy local" in New York—one of those paper organizations designed to exact tribute from employers—heavily implicated Corallo, and until he was convicted the committee held back its report.

This was Bobby's problem when Sam Baron, a thirty-year veteran of the labor movement, approached him. Baron came from the ranks of the Socialist movement. Personal courage he had in plenty, having served in the Republican forces during the Spanish Civil War. After capture by General Francisco Franco's Nationalist troops, he was sentenced to death and would have faced a firing squad except for the intervention of the American Socialist leader, Norman Thomas. His last eight years had been spent in uneasy service with the Teamsters where he had risen to the post of Field Director in the Warehouse Division. He could rationalize his acceptance of the Teamsters only to a point. But when Dave Beck was replaced by the activist Jimmy Hoffa, Baron decided that the time had come for him to get out. With this in mind, he had volunteered his knowledge of internal Teamsters affairs to Bobby. This, to Bobby, seemed like a way to light a fire under Hoffa without seeming to be in any way involved, should his litigious plans for the Teamsters boss lead to significant court action. After some thought, he summoned Henry Suydam of *Life* magazine to a back room in the Attorney General's eight-room suite in the Justice Department. Suydam was one of Bobby's trusted friends and he represented more than 7,000,000 readers. He reported the clandestine encounter in a memorandum to his managing editor, E. K. Thompson, on March 6, 1961:

"Here's the story, as related to me by this fellow after a cloak-and-dagger shift of scenery, involving Kennedy slipping us out through back corridors, a drive by a roundabout route to the guy's home in Virginia, and the assigning to me of the code name 'Brown.'" In his initial interview with Suydam, Baron portrayed Hoffa as arrogant, heartless, and shady—but not necessarily criminal. He was, he said, given an account of Hoffa's alleged part in the rigging of the 1957 Teamster election, of wiretapping, of the Cheasty bribery case—but he could prove nothing. "The exposé stuff sounds interesting," Suydam wrote in his memo, "but to me at least, pretty undocumentable and therefore probably very libelous. But the more personal stuff on what Hoffa is like and how he behaves sounds pretty good."

Life published Baron's inside story of life as he saw it lived at Teamster headquarters, and the piece caused considerable excitement. It appeared, moreover, in July 1962, between Hoffa's indictment and his mistrial on charges that he had accepted more than $1,000,000 in illegal payments from a Detroit trucking company. Though not technically damaging to Hoffa, *Life*'s journalistic coup was distinctly bad pretrial publicity. Had the Attorney General's catalytic role in the story's production become known at the time, it would have had serious repercussions. But it remained hidden for two years after publication. Ironically, it was Bobby Kennedy's old antagonist on the McCarthy committee staff, its chief counsel Roy Cohn, who inadvertently effected the discovery.

Cohn had been one of Bobby's minor obsessions. In 1964, Cohn was tried and acquitted on ten counts of perjury and obstruction of justice in connection with a stock fraud case he had handled. Between indictment and trial, the Justice Department had ordered the Post Office Department to "cover" the mail of both Cohn and his lawyer, Thomas A. Bolan. In a mail cover, postal clerks record the names and addresses on all letters sent and received by the subject. Bolan discovered the practice and went to court to stop it. Federal Judge Archie Dawson immediately issued an order enjoining the United States Attorney, Robert Morgenthau, from continuing the mail cover, and he called it a "shocking" invasion of privacy. This postal spying brought no credit to the Justice Department. And it served Cohn as a warning of other possible activities inimical to his case. He usually suspected the Attorney General of the worst, and in pondering what that worst could be he began suspecting that an unflattering piece about him in *Life* might have been inspired by Bobby. Seeking possible proof of Justice Department complicity in the preparation of the critical article, Bolan subpoenaed the magazine's files. Tucked away among these papers, whether by clerical error or not, was the "personal and confidential" Suydam memo to Thompson.

"Last Saturday I got a phone call from Bob Kennedy asking if I could drop whatever I was doing and come to his office," the memorandum began. "I did, and when I got there he closed the door and told me the following: in a back room was a high official of the Teamsters, a man who had been privy to the inner workings of the organization since 1953. He was particularly knowledgeable about Hoffa. This official is honest, said Kennedy, and also quite an idealist. *The man had been working directly with Kennedy and in secret for the last two years.* He was now so disillusioned and disgusted with the corruption he saw all about him, particularly as concerns Hoffa, that he has just about decided to make a public break with the union. *Kennedy said he had suggested to this man that he make his break via an article in* Life *in the form of a personal exposé of Hoffa.* Kennedy asked my personal word that *for the moment* only you and I would know of this matter. Kennedy feels, perhaps melodramatically, perhaps not, that the man's life would be in danger if word leaked out of his intentions." (Italics added.)

In a second memorandum to his managing editor several days later, Suydam was equally explicit:

"I told Kennedy of your high interest and he is delighted. He makes the suggestion that the piece go into Baron's background and philosophy somewhat, to help explain his disgust with Hoffa and his motivation for breaking with the Teamsters. Kennedy believes deeply that this is not a case of sour grapes, but of a man acting out of conscience and principle. Kennedy thinks the break will be understood better in light of his total life in the labor movement."

In due time, the Suydam memoranda passed quietly from Cohn's camp to Hoffa. It surfaced during the Republican National Convention of 1964 in San Francisco when Sidney Zagri, the Teamsters' legislative counsel, appeared before the platform committee to urge adoption of a plank calling for a congressional investigation of the Attorney General's tactics and denouncing "government snooping."

He charged Bobby Kennedy with "provoking incidents, hiring informants and agents provocateurs, and planting a story in *Life* magazine to influence litigation against James R. Hoffa." In the Suydam memorandum, Zagri argued, "we have positive proof that these charges are true." In August, less than a month later, he told the Democratic National Convention in Atlantic City, where a trailer placarded with Hoffa's defiance sat on a lot near the convention hall, that it should do likewise. The Republicans called for the investigation. The Democratic answer was profound silence.

In September, however, the House Judiciary Committee felt enough political heat to vote twenty to thirteen to look into the possible invasion of constitutional rights by the Justice Department, without naming any victims. An ad hoc committee was formed to make the inquiry, but its chairman was Representative Emanuel Celler, a dedicated Kennedy man who had opposed the investigation from the start. Nothing was done about what in another day would have aroused the national legislature. In March 1965, a Senate Administrative Practices subcommittee looking into federal violations of the right of privacy took up what on the face of it seemed like a clear case of meddling with the judicial process.

The protagonists this time were Roy Cohn and Tom Bolan, ready to discuss the propriety of putting mail covers on a man and his lawyer. This entered an area of privilege in lawyer-client relationships which was once sacrosanct. While press and Senators alike acted as if they had never heard of the Suydam memoranda, Bolan placed in the record the offending documents and described their genesis. "Shocking," said the committee chairman, Democratic Senator Edward V. Long of Missouri. "It is obvious that the Department of Justice was attempting to try cases out of court. For me this is a serious charge." In rebuttal the next day, Bobby, now a member of the Senatorial club, employed an offense of injured innocence to cover the disingenuousness of his defense. He resented the inquiry, he said, and he challenged the propriety of allowing "to go out over the country the implication that I had done something improper as Attorney General." This, he said angrily, was truly "trial by press"—a statement that must have brought startled looks to those who had taken the stand before Bobby's committee.

Suydam's memoranda, Bobby admitted, were substantially accurate. Yet he indignantly denied that the idea for the Baron article was his. Explicit mentions by Suydam of Kennedy's advice on the scope and approach of the *Life* piece were brushed aside in Bobby's insistence that he had merely brought Baron and Suydam together for the initial interview. Even more surprising to the Senators was Bobby's assertion that the original agreement had been to refrain from publishing the piece unless "something happened" to Baron. There was no mention of this in the documentary evidence nor had it been suggested by anyone prior to Bobby's testimony. And the piece, after all, had appeared at the time most propitious for the prosecution, without a word of protest from the Justice Department. It made no sense, moreover, to break publicly with Hoffa, as Baron informed Bobby he intended to do, and then suppress his reasons for doing so.

Hoping to find an answer to the contradictions, the Long committee pressed Bobby. Did he have any independent evidence on the disputed points? "You have the testimony I have just given here," Bobby snapped. When the committee continued to look for something more than Bobby's word on a matter of conflicting testimony, Bobby decided that the time had come to call retreat. "I have made my statement on this," he said in ill-suppressed pique. "I have given you full information." And he stalked from the hearing room. But he left behind him one exchange with Senator Long which showed his utter lack of responsiveness to the committee's questions. "Is it proper," Long asked, "for the Justice Department to put a person in contact with a magazine to do an article on a man who is under investigation by the department?" Senator Kennedy answered: "The circumstances were quite different from the implication put out by this committee."

The Suydam-Baron episode was but one in a long series of events involving the prosecution of James Hoffa and his Teamster officials. The Hoffa Brigade moved from one litigation to another. Legally, the cases were unconnected. But in a philosophical sense they were violative of the principle in American law which forbids the government to try a man twice for the same crime. There was nothing the courts could do about this double and triple jeopardy. Each indictment addressed itself to a different crime, and the courts are not empowered to assess inner motivations or reject legal vendettas. Hoffa had been acquitted of attempting to bribe Cheasty, the man he had presumably planted in the Labor Rackets Committee. He had been acquitted of the wiretapping charge. The Justice Department had failed to make a case against him of mail fraud and of the misuse of union funds in promoting a Florida senior citizens community, when the court found the indictment faulty.

But there was no doubt in anyone's mind that Bobby would continue to pile up indictments until one of them stuck. Most important to this chronicle was the next attempt—the Test Fleet trial in Nashville, Tennessee, in late 1962. The indictment accused Hoffa and his Teamster associate Owen Bert Brennan of setting up a truck-leasing firm which supplied equipment to Commerical Carriers, a Detroit company which specialized in hauling new cars from plant to dealer. The Test Fleet leasing firm was owned by the wives of the Teamster leaders in their maiden names, Josephine Posyzwak and Alice Johnson. The Government contended that this was a subterfuge, and Hoffa's sardonic answer did not help him. "I once heard of a doctor that had a piece of an undertaking firm," he said. "Some of his professional patients became his business patrons, but nobody accused him of anything wrong. I know a lot of guys put property in their wives' names. I heard women own most of the wealth in this country. I happen to be the husband of Mrs. Hoffa." This avoided the point completely. The Taft-Hartley Act specifically forbids a labor leader from accepting money from an employer with whom he bargains. It was the governments contention that Test Fleet was a cover for these payments and a way to collect large sums of money in return for a guarantee of industrial peace.

Bobby had complained that the government was badly prepared in the Cheasty litigation. Now the prosecution's case was thorough and Bobby expected that the trial would present him with his long-delayed revenge. The government had evidence that Commercial Carriers had paid Test Fleet more than $1,000,000, ostensibly for equipment and services rendered. It had what it believed was good and sufficient proof to establish that the money had indeed been paid as a kind of illegal insurance against Hoffa-inspired strikes. But there were troubling aspects to the case. A few days before the trial began, Hoffa had negotiated an unprecedented nationwide contract which brought 400 trucker locals into a single bargaining unit, thereby immeasurably enhancing his power over the trucking industry. The trial was certainly with some justice, seen by some as a means of cutting him down. In the course of the trial, Hoffa was attacked by a fanatic who pumped three shots into him from an air-powered pellet gun. Hoffa himself subdued his assailant while the United States marshals took cover. And to this drama there was added a seedy episode which could not have failed to impress the jurors. On the first day of the Test Fleet litigation, a person representing himself as a reporter for the Nashville *Banner* telephoned some of the jurors. Acting to protect the reputation of his staff, James G. Stahlman, publisher of the newspaper, announced a $5,000 reward for the arrest and conviction of the impostor. To everyone's surprise, Bobby called Stahlman, asking that news of the incident be suppressed. The Attorney General felt, Stahlman later disclosed, that "if a detailed story in connection with this matter were made, it might very well lead to a mistrial."

"What has happened," Stahlman answered, "has made it necessary for me to defend the reputation of my newspaper, which has existed for eighty-six years, and I don't intend to have it sacrificed for Jimmy Hoffa, the federal government, or anybody else."

The Nashville trial did, of course, end in a hung jury, with seven of the panel voting to acquit and five to convict. But the trial was inconclusive in another way. While the jury was being selected, James Tippens, one of those tentatively selected, reported to the judge that a friend had told him that it would be worth $10,000 to Hoffa if he sided with him. This was a bribe attempt, and the trial judge disqualified Tippens. Two similar "incidents" were brought to the judge's attention and he replaced the jurors with their alternates. But had these attempts been made by Hoffa's people? Or were they planned by some overzealous member of an anti-Hoffa group to earn his pay? Federal Judge William E. Miller, as he presided over the case, was disturbed; and when the jury brought in its split verdict, he ordered a federal grand jury to make a complete investigation.

The hardly unexpected indictment of Jimmy Hoffa for jury tampering followed. What came as a shock from the start was the realization that Federal Judge Frank W. Wilson, for all his absent-minded unconcern, had taken to heart the old frontier role of "hanging judge." These are hard words, but the record sustains them. The accused in the case were James Riddle Hoffa; Ewing King, head of Nashville Teamsters Local 327; Larry Campbell, business agent for Hoffa's own Detroit Local 299; Thomas E. Parks, a Nashville funeral-home employee and Campbell's uncle; Allen Dorfman, a Chicago insurance broker with close personal and business ties to Hoffa; and Nicholas J. Tweel, a West Virginia business associate of Dorfman. Defense counsel for these men had asked and gotten a change of venue, from Nashville to Chattanooga. Perhaps they expected that Judge Wilson, who owed his job to the Kennedys, would lean over backward. They also must have reckoned that in the federal courts, it is the practice—and a sound one—to give the defense all the latitude possible and to hold the prosecution within the rigid restraints of procedure.

To their surprise, they discovered that just the opposite would be the rule in Judge Wilson's courtroom. Before the trial was over, they would also learn that the most hallowed of trial principles, the privilege of confidential communication between the accused and his attorneys, would be repeatedly violated without so much as a murmur of disapproval from the trial judge. As the trial proceeded, it became apparent that Walter Sheridan and the "get Hoffa" forces he commanded, under the overall supervision of Bobby Kennedy with whom he consulted on a daily basis, were taking law and the established practice of Anglo-Saxon justice into their own hands whenever it suited their purposes.

In line with Bobby Kennedy's conviction that Hoffa was guilty, the prosecution acted as if there were no need to allow him the due process which the Constitution guarantees. To begin with, the panel from which the jury would be selected was not drawn by lot. Instead, two private citizens, a Democrat and a Republican, were asked to submit 100 names each. These were then screened by three local industrialists and checked by the FBI. The defense, which had a right to knowledge of the backgrounds of the men selected, was denied this information. Though the names were made known to the defense, addresses were not. Hoffa's lawyers, therefore, were unable to exercise intelligently their right to challenge those jurors who might be prejudiced against the defendants. As it happened, two of the jurors who weighed the testimony had histories of anti-labor activity. The jury was, in fact, a "blue-ribbon" panel which would hardly look with sympathy on a man like Hoffa or have patience with his ungrammatical sentence structure and his slum origins. Very early in the questioning of jurors, Judge Wilson lost patience and insisted on handling it himself, and the objections of defense counsel were overruled with deadening regularity.

Three witnesses were called to give evidence of jury tampering. Even on direct examination, their stories were shaky. On cross-examination, they fell all over their previous testimony. One witness withdrew his statement that he had been approached by Ewing King and swore that he had initiated the contact. It was shown that in pretrial questioning by the prosecution, these witnesses had offered no evidence of any attempt at tampering. Their earlier signed statements had, in fact, said just the opposite. An alleged "fixer" for King, Oscar "Mutt" Pitts, testified that Walter Sheridan had said to him on the evening preceding his appearance before the grand jury, "If you don't tell me the truth, I will get you and your wife both indicted." A state trooper who had given positive testimony of an attempt to fix the Nashville jury admitted that he had never so reported to his superiors, that his statements to the FBI clearly denied what he had later stated under oath, and that "I knew that I was deliberately perjuring myself when I was in the U.S. District Court." The third witness to the alleged jury tampering told a muddled story but could offer no explanation for not having made a report to his superiors or to the FBI.

This was the tenor of the testimony—contradictory and full of lies compounded and truth confounded. From this kind of performance, no jury could have in conscience arrived at a conclusion. Most conspicuously, none of the witnesses, even when they were telling their stories under the direct examination of government lawyers, had linked Hoffa to the crimes charged under the indictment. The government's case had so little substance that the defendants and their lawyers began to wonder at Bobby Kennedy's folly in allowing the matter to come to trial. At that point, there was enough on the record to warrant a congressional investigation of the Justice Department's tactics, and this became even more evident when the defense put Frederick Michael Shobe, for two years a member of Sheridan's Hoffa Brigade, on the stand. Shobe had served a term in Michigan State Prison for forgery, burglary, and armed robbery. After his release, he was accused of violation of parole, threatened with a return to prison, then offered a way out.

That way was to join Sheridan's "investigative" unit. In his testimony at the trial, Shobe described his career in that unit. His job was to travel about the country as an *agent provocateur,* stirring up trouble in Teamster locals, Shobe told the court. Once past the time period of his parole, Shobe had asked his superiors in the Justice Department to get him another job, out of the government. He was finally offered one—in Japan. He suspected then that the Justice Department wanted him out of the country, far away from any opportunity to speak up. At this point, Shobe testified, he had poured out his story to William Buffalino, one of Hoffa's lawyers. That he had worked closely with Sheridan was evident when Shobe supplied the court the unlisted phone number of his superior. Shobe's testimony was very damaging to the government. For he told of being sent by a Justice Department aide to Louisville and Nashville in order to get evidence against Hoffa. When he tried to recount his conversations with Sheridan in Nashville, the government objected, and as he so frequently did, Judge Wilson sustained the objections. Shobe was not permitted to testify to anything that might incriminate the government except in *voir-dire* proceedings, after Judge Wilson had sent the jury out. (The judge later admitted that at least sixty percent of the trial record was made with the jury not present.)

The defense argued in vain that it had an absolute right "to ex-

pose any attempt by the government to do something wrong or illegal. . . . Where they attempt to fabricate testimony and suborn
perjury, it is for this court to take such testimony and for the jury
to hear it directly because it bears very materially upon all the credibility of the testimony of all the witnesses put in here up to this
point by the government." But Judge Wilson was adamant, and
Shobe's testimony never reached those who were entrusted with de-
ciding on the guilt or innocence of the men at the bar. Shobe's story
included a plot to kidnap a needed witness and to frighten him into
playing ball with the government, as well as other details. Of importance to this account is the following exchange:

> Q. Let me ask you this: As you sit here now can you tell us
> whether you had discussed with Walter Sheridan a plan to frame
> Mr. Hoffa?
> A. . . . It was my understanding that the only reason for the
> existence of the particular department that Sheridan headed was
> to get Mr. Hoffa.
> Q. I see. Was that made plain to you by Walter Sheridan that
> the purpose was to get Mr. Hoffa?
> A. That is correct.
> Q. And was it indicated to you that it made no difference whether
> he was—they used legal or illegal means?
> A. Well, preferably if there was something found that incrim-
> inated Mr. Hoffa, well and good. However, if there wasn't, the
> feeling in the department was that Mr. Hoffa should be in jail
> anyway and that we—if we had to resort to unfair tactics, well,
> that's where a person like myself came in at.
> Q. I see. And that is why they called you into service, because
> they wanted you, as you described, 'that's why they wanted me in
> the service, to frame Hoffa,' is that correct?
> A. Well, to get him by any means, fair or foul, that was my
> understanding of the matter.
> Q. And you were directly told this by Walter Sheridan?
> A. That is correct.

The jury was not permitted to hear this. When Shobe had finished
his direct testimony, the government had no questions to ask him.
James Tippens, the man who had first raised the jury-tampering issue in the Test Fleet case, was allowed to testify, however, even
though the prosecution could not link the alleged bribe offer he
described to any of the defendants. As a point of law, Tippens'
testimony should not have been permitted by Judge Wilson until

he had received reassurances from the prosecution that it could be linked to the defendants. But matters such as these did not upset the trial judge.

And then the prosecution sprang its surprise. He was Edward Grady Partin, and on him the entire government case rested. In any other court of law, Partin would have been cut to ribbons. For Partin's record, and the manner in which he became involved in the Hoffa case, was such that had the jury been allowed to hear of it, there would have been no case. *Life* magazine later wrote that Partin had been in jail "because of a minor domestic problem" and had been indicted on charges of embezzling $1,600 in union funds." Walter Sheridan painted him as a kind of hero, ready to do his duty and asking for nothing. The facts were something else again.

In December 1943, he had been arrested in the state of Washington for breaking into a restaurant. He pleaded guilty and was sentenced to fifteen years. After two attempted jail breaks, he was finally released.

He joined the Marines and was dishonorably discharged.

In 1961, he had been shot, but told police that the wound was accidentally self-inflicted. At the time, the Teamsters local he headed in Baton Rouge was in turmoil. Several members had charged him with embezzling union funds and of having gone to Castro's Cuba to consult with one of Castro's aides about an arms-smuggling deal. The 600-pound safe in which the union kept its books disappeared from the union's offices and was later found empty at the bottom of the river. Two men who testified against him at grand-jury proceedings were savagely beaten and subsequently one of them was killed by a truck.

On June 27, 1962, he was indicted on twenty-six counts for embezzling union funds and falsifying union records. He was released on $50,000 bond. His conviction would have had a maximum sentence of $260,000 in fines and seventy-eight years in prison.

On August 14, 1962, damage suits were filed against him for driving a car off the road, injuring two occupants, killing the third, then driving off. On September 26, he was indicted in Alabama for first-degree manslaughter and leaving the scene of the accident that had inspired the damage suit.

On September 25, the day before the indictment for manslaughter was handed up, Partin had surrendered himself to Louisiana authorities on a charge of aggravated kidnapping. (He had kidnapped from their mother, who had legal custody, the two sons of an associate.)

His troubles ended when he announced to his jailers that he had knowledge of a "plot to kill" Bobby. After conversations with police, Louisiana law-enforcement officials, and A. Frank Grimsley of the Justice Department, Partin's previously revoked $50,000 bond, as well as $5,000 bail for the Alabama manslaughter charge and $5,000 bail for the Louisiana kidnapping charge, suddenly and mysteriously materialized. On October 7, he walked out of jail. On October 8, he called Jimmy Hoffa in Newark, while Justice Department investigators recorded the conversation. After a second telephone call, ten days later, Partin set out for Nashville to make contact with Hoffa. He carried with him Walter Sheridan's Nashville telephone number and instructions, so he said, to report any evidence of jury tampering. His good luck was boundless. On the day he arrived in Nashville, he ran into a stranger in the hotel lobby, Nicholas Tweel, who generously, and out of a clear sky, volunteered Hoffa's plans to "fix" the Test Fleet case jury. Within forty-eight hours of his arrival, the first talk of jury tampering reached the trial judge—a coincidence worth noting.

Partin, however, had other jobs to do for Bobby Kennedy's trusted special investigator. Partin had made himself the indispensable hanger-on at Hoffa's legal headquarters, and every night he reported to Walter Sheridan. This must have been of tremendous help to the prosecution, but it was both illegal and unethical. When Partin took the stand in Chatanooga, he could claim to be an expert on the internal strategy of the Hoffa defense operation. His appearance in court shook Hoffa and his lawyers. When Partin began to testify to his great good fortune in finding a loquacious jury-rigger ready to confide in him, the defense rose up to object. They said that Partin had been present when defense strategy was being discussed and was therefore an "improper intrusion on the defendant's rights." It was pointed out that the prosecution in the Test Fleet trial had reassured the court that there was no illegally obtained evidence, no wiretapping, no eavesdropping.

The prosecution countered with an explanation that under ordinary circumstances would have been laughed out of court. The United States Attorney said that Partin had reported only on matters referring to jury tampering, but had studiously refrained from mentioning anything else. (This was thoroughly disproved later in the trial.) The prosecution also tacitly admitted that the presence of an informer in the inner defense circle was grounds for keeping Partin off the stand by its tortured argument that his appearance at the Test Fleet litigation would have been improper, but that this was another trial and therefore there could be no taint to his testimony. It was no surprise that Partin, when questioned on the kind of informing he did, remembered with phenomenal detail all that had allegedly been said by the defendants about the jury but suffered a complete loss of memory about everything else. Did that case come up at all in his conversations with the defendants and their lawyers? he was asked. "I don't think it ever did," Partin said, "[I] wasn't interested."

The evidence spoke differently. William Buffalino, a Hoffa lawyer, took the stand to swear that "on the night of the fourth of December, he [Partin] was in our room . . . and I was in the process of preparing, interviewing several witnesses, truck drivers, that were in from Detroit. . . . I asked questions and made notes. These notes were typed in question and answer form. . . . Ed Partin helped me type them. He was carrying copies back and forth from one place to the other. . . . The record will show, on the fifth . . . when Mr. Neal [the Nashville prosecutor] was interrogating defense witnesses, he asked, 'Isn't it a fact . . . that, or were you supplied with questions and answers as to what your testimony should be?' "

Buffalino recalled a second instance. Several of the Hoffa attorneys were discussing defense strategy while Partin sat with them. Buffalino laid out the approach he planned to take with a witness. "The next day," he testified before Judge Wilson, "when I got on this particular area I started, 'Now,' and this is the language, 'Now, witness, I bring you back to 1953,' and that is all I had to say and Mr. Neal jumped to his feet and said, 'I object, Your Honor, they are getting into a different area.' I said, 'How do you know where I am going, what I am going to ask?' He said, 'I am psychic.' That's in the record." There was no rebuttal from the government, and when Walter Sheridan took the stand, he reluctantly conceded that Partin had passed on to him information dealing with defense strategy and activities, including the "comings and goings of people," which had no conceivable connection with jury tampering.

Seeking to get at the question of motive, the defense tried to ask Partin about his previous indictments and his discussions with Frank Grimsley and Bobby Kennedy's representatives. The judge sustained objections, ruling out this testimony on the preposterous ground that it was not "material to the issue that is before this court." Its materiality was eventually established when it was finally conceded by the "get Hoffa" brigade in open court that Partin had been acting as a secret agent for the Justice Department before he had made his first approach to the Teamster chief. When Partin's denial that he was on the goverment payroll blew up, his reliability as a witness was destroyed, on the legal principle that if a man once lies on the stand the jury can reject his entire testimony, Judge Wilson tried hard to prevent this disclosure, since it involved the Justice Department in a clear violation of law. The colloquy is interesting:

> THE COURT: Were you in any way in the employ of the United States at that time?
>
> PARTIN: No, sir, I wasn't. . . .
>
> THE COURT: But was there any arrangement for the government paying your expenses and *compensating you in any way* in your trip to Nashville? (Italics added.)
>
> PARTIN: No, sir.
>
> THE COURT: At whose request did you go to Nashville?
>
> PARTIN: Mr. Hoffa's. Telephone conversation at Newark, New Jersey.

(This conversation was monitored by Justice Department agents, with whom Partin was already working.)

The matter of payments to Partin was of vital importance. Under a 1962 law, no witness in a federal case was to be reimbursed for anything more than his actual travel expenses. Under oath, Walter Sheridan, Bobby's man in Chattanooga, testified that no money was paid to Partin nor were any promises of money made to him. Yet in Sheridan's files was a memo authorizing a check to be drawn against the Justice Department's "confidential fund" for $300 a month. In time, at least $1,500 was drawn from that fund. Much later, the Justice Department would admit that checks for $300 a month, made out to Frank Grimsley, were paid over to Partin's ex-wife. The government tried to argue that these funds had been paid to cover Partin's expenses, although he and Sheridan had also denied that any expense money had been paid. But this belated "explanation" failed to stand up, since the government could produce no expense vouchers. Nor could it explain why the "expense" checks had always been for exactly the same sum, or why such an effort had been made to hide these payments, or how it was that the sums exactly coincided with the amount due Mrs. Partin for alimony.[1]

---

[1] When the checks were produced by the government, they showed that they had been issued to A. Frank Grimsley. He had taken them to the First National Bank of Atlanta with his endorsement, and had then gotten cashier's checks made out to Mrs. Partin, which he wrapped in plain pieces of paper. He inserted them in envelopes and mailed them to Mrs. Partin. Grimsley never signed any vouchers, receipts, or other forms to show where the $300 was going every month.

Judge Wilson's duty was clear: to take action against both the government attorneys and the government's star witness. But he remained mute.

The judge seemed at times to be the mainstay of the prosecution. Partin had testified that Hoffa told him of the "fixing" of the one Negro juror. But at the time given for this disclosure by Hoffa, the jury had not even been selected. Then the defense asked Partin: "How could he fix the jury when he didn't even know who was going to be on the jury?" The government objected to the question, and Judge Wilson sustained the objection. When Partin was being cross-examined on his criminal record, the judge again intervened. The defense had just asked: "And one of those [offenses] was assaulting a Mr. Colotto which you pleaded guilty to on December 2, 1955?"

THE COURT: "Sustain the objection."
DEFENSE COUNSEL: "I didn't hear any, Your Honor."
THE COURT: "Well, counsel stood up."

All of Partin's testimony except for his accusations against Hoffa was withheld from the jury, and efforts by the defense to inform the jurors of what had been brought to light during the *voir-dire* proceedings were frustrated by Judge Wilson. His activities as what has been called "an arm of the prosecution" reached its high point when he withheld vitally important evidence from the defense. Partin had repeatedly insisted in his testimony that he had gone to Nashville at Hoffa's invitation. This Hoffa denied. The defense, knowing that the two telephone calls had been recorded, demanded that the recordings be made available to them to check Partin's veracity —a standard procedure. The prosecution thereupon secretly gave a sealed packet with the recordings to Judge Wilson. Repeatedly, the defense moved that the recordings be made available. But neither Judge Wilson nor the prosecution divulged that this incriminating evidence was in the hands of the court. Finally, after Partin was off the stand, and just before the trial ended, the prosecution was forced into admitting that Judge Wilson had the recordings. The judge lamely said *he* "hadn't known" that *the defense* didn't know that *he* had this evidence in his possession.

The defense could rail that the United States Attorney "knew Partin, when he testified, was perjuring himself, he had the physical documents and hid them in a sealed envelope and then gave them to Your Honor and hid them there, kept the contents from you, kept it from the defendants when he knew that the physical evidence refuted and showed his star witness was perjuring himself and he, as government counsel, put the perjurer on the stand knowingly." When the recordings were played, moreover, they showed that Hoffa had told the truth and that Partin had lied. In his conversations with Hoffa, Partin had repeatedly stated that he would like to meet with him—"If you get an opportunity or something, I would like to get with you and talk with you," and again, "I hate to interrupt you, Jim, but I need to talk to you"—and this evidence placed him in the category of *agent provocateur*.

With this background, Partin's testimony that he had heard Hoffa discuss with others ways and means to tamper with the jury lost all merit. From beginning to end, the prosecution's hands were legally dirty. The jury heard less than forty percent of the testimony, and therefore could come to no conclusions of its validity. The subsequent contention of Hoffa's attorneys that the jurors while they were sequestered during the trial were wined and dined, given gifts, and furnished with prostitutes—unbelievable under most circumstances—becomes secondary in the context of the Chattanooga trial and the activities of Robert Kennedy's Hoffa Brigade. Burning acidly are the words of Judge Wilson after he had fined Hoffa $10,000 and sentenced him to eight years in prison. "You stand here convicted of seeking to corrupt the administration of justice itself. You stand here convicted of having tampered with the very soul of the nation." If this were true of James Hoffa, a slum boy who had clawed his way to the top in the jungle of Teamster politics, how much more true was it for those who turned an American court into a drumhead court martial?

Three of the codefendants were sentenced to three years in prison and received $5,000 fines; two of the defendants were acquitted for reasons best known to the jurors. Jacques Schiffer, counsel for Parks, was fined $1,000 and sentenced to sixty days in jail because he had energetically attacked the judge's conduct of the trial. When he asked for a hearing before another judge, Wilson denied it.

Walter Sheridan's reaction to the verdict surprised no one. Leaping to his feet, shouting and laughing, he raced to the telephone like a Hollywood-style reporter to inform Bobby. The Attorney General congratulated him for his services to the cause of justice. Hoffa's reaction was understandably somewhat different. "If this is justice in the United States," he said, "then I pity those who haven't the money to pay for an appeal, because this is a railroad job."

The congressional outcry against the conduct of the Chattanooga trial, to the surprise of many, was bipartisan. The most detailed speech on the floor of the House was delivered by Representative Roland V. Libonati, an Illinois Democrat: "What is on trial here is the American system of justice," he said. To make his point, he listed thirty questions which have so far remained unanswered. Among them were these:

"Is there, in fact, a 'get Hoffa' squad in the Justice Department?

"Did the payments . . . to Mrs. Partin violate an act of Congress?

"Did the [Justice] Department induce Partin's testimony by promise of immunity?

"Did the government forgive Partin $5,000 in back taxes?

"What happened to pending indictments against Partin in two states?

"Is there an investigation into Partin's gun-smuggling plot into Castro's Cuba?

"Was there a relationship between Partin's release from prison on October 7, 1962, and a call to Hoffa by Partin the next day?

"Were two government witnesses threatened with indictment and reprisal if they did not cooperate?

"Were three defendants offered immunity if they cooperated and since they refused were indicted?

"Was there a 'Mr. Bug' who operated [electronic eavesdropping equipment] from the 10th floor of the Read House, where the jury was sequestered?

"Was money authorized for labor spy activities?

"Why were over 24 marshals brought in from all over the nation?

"Were these marshals brought for any purpose other than guarding the jury?

"Did the marshals conduct themselves in a manner befitting their office or did the behavior include lewd conduct, immoral conduct, and at least one wild all-night party on the 10th floor of the Read House?

"Was the 'locked up' jury really locked up, or could they come and go individually?"

On March 23, 1964, Chairman Emanuel Celler of the House Judiciary Committee appointed a committee to investigate these allegations. Celler has always been a defender of Democratic party causes and, in 1948, was vocal in his attacks on Whittaker Chambers and Elizabeth Bentley after they had testified to the existence of two Communist espionage apparatuses in the federal government. Appointment of the committee, therefore, was all that Chairman Celler did. He could guarantee this inactivity by naming himself chairman.

His sop to congressional indignation had been prompted by a letter from Sidney Zagri, the Teamsters' legislative liaison man. Representative James Roosevelt, who answered the letter on behalf of the House Labor Committee, noted that Teamster charges "were made under oath, and that the government did not offer any rebuttal to them during the course of the trial." Roosevelt supported an investigation because justice "must be for the accused just as much as for the individuals who are recognized to be innocent without too much probing."

There was other congressional comment.

"It is questionable whether a man can have a fair trial in this country if he does not have the opportunity to confer with his lawyers in complete privacy," said Representative William Brock. Representative Michael A. Feighan said: "I am informed that witnesses who are prepared to testify with respect to certain matters in the Hoffa trial have been threatened and that economic reprisals have already been taken against some key witnesses." And Representative S. M. Matsinaga added: "The real issue under discussion is not the guilt or innocence of James R. Hoffa; it is whether or not an agency of government has taken illegal means to convict a man."

One of the few members of Congress to defend the Justice Department was Representative Tobert Macdonald of Massachusetts, a long time Kennedy intimate. In a long paraphrase from Bobby's *The Enemy Within* he justified the government's position on Hoffa, and then called for less noise about the case while it wended its way through the appeals courts.

In the upper chamber, Senator Wayne Morse raised the question of the "get Hoffa" squad and the successful efforts of the Justice Department to win its verdicts in the press. "The issuing of press releases constitutes a trial of the defendant in the press by the Department of Justice," he argued in presenting a bill to end what he believed were abuses of constitutional rights. Such activity "has a detrimental effect upon the defendant and makes it difficult for him to obtain a fair jury—and without a fair jury there can be no fair trial." Morse, in his indignation, was prepared to throw out the baby with the bath water. Needed far more than any legal inhibition on the release of press materials was greater exposure of Justice Department practices and less of the censorship which the Kennedy Administration imposed on all information that might damage it in the public eye.

Labor leaders, on other matters antagonistic to both Hoffa and the Teamsters, reflected the views of Representative Alvin O'Konski, who saw in the litigation "persecution and not prosecution." That Bobby Kennedy had assigned more than 300 people to the Hoffa case was seen as "a willful violation of the intent of Congress and a misuse of public funds. . . . If the rankest Communist had been treated the way Jimmy Hoffa has been treated, using police state methods, you can be sure the American Civil Liberties Union, the Americans for Democratic Action, and all the people who are constantly crying of violation of civil rights . . . would be heard."

They all missed the point. It was best summed up by Joseph P. Kennedy when he made two observations: "Bobby never likes to lose," and "Bobby doesn't care how he wins."

Among lawyers, however, it was assumed that Jimmy Hoffa's conviction would be reversed by the Supreme Court. The record of the case cried for a new trial in which the evidence could be fairly presented to the jury. With the American Civil Liberties Union crying out that Hoffa had been deprived of his civil rights, and filing an *amicus curiae* brief in his favor with the Supreme Court, a cross section of public and legal opinion seemed to be arrayed against the conviction. But by one of those ironies which tend to cast doubt on the validity of due process, the high court sustained the conviction by a highly unusual four-to-one vote. In short, a minority decided the issue.

Justice Byron White abstained because of his association with the Justice Department during the litigation. Justice Abe Fortas also abstained, for similar reasons of prior involvement. And Justices William O. Douglas and Tom Clark voted separately to dismiss the writ of review granted by the Supreme Court on the technical ground that, innocent or guilty, Hoffa's appeal should not have been heard—even though they found that Partin's testimony was "an affront to the quality and fairness of Federal law enforcement." By this legal freak, therefore, James Riddle Hoffa finally fell before Bobby Kennedy's attack.

There is one postscript to the Hoffa trial. To date, Edward Grady Partin has never been brought to book for manslaughter, embezzlement, income-tax evasion, or kidnapping. Repeated postponements have been followed by dead silence. For a man of his talents, after all, virtue could hardly be its own reward.

10

---◆◄◉►◆---

Prime Minister of Everything

T HE Department of Justice," Joseph Kraft wrote for
Harper's in 1963, "consists of seven specialized divisions (Antitrust,
Civil, Civil Rights, Criminal, Internal Security, Lands, Tax), three
offices (Solicitor General, Legal Counsel, Pardon Attorney), three
bureaus (Prisons, Immigation & Naturalization, Investigation or
FBI), and a national network of more than ninety field offices, each
heading up in a U.S. Attorney and Marshal. In one way or another, all these units are devoted to a single task—enforcing the
Federal laws. . . . Except for the rare cases involving a well-known
figure, the work of the Justice Department seems routine. . . . To
the insiders, however, Justice has always worked close to the bone of
national politics. . . . Justice has its special client, not any particular segment of the community, but the whole rest of the government. So mixed up are law and government in the American
system that from the President on down there is hardly an office of
any kind in the Executive that can take action without calling in
some way on the Justice Department. . . . For that reason, Justice
is a strategic point for policing the rest of the government. . . .
Alone among the Federal departments, Justice bears the attributes
of a staff arm of the White House."
The powers and responsibilities of the Attorney General
are, therefore, awesome. But when the greater latitude which a fra-
ternal relationship with the President invokes is added, it is easy to
understand why from the early days of the Kennedy Administration
reporters and pundits commented on Bobby's vast and unprece-

dented powers in the federal Establishment. In a sarcastic mood, President Kennedy had alluded to these comments when receiving a call from the Attorney General by saying to a friend, "This is the second most powerful man in the nation calling." The irony was lost on those who had seen Bobby Kennedy expanding his grip on the federal Establishment every day in every way. The powers resident in an Attorney General and the ramifications of the post did not satisfy him or consume his restless and questing energy. Before this glory had ended in the tragic and senseless death of his brother, Bobby would have in his hands more *actual* power, as opposed to the constitutional and traditional powers of the President, than any single man in the United States. Ambassadors, labor leaders, tycoons, politicians of rank, everyone who had, or thought he had, business with the government or the President, beat a path to Bobby Kennedy's door. And the President, in times of crisis, invariably said, "Get Bobby" or "Get my brother."

In this almost physical craving for control, Bobby was aided by the President's physical condition and personal morale in the first years of his tenure. Hugh Sidey, in a sympathetic biography of John F. Kennedy, describes the long periods of discouragement and disillusion which the President suffered. The Presidency was not what he had thought it would be. As Harry S. Truman had commiserated when delivering the office to Dwight D. Eisenhower, the distance between an order and its performance was usually the longest between the two points. Never having served in an executive capacity, Jack Kennedy was baffled. "I think I'll give the job to Lyndon Johnson," he would say, and it was not completely in jest. The exhilaration of the campaign, of his great moment before the Capitol when he took the oath of office, of the crowds and the cheers and the brave talk about the New Frontier—this had fled and there was only the drudgery of paperwork and the rack of decision. His health had never been good, and to the pain which accompanied him everywhere was the added burden of hiding from the public those ills which so much flesh is heir to.

For Bobby, whose life was conditioned to struggle, conflict, and combat, it was all challenge. The President's sardonic rejections and abrupt withdrawals created a vacuum which no man could have normally filled. But Bobby was not a Harry Hopkins, whose political ambitions needed watching, or a Colonel House, whose manipulations of policy were delimited. He was the President's brother in a family taught to trust only the ties of blood. He had no ambitions which could possibly clash with those of John F. Kennedy. The President was ready to depend on him as he did on the crutches which became necessary when his back injury struck hard. Politely, this was called "reliance," but its psychological roots went deeper than that.

The humdrum tasks in which a born executive takes pleasure bored the President. The matter of receiving the incessant calls from those needing guidance and direction, and the calls which a President must make, taxed his patience. Early in the Kennedy Administration, Jack Bell, veteran correspondent for the Associated Press, wrote: "Since he doesn't have time to make calls of this nature himself, Mr. Kennedy has confided that it would be handy to have Bobby around to pick up the phone on such occasions. He even thinks the most hardened bureaucrat would respond quickly to what would be regarded as his other voice." A year after President Kennedy took office, the authoritative *U.S. News & World Report* could devote four of its pages to an analysis of Bobby's role in a searching analysis of the question, *Is he the "Assistant President"?* "There are few fields in which high policy is set where you do not find, on investigation, that Robert Kennedy has an active interest—expressed either directly or through a group of young men scattered through many branches of government who are very closely aligned with the Attorney General.

"Bobby is known to the capital as a hard-working, decisive official, always ready to take on more responsibility. [He] is also frequently described in Washington as a man who plays an important role in shaping major decisions of the Kennedy Administration. One very important political figure, a Democrat, put it this way: 'John Kennedy, the President, finds advice pushing in on him from all sides of every question. The President consults a wide variety of people. . . . Then he calls Bobby to get his idea about what decision to make.'" One of Bobby's closest associates told the magazine, "There has never been anything like Robert Kennedy in the nation's history."

High government officials, in the constant warfare of the government's higher echelons, were ready to feed Bobby information about the shortcomings of their colleagues, and this was filed away for future use. He was, again according to *U.S. News, & World Report*, "credited with an influential role in shaping national military strategy" although his experience in that field was less than minimal. In those early days of the Kennedy regime, he advocated a hard line against Communist aggressors in Laos and Vietnam. Fields such as agriculture, unrelated to his post as the nation's first legal officer, received his attention and intervention. At the Democratic National Committee, it was made manifest that the real boss in political matters was not Chairman John Bailey, but the Attorney General. The first question there quickly became, "Have you cleared this with Bobby?"

"Of course, Bobby controls most of the patronage," a close friend said. "Why shouldn't he? It was Bobby who went out across the country, worked in the primaries, lined up the politicians and got the votes that elected his brother. He knows who was with the Kennedys when the chips were down. Just after the election he told Jack that the people who sweated it out in the primaries with them should have first call on jobs."

The Attorney General's interest in patronage did not stop there. In the past, it had been the custom to appoint the national chairman of the party in power to the Postmaster Generalship. (Truman, an exception to the rule, gave that office to a career man in the department.) The Post Office Department was rich in patronage, for there are 35,000 postmasters and 33,000 rural letter carriers to appoint, contracts to be let, and property to be bought and sold. When the Kennedy Cabinet was named—made up, it was remarked, "of nine unknowns and a brother"—the new Postmaster General, J. Edward Day, considered himself the least known of all. He also thought for a very brief period that, breaking with tradition, the political manager of the Administration would not handle patronage. Day learned quickly enough that the nation's chief law-enforcement officer, by concept above partisan considerations, had taken over the patronage function. In his book, *My Appointed Rounds*, Day described how it worked:

"He passed on applications for the top appointive positions in the [Post Office] Department. He telephoned in person or sent word through his staff about certain appointments of postmasters and rural letter carriers. One afternoon I talked to him three times by telephone about a single rural letter carrier who was to be appointed in Mississippi in which Bobby was intensely interested. He took an occasional interest in appointments to intermediate jobs in the Department and in those who were going to sell or lease property to the Post Office.

"During the flight to Palm Beach on December 16, 1960, with the President-elect and his brother in the Kennedy family's plane, both Kennedys briefed me about my new job. Significantly, Bobby did most of the talking. When we had a major internal crisis in the Department in 1962, it was Bobby who came over from the Justice Department personally to straighten the problem out. When the controversy arose over continuation of a particular one of the Department's 25,000 separate leases, Bobby sent his personal representative to look into the matter. When too many members of the White House staff were giving orders to various people in the Post Office Department, it was decided that the liaison between the two offices should consist of one man. Bob Kennedy named that man.

"It should have been clear where the power was, but learning who doled out the plums of patronage was a hard lesson for some. The new Democratic State Chairman from a large and populous state visited President Kennedy at the White House. Emerging from the President's office he told a White House staff man that he would have the final say on Federal patronage in his state. The President had so assured him, he claimed.

" 'You've got it wrong,' the White House staffer said. 'All recommendations are to clear through the Attorney General.' "

New York Democrats had good reason to remember who was boss. Though Tammany leader Carmine De Sapio had thrown his weight behind Kennedy at a crucial time at the 1960 convention, Bobby felt that he had not come in early enough. Bobby also wanted full control of the party organization in what he considered the nation's politically most important state, something which De Sapio was not ready to surrender. White House displeasure was not enough to topple the leaders of New York's machine. Bobby's strategy therefore was to starve it of patronage and to stimulate the feuding that existed among the various factions in the New York Democratic party. New York's patronage list, submitted routinely to the Democratic National Committee chairman, John Bailey, was ignored—at Bobby's orders—and the jobs went to others. This shook the "regular" organization and destroyed its prestige. From that moment on, De Sapio was marked for extinction. Like a gangland satrap who falls out of favor, he saw his subordinates begin to edge away from him. Until Mayor Robert F. Wagner of New York was able to pull the pieces together, the Democratic organization was a shambles. In the end, it cost the Democrats the New York City mayoralty in 1965. It also cost Charles Buckley, the most loyal of the Kennedy men in the state, his seat in the House of Representatives.

Patronage had always been the soul of Democratic success in politics, and President Eisenhower's rejection of a patronage role was regarded as a major cause of defeat in the congressional elections and the legislative battles of his two terms. Even in matters where the right was on his side, Eisenhower refused to master the art. One such case concerned the federal judiciary.

Overworked and with a growing backlog of cases on the calendar, the federal courts badly needed new judges. But when the President proposed that thirty-five new seats be created on the federal bench, the Democrats, who controlled both houses of Congress, refused to give legislative sanction. The President might have taken the issue to the people, calling for public pressure to end a situation which was endangering the proper course of legal justice. He might have made political capital by showing that Democratic lust for power was blocking the appointment of judges, presumably above party politics. Instead, he "compromised" by offering the Democrats half the new judgeships. The party with a heart remained adamant.

The election of John F. Kennedy, however, gave the Democrats what they had been panting after: a chance to change the character and ideology of the judiciary by appointing judges who saw the law in New Frontier terms. In the words of Chairman Emanuel Celler of the House Judiciary Committee, who had been in the forefront of those denying Eisenhower's request, the Democrats had "gambled and won," a slightly chilling view of the manner in which the new judges would be appointed. The Justice Department, clearly, shared Representative Celler's attitude. Instead of the thirty-five judges Eisenhower had sought, Bobby asked for seventy-three and got them. Whatever lingering bipartisanship rested in the federal judiciary was thereby destroyed in one move. This does not mean that Bobby's nominations and Jack Kennedy's appointments to the federal bench were all political choices or in any way venal. They were, however, men of a particular bent who could be counted on to interpret the law in Bobby's way. True, some of his appointees, particularly those to Southern districts, turned on the Administration in such matters as civil rights. But the intent was there. Appearing before the House Judiciary Committee in March of 1961, Bobby was asked by Representative William M. McCulloch, an Ohio Republican, if he felt that the federal bench should reflect "a reasonable political balance." The Attorney General, with the sudden opacity of eye that is his response to questions he does not like, answered: "The best qualified individuals should be selected."

His tally at the end of the first year underscored Bobby's idea of what those qualifications consisted of. As President Kennedy's major judge-picker, he had named seventy-nine Democrats and two Republicans to fill the newly created judgeships, as well as vacancies on the federal bench. Even the most partisan Democrat could not

claim that there were only two Republicans whose legal background, integrity, and professional standing measured up to
Bobby's standards.

Though he was untried and suspected on Capitol Hill, Bobby was
called in by the President to lead the fight for packing the House
Rules Committee. To the average newspaper reader, this meant
little. But control of the committee was vital if the Kennedy program was to have any success in Congress. For the Rules Committee
not only decided what measures would reach the floor for a vote; it
also decided how they would be debated, and whether they could
be amended on the floor by the members. The Rules Committee
also served a useful political function. From time to time, legislation
whose controversial nature could embarrass Congressmen would be
proposed. To vote for or against these measures publicly involved
hazards which jeopardized individual chances for reelection. In
labor matters, for example, Congressmen indebted to the AFL-CIO
for money and campaign help knew that repeal of the Taft-Hartley
Act provision allowing the states the right to bar compulsory unionism was unpopular with the voters. They did not want to be compelled to go on record against repeal, thereby antagonizing the
labor hierarchy. In such instances, the Rules Committee saved them
by "bottling up" offending measures.

There might be vociferous criticism of the Rules Committee for its
"arbitrary" and "dictatorial" stand, but the rest of the House of
Representatives was spared reprisals. The members approved of
the system, however "antiquated" or "undemocratic" it might have
seemed to the White House. The New Frontier strategists knew, however, that they stood no chance of getting congressional approval
of their program without putting reluctant members on the spot.
This could be done only if the Rules Committee were packed by Congressmen loyal to the White House who could overrule the chairman and his usually docile fellow members. With some fanfare and
much reluctance, the party leadership set out to change the composi-
tion of the committee by increasing its size. The wise money, however, believed that President Kennedy would not succeed, and even
the powerful Speaker of the House, Sam Rayburn, confessed himself
defeated. When this was reported to the President, he asked Vice
President Johnson to make his own count. His thorough check, as he
told the President, showed that it couldn't be done.

Bobby, however, plunged into the fight. Working with the White
House congressional liaison man, Lawrence O'Brien, a plan of attack
was devised. The President was to get on the phone to twist the

arms of key members. Representative Frank Thompson, a faithful
Kennedy hewer of wood and hauler of water, was assigned to specific
men who might listen to his pleading. And the system which had
succeeded so well in the preconvention drive for delegates was
dusted off. The name of every antagonistic or doubtful member
was placed on a card. His strengths, weaknesses, prejudices, and peccadilloes were noted. Powerful politicians in his district, mindful
of Bobby's patronage-dispensing powers, were ordered to bring
pressure to bear on the recalcitrant. Careful charts were kept, and
as each new "convert" to the packing plan was made, those still holding out were informed. Deals were made with Republicans near-
sighted enough to relish the future discomfiture of their Democratic colleagues. And a skillful propaganda campaign began playing up the struggle, as it had the religious issue during the election.
To be against the packing of the Rules Committee was made
to seem like a manifestation of subservience to the "interests" and
their lobbyists on the Hill. To be for it was made to seem a mark of
liberal virtue.

By this means, Bobby was able to snatch a victory from what
had seemed like certain defeat. With the help of twenty-two Republican votes, the once-independent Rules Committee was made
an adjunct of the White House. The vote was 217 to 212. The margin was five votes, but a change of three would have reversed the
decision. It was, as everybody noted, hardly an overwhelming indication of Kennedy strength in the House. And there is reason to
believe that it hurt the New Frontier in the long run and led to the
paralysis of its legislative will during the three years that John F.
Kennedy was President. But the Rules Committee fight also established Bobby Kennedy as the real muscleman in the Kennedy team.
For there was no doubt on Capitol Hill that it was he, rather than
the President, who had engineered the triumph.

Untypically, Bobby did not gloat over his victory as he had over
the rout of Richard Nixon in the first television debate with Jack.
Instead, he paid a visit to Representative Howard Smith of Virginia,
the conservative chairman of the Rules Committee. Nothing was said
of the battle which had partially shorn the veteran of many legislative wars of his power. The contrast between the two was striking.
On the one hand, the quiet Virginia gentleman discussed his basic
philosophy and the restraints which he felt were necessary to slow
down the brash young politician from Massachusetts and his group
of liberal activists. Bobby listened and defended the revolutionary
change which he saw as mandatory in today's world. There was

really no communication between them. For where Judge Smith had made a career of persuasion and caution, Bobby saw government in terms of total power. "What is really needed," he said later in discussing the backing and filling which characterized Cabinet meetings, "is a minor dictator who listens to everybody involved, then decides, and says, 'Well, this is what has to be done now, and this is what you are going to do.' "

To Bobby's frequent annoyance, dictatorial rule was not John F. Kennedy's strong suit. He might occasionally lay down the law in anger, but for the most part, he tended to put off unpleasant decisions, to delegate power to subordinates, and to see all sides of a question until catastrophe forced his hand. This was particularly true in the foreign-policy field, where trouble is subterranean until the volcano erupts. President Kennedy might take sharp action in domestic matters, but where the issues of war and peace, of possible American involvement were concerned, he was deliberate of thought and hesitant of action. Bobby, who saw virtue in motion for its own sake, served an important function in stirring the Kennedy Administration to act.[1]

In those days, there were no "hawks" and no "doves" in the foreign-policy debate. The terms are misleading, but before the Cuban missile crisis, Bobby definitely belonged to the activist group in foreign policy. He was aware, as few others were, that on January 19, 1961, the day before the Inauguration, President Eisenhower had warned President-elect Kennedy that action was essential in a number of critical areas. Although there is no exact record of the conversation, its substance is known to those who later discussed it with General Eisenhower at Gettysburg. He told Kennedy then that he had refrained from moving in the Laotian crisis because he did not want to saddle a new President with a policy made by a predecessor. Nevertheless, something had to be done and immediately. Kennedy had been briefed by CIA during the campaign on an invasion of Cuba by refugee forces already training in Central America. He was urged to give this operation very close attention, and he was advised that hard decisions on the future of American aid to Vietnam could not be delayed.

There were other plague spots to which Eisenhower alluded. But not until April did the President turn his full attention to them, and

---

[1] Seeing a secretary reading a book—she had nothing else to do at the time—Bobby shouted: "Sack her." And once, as *Newsweek* reported, he spotted an aide waiting to use a phone. "Kennedy pitched a copy of his book, *The Enemy Within*, across the room. It caught the idler in the stomach, doubling him over. 'Get to work and start doing something useful,' " Bobby called out.

then only when his hand was forced. Once the focus of world interest had shifted, moreover, the President delegated responsibility to his brother. Foreign policy then became a major part of Bobby's duties. The catalyst, of course, was Cuba.

The Cuban bungle had begun on March 17, 1960, when President Eisenhower authorized the Central Intelligence Agency to organize, train, and equip a guerrilla force of Cuban refugees to overthrow the Castro regime. This was not a new departure for CIA. Six years before, it had done the same thing in Guatemala, toppling the Communist government of Jacobo Arbenz and removing a threat to the Caribbean and to American security. The job had been done efficiently and well. There were no hitches because the Eisenhower Administration had backed the CIA to the hilt. An invasion of Cuba could have been just as successful.

From the inception of the Cuban planning, it was understood by the President, by the CIA, and by the Joint Chiefs of Staff that any strategy developed by them must be sufficiently flexible to allow for the vagaries of time, tide, and politics, but must flatly preclude the possibility of defeat. An attempt that failed would immeasurably strengthen Fidel Castro's hand and damage the world position of the United States. With this in mind, secret orders made it clear to those involved that the measure of their efforts was not to be cost or size, but a preponderance of force that would make success absolutely certain. What had therefore begun to be planned as an exercise in infiltration and internal overthrow developed, at least on paper, into a full invasion. As such, it demanded the full logistical support of the United States Navy and adequate cover on the beaches from the United States Air Force. Without the two, even the rankest military amateur could foresee the result—tragedy for the invading forces.

With doom the product of failure, only a wholehearted commitment to the invasion could bring it off. But this was never forthcoming. President Kennedy allowed the CIA to go ahead, remarking to his advisers, "You know, I've reserved the right to stop this thing up to twenty-four hours before the landing. In the meantime, I'm trying to make some sense out of it. We'll just have to see." Bobby declared himself in favor of the invasion, characterizing it as a "worthwhile venture." The Cabinet was divided. Fearful that he would seem weak, Kennedy gave the plan a green light. But the continued attrition of Arthur Schlesinger and others who opposed the invasion led Kennedy to begin changing the ground rules, "successfully paring it down from a grandiose amphibious assault to a

mass infiltration," in Schlesinger's words. With a cynicism that may
have been more apparent than real, the President said, "If we have
to get rid of those eight hundred (Cubans), it is much better to
dump them in Cuba than in the United States, if that is where they
want to go." It was at this time that he made his decision to withhold direct American aid and the absolutely essential air cover—a
classic case of half measures halfheartedly brought to bear.

Those who had tried to dissuade the President from embarking
on the venture should have then spoken up bluntly and forcefully.
But they had Bobby to cope with. At a birthday party for Ethel
Kennedy, Bobby took Schlesinger aside and said, "I hear you don't
think much of this business." When Schlesinger gave his reasons,
Bobby answered, "You may be right or you may be wrong, but the
President has made his mind up. Don't push it any further. Now is
the time for everyone to help him all they can." This ended the
interminable debates, but it was too late. The White House, surrounded by the eyes and ears of the press, was a security sieve. More
than a week before the invasion, a New York *Times* correspondent
had enough of the basic elements of time, place, and strategy to
pass them on to Edward R. Murrow, chief of the United States Information Agency. Washington seethed with rumors, most of them
relatively accurate and many of them relayed to Castro's Intelligence
operatives.

If there was any further need for nails to seal the coffin of the
Cuban invasion, it was forthwith supplied. First, Schlesinger and a
contingent of advisers descended on the leaders of the Cuban Revolutionary Council, presumably the group which would act as a pro-
visional government, to impose political, social, and economic standards of such a socialist nature that they out-Castroed Castro.
(Schlesinger was impressed by the "social gains" made by the Communists in the first two years of their control of Cuba.) Secondly,
the President, at one of his press conferences, completely destroyed
any possibility of the uprising which was being planned to coincide
with the invasion. "There will not be, under any conditions, an
intervention in Cuba by the United States Armed Forces," he said.
"The basic issue is not between the United States and Cuba. It is between [*sic*] the Cubans themselves." This attempt to placate "world
opinion" was just what Castro wanted, and the President's words were
broadcast far and wide in Cuba—a warning that those who took
up arms against Castro's regime would be fighting alone.[2]

[2] Blame for the failure of the invasion has been skillfully laid on the doorstep of
the anti-Castro leaders and their predictions that the Cuban people would rise up
once they learned that an expeditionary force had landed on their shores. Since there

There was still hope for the invasion, however. But on the matter of logistical support and air cover, confusion was everywhere—with Secretary of State Dean Rusk citing his wartime experience as a colonel in the Burma-India theater to give authority to his negative advice. On the logistical side, the picture in the final days was grim.

The Navy's role was systematically reduced. At first, its vessels were to escort the invading forces, now increased to 1,400 men, but to lie off the coast of Cuba just beyond the three-mile limit. This was changed to a twelve-mile limit, then a twenty-mile limit. Pressure from Secretary of State Rusk finally led to cancellation of the escort entirely. Submarines, which were to have moved in close to survey the landing, were withdrawn from the operation. Chief of Naval Operations Arleigh Burke felt that the landing of Cubans might fail, but that once committed, the United States would have to follow through. He therefore ordered elements of the Atlantic Fleet and a battalion of Marines to move into position for instant supporting action. He was never given authority to use them.

Cuban pilots were given antiquated B-26 bombers, with no jet fighter cover. There is good reason to accept the report of David Wise and Thomas B. Ross, in *The Invisible Government*, that in "the final week before D-Day, the Joint Chiefs of Staff were, by and large, an unhappy group. Some of them were irritated by the continual changes in the invasion plan." These changes even included shifting the invasion site from the militarily acceptable Trinidad to the Bay of Pigs—a decision prompted by the White House rather than by the CIA, as popular myth has it.

On April 15, D-Day minus two, eight B-26s struck at Castro's air force, destroying some planes but leaving his rocket-armed converted training jets untouched. A second bombing raid was planned for the day of the invasion, but twenty-four hours before, the President cancelled it, cutting himself off from appeal by making Secretary Rusk his intermediary. Richard Bissell, the CIA's director of operations, was shaken. He and Deputy Director Charles Cabell immediately took the matter up with Rusk. They warned that if the order stood, the invasion would fail. Charles Murphy described their meeting in a *Fortune* analysis of the Bay of Pigs fiasco:

was no uprising, it is assumed that these leaders were overly optimistic and had misled President Kennedy. In the last stages of preparation, however, the White House sent an experienced officer to evaluate the Cuban exile fighting forces. His report, which has been cited as the cause for President Kennedy's misconception, is very clear on that point. "[The Brigade and battalion commanders] say they know their own people and believe that *after they have inflicted one serious defeat upon the opposition forces, the latter will melt away from Castro.*" (Emphasis added.) All the defeats were suffered by the invading forces.

"[General] Cabell was greatly worried over the vulnerability to air attack first of the ships and then of the troops on the beach. Rusk was not impressed. The ships, he suggested, could unload and retire to the open sea before daylight; as for the troops ashore being unduly inconvenienced by Castro's air, it had been his experience as a colonel in the Burma theater, he told the visitors, that air attack could be more of a nuisance than a danger. One fact he made absolutely clear: military considerations had overruled the political when the D-minus-two strike had been laid on; now political considerations were taking over. While they were talking, Rusk telephoned the President at Glen Ora to say that Cabell and Bissell were at his side, and that they were worried about the cancellation."

The President refused to withdraw the cancellation. Subsequently, General Cabell pleaded for cover from planes of the carrier U.S.S. *Boxer*, lying some fifty miles off the Cuban coast, to protect the invasion fleet once it had withdrawn. He pointed out that sixteen B-26s, based in Central America, could not possibly cover the supply ships. President Kennedy still refused. As a result, Castro's planes, forewarned, were able to move in for the kill, sinking two supply ships and driving off two others. Castro's tanks and artillery were able to move with impunity, and combining their attack with Castro's air, his troops successfully clobbered the invaders. Short on ammunition and exposed to land and air attack, the invaders fought bravely. They were even able to seize an air strip. But they could not stand up to the pounding, and their morale was hurt by the refusal of aid from American forces.

There was still a chance, but the President failed to take it. On the evening of the invasion's second day, the President and Mrs. Kennedy were entertaining members of Congress at a white-tie ball. He was interrupted by word that Bissell had an urgent message. Defense Secretary Robert McNamara, Secretary Rusk, Admiral Burke and General Lemnitzer were summoned, and the great debate began. Bissell said that only the use of jets from the U.S.S. *Boxer* could prevent calamity. Rusk battled against this, arguing that the President had pledged himself not to use American forces. Finally, in the early-morning hours, it was decided that the United States jets would be permitted to support the supply ships for one hour—a rather curious "compromise"—from 6:30 A.M. to 7:30 A.M. But when the B-26s arrived a little early, the jets remained on the deck of the carrier, bound by the strict but meaningless time limits of the Presidential directive.

Throughout this bitter session, at which the lives of 1,400 men and the future of Cuba were lost for fear of "world opinion," Bobby was at the President's side. ("He needs me," Bobby had said to his wife when he excused himself from the diplomatic banquet.) By the time the advisers had left, the United States had been stingingly defeated and Fidel Castro had emerged cock of the walk. At this point, a red-eyed Bobby put his arm around the President and said, in a remark that typified the Kennedy attitude toward life, "They can't do this to *you*—those black-bearded Commies can't do this to *you!*"

From that black night of indecision henceforth, Bobby Kennedy became a major force in the making of United States foreign policy. Though the President took the blame for the defeat, there were immediate efforts to pass the buck. Walter Lippmann attempted to pass it to Schlesinger and Rusk, for not having tied the hands of the military and the CIA completely. While President Kennedy appealed to General Eisenhower and other Republican leaders for bipartisanship, which they generously agreed to, Administration sources inspired newspaper stories that the real culprit was the former President. Simultaneously, Bobby made the rounds to silence any of the participants who, while the wound was open, might have confided the facts to the American people. When Chester Bowles, still floundering in the State Department, announced to the newspapers that he had opposed the invasion from the start, he was confronted by Bobby, who poked a finger in his chest and said roughly: "So you advised against this operation. Well, as of now you were all for it."

The collapse of the Cuban invasion left a train of anger and disillusionment among some. Most Americans, however, tended to agree with General Eisenhower. His first reaction had been voiced privately. "A second lieutenant could have handled it better," he said. But mindful that the blow to America's prestige had been sufficient, he said publicly, "Don't go back and rake over the ashes, but see what we can do better in the future. To say you're going into methods and practices of the Administration—I would say the last thing you want is to have a full investigation and lay all this out on the record."

Both the President and Bobby were mindful of the political dynamite that full debate of the Bay of Pigs invasion might have set off. The Cuban fiasco, moreover, had become traumatic in their minds. Each in his own way felt the guilt of the lost men and the missed opportunity. The events during the Cuban adventure had also marked a turning point in John F. Kennedy's Presidential career. In the course of a few days, he had discovered that life in the White House would not be roses, roses, all the way. He began looking about him with suspicion, arguing that he had been misinformed by the Pentagon, the CIA, the Cuban exiles, or almost everyone involved. It was necessary, therefore, to satisfy himself by investigating the causes of the terrible failure. A commission of respected and eminent citizens, headed perhaps by a retired Supreme Court justice, would have guaranteed an impartial and painstaking inquiry. Instead, Kennedy named General Maxwell Taylor, long at odds with the Joint Chiefs of Staff, and Bobby to head the group. The other two members were CIA director Allen Dulles and Admiral Burke.

All four therefore had a stake in the inquiry. The results of the group's work could hardly be considered unbiased, and it was clear from the start that there would be continual conflict among the participants, no matter how scrupulously they hid their disagreements from the public. It was also clear that Bobby Kennedy would dominate the proceedings, first as the President's stand-in and secondly because he would work harder than the others. There were enough survivors left to give a cogent story of the invasion attempt, and there were the dubious records of the high-level participants. When the first of the Cuban witnesses appeared, it was Bobby who led the questioning. Later, Roberto San Román would describe his appearance before the Taylor-Kennedy board to Haynes Johnson, author of *The Bay of Pigs:*

"They wanted to know," he said, "the reaction of the enemy, how soon they reacted with tanks and artillery. How much did they fire and how much did we fire? How many did we kill and how many men of ours died? The reaction of the population—and this was a question of Mr. [Robert] Kennedy—he wanted to know the reaction of the people. They wanted to know if we thought we could have won the battle. I told them we needed only three or four jet planes, that's what we needed to win. Three or four jet planes that could knock out the little air force that Castro had at that time. I told them I didn't know they could do this to us. Our troops were so good —because they involved people from every class, rich and poor, rebels and soldiers and everybody together against the common enemy—and they didn't answer these questions."

But far more telling than the questions and answers, and the little pins on the map which would aid future historians in following the ebb and flow of the battle, was a small episode that took place the night after Roberto San Román had testified. He and other

Cuban witnesses were invited to a party given for them by the Robert Kennedys at Hickory Hill, their Virginia estate. "I thought they took us there to forget about the invasion," San Román told Haynes Johnson, "but [Ethel Kennedy] was the one that talked about it. She kept asking me questions and putting Mr. Kennedy in a very rough situation. She said that she had read about the invasion and she asked me if it was true that with some planes we could have won. I told her yes and explained. I thought they were going to avoid this point, but that was the point that she talked about first. She is a wonderful woman."

In the weeks that followed, most of Bobby's time was taken up with the investigation and with the problems raised by the failure of the invasion. The President summoned him to meetings of the National Security Council, and he sat with lowered eyes while the entire structure of the complex of organizations dealing with the national security was discussed. From time to time, he asked a question. Sometimes the President was not present, and Bobby controlled the meeting. New policies were demanded on all phases of America's world involvement. When Chester Bowles presented a paper to the council outlining his approach to the Cuban problem, Bobby sat quietly in a corner as the unimaginative clichés rolled off Bowles' practiced tongue. When the last page had been read, Bobby said, "This is worthless. What can we do about Cuba? This doesn't tell us." Then, for five minutes, he took the Bowles report to pieces, demonstrating its inanities and its paucity of concrete suggestion. Bobby's criticisms may have been valid, but everyone in the room knew that he was also punishing Bowles for his remarks to the press dissociating himself from the Bay of Pigs tragedy. Finally, the President broke in, relieving the embarrassment of the council.

No report of the Taylor-Kennedy group has ever been made public, nor were its findings released. A secret report was prepared by Roger Hilsman of the State Department, but on Bobby's insistence it was suppressed. Instead, there were leaks to the press and stories based on gossip, conjecture, and dubious evidence. Bobby would say, "Victory was never close." But there were many who disputed this. Everyone was to blame and no one was to blame. This was the official consensus. Yet Bobby plowed ahead—mornings at Bay of Pigs business, afternoons with the President, evenings at his Justice Department desk to receive reports from his deputies and to make decisions they lacked the authority to make. In the executive branch, functions were reshuffled, with McGeorge Bundy assuming responsibility in the White House hierarchy for national security matters. Taylor joined the staff as a special consultant and then moved up to the post of Chairman of the Joint Chiefs of Staff. Bowles was bundled off to India and an ambassadorship. But as future events would prove, it was all wasted motion.

Two years later Bobby returned to the subject of culpability in the Bay of Pigs. To David Kraslow, correspondent for the Knight newspapers, he gratuitously offered a new version which stirred up controversy once more. Lack of air cover for the invaders had not been the cause of the defeat, he said. The Central Intelligence Agency and the Joint Chiefs had erred. The invaders, he added, "got all the air cover the plan called for." It was, he said, "just a bad plan." Then Bobby made one disclosure that raised eyebrows. "The President received one call informing him that the first raid was causing us serious problems at the U.N. and elsewhere," he said. "It was suggested that the second raid be postponed. . . . The President said that if those who had the responsibility for the plan had strong objections to postponing the raid, they should let them be known. No strong objections were registered." (This must have been news to General Cabell, Russell, and the Joint Chiefs.)

More controversial was Bobby's flat statement to Kraslow that no Americans were killed in the Bay of Pigs adventure. In point of fact, four Americans had been killed. Their widows and families had tried vainly to learn of their whereabouts from a dummy corporation, set up by the CIA, which had hired them to fly planes for the invading forces. The State Department, the Pentagon, and the CIA had denied knowledge of the dead men's activities or the manner in which they had met their death. The White House had written that "neither the CIA nor any other government agency possesses the slightest pertinent information on your disappearance." When Senator Everett Dirksen, in March of 1963, laid the facts before the public, the White House panicked but stuck to its denials. It could not expunge from the record, however, Bobby's January 20, 1963 statement that "it was made absolutely clear that under no condition, no condition whatsoever, would Americans be used in the invasion." Nor did the White House explain why, if the Administration had not the "slightest" information, it was paying pensions to the widows of the dead fliers.

On March 6, President Kennedy was asked flatly by a reporter at his press conference, "Can you say whether the four Americans who died in the Bay of Pigs invasion were employees of the government or the CIA?" The President hemmed and hawed, then said: "The flight that cost them their lives was a volunteer flight, and that while because of the nature of their work it has not been a matter of public record, as it might be in the case of soldiers or sailors, I can say that they were serving their country." He did not say why, if CIA agents took part in the invasion, it was wrong for better equipped troops to do likewise.

All of this came later. During the Bay of Pigs inquiry, Bobby's power within the government grew. His brother had offered him the post of CIA director, but he turned it down. It would have shuffled Bobby off into one corner of the Intelligence community. By refusing, he remained what David Wise and Thomas B. Ross called "the untitled overseer of the Intelligence apparatus in the Kennedy Administration." When Allen Dulles was replaced as director of the CIA by John McCone, Bobby's grip on the organization increased. For McCone, an able and dedicated American, lacked the aggressiveness necessary to cope with so politicized an Administration. What improvements in its structure derived from his stewardship, or how involved Bobby was, is a matter for conjecture. The CIA does not issue reports, and its officers do not make their observations public. Bobby did accomplish one thing. Driving to and from work in the morning from Hickory Hill, he passed large green-and-white signs pointing the way to the CIA's new headquarters near Langley, Virginia. The incongruity of these road guides to what was presumably the nation's most hush-hush agency must have struck him because, by his order, the signs disappeared.

The CIA's tarnished image, however, needed more of a polish-up job than that. A television show based on the agency's exploit was quietly proposed to NBC, which then dutifully sought the Attorney General's views. He officially approved and assigned to the show Reino Hayhanen, a former Soviet spy who had defected to the United States when his boss in New York, the *apparatchik* Colonel Rudolph Abel, ordered him back to the Soviet Union. It was Hayhanen's confession to the CIA which led to the arrest and conviction of the Soviet spy master. Hayhanen was therefore marked for extinction by the KGB, the Soviet espionage arm, which does not like to see its operatives become informers to the "enemy." Following the Abel trial, Hayhanen was given a suitable cover and put under the twenty-four-hour protection of two CIA bodyguards. Bobby nevertheless allowed an NBC camera crew to take pictures of Abel in Atlanta Penitentiary for a television presentation, an unprecedented act. On the CIA program, Hayhanen's face was kept dark, but he was visible to anyone in the television studio, thus breaking his cover. Between the filming of the program and its showing, however, the protection of the darkened face became academic. Hayhanen was mysteriously killed in an automobile "accident" on one of the major Eastern turnpikes. The public was not informed of this, and neither was the show's narrator, David Brinkley; but this made no less gruesome his concluding plea to other agents, urging them to defect and offering them "guaranteed security, physical and financial."

The shadow of Colonel Abel touched Bobby Kennedy again, though tangentially, in June 1962. A group of exiles had come to him for aid in arranging for the release of the Bay of Pigs prisoners, still being held by Fidel Castro. Bobby sent the exiles to James Donovan, a New York attorney who had negotiated the trade of Colonel Abel for Francis Gary Powers, a U-2 pilot shot down over Russia, and Frederic Pryor, a Yale student arrested by the East German Communist regime. Donovan agreed to become counsel for the exile group—the Cuban Families Committee for Liberation of Prisoners of War, Inc., a tax-exempt organization working under the tutelage of the CIA. In August 1962, he was in Havana, dickering with Castro and offering drugs and baby food for the prisoners. The Cuban dictator agreed, but insisted also on the $2,900,000 he had already been promised for the prior release of sixty prisoners.

Back in New York, Donovan and the CIA, working separately, began getting the drugs and baby food as contributions from the producers of these necessities. In October, Donovan was back in Havana, making final arrangements as $2,000,000 worth of drugs were being shipped to Idlewild Airport for air-cargo flight to Cuba. Though Donovan claimed to be acting as a private citizen, the ransom of the prisoners was a Bobby Kennedy operation. During the missile crisis, however, the transfer of drugs for men was put on ice. When, after the November 1962 election, the negotiations were resumed, the drug companies had second thoughts. They were under attack by the federal government and they wanted no part of what might be interpreted by the public as subservience to Communist Cuba. Before they delivered the drugs, they told the Attorney General, they wanted a public acknowledgment by the government that they were acting in the national interest.

Bobby, who had repeatedly voiced concern for the fate of the Cuban freedom fighters abandoned at the Bay of Pigs, worked fast. He summoned representatives of the Internal Revenue Service, the State Department, and the CIA to meet with Deputy Attorney General Nicholas Katzenbach. They were presented with Castro's bill for the exchange: $53,000,000 in drugs. Wholesale, it was reckoned, this would come to $17,000,000. A memorandum was prepared for Robert Kennedy which noted that the drug companies would enjoy a tax "windfall" if their contributions were classified as charitable. The drug companies would not act, however, unless they had approval of the Kennedy Administration and were guaranteed "maximum protection from legislative and public criticism in two particular directions: (a) charges of pro-Communism and (b) criticism for inferences drawn from any price mark-up exposed in the transaction."

Shuttling between the White House and the Justice Department, Bobby made the arrangements for the exchange. The American Red Cross agreed to take the drugs as charitable contributions. He informed the drug companies and the nation that the United States had a responsibility for the welfare of the prisoners. The baby-food manufacturers were given similar reassurances. An Assistant Attorney General was assigned full-time to the project, ending the fiction that the exchange was a private matter between a group of exiles and Fidel Castro. Air carriers were told that transportation costs would be considered charitable contributions. The CIA, the Air Force, the Immigration and Naturalization Service, and the Commerce Department were mobilized. Everything was going according to plan. But there was one tremendous hitch. Castro was still demanding $2,900,000 in cash.

At 5:00 A.M., December 24, one of the negotiators called Bobby from Miami. Unless the money was raised by 3:00 P.M. of that day, all bets would be off, he said. Bobby promised to get the money, and he did—from Richard Cardinal Cushing, a Kennedy family friend, who pledged $1,000,000, and from General Lucius Clay, who borrowed $1,900,000 and then solicited contributions from major American corporations. On Christmas Eve, 1962, the prisoners were all on American soil. By main force, Bobby Kennedy had rescued them. It had been simple blackmail on Castro's part, but on that day no one reckoned it so.

The ransom of prisoners was but a side excursion for Bobby. After the Bay of Pigs, Arthur Schlesinger has written, "the President wanted [him] at every crucial meeting." Bobby put it another way: "Obviously it would have been better if it hadn't happened, but it would have been disastrous if [the President] hadn't learned the lesson of Cuba." It had taught John F. Kennedy, Bobby reasoned, two things: (1) not to take anything for granted, and (2) "simply because a man is supposed to be an expert in his field it will not qualify him to the President." Ironically, the President turned to Bobby because he considered him a "hard liner." "The men at the State Department," said biographer Hugh Sidey, reflecting this attitude, "spent their lives trying to solve problems without fighting. It was against the nature of the department personnel to want to use or show force." Rejecting the diplomatic arm of his own government, rather than making it effective, the President set up an informal cold-war council made up of General Taylor, Edward R. Murrow of the United States Information Agency, and Robert Kennedy. They met frequently, though at irregular intervals, with the President.

Some of their ideas were of considerable value. General Taylor was convinced that American troops would be compelled by the Communist strategy of brushfire wars and guerrilla tactics to develop new techniques of defense and offense. The mechanized techniques of World War II were entirely unsuited to the jungle terrain of Southeast Asia. The answer to Mao Tse-tung and Ho Chi Minh, he argued, was "counterinsurgency"—a fancy word for the application of military muscle against Communist hit-and-run forces. Bobby seized on this idea and pushed it hard. "Counterinsurgency" became the thing in the United States armed forces, glorified in the Green Berets. That much of what was now being advocated came almost directly from the Marine Corps is not the point. More important was the recognition that Army combat forces needed toughening. If Bobby reveled in the new form of the "strenuous life," defense-minded members of the executive branch did not mind.

But for a time, "counterinsurgency" became a substitute for long hikes, touch football, and immersion in the Hickory Hill swimming pool. The word went out that State Department and Pentagon civilians were to be "encouraged" to take counterinsurgency training whenever possible. To underscore his support of this, Bobby told a North Carolina Cold War Council gathering in May 1963 that "by next month, some fifty-seven thousand government officials will have completed counterinsurgency courses." The Justice Department dutifully sent out copies of the Attorney General's speech. A check showed that Washington officialdom was not that anxious to learn guerrilla tactics. The public-relations officers of both the Justice and State Departments had no idea where the "fifty-seven thousand" figure came from. Dr. Myron L. Koenig, dean of the Foreign Service's School of Foreign Affairs, which handled the counterinsurgency courses, said that since the inception of the program only 400 to 500 people in all had participated. Each increment had been made up of some sixty students—ambassadors, directors of foreign-aid missions, high-level foreign service officers, and others in that general category. Dr. Koenig was puzzled by the Attorney General's figure but could find no way to substantiate anything that was remotely close to that.

Bobby's own taste of counterinsurgency training was somewhat more disconcerting. Visiting the Army's Tropical Warfare School in Panama, he was ushered to a front seat. The school had developed a special technique for giving important guests a feel of the curriculum: it handed them a live boa constrictor. When Bobby was offered a wriggling armful of snake, he leaped to the seat of his chair yelling: "Get it away. I don't want it. I hate snakes."

But training American troops in the kind of warfare their great-grandfathers had used against the Indians was the total of his contribution. Speaking at Fordham University in November 1961, he had said: "To muddle through a crisis was once a democratic people's boast. That self-indulgent day is gone. There is no time now for confusion and no place for perplexities." These were brave words, and they promised much. But the Administration record did not sustain them. Three months earlier, the Communist regime in East Germany had built a wall across Berlin, with no response other than anguished cries from the democracies. Less than a month later, the Kremlin announced that it was breaking a three-year moratorium on nuclear testing. At the United Nations, the Soviets were busily sowing malice and confusion, demanding a "troika" to give the Secretariat's leadership a three-way stretch and to make it more responsive to Soviet pressure.

With more energy than know-how, Bobby held the fort during this troubled period as a behind-the-scenes Secretary of State. When Rafael Trujillo, dictator of the Dominican Republic, was assassinated, President Kennedy was in Paris conferring with President de Gaulle. The murder was not as unexpected as the general public believed, and there was behind-the-hand talk in official Washington that the CIA had been more than an interested bystander. Immediate and decisive action was necessary to forestall a Castro-Communist takeover and, conversely, to prevent any attempt by the *Trujillistas* to retain power. Either would have precipitated a bloody civil war. There was also the need to seize those Trujillo dictatorship's records which involved men high in American public life who had received substantial sums of money from the Dominican treasury. A fleet of United States battleships, bearing contingents of Marines, went into patrol duty off the Dominican coast, and the

crisis was averted. In the feverish meetings in State Department conference rooms, Bobby and Allen Dulles controlled the decisions.

The Attorney General demonstrated a willingness to speak out
where the State Department pussyfooted, and he did so on a "Meet
the Press" appearance during the Berlin crisis. "The President and
the free world are willing to use nuclear weapons to preserve our
position in Berlin," he said, "to insure that the people of Berlin remain free and that we have access to that city." (He later retreated
agilely from this position, attacking those who held it as war-
mongers.)

"Especially in foreign politics," Schlesinger said, "if a good idea
was going down for the third time in the bureaucratic sea, one
turned more and more to Bobby to rescue it." The rescue was real
enough, though there were some who questioned the *cui bono* of its
merits. As Bobby ventured deeper and deeper into foreign policy, it
became apparent to him and to the President that the world they
were dealing with had become less an abstraction and something to
know at first hand. This, and the President's need for on-the-spot
reports from someone he trusted, launched Bobby on his series of
world trips.

Bobby saw these trips as a means of showing the world that the
"United States is not, as described by the Communists, run by a
tired and old government." In February 1962, after his trip to Japan
and Indonesia, he told Schlesinger that America's contact with the
intellectuals and young people of Asia must be made by stressing
the "progressive" nature of this country. "I kept asking myself," he
said, "what a conservative could possibly say to these people. I can
talk all the time about social welfare and trade unions and reform.
But what in the world could Barry Goldwater say?" But he also
found serious sins in American policy and what he described as this
country's association with "tyrannical and unpopular regimes that
had no following and no future." Bobby was referring, of course, to
"reactionary" regimes. Presumably Indonesia's dictatorship had
both a following and a future.

In Japan, the thirty-six-year-old Attorney General undeniably
succeeded in conveying an impression of youth and vigor. But in a
country seeking to maintain its equilibrium against the twin forces
of Communoid radicalism and technological advance, Bobby's performance contributed little. At Tokyo's Waseda University, he invited a twenty-one-year-old member of the extreme leftist Zenga-
kuren student movement up to the podium with him—the better
to receive a raucous and sustained heckling from the young man.

Bobby even held the microphone for his antagonist, winning the cheers of the audience but losing face—and lending his prestige to an enemy of the United States. The same day, Bobby made the rounds of working-class bars in the Ginza district, singing "When Irish Eyes are Smiling" in his monotone and drinking *sake* in place of his usual glass of milk. This drew applause at the moment, but the Japanese government was not ecstatic. And in Washington, even the ultra-liberal Representative John Lindsay wrote to Secretary Rusk wondering whether it was necessary "for you and your office to be burdened or embarrassed by free-wheeling foreign missions on the part of highly placed amateurs who do not have the background, training, language ability, or capability."

There were, however, sacrifices that Bobby had to make. Given to a diet of steak and chocolate malteds, he was forced to eat foods that left him queasy. To a group of foreign correspondents in Tokyo, he confessed his difficulties. "I had seaweed for breakfast yesterday. To tell you the honest to goodness truth, it didn't taste too bad. When I went to Central Asia with Justice Douglas in 1955, they brought in a goat, very dead, plucked out its eyes, and served them to us. Justice Douglas turned to me and said, 'For the sake of America, Bobby, make like it's an oyster!' So things have gone up since then."

But, as Lindsay had noted, background and capability were certainly lacking when Bobby Kennedy moved on to Indonesia for conferences with President Sukarno, the sex-obsessed, pro-Communist and megalomaniacal despot. Even in the liberal confines of the White House, Sukarno was recognized for what he was, an adventurer who ignored the wellbeing of his people, made no effort to develop his country's vast resources, and perpetuated himself in office by an aggressive foreign policy. Here, presumably, was one of the "tyrannical rulers" that Bobby should have inveighed against. But he had journeyed to Djakarta, under cover of a world tour, specifically to deliver to Sukarno the people and territory of West New Guinea, to which Indonesia had no conceivable claim except Sukarno's desires. The United States, in the postwar years, had engineered the expulsion of the Dutch from Indonesia and the delivery of this vast archipelago to Sukarno, a project conducted to the great financial profit of several New/Fair Dealing lobbyists in Washington who had been retained by the dictator-to-be. Now Sukarno wanted more.

Sukarno's claim on West New Guinea had been rejected out of hand by the Dutch, who saw no reason to appease an imperialist

Indonesia. The Australians were even more opposed. They remembered General Douglas MacArthur's words. "The battle for Australia will be fought in New Guinea." And they were aware that Indonesian occupation would breach their defensive shield. The aborigines of West New Guinea had no desire to be absorbed by the Indonesians. Even the State Department was opposed. But when Sukarno began to rattle his saber, the foreign policy team of Kennedy & Kennedy decided to deliver the territory to him—as a gesture of American friendship. It was Bobby's assignment to negotiate the surrender and withdrawal of the Dutch, who administered West New Guinea.

The first step was to remove Australian objections. The Australians were and are America's most steadfast allies, but, in words that shocked diplomatic discourse, they were bluntly informed that the United States would not come to Australia's defense if Sukarno should attack them over the issue of West New Guinea's future. The second step was to get Sukarno to agree to go through the motions of "negotiating" with the Dutch, with assurances that they would be brought into line. Finally, according to the Kennedy plan, the Dutch would be sandbagged into an agreement to withdraw.

In Indonesia, Bobby made the speeches to student groups—now a standard part of his travels—debating the leftists who heckled him and making jokes. In the course of one of these exchanges, he revised American history by accepting a student's remark that an Indonesian seizure of West New Guinea would be no different from the United States annexation of Texas. The American role in Texas, he said, was not "a very bright spot in our history, not one to be proud of." He insisted that neither he nor the United States was taking sides in the West New Guniea dispute—and then he quietly delivered a letter from the President to Sukarno. Graciously, the Indonesian dictator agreed to go through the motions of negotiating.

From Indonesia, Bobby moved on to the Netherlands. In his public statements, he hinted that the United States favored a plebiscite of the Papuans, natives of West New Guinea, and added that Sukarno would not oppose such a settlement. He also said that Indonesia's leaders would like a peaceful solution. But he refused to say what the Kennedy Administration would do if the Dutch were attacked by the Indonesians. In his conferences with Dutch officials, he reportedly asked them merely to sit down at the conference table with Sukarno. The Netherlands government was fully aware that this was simply the prelude to an American-directed surrender, but eventually they were forced to capitulate. The "solution" turned out to be all in Sukarno's favor: an eight-month transition period under the United Nations, then Indonesian annexation, to be followed in 1969 by a plebiscite to determine what the Papuans wanted. The last point was universally recognized as a sop to public opinion; once the Indonesians had taken control, no one expected them to relinquish it. (Schlesinger characterized the settlement as "a shameful legalization of Indonesia expansionism.")

Between Djakarta and The Hague, Robert Kennedy stopped off in Rome for an audience with the Pope. On Washington's Birthday, while snowflakes flurried, he visited the Berlin Wall, which he called "the most shameful object of mankind." To the thousands who turned out to hear him, he said: "An attack on West Berlin is an attack on Chicago, New York, Paris, and London." But in Bonn he took it all back by adding that the United States was "not willing to go to war for German unity."

Back in Washington, the Attorney General put down his thoughts on the trip in his second book, *Just Friends and Brave Enemies*. It contributed little to the nation's knowledge of the sad new world the cold war had created. Its concluding chapter, taking its title from the Declaration of Independence, "Let Facts Be Submitted to a Candid World," summarized Bobby's findings on the "appalling" lack of information current abroad about the United States, as well as the rampant misinformation which the leaders of the world and their subjects held to be gospel truth. Bobby's information about the world in which he voyaged sometimes matched the misinformation he found. In Paris after a trip to the Ivory Coast where he represented the President at an Independence Day celebration, Bobby was discussing his experiences with an American correspondent. When the name of Kwame Nkrumah, president of Ghana, came up, Bobby said flatly, "We're against him."

"No, Bob, we're not," said the correspondent. "Why, your brother had him on a state visit to Washington."

"Well, I think we're against him, but I'll check," said Bobby. He went to his hotel room, returning in about ten minutes, and said: "Yeah, you're right. I looked him up on the cards and we're for him."

"No one is prepared to counter the Communists' arguments with facts and figures," wrote Bobby, forgetting that this was precisely the job that Edward R. Murrow, his associate in cold-war matters, was supposed to be doing. "No one raises questions or stresses opposite opinions or positions. . . . We are victims of a smart, articulate, well-organized minority which has kept us continually on the

defensive. . . . If we are not ourselves imaginative, tough, dedicated, willing, and self-sacrificing, the struggle with the enemy will
not be won by them, but lost by us." This was the rhetoric of debate,
all too often employed to discredit those who argued that the Communists must be faced down in every field, that the apologetics of the
State Department and successive Administrations simply played into
the hands of Moscow and Peking. His own ideas for bridging the information gap added little. For the most part, they merely rang
changes on the theme that the cold war would be won by educational
and cultural exchanges between countries. He also lectured those
members of Congress who travel about the world without adequate
knowledge of American history. He praised the Peace Corps but retreated into cliché again by warning that its efforts would be useless
unless the country "live[d] up to our ideals within the United
States . . . by solving the problems of racial discrimination, chronic
unemployment, and crime."

None of these problems had approached solution, however, when
the United States was confronted by the gravest threat to its survival
in all the years of its history. It was a threat, moreover, compounded
by an Administration which resolutely blinded itself to all the facts
and then heaped vituperation on those whose eyes remained open.
The newspapers would call it the "Cuban missile crisis," but in fact
it was a failure of nerve and a shortage of the very knowledge which
Bobby Kennedy had urged on his countrymen in *Just Friends
and Brave Enemies*. To make matters worse, men skilled in lan-
gauge substituted semantics for good sense in a vast exercise of self-
deception. [3]

This is the story.

Early in 1962, there were incontrovertible reports that a great
military build-up, financed, equipped, and manned by the Soviet
Union, was taking place. This was reported in the press but played
down by Administration sources as politically inspired or the work
of Cuban exiles who were attempting to stampede the United States
into a war to liberate their homeland. (General Thomas D. White,
former Air Force Chief of Staff and an expert in military Intelligence, subsequently wrote that "long before October there was
enough information available in the daily press alone to have led
to a military conclusion that the Russians in Cuba were posing a

---

[3] Let it be noted here that this account of the missile crisis is not based on hindsight. In its early stages, while denials poured from the White House, both the Intelligence community and those members of the press not inextricably tied to the
Kennedy Administration were aware of the essential facts.

serious threat to the States.") By August, the word was out in Washington that thousands of Soviet troops, with matériel brought in at a rate of some thirty ships a month since the beginning of the year, were at work building missile launchers for weapons already on the island.

Between August 31 and October 12, 1962, Senator Kenneth Keating, a respected New York Republican, made ten speeches on the Senate floor and fourteen public statements, warning the country of the developments in Cuba. He was merely saying publicly what the American Intelligence community, his major source, was muttering as loudly as Defense Secretary McNamara would permit it. White House press secretary Pierre Salinger, however, was volubly criticizing the television networks for giving time to Keating and others to express their worries. The reports of newly arrived Cuban refugees that they had seen missiles, as early as mid-July, were laughed away, and it was officially said that they had mistaken "sewer pipes" for more lethal objects. At the White House, the President's aides systematically ignored the mountains of evidence and the clouds of witnesses, thereby lulling the President into a false sense of security. The State Department contributed its mite by assuring all and sundry that the Kremlin would never embark on such a rash venture. But concern mounted, and Senator Keating's speeches began to have their effect.

At this point, semantics entered the controversy. The President admitted the arms build-up in Cuba but insisted that it was defensive, not offensive. No explanation was offered as to the "defensive" nature of Soviet heavy bombers being uncrated in Cuba, and efforts at eliciting a definition of the difference between an offensive and defensive weapon were met with anger or ridicule. Those in the know were assured that any missile emplacements would have been discovered by the U-2 reconnaissance flights over Cuba, but they were not told that these flights were bypassing the important areas in order to avoid batteries of surface-to-air missiles installed by the Soviets before emplacing the intermediate missiles. Early in October, when U-2 flights were ordered over the key areas, they were inexplicably canceled. (After the crisis, the White House "explained" this by saying that hurricane Ella had prevented air surveillance. The fact was that Ella did not form until October 16.) In line with this downplay of the threat, the New York *Times* informed its readers on October 14 that "extremely thorough" aerial reconnaissance showed that Castro had gotten "not even a water pistol."

One reason for the stubborn refusal of the White House to believe what was so apparent can be found in Bobby Kennedy's relationship with George Bolshakov, then of the Soviet embassy in Washington. It was Bobby's belief that he was "using" Bolshakov to funnel Administration attitudes to the Kremlin. The exact opposite was true. Very early in October, Bolshakov, who had just returned from Moscow, gave Bobby a "message" for the President from Nikita Khrushchev. The Soviet dictator particularly wanted Kennedy to understand that the weapons he was sending to Cuba were only for defensive use.

When a U-2 reconnaissance flight returned with photographic evidence of the Soviet missile build-up in Cuba, the Administration's spokesmen were still vociferously denying facts known all over Washington. Since most of the Paul Reveres had been Republicans, the final admission at the White House created political as well as military problems. Almost twelve hours after confirmation by the Pentagon and the CIA of the bad missile news, McGeorge Bundy, the White House man on national security matters, reported the facts to the President. Writing of that stark moment, James Daniel and John G. Hubbell, in *Strike in the West,* suggest John F. Kennedy's state of mind:

"As he watched the bespectacled 'Mac' Bundy leave, the President might have had much cause for reflection, some of it bitter. His Intelligence forces seemed to have been on the job gathering evidence. But somewhere along the line, in the evaluation, interpretation, or response, there had been a serious lapse. It was subsequently calculated that the Russians could hardly have devoted less than a year to their Cuban missile project . . . all without rippling Washington's serene confidence that Nikita Khrushchev would never do such a thing."

It was no fault of United States Intelligence. The State Department had sufficient information to pinpoint the forty-seven locations in Cuba where Soviet "technicians" were at work on missile sites, plus an abundance of corroboration. Why this never reached the President is one of the bureaucratic mysteries of Washington.

This time, however, the President could not lay the blame on any scapegoats. After the Bay of Pigs fiasco, he had turned over the management and coordination of all Intelligence activities to Bobby. He had accepted Bobby's evaluation of Bolshakov's "information." The President himself had made political capital of Republican warnings by ridiculing them at his press conferences, and his comments had been taken up by New Frontier spokesmen. Among all those at the White House, he was perhaps the only one who recognized that there was no hook on which to hang the blame, even if he were ready to sacrifice Bobby. Bobby was his man, his brother, his assistant President. They were in it together. And together they would have to make an overwhelming decision: to withhold or not to withhold the fateful news from the American people until after the congressional election, just two weeks off.

He and Bobby decided to call together what became known as the Executive Committee—in later newspaper shorthand, ExComm—an ad hoc group made up of the Secretaries of State and Defense, sub-Cabinet-rank officers, the Joint Chiefs of Staff, the CIA, ambassadors, and several "outsiders." (The two leading outsiders were former Secretary of State Dean Acheson and former Defense Secretary Robert Lovett.) Also included was Vice President Lyndon Johnson, who had not been consulted during the Bay of Pigs crisis. Signally a member of ExComm, of course, was Robert Kennedy. It was the function of the committee to evaluate the facts, to take stock of the situation, and to come up with a course of action. If delay were possible, then the President would do nothing until after the November election. If action were mandatory, he was prepared to move no matter what the political consequences. Hope of postponement vanished as U-2 reconnaissance photographs showed that almost every hour brought signs of new Soviet readiness, new Soviet installations. The very first meeting of ExComm brushed aside the no-action possibility. But in the discussion of other alternatives, it found some support in a modified form.

The choice of policy, as seen by ExComm, consisted of five other alternatives:

1. To protest privately to Comrade Khrushchev, with a demand for immediate removal of the missiles and the Soviet troops manning them in violation of the now-tattered Monroe Doctrine. This course was favored by United Nations Ambassador Adlai Stevenson, who proposed privately to the President that a personal emissary be sent to the Kremlin.

2. To call the Soviet Union and Cuba before the United Nations Security Council, thereby establishing America's "moral" position when the Soviet delegate, Valerian Zorin, exercised the veto.

3. To embargo arms shipments to Cuba, with the eventual possibility of a full blockade which would strangle the Castro government. Since the Kennedy Administration had berated Senator Keating for having made this suggestion previously—it was denounced as an "act of war"—acceptance of this alternative might have had serious political consequences in the November elections.

4. To launch a powerful surprise air attack on the missile sites. This would mean the death of Soviet troops in Cuba, a thought that brought shudders to some of the participants at the ExComm meetings.

5. To invade the island. This, too, would result in casualties among Soviet military units. It would also take time.

The first decision of ExComm was a political one. Nothing would be said until a decision had been made. Meanwhile, the Administration would continue to decry Senator Keating's warnings, deny the facts he was steadily bringing to the American people, and on the surface continue to maintain a "business as usual" posture. The President would honor his campaign commitments and keep the lid on any disclosures by the Administration. While he was away, and even when he was physically present in Washington, the President would turn over chairmanship of ExComm to Bobby. The assistant President would become, in effect, the co-President.

Almost from the start, the Executive Committee agreed that there were really only two immediate alternatives: blasting the missiles out of Cuba by a series of air raids on the sites, or imposing an embargo. The proponents for Air Force action were General Taylor, the Joint Chiefs of Staff, Treasury Secretary Douglas Dillon, and Dean Acheson. They had a majority of ExComm behind them. Opposing it, though not fully committed to the embargo, were Defense Secretary McNamara—as usual disagreeing with his service chiefs —and Bobby Kennedy. In the debate, Bobby quickly became the spokesman for the minority view. He argued that to bomb the sites would be a "Pearl Harbor in reverse." And he said violently at one point: "My brother is not going to be the Tojo of the 1960s."

It was on this principle that he based his case and not, as the Administration would later contend, that an air strike would risk nuclear holocaust. Bobby was well aware that any of the alternatives, including submission, would involve danger. "We all agreed," he subsequently stated, "that if the Russians were ready to go to nuclear war over Cuba, they were ready to go to nuclear war—and that was that, so we might as well have the showdown then as six months later." His basic objections were neither military nor diplomatic; he was thinking in terms of what history would say of his brother. This seemed more important to him than the arguments advanced by Acheson, the leader of the air-attack forces, who pointed out that a "surgical" strike would not only eliminate the missile sites but also topple the Castro Communist regime and remove a chronic threat to American security.

In the President's absence—he was receiving the boos of Yale students and parrying embarrassing questions about Cuba from those who turned out to see him—Bobby became the dominant voice in ExComm. He and those who sided with him pressed strenuously for a Navy "quarantine" of Cuba. This, it was said, would give the United States a chance to maneuver and to "negotiate" with the Kremlin. To soften the blow to the Soviets, the United States would offer a concession to Nikita Khrushchev (the dismantling of United States missile bases in Italy and Turkey) and another to Fidel Castro (surrender of the Navy base at Guantánamo, which the Communists vigorously demanded). Publicly, the Kennedy Administration passionately denied that a deal to shut down the Italian and Turkish bases had been made with Khrushchev, or that this had been his price for "withdrawal" from Cuba. But after the Cuban crisis had been resolved, those bases *were* dismantled—to the consternation of the Turkish government, which privately insisted that this seemed to anticipate a writing off of the eastern Mediterranean by the United States. (And four years later, Castro himself would confirm the existence of secret commitments between Khrushchev and Kennedy.)

By the time President Kennedy returned to Washington, the decision to employ a naval blockade had been made. In spite of Bobby's pressure on ExComm, it had voted only seven to five for naval action, with the five opposed still pressing for a "surgical" series of air strikes and the invasion which would end the menace of Castro Communism to the Western Hemisphere. The President gave his approval, and history was made. Dean Acheson was sent to Europe to inform America's allies of the "quarantine" and discovered that Bobby's obsessive fears of allied reaction to America's stand were groundless. President Charles de Gaulle warmly greeted Acheson and told him: "If there is war, I will be with you. But there will be no war." When the President informed Senate and House leaders of his decision, there were strong objections from Chairman Richard Russell of the Senate Armed Services Committee and—surprisingly —from Senator J. William Fulbright, leader of the Senate's professional pacifists, that a quarantine was too slow and more risky than air attack and invasion.

It was the very inconclusiveness of a naval blockade that bothered those with a realistic approach to questions of war, peace, and diplomacy; this the President and his assistant President were to discover in the days that followed. For once having announced the blockade, in a dramatic evening television address to the nation, the White

House was left dangling while it awaited the reaction of Nikita Khrushchev and the Kremlin. In his speech, the President had announced that no more missiles or heavy bombers would be allowed to reach Cuba. He had delivered an ultimatum warning the Soviets that should the missile arming of Cuba continue, "further action will be justified," although he had never specified what he meant by that phrase. And as a gesture to those who saw in his decision a sign of weakness, he had added:

"It shall be the policy of this nation to regard any nuclear missile launched from Cuba against any nation in the Western Hemisphere as an attack by the Soviet Union on the United States, requiring a full retaliatory response upon the Soviet Union."

But this could only be taken as rhetoric until the Kremlin had made its formal response to the text of the President's television address, as delivered in Washington to the Soviet Ambassador and in Moscow to the foreign ministry. Until Khrushchev made his answer, the President and his surrogate, Robert F. Kennedy, could only make preparations for terrible eventualities. Soviet ships carrying "offensive weapons" were on the high seas, moving toward Cuba. A U-2 plane was shot down by Soviet surface-to-air missiles, the SAMs that had been spotted much earlier by United States air reconnaissance. The President had promised to retaliate against any action against American planes, but after conferring with Bobby, he overlooked this hostile act. The first of the Soviet freighters was allowed to go through the naval screen and unload in Cuba. The initiative was lost.

The first substantial reaction from the Kremlin, a long letter to the President from Khrushchev, indicated that the Soviets were neither willing nor able to confront the United States eyeball to eyeball. As the Joint Chiefs had predicted, Khrushchev was not ready for nuclear war. He was, however, ready to make a deal. Stripped of its bluster, the Soviet proposal agreed to a withdrawal of all missiles and heavy bombers, under United Nations supervision, if the United States would make a formal commitment that it would never invade Cuba or allow Cuban exiles to mount their own invasion from American soil. These conditions were repeated to John Scali, an American Broadcasting Company reporter friendly to Soviet diplomats in Washington.

The first letter arrived on October 26. Before the President could indicate his acceptance of the Soviet proposal, however, Khrushchev had sent another letter demanding as a price for withdrawal the shutting down of United States bases in Turkey. This the President was not opposed to, but he could not trust the Kremlin not to divulge to the world the price that the United States was willing to pay. Worried and indecisive, he laid the matter before ExComm. "Ignore the second letter and answer the first," Bobby said. Whether or not this advice was taken by the President will never be known, or not until the secret Kennedy-Khrushchev correspondence is made public by the White House. Obviously, a deal was made which satisfied the men of the Kremlin.

In a great public show, the Soviets began to pack up their missiles and bring back their technicians. The American people breathed a sigh of relief and blessed Jack Kennedy for averting nuclear war. But the key American condition for lifting the blockade and licensing Fidel Castro in perpetuity to rule his Communized island was forgotten. United Nations inspection teams were never allowed to do their work. The missiles, as Intelligence sources reported within months, had simply been hidden in the vast network of caves which laces Cuba. And United States missile bases in the eastern Mediterranean were dismantled. At home, the American people returned to business as usual—and showed their gratitude to those who had first warned of the Cuban missile build-up by voting them out of office. The November 1962 elections, which had promised catastrophe for the Kennedy Administration, were instead a triumph. In the context of everyday political reality, an observer could quote the tellingly cynical lines of the Elizabethan dramatist, Christopher Marlowe: "Thou has committed fornication—but that was in another country, and besides the wench is dead."

In the months that followed, Bobby could turn to other matters. The 1964 Presidential election lay ahead, another hurdle to be negotiated by the Kennedy team. The missile crisis had restored some of the President's prestige. But the Administration gravely conceded that the months ahead could bring trouble for the Democratic party unless fences were mended, the conservative wing placated, and the noisy battles between machine politicians and reformists halted. This was Bobby's job, and he approached it confident that he could knock heads together with sufficient energy to end intraparty strife and reweld the machine which had brought Jack Kennedy to the Presidency in 1960. As Attorney General and as political boss, he was under fire, but he felt jovial enough early in 1963 to tell the audiences he addressed a little anecdote.

He had been talking to a businessman, Bobby said.

"I don't trust your brother," the businessman scolded.

"My brother, the President?" Bobby asked.

"No, your brother Ted," he was told. "And furthermore, you're listening too much to Arthur."

"Arthur Schlesinger?" Bobby asked.

"No, Arthur Goldberg," the businessman replied. "What's more, you should take more advice from Rose."

"Alex Rose, the New York Liberal party leader?"

"No, your mother Rose," the businessman said.

This brought a laugh. But as Bobby contemplated the year ahead, he knew that the mythical businessman had touched on a point. Alex Rose, head of the influential Hatters Union in New York and leader of the Liberal party, was an important factor in Kennedy plans for the 1964 election. Of more direct importance to Bobby was the role Alex Rose could play in planning the succession in a Kennedy dynasty. As Attorney General, he had held great power in his hands. In his brief tenure as co-President during the missile crisis, he had moved in that heady field of international relations in which the fate of nations are decided by determined men. The Presidency was no longer beyond the scope of his ambition and the ambience of his dreams.

And Bobby knew that Rose was already thinking in terms of 1968. At a Hatters' convention, he had introduced Bobby by offering him a union-made hat to throw into the Presidential ring. "After all," he had added, "we had Franklin Roosevelt for sixteen years. We may want sixteen years of Kennedy." This, moreover, had not been platform joviality. In private conversation with Victor Riesel, the labor columnist, Rose had made his intentions clearer: "Of course there's a constitutional amendment against more than two terms for a President. But eight years of John and then eight years of Bob—eight times two—that gives us sixteen years of Kennedy. In eight years, the country will be addicted to Kennedys. Bob Kennedy will have such an energetic image and impact on the country that we feel he will make a fine President."

Bobby knew of Alex Rose's sentiments. And in this case, they did not differ from those of another Rose—Rose Kennedy, his mother. The idea of his succession to the White House had been discussed by President Kennedy, both in seriousness and in jest. Bobby did not reject it as beyond the realm of possibility. He accepted it, in fact, as something that could be pushed over into the neighbor realm of probability if he continued to act with energy, to run the country with vigor, and to reelect "Johnny." The target was 1968, with the

President using his powers to facilitate the changeover. It might have been more than a dream but for the pull of destiny which led John Fitzgerald Kennedy, on November 22, 1963, to a strange and fatal interview on a road in Texas from which there was no returning.

11

Sorrow—and a New Life

DEATH is never kind, nor can philosophy quench its sorrows. On November 22, 1963, an assassin's bullet struck down John Fitzgerald Kennedy. He was as much a victim of the war with Communism as any of the unknown men and women who were shot down at the Berlin barrier, in Korea, or along the curtain of destruction which the Communists had lowered around their empire. For whatever has since been said or written about Lee Harvey Oswald—and some of it by Robert Kennedy—he was a product of the ideology which for four decades has deprived the world of peace. He had deserted his country for the Communist homeland, and his return under conditions which only the naïve could find lacking in suspicion was a step down that road which ended in a simple deed and its complex consequences.

The man to suffer least from the assassin's bullet was President Kennedy. The man who suffered most was Robert Kennedy. In every conceivable way, he was grievously wounded, perhaps irreparably so. For Bobby Kennedy's entire adult existence had been a function of his brother Jack's life. The friends he had made, the enemies he had collected, his acts both brash and subtle, the obsessiveness of his political thought—these were not his own. Or, more accurately, they were his own simply because his every waking moment had some motivational connection with Jack. Even the drive which from time to time made him more powerful than the President was harnessed to Jack's best interests as he saw them. Death put an end, if only temporarily, to Bobby's reason for being.

Ironically, the Washington *Post* of the 22nd had carried a story of Bobby's public plans. "Right now I plan to stay on this job at least through the election," he had told the newspaper the previous day. "I'm not sure what will happen after that. Of course, something could come up between now and then, but as of now I definitely plan to stay here through the election." He had no intention of running the President's 1964 campaign, he added, and suggested that this would be the assignment of Stephen Smith, his brother-in-law. As Attorney General, he could not become too involved in a partisan contest, "but I must admit that I have a definite interest in who wins."

He was at lunch with his wife and Robert Morgenthau, United States Attorney for the Southern District of New York, when the news from Dallas reached him. A maid came out of the house to the poolside dining table to tell him that J. Edgar Hoover was on the private line from the White House. Bobby picked up an outside phone. Suddenly he covered his face with his hand in a gesture of terrible anguish. Ethel ran to him, throwing her arms about him. His head down, Bobby dragged himself back to the table. "The President was shot in Texas," he said. "It may be fatal."

In this moment of agonizing sorrow, he walked slowly into the house, his wife at his side. While his guests turned to television for news, he was on the phone. The news reports were then holding out some hope for the President's life. As they listened to the conjectures of the news commentator, Bobby said from the doorway, "He's dead." But there was little time for grief. Lyndon Johnson was on the phone to ask about the legality of taking the Presidential oath in Texas. Bobby called the Justice Department, then spoke to Johnson again. It would be all right, he reported, and suggested that he take it immediately on board "Air Force One," the jet which would bring back John F. Kennedy's body. This, perhaps, was the hardest moment of all.

For an hour, he paced back and forth, his dog Brumus with him. Then his close personal and official friends began to arrive, and to them he said, "He lived such a wonderful life." Then he was back on the phone, speaking to his mother. He took a call from Defense Secretary McNamara, who told him when "Air Force One" would be landing at Andrews Air Force Base. "There will be no long faces here," Bobby said to his friends. He went up to his bedroom to change his clothes and to cry. Now in heavy black, he drove to the Pentagon where a helicopter flew him to Andrews. When the plane put down, it waited for him to board, then taxied to its berth. It was dusk and the floodlights garishly picked up the scene—the heavy copper coffin, Jacqueline Kennedy in her blood-stained pink suit. From that moment on, Bobby was continually at Jackie's side.

Although President Johnson made no move to occupy the White House, it was obvious that Jacqueline Kennedy could not remain there for long. (Johnson waited patiently for her to act, though he was rewarded for this kindness by Kennedy-inspired rumors that he had shoved her out as quickly as possible.) The task of searching for a house for John F. Kennedy's widow fell to Bobby, and he found one quickly. Averell Harriman, an Assistant Secretary of State in the Kennedy Administration after a notable career in the Roosevelt and Truman Administrations, had remodeled and furnished a town house in fashionable Georgetown. Bobby approached him to ask if he would relinquish it to Mrs. Kennedy until she had bought a house of her own. The Harrimans, who had just moved in, were a little reluctant. Bobby settled the matter by announcing to the press that Harriman had "offered" the house to Jacqueline. The Harrimans could not contradict Bobby without appearing boorish and hard-hearted, but relations between them and the Kennedys were never the same.

It was a dismal Thanksgiving at Hickory Hill. Friends rallied around and columnist Mary McGrory tried to fold Bobby to her bosom, but he remained remote from the chatter. His look on that day has been described as haunted and full of what Jimmy Breslin called "the great doom of the Irish." At one point, a Justice Department colleague asked Bobby when he was going back to his official duties. "I don't know," said Bobby. "I don't know. I don't have the heart now." Some of those around him, who knew his driving commitment to work, began wondering whether or not his withdrawal from his duties as Attorney General were perhaps connected with his feelings about Lyndon Johnson. Bobby's opposition to the nomination of Johnson for the Vice Presidency was known in Washington official circles. So, too, was Johnson's bitterness over the cavalier way he had been elbowed aside by the young "assistant President." The thousand days of President Kennedy's Administration had been galling to a man accustomed to the uses of power. Johnson had not been so much thwarted as ignored by both the President and the Attorney General. Could the new President and Bobby work together? The answer, everyone suspected, was a flat no.

This estimate of the relationship between the two men found some corroboration in Bobby's public behavior. "While newspapermen and politicians speculated about his future, and his closest friends worried and wondered, Bobby wandered erratically in and out of his office in the Justice Department, his expression glazed, his eyes puffed," biographers Timmesch and Johnson have written. "Some days he took off three hours to have lunch with his family. He had always been a walker, but now he took many walks—around the courtyard at the Justice Department, across the street from the Smithsonian Institution, down Constitution Avenue. Sometimes Brumus was along, but always Bobby's head was down and his hands were in his pockets." Even those who had been most critical of him in the past understood that with one blow he had been deprived of a beloved brother, a *beau idéal*, and his personal dreams of glory. They sometimes suspected that Jimmy Hoffa had been brutally right when, after the assassination, he had described Bobby as "just another lawyer."

Much of the speculation went by him with no effect. The papers were full of stories about his plans. He was preparing to run for Governor of Massachusetts, or he was seeking a position as head of the United States foreign aid program. He had his eye on the Senate. Whatever he may have wanted to do, he made it clear that he intended to leave the Justice Department. "I'm tired of chasing people," he said to James Reston of the New York *Times*. "I want to go on to something else." Meanwhile there was his family at Hickory Hill and his concern over Jackie. Their two names were continually linked in newspaper stories, always sympathetically and with few raised eyebrows. He helped her move into the Georgetown mansion rented to her by the Averell Harrimans after Bobby had announced the transaction as a *fait accompli*. When Jackie decided to vacation in Antigua with her sister, Princess Lee Radziwill, and her husband, Bobby accompanied her. Caroline and John, the late President's children, spent days and weeks at Bobby's house. He took over the management of her business affairs. When she called him at the Justice Department, all other matters were put aside. It seemed almost as if Bobby had made of her a symbol of his dead brother, but one infinitely more in need of help and protection.

Those very close to them knew that there was a bond far deeper than the world realized. For in the trauma of her ordeal, Jacqueline Kennedy had conceived a great hatred of Lyndon Johnson. It was her feeling, and Bobby shared it, that Johnson was somehow responsible for President Kennedy's death. It was Johnson who had insisted that Kennedy visit Texas to extricate the Vice President from political troubles of his own making. He should, they felt, have known of the danger lurking in his state. From the moment that Johnson had stepped into "Air Force One" to take the oath which made him President of the United States, both Bobby and Jackie looked on him as a usurper. Bobby always and very pointedly referred to his dead brother as "President Kennedy" as if there had been no succession. The new President's every act seemed like an affront to the memory of a departed hero and fed their antagonism. The two, Bobby and Jackie, found it difficult to maintain the pretense of public courtesy. In private, as President Johnson began to take hold of the reins of government, there was calculated rudeness. Whether Bobby led or was led down the road of this destructive emotion will never be known.

The world of Washington affairs watched and waited for a sign from him. His every utterance was thought to be a valedictory. He was also being watched for signs of antagonism to Lyndon Johnson. But the tough-minded new President would not be baited into an open break with the man who represented John F. Kennedy's surrogate on earth. The Administration was in a state of transition, and Bobby was a necessary bridge between the fanatically loyal Kennedy forces and those allied to the steadily increasing power of the new President. The appearance of continuity was important as the new Administration took over job by job and strategic post by strategic post. In every department and agency there were key men, appointed at Bobby's behest and loyal to him rather than to what New Frontiersmen thought of as the Texan upstart. They looked to Bobby for guidance. Bobby was also necessary to help in the maneuvering to enact a new civil rights bill, necessary if Johnson was to win over the Northern ideologues. By having Bobby carry the ball, the President could maintain cordial relations with Southern legislators.

The President wanted Bobby to remain in his Cabinet for other reasons. The most pressing of these was the Bobby Baker case. Its turgid waters had lapped about Lyndon Johnson's bastion from the time the case had welled up from the Senate's privileged depths. As Secretary of the Senate, Baker had been Lyndon Johnson's man during the years of his majority leadership and his Vice Presidency. That he had used his position, and his close association with other Senate powers like the late Senator Robert Kerr, to make a multimillion-dollar fortune was well established. The degree of Johnson's awareness of Baker's wheeling and dealing was something else again. When the scandal became public property under President Kennedy, Bobby ordered a thorough FBI investigation. The report remained secret, although a copy was reportedly in the Attorney General's safe. But the leaks to favored reporters and to Senators who wished to make an issue of Baker's activities began to cause considerable concern. After Johnson became President, the leaks continued, and the White House became convinced that the Attorney General was the source of much that was being aired on Capitol Hill.

Whatever President Johnson's connections with Baker may have been, the efforts of his Attorney General to make political capital of them only added to the bad blood between the two. Nevertheless, it was essential to keep Bobby where he could be controlled, rather than to edge him out of his post. It was important as well to keep the Attorney General's mantle on him, to limit the extent of his political adventuring. It was clear, almost from the time Bobby returned to his duties, that he was interested in high public office—the Vice Presidency, in fact. Johnson could tell his friends, "I'll never have a Kennedy on the ticket." But the continued national adulation for the late John F. Kennedy did not subside, as many thought it would, and some of it was obviously rubbing off on Bobby. It would not do to have Bobby out of the Cabinet and a free agent.

President Johnson hoped, moreover, that in time, the antagonism toward him covertly demonstrated by the pro-Kennedy wing of the Democratic party would be dissipated, and that Bobby himself might decide to put aside the vendetta and pitch in during the 1964 Presidential campaign. To keep him on the Johnson team, however nominally, the President allowed Bobby to retain most of his prerogatives, although without the influence that went with them when his brother was alive. Bobby was asked by the President to continue attending the meetings of the National Security Council, although the Attorney General is not a statutory member. Although Bobby had ridden roughshod over Intelligence and national security forces, ignoring the recommendations of security officers in order to appoint some characters of dubious loyalty to sensitive posts, he was allowed to remain their "faculty adviser," particularly in the Central Intelligence Agency. The President also promised to give him a major voice in the making of Latin American policy. As part of the Kennedy "package," such family and political intimates as Kenneth O'Donnell and Lawrence O'Brien were guaranteed their jobs as Presidential aides.

In a spirit of conciliation, and to push Bobby back into the world of affairs, President Johnson sent him on a mission to Asia, where President Sukarno of Indonesia was leading his country into guerrilla warfare against the newly born Federation of Malaysia. It was an assignment of the utmost delicacy, for the vain and arrogant Sukarno was completely in the wrong, the Malaysians completely in the right; yet Sukarno had to be wheedled to the conference table and the Malaysians had to agree to negotiate. The meeting place between Bobby and Sukarno was Tokyo's Imperial Hotel. They talked for more than an hour, but achieved nothing. At a second meeting, the menu made more news than the discussion between the two men; bean-paste soup and dried seaweed were on the bill of fare and Bobby ate them with equanimity, while telling "elephant" jokes.

With a third meeting scheduled for five days later, Bobby went on to the Philippines, a worried bystander in the Indonesian-Malaysian clash. There he conferred with President Diosdado Macapagal and was mobbed by squealing schoolgirls. In Malaysia, to meet with Prime Minister Tunku Abdul Rahman, Bobby found Prince Norodom Sihanouk, dictator of Communist-leaning and anti-American Cambodia, seeking to elbow his way into the negotiations, but Bobby refused to see him. From Malaysia, Bobby flew to Djakarta to plead with Sukarno for negotiations. His aim, he stressed, was to "take this controversy out of the jungle, out of the warfare that is now taking place, and put it around the conference table," but he let the participants know that he and the United States government felt that it was "an Asian dispute and should be settled by Asian countries."

At his third meeting with Sukarno, Bobby received reassurances that Indonesia would sit down with the Philippines and Malaysia to find a solution to the border dispute. But he was airborne, en route to London, when Sukarno predictably broke his word and called on his people to "crush Malaya." Bobby's reaction to this stirred up a diplomatic hornet's nest. "I never assumed that President Sukarno had given up his hostility to Malaysia," he said. "If the conference [of the three countries involved] is not successful, everybody can go back to the jungles and shoot one another again. So nothing has been lost but two weeks of shooting and killing." The Malaysians were up in arms over Bobby's calm acceptance of Sukarno's betrayal and of the manner in which he equated Indonesia's actions with those of a country defending itself against an invading army. The Straits *Times* characterized Bobby's remark as "insensitive." It editorialized: "He seems to have little enough knowledge of the Malaysian dispute, judging by his comments . . . and to be much taken up with his success in bringing about a cease-fire.

. . . He seemed to give Sukarno every reason for believing Washington looks upon Indonesia and Malaysia with at least equal favor. We know (or trust) that this is not so, and that Indonesian aggression in the Borneo states is as little liked . . . as Communist aggression in Vietnam."

President Johnson, however, gave Bobby a warm greeting and praised him for carrying out "his assignment constructively and with real achievement." Bobby appreciated the welcome, and the vendetta that had been foreseen by everyone seemed a thing of the past.

By early January of 1964, Bobby Kennedy had made his "peace with the situation" and agreed to stay on under Lyndon Johnson. The polls showed that Senator Hubert H. Humphrey had a slight edge over Bobby among Democrats, although both men were aware that the choice of a running mate would be the President's. But Bobby, even then, hoped to condition the President's thinking by showing that there was strong support for him from the public and the politicians. Less than three weeks after he had agreed to remain as Attorney General, the first trial balloon in his behalf was being floated by an upstate New York political boss, Peter Crotty, the man who had started the bandwagon rolling for John F. Kennedy in 1960. Crotty belonged to the old school of party leader—a Buffalo version of Tammany Hall's grand sachem—and his support of Bobby so early in the game was designed to show that the Democratic machine stood behind Robert Kennedy.

Early in February, a second play was made in New Hampshire, the state holding the earliest primary and therefore one that is watched by the public with tremendous interest. Into that wintry countryside went Paul Corbin, a Kennedy hanger-on who had been protected by the Attorney General even after the House Committee on Un-American Activities published testimony questioning his citizenship status and linking him with Midwestern Communists. Corbin was an employee of the Democratic National Committee, and therefore presumed to be neutral in primaries. What authority he had to venture into New Hampshire, or what encouragement he received, was never clear. But Corbin roamed the state openly campaigning for Bobby and urging all who would hear him to cast a Vice Presidential write-in vote for his candidate. A big write-in for Vice President Richard Nixon in the 1956 New Hampshire primary had silenced those urging President Eisenhower to find another running mate, and Bobby's supporters argued that a similar turnout for the Attorney General would force President Johnson's hand.

Whoever conceived this strategy failed to foresee the effect it would have on the President. According to the New York *Herald-Tribune*, he became so furious when he learned of the Kennedy ploy that he refused flatly to communicate directly with his own Attorney General. His response was quick and sharp: a call through intermediaries to Bobby demanding that Corbin be fired from the Democratic National Committee. The loss was not great, for Corbin had hardly added luster to Democratic politics. But it was a blow to Bobby's pride. He nevertheless complied with the President's demand. The bandstand had begun to roll, however, and the "Robert Kennedy for Vice President" movement continued to pick up steam.

Corbin, now on the payroll of the Joseph P. Kennedy Jr. Foundation, joined forces with New Hampshire's Governor John King to push for the write-in vote. This time, Bobby protected his flanks by calling the White House to ask if he should issue a statement disclaiming any interest in the nomination. Knowing how Bobby's friends in the Washington press corps would interpret this, the President let it be known that he did not favor such a move. But when political scouts reported to him that Bobby might well poll more Vice Presidential preference votes in New Hampshire than Johnson would at the head of the ticket, Bobby was asked to withdraw formally. Five days before the primary, the Attorney General's public-relations officer at the Justice Department, Ed Guthman, called in reporters and read them a statement.

"The Attorney General has said," Gutham told the press, "that the choice of the Democrat nominee for Vice President will be made and should be made by the Democratic Convention in August, guided by the wishes of President Johnson, and that President Johnson should be free to select his own running mate. The Attorney General, therefore, wishes to discourage any efforts on his behalf in New Hampshire or elsewhere."

It was hardly a General Sherman kind of disengagement. And it came in the context of such Kennedy moves as his appearance before a United Auto Workers meeting at Washington's Hotel Mayflower in which he acted very much like a candidate on the move. ("You played a major role in putting [John F. Kennedy] in the White House," Bobby said. "He always had a very special place in his heart for the UAW.") Taking nothing for granted, but irritated by this turn of events, President Johnson ordered a stepped-up campaign to get out the vote for him in New Hampshire. Despite this effort, the President's vote of 29,635 looked weak next to Bobby's 25,861 write-ins. Now more than irritated, the President took to television to tell his party that no Democrat should be campaigning for the Vice Presidential nomination at that time.

The point was lost on Paul Corbin, who now surfaced in Wisconsin, his home state, to organize a "Draft Robert F. Kennedy for Vice President of the United States Grass Roots Groundswell Committee." This attempt stirred up the old talk of a "feud" between Johnson and Kennedy. Eyebrows were lifted in the White House, and few in political Washington were ready to believe that Bobby was an innocent bystander. The committee died an early death, but not before it had made coast-to-coast headlines. Also noticed was the announcement by Robert Blaikie, a dissident Manhattan Democratic leader, that he was forming a "draft Kennedy" committee of his own.

Since then, both Bobby and his associates have insisted that he had no such idea in mind. But all the signs were there. He appeared on "The Jack Paar Show" to talk about his brother, about Jacqueline Kennedy, and about his vaguely defined future. "I'm just not prepared to decide yet," he said, "so I am just going to stay on as Attorney General until the end of the this year, and then I'll decide what I'm going to do."

As of that spring, however, Bobby knew quite well what he intended to do—and did. He set out on a tour of the nation, almost as if he were campaigning for the Presidency, touching base wherever there was strong Kennedy feeling and playing directly to minority groups. On St. Patrick's Day, he appeared in Scranton, Pennsylvania, whose heavily Irish population turned out for him almost en masse, as it had for John Kennedy in 1960. Everywhere there were the signs, "Let's Keep the Johnson-Kennedy ticket in 1964" and "Mr. President, Please Ask Bobby to Be Vice President." He shook the politically powerful hands and beamed at the crowds that stood in the snow to see him.

That night, at a dinner of the Friendly Sons of St. Patrick, he made a boldly direct pitch for the sympathies of his audience. He spoke of the Irish as "the first of the racial minorities" in America—a slight distortion of history—and recalled the days when "No Irish Need Apply" signs were to be seen in the great Eastern cities. There were repeated references to his brother and an oratorical climax when he compared the late President to Owen O'Neill, the

Irish patriot. Both men had left behind ideals and principles which survived their deaths, Bobby said, and he promised a continuation of the New Frontier. Then, as strong men wept, he read the old ballad of Ireland's sorrow for Owen O'Neill:

> *Oh, why did you leave us, Owen?*
> *Why did you die? . . .*
> *We're sheep without a shepherd,*
> *When the snow shuts out the sky.*
> *Oh, why did you leave us, Owen?*
> *Why did you die?*

His brother was Bobby's theme everywhere. In West Virginia, he visited the areas that had given them both a victory in 1960. To a four-year-old girl with cerebral palsy, he gave his PT-109 clasp. To audiences, he said, "Coming back to West Virginia for a Kennedy is like coming back home. There is a close association with my family, particularly my brother." He recited Jack Kennedy's favorite poems. Visiting campuses, he was given hysterical receptions by girls and their elders, none of whom seemed to care very much what he said just so long as they could shake his hand, tear at him, and unleash emotions pent up since the last visit of a young and attractive celebrity. In the South, he spoke on civil rights, but the enthusiasm of the young people did not abate. Though they made their opposition to further legislation clear, they still cheered Bobby and accepted his criticisms almost happily.

Moving north and west, he addressed commencement exercises at Marquette, a Catholic university, calling on the students to enter public service—"the most meaningful and effective way of achieving involvement" in the community. The applause was tremendous, and as he left the hall the press of students was so great that Bobby's coat was torn off him. In Los Angeles, students clamored that he be nominated the Democratic Party's Vice Presidential candidate. He spoke to student audiences of President Kennedy's efforts to avoid war, of the Cuban missile crisis, of the need for military power as a deterrent, but then took up a theme which would be his in the months to come, as campaigner and a United States Senator.

"Far too often, for narrow tactical reasons, this country has associated itself with tyrannical and unpopular regimes that had no following and no future," he said. "Over the past twenty years, we have paid dearly because of support given to colonial rulers, cruel dictators, or ruling cliques void of social purpose. This was one of President Kennedy's gravest concerns. It would be one of his proudest achievements if history records his Administration as an era of political friendships made for the United States." He quoted then from John Kennedy's undelivered Dallas speech, attacking unspecified voices "preaching doctrines wholly unrelated to reality, wholly unsuited to the Sixties, doctrines that apparently assume that words will suffice without weapons, that vituperation is as good as victory and that peace is a sign of weakness." Though the rhetoric was factually weak, the lunge at conservatives was unmistakable.

That spring, it was Kennedy time wherever Bobby appeared. Syracuse, New York, greeted him with a newspaper headline, "Bobby Brings City $750,000." The largesse had come from the federal government, but the people neither knew nor seemed to care. For those politicians dedicated to Bobby's future, he was on a winning streak, a candidate who seemed to embody all the appeal of Santa Claus and John the Baptist, of the Fighting 69th and Mother Machree. While Bobby traveled, keeping alive the homage to his brother, Stephen Smith, his brother-in-law, was busily at work. Private polls were taken to discover the temper of the people. By May 1964, these samplings showed that Bobby was the overwhelming favorite among Democrats for the Vice Presidential nomination. More significantly, there were party officials ready to risk the loss of federal patronage by openly supporting him, once he gave the sign. Pennsylvania gave Bobby fifty-three percent of the polled voters. In Missouri, where he ran in a field of nine, he received thirty-seven percent, the highest, to Senator Humphrey's seventeen percent. A Michigan poll gave him fifty-four percent.

In spite of the President's determined opposition to having as his Vice President a man whose feelings toward him had fluctuated from contempt to enmity, Bobby might have made it, had he been ready to do battle. The astute Kenny O'Donnell, now a Johnson aide but still a Kennedy man, urged Bobby to make the fight and assured him that there was enough Kennedy power to force President Johnson's hand. O'Donnell pointed out to Bobby that Johnson could not afford an open break with a Kennedy if he wanted to retain the Catholic vote. Without that vote, he would stand a good chance of losing the election. But Bobby was buffeted by doubts. He wanted the Vice Presidency, but he was not sure he wanted it that much. He wanted to remain in government service, but other possibilities appealed to him. He discussed with friends the idea of becoming Secretary of Defense, of State, of the ambassadorship to Vietnam, of running for the United States Senate. But, "He had difficulty coming to grips with any decision," Eunice Shriver, Bobby's sister, said. "If ever there was a lost soul at any time, it was Bobby. He was out of it. He was hard to talk to on anything."

In this state of mind, he saw his weaknesses rather than his strengths. In an interview with *Newsweek*, Bobby could say: "Actually, I should think I'd be the last man in the world Johnson would want . . . because my name is Kennedy . . . because we travel different paths. . . . Most of the major leaders in the North want me—all of them, really. And that's about all I've got going for me." This should have been enough—the Kennedy appeal and the support of the most powerful bloc of Democrats in the country. The desire was there, but not the heart. He could speak unblushingly of what his role might be, but he failed to see the contradiction. "I'd like to harness all the energy and effort and incentive and imagination that was attracted to government by President Kennedy. I don't want any of that to die. It is important that this striving for excellence should continue, that there be an end to mediocrity. The torch really has passed to a new generation. People are still looking for all that idealism. . . . And I became sort of a symbol, not just an individual."

Bobby's lack of decision played directly into President Johnson's hands. Older, careful, and with the experience of years in the Senate, Johnson did not wear his sentiments on his sleeve. When growing participation in the Republican Presidential stakes made it improper for Henry Cabot Lodge to remain as Ambassador to South Vietnam, Bobby grasped at a straw. In a letter to the President, he volunteered his services as Lodge's successor. Johnson telephoned him immediately, thanked him, but asked him to remain as Attorney General. As the White House explained it to James Reston of the New York *Times.* "There has been a lot of speculation that the President was on bad terms with the Attorney General—he denies this—and that he was opposing those who wanted Mr. Kennedy to be the Democratic Party's Vice Presidential nominee. In the light of this, the President did not want to send the Attorney General to Saigon and be charged, as he believed he would be, with banishing him from the country during the nominating convention."

This was a point for Lyndon Johnson in the game of oneupmanship he was playing with Robert Kennedy. It showed a generosity that Bobby was unable to reciprocate. Subsequently, when the President met Kennedy in New York, he talked to him at length about the civil rights legislation then undergoing Senate surgery and expressed his pleasure over the manner in which Bobby was handling it. In both instances, he was the kindly older man overlooking the excesses of youth and ambition. Bobby, for his part, seemed determined to carry on the vendetta and to make indecisive gestures toward the nomination. But the President did not intend to let Bobby take away the play. To visiting friends, who repeated his remarks to reporters, he said that he was interested only in three factors: Was the potential candidate qualified for the Vice Presidency, would he clash with the Administration and attempt to impose his own policies, and would he hurt the ticket?

The questions almost answered themselves. But the President was ready to spell them out. Bobby, he said, had a tendency to ride roughshod over people, to come to snap judgments, to stir up controversy. He had already shown, Johnson argued, that he was not a part of the Johnson team. Bobby was not flexible enough to modify Kennedy policies so that they fit new situations. After the nomination of Barry Goldwater in San Francisco, the President took his second step against Bobby. On July 27, he telephoned to invite the Attorney General to the White House. A Presidential invitation has the weight of a command, particularly for a federal officeholder, but Bobby muttered some excuse about being busy preparing for another one of his journeys. The President showed no offense but suggested July 29. He received Bobby in the Oval Room and read him a very brief prepared statement, almost as if posterity or the press were present.

"Ever since San Francisco," he said, "I have been thinking about the Vice Presidency. You have a bright future, a great name, and courage, but you have not been in government very long. I have given you serious consideration, but find it inadvisable to pick you."

There was dead silence for a moment, as Bobby's opaque blue eyes fixed themselves on a spot just below the President's tie. Then Johnson changed the subject, and the two men chatted formally. It was the President who returned to the matter at hand. Didn't Bobby think it would be a good idea if he told the reporters as he left that he was no longer interested in the Vice Presidency? Bobby did not think it was a good idea at all. But as he left the office he said almost ominously, "I could have helped you a lot." That afternoon, McGeorge Bundy, one of the President's assistants, called Bobby to advise strongly that he withdraw from the race publicly. "Go to hell," Bobby answered. This was no longer determination, but pique. It was the last protest of a man who sees power slip-

ping from him, the power that had made federal officials jump
when he beckoned, but refuses to accept the loss.

The press knew that Bobby had been rejected. It was now a question of wrapping it up, and the President did so in two moves the
following day. In the morning, he told the group of correspondents
who cover the White House what he considered the qualifications
of a Vice President. They were carefully tailored to exclude Bobby.
"I think he should be a man that is well received in all States of
the Union, among all our people," he said. "I would like to see a
man that is experienced in foreign relations and domestic affairs. I
would like for him to be a man of the people who felt a compassionate concern for their welfare and who enjoyed public service and was
dedicated to it."

Early that evening, the President made it final. Again he called
in the White House press corps to hear his statement: "With reference to the selection of the candidate for Vice President on the
Democratic ticket, I have reached the conclusion that it would be
inadvisable for me to recommend any member of my Cabinet or
any of those who meet regularly with the Cabinet. In this regard,
because their names have been mentioned in the press, I have personally informed the Secretary of State, Mr. Rusk, the Secretary of
Defense, Mr. McNamara, Attorney General, Mr. Kennedy, and the
Secretary of Agriculture, Mr. Freeman. I have communicated this
to the United States Ambassador to the United Nations, Mr. Stevenson, and the head of the Peace Corps, Mr. Shriver. In this manner,
the list has been narrowed. I shall continue to give the most thoughtful consideration to the choice of the man who I will recommend,
and I shall make my decision known in due course."

The logic of this statement was never explained, but its effectiveness was abundantly apparent. By downgrading five men in order
to place Bobby in the group, the President had shifted press interest from the intended slight of a Kennedy to other questions:
Why say the other five are not qualified? Did service in the Cabinet
automatically carry a stigma? Robert Kennedy's reaction was
ambiguous: "As I have always said, it is the President's responsibility to make known his choice for Vice President. It is in the interest
of all of us who were associated with President Kennedy to continue
the efforts to advance the programs and ideals to which he devoted his life and which President Johnson is carrying forward."
In other words, the President had exercised his responsibility, but
this did not bind those who hoped to advance John F. Kennedy's pro-

gram. But this was whistling in the dark, as Bobby knew. There was one last hope that the convention, when it met in August, could be stampeded by the showing of a film on John F. Kennedy's life. In the outburst of emotion, Kennedy strategists thought, Bobby could ride to the nomination, unless Johnson was ready to take the risk of splitting his party in two.

But even this was not to be. Johnson was as fully aware of the emotional potential of the Kennedy film. He therefore ordered John Bailey, chairman of the Democratic National Committee, to change the scheduling. Instead of being timed for the second night of the convention, it would be shown on the fourth night—after he had designated his Vice Presidential choice and the convention had confirmed it.

So ended Robert Kennedy's dreams of standing one heartbeat away from the Presidency. Before the curtain had been rung down on that one act, there were some who said that the convention might have broken its tether. Afterward, however, no one would concede that possibility. But Bobby Kennedy and his supporters had not been too far wrong in gauging the great surge of emotion that one man's memory could evoke. In the carnival atmosphere of Atlantic City, tawdry and ill equipped to hold 5,500 reporters and 5,300 delegates, the two Kennedys once more worked their magic. There is no better brief description than Theodore White's in *The Making of the President, 1964*:

"Of the last day of the Convention there remains in this reporter's memory only a succession of scenes without any real connection —as if they were all patched together from fragments of a broken stained glass window:

"The first abashed bow of the convention to the memory of John F. Kennedy. Robert F. Kennedy standing before the gathering, trying to speak, unable to speak, the applause building and building and building (one Chicago delegate to another: 'Let's not let them stop it—first our row will clap and then when we get tired we'll get the row behind us to clap') and going on for twenty-two minutes until finally Bobby could deliver an evocation of his brother's memory which he climaxed with a passage from *Romeo and Juliet*:

> . . . *when he shall die*
> *Take him and cut him out in little stars,*
> *And he will make the face of heav'n so fine*
> *That all the world will be in love with Night*
> *And pay no worship to the garish Sun.*

(Whereupon one of the Chicago delegates growled, 'See? I bet no-body else could quote Shakespeare to a Democratic Convention and get away with it. . . .')"

This was perhaps the greatest hour in Bobby Kennedy's life, the greatest he would know. For politics had ceased at the water's edge of emotion. A convention of politicians—the old and cynical, the young and grabbing—had put aside their noisemakers and their deals and surrendered themselves to a great outpouring of sorrow for a man they may or may not have loved but who represented to them, at that moment, a spirit of youth and adventure which they would never really know for themselves. For Bobby, it was almost a laying on of hands. He stood before this inchoate mass of people, and he was in fact a symbol. He could not bend the delegates to his purpose; Lyndon Johnson had seen to that. But the moment was his.

How he had approached it is a secret shared by his intimates, of which there are few. In the period between his rejection by the President and the convention, he had treated his future with light irony. Not many days before, in speaking to a group of Democratic Congressional candidates, he had said wryly: "I must confess I stand in awe of you. You are not members of the Cabinet and you don't meet regularly with the Cabinet, and therefore you are eligible for Vice President." When the laughter had subsided, he grinned and went on: "I decided to send a little note to the Cabinet members in general saying, 'I'm sorry I took so many nice fellows over the side with me.' "

Between that rejection and the convention, too, he had come by small and hesitant steps to a declaration for New York State's Democratic Senatorial nomination. It could almost be said that the decision was made for him out of a combination of pressure from friends, the desperate need of New York Democrats for a candidate who could stand up to Republican Senator Kenneth Keating, and the desire of the Kennedy clan to find a new place for him in the world of affairs. As late as May 20, he had somewhat equivocally denied any real interest in making the race. To re-porters who cornered him when he appeared in New York to campaign for one of the last of the major big-city bosses, Representative Charles Buckley of the Bronx, he had said, "All things being equal, it would be better for a citizen of New York to run for the position. I have no other plans than staying on as Attorney General." The "all things being equal" clause was a qualifier wide enough to run a truck through, but both the public and the newspapers considered it as definite a statement as could be expected from a man in public life.

It seemed all the more binding because it took cognizance of the charges already being made that he was a carpetbagger from Massachusetts seeking to restore his political fortunes in a state that was his only by the biggest stretch of electoral tolerance. At the time, in fact, he was in line to become a delegate from Massachusetts to the Democratic convention. His residence, moreover, was Hickory Hill in Virginia. Under New York's election law, he was not qualified to vote, but he could be a candidate if he was a resident on Election Day. This was a tenuous claim to one of New York's Senate seats. To open himself to a carpetbagging charge was doubly perilous, for another member of President Kennedy's official family, former White House Press Secretary Pierre Salinger, was running for the Senate in California under an equally flimsy pretext of residence in the state.

But there were forces at work for Bobby. Stephen Smith, his brother-in-law and Joe Kennedy's business and political eyes and ears in New York, had been quietly sounding out opinion among Democratic leaders. The old party hacks, the machine politicians, and the opponents of the so-called Reform group favored Bobby. They had been badly treated over the years by the highly vocal and well-heeled "Reformists." They had seen Mayor Robert F. Wagner desert their ranks. And they wanted no part of the Adlai Stevensons, the Frank Hogans, the Ralph Bunches—or even Wagner himself. These were the candidates who would cut them out. With Bobby, they felt they had a winner and a man of party loyalty. That he was ready to brave the wrath of the Reform group and its mouthpiece, the New York *Times,* in order to campaign for Representative Buckley was proof positive to them that he could be counted on to side with them in their internecine wars. The Liberal party, which could deliver some 400,000 votes to the candidate of its choice, was also ready to give the nod to Bobby if he decided to run for the Senate. Against these forces, the *Times* could thunder that Robert Kennedy "would merely be choosing New York as a convenient launching pad for the political ambitions of himself and others." But how many divisions could the *Times* muster?

Stephen Smith's strategy was to confer with Democratic leaders and to fly trial balloons. Bobby was willing to allow this, but not to commit himself in any way. By mid-June, however, it became apparent that should he make a fight for the nomination, no one could stop him. The Kennedy influence and the mystique that seemed to cloak all those intimately connected with the late President were doing their work. But it was precisely at this moment that near-tragedy struck the Kennedys. On June 19, Senator Ted Kennedy, flying a private plane from Washington to Boston, crashed near Springfield. Bobby was at Hyannis Port when he received the news that his brother was seriously hurt. He flew immediately to Boston and was driven to the hospital by state police. To his relief, Teddy's injuries were not permanent—three broken vertebrae and two fractured ribs—and there was no paralysis, no nerve damage. The impact of Ted's accident, however, thrust Bobby back into the mood that had possessed him for so many months. "Somebody up there doesn't like us," he said to a friend. "It's been a great year for giggles, hasn't it?" Several days later, "in fairness to the people who have urged me to run" and "to end speculation," Bobby announced that he would "not be a candidate for United States Senator for New York."

That seemed to end it. To make the point even clearer, he took his second trip out of the country, a semiofficial visit to Chancellor Ludwig Erhard and former Chancellor Konrad Adenauer of West Germany. Berlin was his destination. His mission was to unveil a plaque at the Free University commemorating his brother's "Ich bin eine Berliner" visit. But also on his itinerary were four days in Poland at the touchiest of times, when Premier Tito of Yugoslavia was an official guest. In Berlin, Bobby was wildly cheered for a speech of untypical lyricism whose theme was Goethe's famous dictum: "The destiny of any nation, at any given time, depends on the opinions of its young men under twenty-five." This idea was to recur with growing frequency in Bobby's public utterances. And as always, he spoke about his brother. With "the torchbearer for a whole generation" gone, he said, it seemed that "the world might lapse again into the empty poses and vain quarrels that disfigured our yesterdays and made of our past a litany of anguish." But the "hope that President Kennedy kindled" was "not a memory, but a living force" still.

It may be that the trip to Poland was the turning point in his life —or the life he had led since John Kennedy's assassination. The adrenalin began working in his system again as he stepped down from the plane, unannounced by the Polish authorities, and found a hysterically enthusiastic crowd waiting for him. The grapevine had brought them the news of his visit, and of the day of his arrival. And the welcome he got matched the one Vice President Nixon received in 1959, for much the same reason. To the Poles, both men represented America, liberation, and hope for the future. Both men gave the people a chance to demonstrate for freedom without openly confronting their Communist government. The parallels were there at every step. Nixon's arrival had followed Nikita Khrushchev's, and the contrast of grudging official duty and genuine greeting was apparent to all. Bobby's visit followed Tito's and the contrast was as apparent. But Nixon's visit had been official, a Vice President seeking to reach the Poles and their government with a message of America's good intentions. Robert Kennedy was a "private citizen," and it was discernible from the start that he was there to stir up popular enthusiasm, almost saying, as liberal columnist Marquis Childs noted, that he could "appeal to the big urban centers [in America] with their big Catholic majorities."

The result, the New York *Times* reported, was predictable. "In three days," correspondent Arthur Olsen wrote later, "he ripped to shreds the elaborate web of carefully articulated relationships that the United States and Poland have spun in the past eight years. . . . Robert Kennedy, sensing he was among friends, responded [to the crowds] like an Irish politician running for Mayor of Boston. He climbed onto the roof of the nearest automobile and spoke in simple, warm-spirited sentences of friendship and Polish virtues and of historic ties between the two countries." He visited an orphanage, a children's hospital, a farmer's market, a student graduation ball (where he showed up uninvited), Warsaw's cathedral, and the beautiful medieval square. While the United States Ambassador, John M. Cabot, and other embassy officials ground their teeth in frustration and the Ambassador protested Bobby's practice of leaping to the roof of the official limousine whenever a crowd gathered, what one biographer has called "a carnival" continued. In his impromptu speeches on these occasions, Bobby spoke of Poland's minority government, discussed church-and-state relationships, and tossed off remarks on other touchy areas of Polish-American policy.

When told by Polish officials that "Premier Gomulka doesn't play to the crowds," he answered, "Well, perhaps that's his problem." He was brusque to Communist dignitaries and snarled at one, "Please let go of my arm." Angrier by the minute, the Polish government sent its Vice Minister of Foreign Affairs, Jozef Winiewicz, to tell Bobby that he had gone much too far. By breaking all the rules, Winiewicz told Bobby, he was "seriously damaging" United States-Polish relations. And he was told that it would be "very ill-advised" if he visited Cardinal Wyszynski, in semi-house arrest at the Pauline Monastery in Czestochowa. Bobby went anyway, but the *Times* report notes that "thereafter he did not go looking for crowds and abstained from forthright comment on church-state relations."

At public and private meetings with Polish officials, Bobby lectured them on their evasion of responsibilities to the cause of peace. He brought up the question of the Polish-German frontier, imposed on the Germans by the Soviet Union in violation of all ethnic determinations. Premier Gomulka replied huffily to this, and one official said to Bobby, "You may be winning votes in America, but this kind of thing is not done in Poland." To all of this, there were grumblings from American diplomats. But there were some who felt that it did not hurt the United States to have one forthright and unabashed representative speak his mind. That he showed no concern for Communist sensibilities and sensitivities was to his credit, despite his small-boy show of bravado.

There was one curious episode, however. At a press conference, the Polish party hacks who pass themselves off as reporters tried to throw him off balance with questions which were at best needling. This did not bother Bobby, who could give back as much as he received. When asked about Lee Harvey Oswald, President Kennedy's assassin, Bobby was forthright in countering the prevalent European view that someone else, in the pay of fascists or right-wing extremists, had committed the crime. There was no doubt of Oswald's guilt, Bobby said flatly. Oswald was "a misfit," Bobby added, and "ideology, in my opinion, did not motivate his act. It was the single act of an individual protesting against society." That he tried to lay to rest the anti-American rumors about a "frame-up" of Oswald was highly praised by the American press. But few asked what Robert Kennedy meant when he said that the assassin was "protesting against society."

Back at Kennedy International Airport in New York, Bobby dropped his Polish manner and returned to conciliation. "Now is the time to really achieve something [in East-West friendship]," he said. "We should do it at this time, during a period of relative calm, instead of at a later time when some crisis arises which might mean that we could lose control of the situation. Don't let us leave this problem to others to sort out."

In Bobby's absence, Steve Smith had been at work. Democratic leaders and opinion-makers were reassured that Bobby hadn't really meant it when he categorically withdrew from the Senate race.

Smith was also getting pledges from county leaders and delegates to the New York State Democratic convention. But the exhilaration of his Polish experience had not yet crystallized Bobby's thinking. Stubbornly, he held to the thin edge of hope, still dreaming of the Vice Presidency. He also spoke of spending a year abroad, of teaching, of a variety of ventures. None really appealed to him. He was aware, too, that he had worn out his welcome in the Johnson Cabinet, that there was "no future for me in Washington any more." This was the attitude that Steve Smith and the other "Kennedy for Senator" sponsors were waiting for. In the days before the Democratic convention, he was shown statewide polls to prove that he would beat Senator Keating. Tally sheets showing his delegate strength—almost a clean sweep—were thrust upon him. The only opposition came from Mayor Wagner, who realized that with Bobby in the Senate, his own hold over the New York Democratic party would be broken. To save face for Wagner, an elaborate ballet was arranged in which Bobby said, "Under no circumstances would I ever have considered, or would I now consider, coming into the state of New York against the wishes of the mayor." The mayor, bowing politely, answered with his own statement to the press, "If he is available, he is the type of person who would make an exceptionally fine candidate. I'm sure that he would win."

At this point, by prearranged signal, the pieces began falling into place. Adam Clayton Powell, Harlem's representative in Congress and its political boss, ticked off the names of the powerful political bosses behind Bobby, including himself. "I urged him to make the race three months ago," he said. To win over the Jewish vote, Alex Rose and David Dubinsky gave private assurances of Bobby's liberalism to those Jewish leaders who had their doubts. A star-spangled list of prominent and wealthy liberals formally endorsed Bobby. Behind the scenes, while anti-Kennedy forces—badly split and unable to find a candidate of their own—fulminated and made colorful news stories, Smith had sewed up 700 delegates to the nominating convention, with only 563 required. Finally, on August 21, Mayor Wagner gave his formal though hardly joyous endorsement. At that point the convention was no more than a formality.

The scene on the steps of Gracie Mansion—Bobby, his wife Ethel, and His Honor, the Mayor—was almost anticlimactic. Bobby read a statement announcing his candidacy. He was nervous and his voice shook almost as much as his hands. He spoke of President Kennedy, of peace and enduring prosperity. He made the usual obeisance to New York, the greatest state in the union. Then he answered routine questions from the press and wandered about the trampled grass of the mansion grounds, shaking hands with admirers who had gathered outside the iron fence. On the "Caroline," the Kennedy family plane, he plumped himself down in what had been Jack Kennedy's usual place, and plunged into the mechanics of the campaign.

At the Democratic National Convention in Atlantic City, Bobby conferred that day with members of New York's delegation, with Averell Harriman, with the hard-core political bosses. He visited the Kennedy Library exhibit on the honky-tonk boardwalk, pausing for a moment before the movie screen which showed Jack Kennedy delivering his moving Berlin speech, and tears came to his eyes. At a reception in his honor, labor leaders, New Frontier intellectuals, society, show-business people, and the owner of the New York *Post,* Dorothy Schiff, gathered around him. The discordant note was struck elsewhere when Mayor E. Dent Lackey of Niagara Falls continued to battle the inevitable with a denunciation of Bobby for "coming in here riding an aura of an assassinated President we all adore," adding, in greater indignation, "I don't believe anyone should ride an aura this way"—a metaphor both mixed and confusing, as if there were an acceptable way to ride an aura.

The climax came the next day. President Johnson had been nominated and his Vice Presidential running mate named. There was no longer any fear of a runaway convention. And those who had hidden their advocacy of Bobby could now show it without fear of offending the President. For thirteen minutes, while the television cameras tried to record the scene, the crowd went wild, drowning out an introduction with a sustained drumbeat cry of "We Want Kennedy." Bobby wept, but few people in the convention hall noticed it. They were weeping themselves. Then it was over.

On September 1, at another convention, on the neglected, splintery boards of a hot and dirty New York armory, the Democratic party nominated Robert Francis Kennedy for the first elective office he would ever hold. There was some opposition, but few paid it any mind. For it was clear to all that whether Bobby won or lost, the Kennedy dynasty had returned.

And this precisely described the campaign. It was not Bobby who was running for office but his brother. And in a way, it was not even Jack Kennedy. A high-powered political machine and some sort of disembodied spirit had contrived to turn a Senatorial race into a kind of Elvis Presley hysteria. Although Bobby paid $10,000 to Gerald Gardner, a television gag writer, for one-line jokes to toss out to the crowd, the money was wasted. Bobby did not have to speak, did not have to discuss issues. He merely presented himself to the crowds and they went wild. The newspapers tried to make a contest of it, to inject issues, to quote Bobby's ghosted quips. But the public wasn't interested. Senator Kenneth Keating, who had in the past also purchased his wisecracks, did the best he could. But no one was really interested. The electorate split up into those who were for Bobby and those who were against him. Keating was hardly a factor.

Working against the Republicans, of course, was Keating's refusal to endorse or to reject Barry Goldwater. Either one would have been better than the studied "neutrality" which antagonized conservatives and liberals alike. The Conservative party, which could swing 300,000 votes to its candidates and away from the Republicans, nominated Henry Paolucci for the Senate—and this was bad news. Keating's middle-of-the-road voting record, the many services he had rendered the state, his wartime background, his legal abilities, and his Senatorial mien could not possibly prevail against the kind of reaction that Bobby evoked, particularly among women voters. Those who had covered the squealing mobs and the hysterical outbursts which surrounded Benny Goodman, Presley, Frank Sinatra, or any of the show-business idols of our times, were struck by the similarity between their crowds and Bobby's.

Girls tugged at their bikinis when he campaigned on New York's beaches. They tore at his clothes and had seizures. But it was not only young girls. In Negro neighborhoods, the crowds burst through police lines just to touch him, as if that contact could cure scrofula or some modern diseases. The "Caroline" flew from city to city, and everywhere it was a triumphal procession. One street was like another, one street crowd undiscernible from another, one speech from another. Bobby's "address" to the business leaders of Buffalo is as good an example of his approach to the voters and the issues as any.

He arrived late, smiled shyly, listened to the introduction from a bank president, ran his hands through his hair, and said: "I've been all over the state talking about Medicare today and when I came into Buffalo tonight I thought I needed it myself. The Kennedys always felt Buffalo was a second home. My brother felt that way. President Kennedy ran on the idea of getting this country moving again. We are now in the longest period of prosperity this country ever enjoyed—forty-two months. People said we weren't the businessmen's friends. How in hell could you have a better friend?

"My brother used to say that when the market went down, it was a Kennedy market. When it went up it was due to free enterprise. Well, we made an effort to get going in the past three and one-half years. We made a start. We must continue with other programs— health, education, too.

"I don't want to retire even though I'm getting old. I could retire on my daddy's money. But I'd rather work. I'd rather be in public service. I want to represent New York. I want to be Senator."

When he told audiences, with tremendous earnestness, that "half the people in South America are under twenty-five years of age," he seemed to be touching on great truths. Keating's distinguished years as Congressman and Senator were irrelevant. Keating had an eighty percent record of supporting labor, but the AFL-CIO which had suffered from the Senate Labor Rackets investigations endorsed Bobby. Keating had demonstrated his friendship for the state of Israel, but the Jewish vote went to Kennedy. Negro leaders privately acknowledged that Keating deserved their support, but publicly they backed Bobby, and so did seventy-five percent of their people. Keating had been consistently anti-Communist and for the captive nations of Eastern Europe, but Bobby invited himself to the Pulaski Day Parade in New York and broke into that ethnic bloc.

It was not even necessary for him to be very logical about some of the charges made against him. He was using New York to establish a power base for a shot at the Presidency, his opponents said. To this, he answered earnestly, though with little eloquence, according to a *Newsday* story: "I intend to serve until my term is up. . . . I don't intend to use it as a stepping stone to go some place. First, I am going to serve a full term. But let's just assume I am going to use it as a stepping stone. Because that is the implication of the question. . . .

"Assume that I was using it as a power base. That's . . . the expression that is used. Using it as a power base, the only thing I can think of is that I want to be President of the United States.

"Let's just assume then—let's just assume the worst—let's just assume that I am using it as a power base—the state of New York— and I am really trying to get some place else, the Presidency of the United States. In the first place, truthfully now, I can't go any place in 1968. We've got President Lyndon Johnson and he's going to be a good President and I think he is not only going to be a good President in 1964 but he is going to be reelected in 1968. . . . And he'll have my support and my efforts on his behalf. . . .

"Now let's go to 1972. Let's assume I am using it as a power base. I'm going to have to be reelected in six years. That means that if I have done such an outstanding job and I want to be President, I've got to do an outstanding job in the state of New York, I've got to do a splendid job for the people of the state of New York, I've got to be reelected in six years. . . . That means that in eight years I have got to do such an outstanding job that people will be demanding all over the country that I be a Presidential candidate. . . . I don't see how New York suffers."

With the same zeal with which he had attacked Jimmy Hoffa, Bobby went after Keating and his voting record. To hear the Kennedy oratory, Keating had opposed every humane measure that came before the House and Senate. Since both men were fighting for the liberal vote, Bobby's charges that Keating had fought federal aid to education and the test-ban treaty were damaging. The charges, incidentally, were not true. Keating appealed to the Fair Campaign Practices Committee, whose chairman, Bruce Felknor, wrote to Bobby that his characterization of the Keating record was "not only false and distorted but also appears to be either a deliberate and cynical misrepresentation or the result of incredible carelessness." These were strong words and, according to the record, justified. Instead of retracting, Bobby applied pressure on Felknor. Ralph McGill, editor of the Atlanta *Constitution,* and Cardinal Cushing, a Kennedy family friend, resigned from the Fair Campaign Practices Committee, and Felknor was forced to apologize to Bobby.

Every possible means was used to propel Bobby into the Senate. Almost every bus in New York City was placarded with Kennedy campaign slogans, at a cost no one has estimated. Daily newspaper ads beat the drums for him. One of them claimed that Adlai Stevenson planned to vote for Bobby, although he had already cast an absentee ballot in the Illinois election. The Fair Campaign Practices Committee reported at length and devastatingly of Bobby's campaign methods—but only after the voting.

Typical of the dead-end-kid methods used by Bobby was the "debate" espisode. On October 24, CBS wired Keating and Bobby, inviting them to a half-hour television debate to be held on October 27 at 7:30 P.M. Keating accepted with alacrity. Bobby ignored the invitation. On the day of the debate, CBS wired Kennedy, urging him to appear and giving him until 3:30 that afternoon to send in his acceptance. Bobby ducked again, complaining that no format had been proposed for the show. His aides, moreover, made it known that he did not intend to appear. Keating seized the opportunity, bought the 7:30-8:00 half hour, and announced that he would debate an empty chair. Whereupon, Kennedy bought the 8:00-8:30 half hour to answer Keating.

One minute before Keating was scheduled to go on the air, Bobby and several dozen newspapermen burst into CBS and marched to the studio where Keating's broadcast was just beginning. Bobby jabbed his finger into the chest of a Keating aide and said loudly: "Inform Senator Keating that I'm here and ready to go on the air." Then he tried to force his way into the studio. A CBS official blocked him and explained that Bobby had not been willing to debate and that the air time was Keating's. "This is dishonest," Bobby spluttered. On his own half hour, he devoted his time to "exposing" Keating's "political trickery." He charged that Keating's staff had barred him from the studio, which was not true, and turned his attempted blitz to his own advantage. (He would admit later that he had no reason for showing up when he did.)

By this time, however, the campaign had developed into a Kennedy Hour. Jean, Eunice, and Pat, his three sisters, ranged the state, evoking the memory of the dead President. Mrs. Rose Kennedy made speeches for Bobby. To climax it, Bobby himself appeared at a Bronx rally leading John-John, Jack Kennedy's little son, by the hand. And all of it was televised, $1,000,000 worth of it in October alone. It all added up. A week before the election, Bobby felt confident enough to stand before a crowd in Ossining and, in effect, stick out his tongue at Keating.

"Who grew up in Westchester? I did. Keating didn't," he said. "Does Keating know the problems of Westchester County? No. Boo-boo, Ken Keating! Boo-boo! Did he go to Bronxville schools as I did? No. Keating is the carpetbagger. He says keep New York's own. Imagine that. Boo-boo! Ken Keating. Boo-boo! Do you want a local boy in the United States Senate? That's me!" And then, one of his famous *non sequiturs:* "There's even some talk about Keating dumping garbage in the Hudson River."

It was as silly a speech as New York had heard since the days of the Tammany Hall hacks. When the votes were counted, however, Bobby had won. But it was also true that but for Lyndon Johnson's phenomenal sweep of all sixty-two counties, Bobby might well have lost. President Johnson won by 2,669,597 votes, Bobby by 719,693 votes. The President carried upstate New York by 1,300,000 votes, Bobby by 8,644. Landslide or not, Bobby failed to win in the three key suburbs of New York City—Nassau and Suffolk on Long Island, and influential Westchester. The political professionals had predicted that Keating would lose if President Johnson's plurality exceeded 1,500,000 votes—and they were right. But Bobby did not see it that way. "We started something in 1960," he said, ignoring the President, "and the vote today is an overwhelming mandate to continue."

In the post-election period, there were three significant analyses of Bobby Kennedy's rise to elective office. The New York *Times,* in a long news story, finally gave the details of the steps by which Bobby had won the nomination. Victor Riesel described the manner in which Bobby had sewed up the labor vote. And Terry Smith, in *Esquire,* analyzed the way Bobby had used television to win over the voters.

The *Times* story, by R. W. Apple Jr., described "secret meetings at Gracie Mansion, hundreds of telephone calls from an office high in the Pan Am Building, thorough political organization and precise timing." And it stated flatly: "The Attorney General's strategy exerted great pressure on those reluctant to support him. They attempted to create the impression of an inexorable drive toward victory, continually telling politicians that they could not afford to be on the losing side." Of more interest was the implication that the Kennedy campaign had really begun to roll—with Kennedy's consent—at a time when he was making his public announcement bowing out of the race.

On July 31, for example, a meeting was held at Hyannis Port to discuss two topics: Could Bobby remain in the Johnson Cabinet? If not, what was his future? Present at this meeting were Bobby; David Hackett, a Justice Department assistant; Averell Harriman, Under Secretary of State for Political Affairs; and Arthur Schlesinger Jr., a refugee from the Johnson White House. The discussion indicated that there was no future for Bobby in the Johnson Administration. He could quit and take a rest, or seize the opportunity that New York presented. "No irrevocable decision emerged from these discussions but the Attorney General—after 'looking down the well,' as one friend put it later—said he was strongly inclined to try for the Senate, if the nomination could be had without a protracted fight."

That was permission enough for the Kennedy cohorts, and for Stephen Smith, in his aerie in the Pan Am Building, to begin the necessary mobilization. Bobby had demanded as the condition for "accepting" the nomination that a broad spectrum of party support be his. Four days later, Schlesinger was in the office of Alex Rose, a power in the Liberal party, to enlist his support. He had no difficulty in getting it. That night, John English, a Democratic leader from Long Island, summoned to a secret meeting in Westchester County the nine county leaders and William H. McKeon, a covert Kennedy adherent. The meeting had been called to find ways and means to create the illusion of wide party support, so that "this thing doesn't look like a coup by the Irish Mafia." At the same time, Steve Smith was meeting with Stanley Steingut, the Brooklyn Democratic leader. Harriman's job was to enlist New York's liberal Democrats. Working with him was George Backer, ex-husband of the New York *Post*'s Dorothy Schiff, and an expert behind-the-scenes operator.

Having touched base with the bosses and the intellectuals, Smith "recruited" William F. Haddad, a Kennedy man since the 1960s, who could reach the so-called Reform Democrats and soften them up for Bobby. "Now," Apple wrote, "Mr. Smith's role became central. Day after day, he sat in his corner office on the thirty-first floor of the Pan Am Building, talking for hours on a cream-colored telephone, urging everyone he could find to bring pressure on [Mayor Wagner]."

To those who had watched the Kennedy steamroller in 1960, this seemed like a smaller version of it. The one hope of the anti-Kennedy forces, as they looked about desperately for a candidate, was that President Johnson would let it be known to his representatives in the New York Democratic party that he did not want Bobby. "Some of those who talked with him," Apple reported, "got the impression that he was reluctant to foreclose the Attorney General from two positions in two weeks, whatever the personal and political strains between them." The President, in fact, was ready to speak well of Bobby, and this wrapped it up. It had taken twenty-seven days to convert a stranger to New York's politics into a Senatorial candidate.

Once nominated, Bobby made his speeches and received the adulation of the crowds. But the real battle continued behind the scenes. The expenditure of effort in just one area indicates how much was done. Victor Riesel saw it as a "story of how Robert Francis Kennedy turned a campaign into a precise science by leading a team which found no errand too meager to run, no trip too fatiguing to make, no hamlet too isolated to visit, no minor leader too obscure to consult with, no issue too esoteric to tackle if a handful of votes were involved." Riesel's beat is labor, and it was into this vastly important segment of the New York population that he turned his attention in analyzing the Kennedy victory.

A United Labor Committee was formed, Riesel reported, under

the chairmanship of two indefatigable men, John McNiff of the Pulp, Sulphite, and Paper Mill Workers union, and Robert Mozer, a labor lawyer. The ULC created its own network of Kennedy workers. Many counties had permanent ULC directors, including the town of LeRoy, population 4,000, which had never been so signally honored by a Senatorial candidate. ULC workers visited more than 800 labor leaders throughout the state. They "walked in and said they represented Bob Kennedy and wanted to know what [the labor leaders] thought, what were the specific issues which worried them and their followers, and what could the candidate do for them and their movement." On the basis of these interviews, the ULC activists filed concise reports, each giving the labor leader's name, the number of union members in his area, wage levels, percentage of union members registered, the issues in order of their importance to the labor leader, and reactions to Bobby as a person and as a candidate.

The activists not only mailed in their reports to ULC headquarters, they also phoned in daily reports. Digests of the written and oral reports were distributed to Steve Smith; to Bobby's press chief Ed Guthman; to David Hackett, Bobby's personal aide in the campaign; and to ULC's cochairmen, McNiff and Mozer. Résumés also went to Bobby, who was consulted directly only when an important policy decision had to be made. When Bobby went into a district, he had a ULC abstract of its voting record in 1960, a breakdown of the population by income, age, and labor penetration. The ground was prepared by 700 personal letters to labor leaders from Bobby. Another 127,000 letters to the smaller labor fry were written by pro-Kennedy labor officials with help from Bobby. At the same time, friendly unions, their activities coordinated by ULC, Riesel reported, "put loud speaker trucks onto the streets and highways, made tens of thousands of telephone calls, poured hundreds of thousands of publications into the mailboxes of members, widely circulated Kennedy's own newspaper The Tabloid, crushed Keating's labor machine, reversed endorsements of the Republican, gave Kennedy full use of the trade union structure for swift contact with vast masses of members, got the usually unseen local labor leaders into the Kennedy caravans."

But it was the advertising campaign, handled by the firm of Papert, Koenig & Lois, Inc., which, according to the New York Herald-Tribune's Terry Smith, sold the public on Bobby Kennedy. After the election, Smith had the agency run off all the television and radio commercials they had prepared at a cost of $1,206,207. "There were about a hundred of them," he wrote in *Esquire,* "varying in length from twenty-second spots to thirty-minute films, plus a score of newspaper ads, radio commercials, and flyers." The cost, said Smith, was "staggering" and set "a record for advertising in a Senate campaign." The aim of the radio-television campaign was to change the candidate's "image as a Little League ogre. They had to warm up the merchandise. The job was not unlike that of getting tunafish moving after a botulism scare." The technique was to show Bobby talking to small groups of people, to individuals, where he could be relaxed and friendly.

"One showed a young man asking about the carpetbagger charge, and Bobby answering by describing his roots in the state, how he had gone to school there and spent twenty years there. Admittedly, he described the good old days in New York in an accent that reeked of Harvard Yard, but it seemed to work. (On the campaign trail, Kennedy often explained to his upstate audiences that although his accent might sound strange to them, it was actually a 'Glen Cove accent.' [Glen Cove is the Long Island town where he had rented a house in order to establish New York State residence.] On another day, he would tell a group of Long Islanders that his was the accent of upstate New York.)"

For the ethnic votes, the agency got Harry Golden "extolling Kennedy's virtues in Yiddish"—and a similar technique was applied to soften up the Puerto Rican, Russian, Polish, German and other foreign-language groups.

To keep the commercials flowing, the agency set up a task force of sixteen department heads, with a staff of more than 200 assistants. They worked seven days a week. The cameras followed Bobby everywhere he went, and the tapes of his speeches and his conversations were carefully edited to give the brief moments which fit the agency's format. A meeting was set up with Columbia University students just to furnish material for the commercials. Bobby answered their questions, supplying the agency with material for a half-hour commercial, broadcast six times, as well as a five-minute segment and many one-minute spots. It was from this taping that the agency got the famous scene of Bobby crying when he was asked about the Warren Commission report on Lee Harvey Oswald and the assassination of President Kennedy. His election-eve broadcast, in which Bobby, his wife, and the children appeared, had to be taped twice to give it the proper informal atmosphere.

"If the voters thought Kennedy ruthless in August, at least they had some doubts by November," Terry Smith wrote. "His public image had undergone a hurried but successful face lifting."

After the election, Bobby could remark, "Now I can go back to being ruthless again."

12

---◆◄◐►◆---

Burr Under the Saddle

A CERTAIN magic envelops the ordinary mortal when he puts on the Senatorial toga. There is prestige to membership in the "world's most exclusive club" and a subtle power which can almost be felt in the corridors of the two Senate office buildings. There is also a mystique which finds expression in the rules and traditions of what was once a truly deliberative body. For Robert Francis Kennedy, however, election to the United States Senate was a temporary expedient, a way station on the way to the high place he saw as inevitably and legitimately his own. The death of John F. Kennedy had deprived Bobby of powers closely linked to those of the Presidency. They included life, death, and the manipulation of a vast bureaucracy for ends good or bad. Before history marched into the President's office during the Kennedy Administration, it made a detour through the Justice Department. Heads of state and greedy politicians made their obeisance to the Attorney General.

But the staid and careful ways of the Senate demand a period of apprenticeship for its new members, a kind of initiation through humility and silence. This, however, was not for Bobby Kennedy. From the moment that New York's votes were counted, he made it clear to his intimates that he had other fish to fry. The question was, how to fry them? The ultimate goal was the White House, as all those close to him knew. Barring the death of President Johnson, he had eight years ahead of him for preparation and action. But even the most casual student of American politics knows that the best-laid plans of men seemingly destined for the Presidency can turn to nothing. The long wait and the slow approach, therefore, were not for Bobby. It was his often-expressed conviction that the race is to the swift, the battle to the strong, and victory to the man who rises earliest and throws the most punches.

To become President, as he saw it, he would have to devote his time and his considerable energies to a multiple effort. First, it was mandatory that he establish his power in his adopted state of New York. There were men in the Democratic party willing and anxious to seize the reins of power for their own purposes. They had resented Bobby's entrance into New York politics. They saw him reaching out for the strings that activate New York politicians, that employ patronage to win votes, that make or break candidates. With New York in his grasp, Bobby could lead from strength in his bid for the Presidency. But New York was only the bastion. He would still have to make his mark on the Senate, assuming such leadership as he could. To do this, he would have to surmount the obstacles placed in the way of a "freshman" Senator by his colleagues.

At the same time, he would have to keep together the "Kennedy underground" in the federal Establishment—that group of officials, high and low, who still acknowledged their indebtedness to the money and power of Bobby's clan. The Kennedy underground was made up of those who had been appointed to federal jobs by Bobby in the days when he controlled patronage, to the doctrinaire liberals who had shared the press' overwhelming admiration for the late President, and to ambitious officeholders who felt that the Kennedy wave of the future would carry them much further than the Johnsonian omnibus. Bobby had fashioned his underground with considerable care, and it had continued to serve him even during the time when President Johnson was carefully attempting to root it out. With Bobby once more on the move, the underground's lines of communication reached into the White House, the State Department, and in many of the major departments and agencies of the federal government. Behind the underground, and giving it strength, was a Liberal Establishment of increasing restiveness whose leaders looked down their noses at what they considered Lyndon Johnson's lack of intellectual polish.

Bobby is essentially a "loner," but he has learned that organization is essential. He could cut as wide a swath as Wayne Morse in the Senate, but he would remain equally ineffectual. To have his words taken seriously by his colleagues, they needed the backing of others who would speak and vote similarly. Bobby was wise enough to realize that he could not build an openly recognizable "Kennedy bloc" in the Senate or exact a 100-percent conformity from those he welded into his machine. Seemingly a participant in a group of younger and more left-swinging Democratic Senators, Bobby hoped to use his group as a political force in Congress but, equally important, as a means of achieving the piecemeal capture of the Democratic party which was a vital element in his drive for the Presidency. Within the Kennedy periphery, and available on key issues as time went on, were Birch Bayh and Vance Hartke, both of Indiana, Gale McGee of Wyoming, and Joseph Tydings of Maryland. His brother, Senator Edward Kennedy of Massachusetts, was not as sturdy a reed as the pundits had predicted. With ambitions of his own, and the politician's natural lack of abrasiveness, Ted occasionally resented Bobby's brash aggressiveness. Frank Church of Idaho was singled out as a part-time ally. Among the older Senators, Ernest Gruening of Alaska and Joseph Clark of Pennsylvania added numbers to the "Kennedy bloc," whether consciously or not. Others joined temporarily, dropped out, and returned.

Through all of them, the Kennedy underground began reaching out into the grassroots where, as the politicians learned in the spring of the Goldwater movement, conventions can be won or lost. But this support is not one that can be synthetically manufactured. The county chairman and the precinct worker can be hoodwinked or manipulated, but he must have a cause or an ideal. He must respond viscerally to an appeal. Bobby Kennedy set out to appeal to youth, the greatest of all American cults. In his late thirties, he still cultivated the young manner, aided by his own durable youthfulness and deceptive shyness. But "youth" was not enough. It was necessary to mark himself off from the Johnson ideology, to make himself as different as possible from the President. Johnson had preempted the so-called middle of the road, and his consensus was built on the aspirations of those fearful of anything that smacked of the "extreme." Left and right were open to Kennedy, and his inevitable course was to swing to the left. No other way would have been possible for a Democrat, and Bobby's natural tendencies, like those of many rich young men, were toward the left.

This was a decision made long before the Senate had become his base of operations. He had tried it on for size in his journeys to the world's troubled areas during his tenure as Attorney General. He was developing it when he thought he might coerce President Johnson into giving him the Vice-Presidential nomination. The portion of the political spectrum which he selected for himself has been labeled by sociologists, Intelligence authorities, and others as "the revolution of youth," ill-assorted but activist and destructive elements in the United States and abroad. Some of it is Marxist-Leninist, some is freakish and disgruntled, most of it is totalitarian. He himself had vaguely but approvingly characterized this attitude in a speech in Toronto early in 1964, the import of which few recognized at the time.

"We must recognize that the young in many areas of the world today are in the midst of a revolution against the status quo," he said. "Their anger is turned on the system which has allowed poverty, illiteracy, and oppression to flourish for centuries. And we must recognize one central fact: They will prevail. They will achieve their idealistic goals, one way or another. If they have to pull governments tumbling down over their heads, they will do it. But they are going to win a share of the new world.

"This affects us: Canada and the United States, and you and me. Our future is tied up with what they think. Like them or not, what they are going to do will have a direct impact on us. We, in turn, are part of their revolution. At least we should, and I believe we must encourage them. They will not be like 'sheep without a shepherd when the snow shuts out the sky.' Someone will share their aspirations and their leadership. If this means that the future is perilous, I must admit that I think it is."

In the months and years that followed this utterance, Robert Kennedy made it clear that he intended to seek directly and energetically the support of a "revolution" which was already manifesting itself on the Berkeley campus and in draft-card burnings, in appeals for sending American blood to save Vietcong Communists, and in the fervid rhetoric of young professors who called for the defeat of American arms in Vietnam. Robert S. Allen and Paul Scott, the syndicated columnists who were among the first to call attention to the Bobby Kennedy line, noted in June of 1964 that, "as proposed by Kennedy in the Canadian trial balloon, he will call for U.S. government support for such controversial revolutionary leaders as:

"Kenneth Kaunda, 39, heard of the Northern Rhodesian Nationalist Movement, and a known pro-Soviet Marxist [now the rabble-rousing president of Zambia]; Oskar Kambona, 32, left-leaning minister of Tanganyika; Joana Savimbi, 30, Angolan exile leader who has secret Russian ties; Sékou Touré, 38, president of Guinea and an avowed Marxist; Tom Mboya, minister of justice in Kenya, and

Rufino Keckonova, 33, left-leaning Philippines minister of finance." [1]

The Kennedy plan for 1972 also included a push for recognition as an expert on foreign policy to show that Bobby could cope with problems of the Presidency in a world grown more complex and more hostile. He had traveled enough to realize that no matter how he was received abroad, he could turn it to his advantage. If he was heckled, he responded with boyishly phrased arguments in defense of America—and made headlines. If he was cheered, and reached the undergraduate New Leftists sufficiently to be sure of a friendly welcome, then he could give them understanding and a few critical slogans to show that his heart was with them—and make headlines again. He was weakest on domestic matters, on the problems of New York State and of the nation. But he was ready to make up for this by frontal assaults on the President, Governor Nelson Rockefeller, Senator Jacob Javits, and others who did not figure in the maneuvers of the Kennedy underground. These attacks, made in violation of Senate protocol and political custom developed over the years, earned him the quiet hatred of those on the receiving end, but to the public, it seemed like a show of youthful courage.

The plans were carefully thought through in brainstorming sessions with the old Jack Kennedy team. The implementation was to remain in the hands of a large staff made up of men he had brought with him from the Justice Department. But like most blueprints for success, the Kennedy Eight-year Plan was subject to forces not in Bobby's control. The election barely over, he was caught in a crossfire from the Defense Department and the White House. Secretary Robert McNamara, pursuing his much-publicized drive for economy, had been itching to close down some ninety-five Army and Navy bases. Among them was the Brooklyn Navy Yard, a venerable relic but of considerable economic importance to New York since it employed 10,000 people. President Kennedy had ducked the issue of the base closures, despite continuing pressure from the Secretary of Defense. During the 1964 campaign, dockworkers and others employed at the Brooklyn Navy Yard had been reassured that with Bobby in office the bases would be saved, whereas a Republican Senator would have no influence on a Democratic Administration.

On November 19, Secretary McNamara called Bobby to inform him that the Brooklyn Navy Yard would be shut down. This an-

[1] "If they get out a coloring book for Bobby," one Washington correspondent remarked, "we'll have to color him pink."

nouncement came despite Bobby's highly publicized trip to Washington, two days after the election, to urge that the base be kept open. And it led to the pointed lead in Philip Potter's Baltimore *Sun* account: "Senator-elect Kennedy's first effort in that post to influence the decisions of the Administration of which he once was a vital part ended today in failure." To make matters worse, Secretary McNamara made it bluntly clear that he had been under great political pressure to back down from what he considered the only solution. The second blow came when Bobby received his committee assignments. He had asked for and gotten places on the District Committee, the Labor and Public Welfare Committee, and the Government Operations' Committee. But his hope that Chairman John McClellan, with whom he had worked so closely during the Senate Labor Rackets Committee days, would appoint him to the powerful and headline-making Permanent Investigations Subcommittee was dashed. Senator McClellan let it be quietly known that he disapproved of Bobby's part as Attorney General in assigning the controversial TFX airplane contract to a company unable to meet the lower bids and better specifications of a competitor. To many the TFX case smelled of political influence.

All did not go as smoothly as Kennedy had anticipated. His office situation, three months after he had been installed, combined the trials and tribulations of the freshman Senator. Bobby's staff was scattered among three rooms on different floors and corridors of the Senate Office Building. This made the necessary work of greeting constituents, answering mail, and attending to routine Senate business triply difficult. The fault was no one's; as low man on the totem pole, the junior Senator from New York had no claim on any office space until those with seniority had picked the accommodations they wanted. But if Bobby did not do so well in Washington, his office situation in New York and Syracuse made up for it. To make Bobby comfortable, the government spent more than $200,000 to provide him with free office space in New York's Grand Central Federal Building and an unspecified amount for other offices in Syracuse, plus $2,500 for new furniture in New York alone. In the first space he dispossessed the operations manager of the New York Post Office. In the second, he ousted the United States Retirement Board.

Bobby's justification lay in post-office regulations which granted that "limited office accommodations" at the Grand Central and other post offices be made "available when convenient" to Senators when they were in the state. Bobby had gone far beyond this by demanding Rooms 401, 402, 403, 404, and 405, which were remodeled for

aultfault

his use. In the process, the two rooms now taken over by the operations manager, who in turn was forced to preempt space from the post-office sign painter and the safety director, had no independent access to the elevators. It was necessary to cut a new corridor to give those rooms that access. The sign painter and the safety director were pushed into a storage room which had to be remodeled. By the time the floor was redesigned thirty-nine rooms had been affected. In Syracuse, Bobby's seizure of three rooms compelled the Railroad Retirement Board to move from the federal complex at the main post office and to take space a quarter of a mile away in a private office building.

Columnist Henry J. Taylor commented: "Neither hail, rain, sleet, nor the gloom of night stay Bobby from the swift completion of his ride on the gravy train. Conscience and money somehow do not seem to mix in politics. But this writer, at least, finds it especially galling when the very rich—silently, oh so silently—spend our money when they should spend theirs."

Bobby, however, seemed little bothered by the bad publicity. He wanted the two offices for his war on Mayor Wagner and as a command post for his operations in New York State. The area north of the New York City line had always been neglected by Democratic Senators, and it was Bobby's aim to take over these once-Republican urban centers in his drive to seize the leadership of his own party from those reform elements which had formed around Mrs. Eleanor Roosevelt, the late Senator Lehman, and Wagner. In his first attempt at Democratic leadership, however, he failed miserably and pushed Wagner and Governor Rockefeller into an anti-Kennedy alliance, which Bobby took with ill grace. At issue was the control of the New York state legislature, Democratic for the first time in twenty-nine years—as a result of the great Johnson landslide.

Under normal circumstances, the majority leadership in the state Senate and the Assembly would have gone without too much controversy to the former minority leaders. In the State Senate, Joseph Zaretski of Manhattan considered the majority leadership his. In the Assembly, Anthony Travia of Brooklyn felt equally certain of his right to the position of speaker. Both were downstate politicians and part of the Wagner wing of the Democratic party. But they had not reckoned with Bobby Kennedy or old-line boss Charles Buckley. With Bobby remaining modestly in the background but pulling the strings, State Senator Julian B. Erway of Albany and Assemblyman Stanley Steingut of Brooklyn suddenly appeared as contenders for the coveted posts. There were vociferous denials that they represented Bobby's bid for control of the Democratic party in New

York, but no one took them seriously. What lingering doubts there may have been that this was a power play disappeared when the two "dark horses" were shown to have more strength in the legislature than the veteran leadership. On a head count, Zaretski could only muster twelve of the state Senate's fifty-eight Democrats, Travia only thirty-five of the Assembly's eighty-eight Democrats. On a showdown vote, however, neither side could muster a majority of the respective chambers.

Making the impasse more impassable was the Kennedy-Buckley choice for the Assembly's speaker. Julian Erway, liberal Democrats charged, was a "Goldwater Democrat"—a thoroughly destructive criticism among Democrats. He had also opposed a bill to prohibit housing discrimination, and sometimes voted with the Republicans. Erway's rebuttal was hardly satisfying to the liberal Democrats. He treated his Negro maid very well, he said, and his farm had served as a way station for the Underground Railroad during the days of the War Between the States. In quick time, even the Kennedy-Buckley legislators turned on Erway and there was talk of a deal in which the pro-Wagner Zaretski would get the majority leadership and the pro-Kennedy Steingut the speakership. But this fell through.

Finally, after twenty-five ballots, the Republican minority cut the knot by throwing their support to Zaretski in the State Senate. There were howls of indignation from the Kennedy-Buckley side, but the Wagner faction, in conjunction with the Republicans, had the votes. Immediately, the cry went up that Mayor Wagner and Governor Rockefeller had made a deal. But this was neither true nor necessary. Having watched the Democrats making a spectacle of themselves, the delighted Republicans had jumped in to heap humiliation on their rivals, to exact a political debt from the Zaretski-Travia leadership, and to demonstrate to the voters that they were the responsible party in the New York legislature.

Bobby Kennedy was skiing in Colorado, presumably unconcerned, while his fellow Democrats were brawling in Albany. His assistants argued with persistent reporters that he was "neutral," that it was not his battle. But these denials, as the New York *Times* editorially noted, fell of their own weight when Bobby, in one of his unpredictable, impulsive, and gratuitous outbursts, took pen in hand to admonish the new Democratic leadership. In long letters to Zaretski and Travia, Bobby lectured them seriously on the evils of patronage —a rather odd position for one who had dispensed so much of it when he was Attorney General. He had "assumed" that the

$4,000,000 a year in jobs available to the majority "would be filled on the basis of merit," he wrote sternly, and "since this is a state matter, I had intended to remain uninvolved." But he had learned that "telephone calls" were being made, and this upset him. "Dealing the jobs out like so many cards off the top of the deck is intolerable and can only contribute to the loss of our party's newly gained majority position." He "suggested" that "full disclosure be made to the public of all the jobs which are involved and of the duties and responsibilities and pay, including expenses, attached to each job." The press and the professional politicians asked themselves why Bobby had taken this opportunity to imply that his own party was venal or why, after the sad showing of the Democratic state leadership, he should inflame old wounds.

Zaretski answered angrily that "he's trying to take over the legislature." And he added bitterly, "You don't see Senator Javits telling the Republicans how to run the state—and he is just as dedicated a man as Senator Kennedy. . . . The letter came like a bombshell. I didn't think he was the Democratic State Chairman. I thought he was just elected to the United States Senate." The professional politicians were not particularly impressed by Zaretski's indignation. But they asked themselves why Bobby had taken that moment to attempt intervention. "Youth," said one, "and inexperience. He counted on taking over the New York legislature—and when he was outmaneuvered he lashed out at those who won. I guess he's just mad —but I wonder what would have happened if he'd been President."

But youth and inexperience were a style that Bobby Kennedy cultivated. Even the uncritical press noted this when he made his first appearance at a Senate committee hearing. This was one side of congressional activity that he knew well from his years as counsel for various Senate investigations. Bobby, however, entered the hearing through the public entrance, along with the press and the gaping tourists, rather than through the committee room as the other Senators did—as, in fact, he had done when he was on the staff of the McCarthy and McClellan committees. His coat was draped over his arm and he looked about helplessly for a place to leave it. As Warren Weaver Jr. of the New York *Times* said, "He seemed perplexed as to how to find his way up to the rostrum with the rest of the Senators." In questioning witnesses, he played the part of a lawyer overwhelmingly conditioned by courtroom experience—though his days in court have been notably few—by rising to his feet, which in the memory of Capitol Hill correspondents no other Senator has done.

In the Senate, Bobby set out to show that he would not be bound by those traditions which help to differentiate politics from jungle warfare. A Senator, though he may be of a different party than the governor of his state, is considered to represent that governor in the Congress. If the state, rather than the ambition of the Senator, is to be served, the two must work together, however antagonistic they may be to each other. They do not attack each other publicly, whatever they may do behind the scenes or through their political henchmen. Yet Bobby, in his maiden speech to the Senate, was openly critical of Governor Rockefeller. Offering an amendment to the Appalachia bill to include thirteen New York State counties in the so-called War on Poverty, Kennedy attacked Rockefeller for being "shortsighted" in not asking for a share of the federal loot. Bobby had his way, but in so doing, he won the enmity of Republican Senator Jacob Javits, who was placed in the awkward position of having to support the Kennedy amendment with its implied criticism of his state's governor or of appearing to be opposed to helping New York's poor. As Rockefeller acidly pointed out, however, twelve of the thirteen counties had no need of federal aid. The thirteenth would have been better served by being included in the federal highway-building program, which would have opened it up to commerce and industry. The Kennedy amendment, however, did make headlines for Bobby in upstate newspapers.

To make matters worse, Bobby moved in rapidly to make capital of the amendment he had pushed through. He scheduled a well-publicized press conference in Syracuse, New York, never disclosing what it would be about. Javits knew that Bobby planned a coup of some consequence, but he was rebuffed at every turn when he tried to discover what Bobby intended to announce. While Javits fumed and fretted, Bobby told local reporters—and voters—of a gigantic antipoverty grant to the city, taking sole credit. Javits was left out in the cold, and so was Rockefeller. Commenting on this political knifing, one Republican Congressman said, "Rockefeller was cut by this thing, too. This is the maddest I've ever seen Javits in his life about a political trick." New York Democratic bosses, however, chortled and counted votes.

But Bobby's anti-Rockefeller onslaught had just begun. He railed at the governor for his failure in dealing with the New Haven Railroad, a major commuter line from Connecticut to New York. He called for a National Scenic Waterway along the banks of the lower Hudson River, opposed by both Rockefeller (who charged that it would violate the state's sovereignty) and President Johnson. Then, calling on members of the Kennedy underground, he caused them to issue a statement in support of his program. Praising California and denigrating New York, he was sharply critical of the Rockefeller treatment of narcotics addicts. And when a bill was introduced in the state legislature to increase the minimum wage to $1.50 an hour, Bobby let fly at the governor for opposing it. "I know I couldn't get by on $1.50 an hour," Bobby said, "and I doubt if Mr. Rockefeller could." He made no mention of the effect that a New York State minimum wage twenty-five cents an hour higher than the federal rate would have on industry. Rockefeller was aware that it would drive out some businesses and lead others to stay out of the state at a time when he was working hard to bring in new industry, and the jobs it created, to New York.

Meanwhile, in Bobby's spacious and well-appointed suite at the Grand Central Federal Building, a staff of eight paid workers and twelve volunteers [2] were adding a new dimension to New York political activity by going far beyond the servicing of inquiries, protests, and requests from constituents. The order of the day at what was nicknamed the "Kennedy clubhouse" was to originate projects which would keep Bobby's name in New York City and upstate newspapers. One such "project" was Bobby's unannounced visit to two state-run schools for mentally retarded children. Then he proceeded to give his account of what he had presumably seen there to the State Joint Legislative Committee for Mental Retardation, which by "coincidence" happened to be meeting in a Bronx hotel, ready to hear what Bobby had to say.

All the news media had also been forewarned, and the New York City papers front-paged what had already been confided to television's anxious ears. The children at these schools, Bobby said, "just rock back and forth. They grunt and gibber and soil themselves. They struggle and quarrel—though great doses of tranquilizers usually keep them passive and quiet." He protested the lack of "civil liberties" for those put into "cells" where, living "amidst brutality and human excrement and intestinal disease," they were "worse off than in a zoo." How, in brief visits, he could have discovered the "brutality" and known of the intestinal disease became clear when it was learned that he was, in effect, quoting from special and unpublished reports to the state legislature which had somehow come into his hands. The shot had nevertheless reached its target, the

[2] Javits has three paid employees and, during periods of peak activity, never more than ten volunteers.

Rockefeller administration. That New York has perhaps the best facilities and gives the best treatment for mental disability of any state in the union was a fact lost in the general furor.

Lost, too, was the rebuttal by Dr. Christopher F. Terrence, Commissioner of Mental Hygiene, that Bobby's out-of-context observations "distorted out of all perspective" the conditions in state schools for the mentally retarded, and Rockefeller's anguished statement that New York's efforts in this area had been of a caliber to serve as "the blueprint for the federal program presented to the Congress by the late President Kennedy." Explanations that the Democratic legislature had refused to appropriate additional funds requested by Rockefeller were bypassed. The director of one of the schools, Dr. Jack Hammond, could protest the effect of Bobby's attack on the morale of his teachers. "To understand the operation at all and be fair, you have to be able to stay a couple of days. He didn't have the time here to make the statements that he did," said Hammond. Others, less restrained, pointed out that some mentally retarded children, under all conditions of care and understanding, act as Bobby described. An inability to control their bodily functions is a part of their sickness and not a result of the treatment they receive.

The climax to the whole controversy came when Bobby released to the press the texts of four communications between himself and the governor. In one letter, Bobby had written that "a brief survey of available federal programs indicates that in virtually every case, New York State is foregoing opportunities for federal assistance which could make a major difference in the lives of the retarded. I am sure that when you are aware of the extent of unused federal assistance available, you will wish to make the appropriate changes in the relevant state machinery to insure that you will be properly informed in the future."

This sarcastic letter, implying that inefficiency or callousness was preventing Rockefeller from requesting federal aid for the mentally retarded, was on the face of it hardly believable. Pressed for funds, Governor Rockefeller was seeking every dollar he could get from the federal government, and he certainly had no ideological objections to dipping into the United States Treasury. His answer, therefore, was equally brusque.

"I trust," he said in an answering telegram, "that the continuing relations of state officials with their federal counterparts and the obtaining of assistance for the mentally retarded will not depend on your acting as the political broker. The state government is aware of these federal programs. The relations between federal and New

York State officials has been a close one over the years, regardless of the political party in power at either level of government. The departments of the state government have been instructed to obtain every dollar of federal funds that the people of New York are entitled to, in the field of mental retardation, as well as in other areas."

Bobby called a press conference forthwith at the Carlyle Hotel in New York. "What he has done is tasteless," he said angrily. "It is wrong. He is jeopardizing the future of children and others for the benefit of his own political administration." He did not explain how Rockefeller would gain politically by depriving mentally retarded children of adequate care, but he had a quick answer to a reporter's question as to why Rockefeller had rejected his "help" in solving the mental retardation problem. "Evidently," Bobby said, "he feels that he doesn't want to cooperate at all in any matter in which I am involved."

The performance was "politics at its worst," as one observer remarked. But this did not deter Bobby. Shifting his position on the welfare state, he made a series of tours of upstate New York, the Republican heartland, visiting city and county officials, farmers, businessmen, labor leaders, and others in areas which, as a result of changing technology, had been slipping economically. To these people, he no longer preached the virtues of government intervention and federal handouts but of local initiative and state help. "I don't think your answer is in Washington," he would say. "Your answer is here." During these trips he was steadily adding to the Kennedy card file of people who could be useful in the future, of problems that could be exploited during an election campaign. He was making himself known to those who might someday make rural New York solidly Democratic territory after generations of allegiance to the Republican party. And he was neutralizing the attitude of those who resented the fact that a big-city boy now occupied the seat once held by upstater Kenneth Keating. The effectiveness of these "fact-finding missions," as Bobby called them, was underscored by the New York *Times* when, early in his Senatorial tenure, it reported:

"The New York Democrat has devoted so much attention to upstate communities and issues already that a loose federation of upstate Republican House members has been formed to combat his influence. In the new Congress, there are only seven Republicans from north of Westchester County, and their administrative assistants have established a group called Congressional Republicans of New York, or C.R.O.N.Y.

"They are not primarily concerned over Senator Kennedy's mounting criticism of Governor Rockefeller; they are afraid the Democrat is getting so much publicity in their upstate districts that he may undermine even these last few bastions of New York Republicanism."

There was always a question of Bobby's ability to transfer his appeal to candidates of his choice, always a difficult and touchy matter, as Franklin D. Roosevelt discovered when he tried to replace several Congressmen and Senators with his hand-picked choices. In the 1965 race for mayor of New York City, Bobby's intervention in the primary battle succeeded in stopping Paul Screvane, Mayor Wagner's candidate; but the choice of the Kennedy machine and the old-line politicians, Abraham Beame, although a reasonably estimable man, was defeated by ultraliberal Republican John Lindsay. Local issues were in part responsible, as they will be in all future contests in the state, whether or not Bobby is involved. But Kennedy and his chief political operative, brother-in-law Stephen Smith, were not interested in winning congressional races. The aim was to defeat Nelson Rockefeller with a Kennedy-picked Democrat and thereby to nail down the New York state government and its delegates to the next Democratic Presidential conventions.

In the Senate and on the national scene, Robert Kennedy was even less tactful. This was reflected in the attitude of veteran Senators who realized from the start that Bobby was not interested in them, not concerned with the customs of the Senate, and had little thought of introducing major legislation. His attention was focused on the press. What they said about him, and what he could get by them, were the important considerations. As Attorney General, he had treated the Senate with what almost amounted to contempt. In his personal relations with the members, he was brusque and chip-on-the-shoulder, frequently attacking Senators even though no one had challenged him. The usual human courtesies, much emphasized in the Senate, were ignored, and Bobby would walk by his colleagues in the Senate subway or the corridors of the Capitol without so much as a smile of recognition or a word of salutation—"as if," one Senator said, "we were enemies or servants." Another Senator remarked, "I expect any day to read that Bobby has set up a Senate of his own. He doesn't give a damn about this one."

There were some sharp observations about his eagerness for newspaper coverage. It was noted, with considerable irony, that, on the anniversary of the assassination, Bobby visited his brother's grave, and then returned for another visit because photographers had not been present the first time.

Astonishing to those who had heard of Bobby's political perspicacity was his reluctance to reciprocate when someone did him a favor. For example, when Bobby submitted his amendment to the Appalachia bill, including thirteen New York counties, it was Senator Javits who came to his aid. The Kennedy amendment was so badly written that it did not list the counties to be included, and it was out of line with the rest of the bill. As a courtesy to a junior Senator from his own state, Javits stepped in to help Bobby rewrite the amendment. But in case after case, Bobby would stop just short of outright rudeness in his exchanges with Javits. And he worked diligently to cut Javits' throat with New York voters whenever possible by directing the Kennedy underground to give him prior news of federal grants to New York. These Bobby announced first, a violation of protocol, particularly from a junior Senator. In the long run, Javits benefited by this "what makes Bobby run" behavior. Javits is a member of the "Senate club," and his colleagues delighted in tipping him off to Bobby's presumably secret moves.

But if Bobby was disliked for his aggressiveness and his unalloyed feistiness, he was grudgingly respected for his willingness to take on the President of the United States and to organize a Senate cabal against him. On both domestic and foreign policy, he was ready to take issue with the Administration, to embarrass it, and to hold forth on problems in a manner which gave foreign governments a bad case of the jitters. Any speech on the affairs of the world, when it was delivered by Bobby, would flood the State Department and Secretary Dean Rusk with questions. Was it a trial balloon? Did it mean that the American people stood in opposition to Lyndon Johnson? Was there more to it than the opinions and prejudices of a United States Senator? Not even Joe McCarthy had caused so much unhappiness among heads of state and their ambassadors plenipotentiary as Bobby did.

When the Johnson Administration announced that it was closing down eleven Veterans Administration hospitals, Kennedy protested loudly, as did other Senators whose states were affected by the order. But Bobby studied the VA reports carefully, right through the small print, and consulted a few experts. At the hearing called to consider the President's action, he plowed into William J. Driver, the Veterans Administrator, with an intensity that would brook no interruption—not even from his brother Senator Edward Kennedy. Of particular interest to Bobby was the Sun Mount Hospital, a VA installation in New York.

The Veterans Administration had said that it was "outmoded" and that shortages in staff made it impossible to operate properly. Under questioning, however, Administration witnesses began to wilt. As the caustic Mary McGrory wrote in the Washington *Star*, Bobby challenged "every other sentence in the V.A. report" and made "every member in the thin gray line of bureaucrats before him wish they [*sic*] had never been born as he taxed them in turn about radiologists, psychiatrists, dental clinics, new ceramic floor, and research on liver." Was Sun Mount, built in 1926 and renovated in 1950 at a cost of $2,500,000, outmoded? After a small pause, James E. Shaw, the engineer of the hospital, said that in his opinion it was not outmoded.

"I don't want to put you in difficulty," Bobby said, "but obviously I have." Was there a shortage of personnel? Shaw said there wasn't. Another witness had testified that Sun Mount had no pathologist. Bobby wrung an admission from him that it did have one, but on part-time. When the hearing had ended, the witnesses felt as if they had been given the third degree in the back room of a police station. The White House was unhappy, too, and more than a little embarrassed—a fact that was not lost to a Washington press corps gathering evidence of the continuing rift between Bobby Kennedy and Lyndon Johnson.

The real break between Bobby Kennedy and President Johnson, however, came in the field of foreign policy. In the domestic field, he could only hop and skip to remain consistently on the left of the Administration. But as his chief aid, Adam Walinsky, a twenty-eight-year-old whiz kid out of Harvard Law, said: "All Bob can do is offer amendments to legislative proposals. How can he do anything else? The Great Society has a program for everything." The Kennedy oneupmanship could go just so far. Foreign policy, in Bobby's mind, offered a clear field. President Johnson remained cautious and conciliatory to the warring left and right wings of his party. He hoped, at best, to keep the debate within legitimate bounds, to impress on both Democrats and Republicans that differences of opinion and approach had to stop at the water's edge. His record in the Senate during the Eisenhower years had been one of responsibility where the nation's security was concerned, and it can be said to his credit that he used his power and prestige to back a Republican Administration when it confronted a hostile world. Bobby had other ideas. They were summed up incisively in a column by William S. White, who more often than not put into print what Lyndon Johnson had on his mind.

"Though once a notable hard-liner," White wrote for his syndicate, "Kennedy's every utterance now comes close to adopting the theory of the liberal left that almost any exercise of American power against Communist expansionism or against the clear danger of Communist expansionism—in Latin America or in Southeast Asia—is perhaps extreme, or unnecessary, or unsympathetic to the spirit of social reform.

"So marked is the Senator's new far-liberalism that one after another he is dropping the positions of the late President. John Kennedy would neither speak for nor gladly deal with the far-out liberal wing. Robert Kennedy is becoming its most precise spokesman—and seemingly intends to become formally its leader.

"His ideological associates are not only out of step with the national Democratic Administration, they are out of tune as well with some of the most faithful of the old Kennedy people, those who were close to the late President. In the Senate itself, moreover, Robert Kennedy has joined the very bloc which gave his brother the most trouble and for whom the late President openly had no stomach at all, either politically or personally."

Bobby, too, had little stomach *personally* for many of the people whose far-out causes he espoused. He referred to the "peacenik" professors and their beatnik allies as "kooky intellectuals," but politically, he was ready to carry the ball for them. How much of this was principle, how much his determination to mobilize behind him the "youthful revolutionaries" of the world, is a moot point. President Kennedy could never have said, as Bobby did, that "to give blood to the North Vietnamese would be in the oldest traditions of this country. I'm willing to give blood to anybody who needs it." Perhaps, never having seen war at first hand, Bobby did not quite realize what he was saying. But when he said it, American soldiers and Marines were spilling their own blood against the enemy that Bobby could regard with such equanimity. The remark endeared him to left-wing students and to those actively seeking to undermine the American war effort. And it probably did him no great harm in the day's antipatriotic climate. It did explain why some one-time Kennedy supporters were beginning to refer to him as "Ho Chi-Bobby." But Kennedy must have realized the effect his casual remark had on his constituents because he formulated a flatly contradictory answer for those who complained. Through an assistant, he replied: "Senator Kennedy has always opposed any direct action by groups in this country to send blood or other supplies to the North Vietnamese."

On Vietnamese and Latin American policy, Bobby's statements

were carefully prepared and delivered with full knowledge of what they implied. Working with Adam Walinsky, he hacked out a political line which called for "negotiations" with the North Vietnamese regime and its puppets, the Vietcong and the National Liberation Front. "I believe that we have erred for some time in regarding Vietnam as purely a military problem when in its essential aspects it is also a political and diplomatic problem." When the North Vietnamese were pouring troops and matériel into the Vietnam war, Bobby could still insist that "victory in a revolutionary war is won not by escalation but by de-escalation." He did not explain how the withdrawal of American troops, at a time when the enemy was building up its forces, could lead to "victory." Nor did he specify who the victor should be. His criticism of the military aspects of the war were all aimed at the United States and the South Vietnamese government.

"If all a government can promise its people, in respect to insurgent activity, is ten years of napalm and heavy artillery, it would [sic] not be a government for long," he said. And: "Air attacks by a government on its own villages are likely to be far more dangerous and costly to the people than is the individual and selective terrorism of an insurgent movement"—a formulation neatly ignoring the organized campaigns of mass murder, the bombings, and the looting of the Communists. Bobby was ready to include the Communist Vietcong and the National Liberation Front in a "coalition" government, forgetting the lessons of Czechoslovakia and Poland in the postwar years: that "coalition" has always been the prelude to Communist seizure of power. When his proposal backfired, he typically resorted to the worn claim that he had been misunderstood and misquoted. He had never, Bobby insisted, really called for coalition. The verbatim text of his statement belies this:

"Whatever the exact status of the National Liberation Front—puppet or partly independent—any negotiated settlement must accept the fact that there are discontented elements in South Vietnam, Communist and non-Communist, who desire to change the existing political and economic system in the country. There are three things you can do with such groups: Kill or repress them, turn over the country to them, or admit them to a share of power and responsibility. The first two are possible only through force of arms.

"The last—*to admit them* [*the Communists*] *to a share of power and responsibility*—*is at the heart of the hope for a negotiated settlement.* It is not the easy way, or the sure way; nor can the manner of the degrees of participation now be described with any precision. It may come about through a single conference or many meetings, or by a slow, undramatic process of gradual accommodation." (Emphasis added.)

Proceeding down the same road, Kennedy began his campaign to bring Red China and the United States into closer diplomatic touch. In this he was aided by elements within the State Department which have steadily pushed for United States recognition of the Chinese Communists and for their admission into the United Nations, policies which run counter to the established policy of this country, to the overwhelming sense of Congress, and to the desires of the American people. Those individuals within the department working toward the goal of giving respectability to Chinese Communism have operated behind the scenes, a middle echelon "Red China lobby," seeking to sway the Secretary of State by the position papers they prepare and the information they allow him to see. Also advising Bobby was William C. Foster, director of the so-called disarmament office, whose goal at times has seemed to be the unilateral destruction of American nuclear weapons.

The vehicle for this drive was a speech delivered by Bobby on October 13, 1965. Present on the floor of the Senate were ten members who have systematically opposed the bipartisan containment policy and have advocated a thinly disguised appeasement. Among them were Senate Majority Leader Mike Mansfield, a thorn in President Johnson's side on foreign policy matters and a prophet of nuclear doom whenever the United States has moved to prevent the further expansion of the Communist imperium. Bobby's speech was reviewed, without the President's knowledge, by McGeorge Bundy, the White House aide entrusted with national security matters. It was, in short, a planned guerrilla operation by the Kennedy underground. Much of Bobby's speech dealt with the controversy inflaming Western Europe over the control of nuclear weapons and their deployment through a multilateral force, complex problems which not one American in a hundred had taken the time to analyze.

But the Kennedy speech also had its built-in kickers. It called for an extension of the unfortunate Treaty of Moscow, which banned nuclear testing in the atmosphere under conditions opposed by the Joint Chiefs of Staff. (Under the terms of the treaty, the Joint Chiefs warned, the Soviets could continue to develop tactical nuclear weapons, a field in which they lagged far behind the United States, while this country would be prevented from carrying on the research and testing necessary to develop a vitally needed anti-missile missile.) The "second step" demanded by Robert Kennedy called for (1) negotiations "at once" with all nations having nuclear weapons and (2) an invitation to Red China "to participate in the disarmament talks in Geneva"—a prelude to the admission of Red China to the United Nations. Bobby also proposed the creation of a nuclear free zone in Latin America, although not including Cuba, the one country in the area which, through its alliance with the Soviet Union, has had—and reportedly still has—such weapons and the capacity to deliver them.

The speech itself, filling sixteen columns in the *Congressional Record*—a somewhat shorter than average length for a Kennedy pronouncement—was a rehash of proposals made by pacifist, left-wing, and "Nervous Nellie" spokesmen. Its only significance was in the source. The ambassador of the Federal German Republic immediately called on Secretary of State Rusk. He was deeply disturbed by Senator Kennedy's remarks and wanted to know if they represented a shift in American policy. In Europe, the speech, as the late Marguerite Higgins reported, was "widely interpreted as advocating the abandonment of the idea of a NATO nuclear force in order to attain a broadened treaty with the Soviet Union. . . . Indeed, Kennedy's speech produced reactions opposite to what he intended. The alarms it stimulated led to the first public hints from responsible Germans that it might not be possible forever to renounce 'acquisition' of nuclear weapons if world circumstances change."

Bonn's foreign minister, Gerhard Schröder, commented pointedly that "Germany desires an effective means of achieving co-responsibility in the Western nuclear deterrent . . . and could renounce acquisition of its own nuclear weapons only if it gained co-responsibility" with the West for control of nuclear armaments—a broad hint that that it was not going to be pushed aside in order to allow the United States and the Soviet Union bilaterally to determine the world's nuclear future.

The "relaxation of tensions" which the speech was to have encouraged increased them instead. And diplomatic circles noted that no new test treaty would have any validity unless it were accompanied by a Soviet willingness to end its attempts to frustrate the economic and political union of Western Europe which many European and American leaders had sought for two decades. What mischief there was in Bobby's attempt to play the role of world statesman and Secretary of State on European and nuclear matters found itself multiplied in his venture into Latin American politics, and his extension there of his "revolution of youth" thesis. The locus of his interference was the Dominican Republic.

In April 1965, a revolt of Communist (Castroite, Moscow, and Peking varieties) and other left extremist groups plunged Santo Domingo into bloody warfare. Behind the uprising was Juan Bosch, a former Dominican president who had been overthrown for mismanaging the government and permitting its systematic infiltration by Communist activists. There was more than adequate Intelligence information that some of Bosch's lieutenants in Santo Domingo were under the discipline of a Castroite-Communist cabal—that without prompt United States intervention, one more Caribbean country would fall into totalitarian, antidemocratic, and anti-American hands. This would have been calamity. President Johnson moved in promptly to save American lives and to prevent the seizure of the country by Red rebels. From the standpoint of the national security, Johnson could do no less.

The outcry from the left, both in Congress and out, was deafening. The President was accused of crushing a "legitimate" revolution, of reviving "dollar diplomacy," of supporting "reaction" in order to thwart the "aspirations of the people." Speeches were delivered and articles written to prove that Johnson had succumbed to evil men in the Pentagon, motivated by an unreasoning anti-Communism. Rejecting incontrovertible evidence, some argued that the Communists were small in numbers and therefore of no consequence. Theodore Draper, once a contributor to the Communist *New Masses* under the name of Repard (the Serutan spelling of Draper), devoted pages of the *New Republic* to this charge, adding the argument that those accused of being Communists were, in fact, anti-Communist. Assistant Secretary of State Thomas Mann and Ambassador to Santo Domingo W. Tapley Bennett Jr. were verbally castigated and eventually forced out of their posts.

Bobby plunged into the fray, taking the leadership in Congress of Administration critics. Communism must be kept out of the Western Hemisphere, he said piously. "But this cannot mean that we plan to act on our own without regard to friends and allies in the Organization of American States." He condemned United States intervention, even though the Marines had been sent in at the request of the Dominican government, and protested that the Organization of American States should have taken the lead. That this would have meant long delay and the success of the Communist-controlled *coup d'état* evidently had not entered his mind. "Our determination to stop Communist revolution in the hemisphere must not be construed as opposition to popular uprisings against injustice and oppression just because the targets of such popular uprisings say they are Communist inspired or Communist led, or even because known Communists take part in them." In the Dominican uprising, he said, "the revolutionary forces include also many non-Communist democrats"—which, he did not mention, had been the case when Castro seized Cuba. That those "non-Communist democrats" had dropped their arms when Communist domination became apparent did not blunt Bobby's rhetoric.

(A year later, as a result of the Johnson policy and the cooperation of the Organization of American States which he had solicited, the Dominican Republic held a free election. The landslide vote elected a moderate conservative and showed just how many "non-Communist democrats" were on the side of Juan Bosch. The defeated candidate cried "fraud," but a team of American observers, invited by Bosch, led by Norman Thomas, and consisting of pro-Bosch liberals, declared that the election had been a fair one, reflecting the will of the people.)

The "revolution of youth," as interpreted by Bobby, had failed in the Dominican Republic. Its most notable successes in the United States had been the obstruction of the educational process at Berkeley in a "free-speech movement" that rapidly degenerated into a "free smut" crusade. But there were other lands and other peoples to be encouraged, and it was toward these far horizons that Robert Kennedy turned.

13

Mountain Climbs and Political Junkets

As a member of the United States Senate, Robert F. Kennedy for the most part devoted himself to those tasks and ventures which related to the political sphere he had chosen for himself. But he put aside these more mundane matters on three major occasions. The first was his ascent of Mount Kennedy, a 14,000-foot peak in Canada, until then the highest unclimbed mountain in North America. This climb, a sentimental journey, had no connection with his work or his ambitions. He wanted to be the first man to reach the top of a mountain named after his late brother. His junket through Latin America and his journeying in sub-Saharan Africa were clearly political in nature and closely related to the "revolution of youth" which he so fervently espoused.

The ascent of Mount Kennedy was one that would provoke the interest of armchair psychoanalysts and their professional cousins. On the face of it, he undertook the arduous and dangerous climb to honor John F. Kennedy. But obviously he was impelled by some inner drive. His wife Ethel, making one of her surprisingly sharp comments, said: "I think he wants to take his mind off the fact that he's not an astronaut." Friends who saw him before and after he had accomplished his mission remarked that his period of personal mourning ended on the icy sides of Mount Kennedy, and he himself spoke of the "exhilaration" he had felt when he was able to stand at the peak of the mountain. Though an advocate of the strenuous life, Bobby had never climbed a mountain before and was subject to fear of high places, hardly a qualification for what he set out to do. Obviously, he was proving something to himself, reasserting his physical courage—although no one had ever questioned it.

For experienced mountain climbers, Mount Kennedy was not very much of a challenge, but for a man who had never trained in the sport it presented terrors and difficulties. Bobby was aware of this, and from the moment that he announced his intentions, he was grim and determined about it. The idea had come simultaneously to both Bobby and his brother Ted. The original plan had been to make the ascent during the summer of 1965, but the date was advanced to late March when Bobby learned that the National Geographic Society was sending a scientific expedition to map the area for the first time, setting up the surveyors' markers which are necessary for this task. Bobby agreed but Ted was not recovered sufficiently from the plane-crash injury which had so nearly cost him his life. Early in March, a member of the Society "visited me," Bobby wrote later, "and said that we should leave within two weeks as there were other expeditions, both in the United States and Canada, planning to climb Mount Kennedy in the immediate future."

On March 22, Bobby took off from White Horse, in Yukon Territory, for the base camp. Mount Kennedy is twenty-five miles north of the British Columbia-Yukon line and slightly east of the Alaskan border. Weather conditions are treacherous and he was risking the possibility of temperatures of fifteen degrees below zero as well as blizzards. The flight itself was dangerous, with low clouds threatening, and Bobby was asked to delay the take off. But he insisted on moving ahead. "If we get to the mountain, we'll get up it one way or another," he said. "If we wait here, we could be stuck for two weeks." Driving him to risk bad flying weather was his desire to reach the base camp that day—just sixteen months after the assassination. The beginning of the adventure was marred also by a phone call from a hysterical woman who reported to the FBI in Denver that two men with guns would attempt to attack Bobby in White Horse. However, the takeoff and one-hour chartered flight to the camp were uneventful.

The next morning, Bobby and the team of climbers pushed up toward their next camp, 4,000 feet above them and 12,000 feet above sea level. The sun was warm as they began the climb, but by the time they reached the high camp, snow had begun to fall. By early evening the snowfall had become a blizzard and there was some dis-

cussion of abandoning the climb. "But during the night," Bobby
wrote for *Life*, "the snow stopped, the stars became visible, and the
northern lights appeared over the ridge of the mountains. The wind,
which continued until early morning, made sleep almost impossible,
yet it really was a blessing. It either cleared or packed the fresh snow
which had fallen and made our climb to the summit that much
easier. We got up at 6 A.M., ate soup, mush, and chocolate bars, put
on packs, crampons (the day before we had snowshoes), and by 8:30
we were on our way."

For three days and three nights, Bobby, with the mountain climbers looking after him, pushed ahead. Tied to Bobby were James
Whitaker and Barry Prather, who had been the first Americans to con-
quer Mount Everest. There were two other teams, one of which
included a National Geographic photographer. Beyond this, there
was solitude. Contact with the expedition base in White Horse was
impossible because of faulty radio equipment. But they had one unexpected participant—good luck. Had the storms and thirty-five-
below temperatures struck then, instead of after the successful ascent
and descent, there might have been failure and even tragedy. Of
course, there were hardships for Bobby—the pressing awareness of
danger about which he knew little, the steady physical exertion in
which every ounce of energy was devoted to putting one foot before
the other, the spill into a crevasse. And looming ahead, the last
500 feet to the top, the steepest and most dangerous part of the
climb.

"We arrived at the final ridge," Bobby wrote, "rising 500 feet above
us, at around 12:15 P.M. (of the 24th). . . . As we approached the
crest, I didn't see how it was humanly possible to climb it. We rested
for a few minutes and then began again. After ten minutes or so of
climbing, we came to a place which I felt certain was going to frustrate us completely. It seemed to go almost straight up for approximately 200 feet and had a small, irregular ledge. To the left there
was a straight drop of more than 6,000 feet and on the right a somewhat more gradual fall of approximately 1,000 feet."

Jim Whitaker took one look at the expression on Bobby's face and
decided to move rapidly, before the impact of what was ahead had
taken hold. He dug the handle of his ice ax into the snow and, it
seemed to Bobby, "started to pull himself straight up." Some thirty
feet up, he turned and shouted to Bobby, "Come on, follow me." As
he did so, Bobby thought of his mother's admonition, "Don't slip,
dear," and of the words of one reporter who told him that his news-

paper had just completed his obituary. "All of these splendid thoughts raced through my mind," Bobby wrote. "Then I began to think, 'What am I doing here?' I stopped and I held on to the mountain with both hands and remained there."

"What can I do now?" he thought.

"Come on, it's not much farther," Whitaker called out. Bobby had only one choice. But as he climbed higher, the ridge widened and the angle of incline became less perilous. Whitaker and Prather held back in the final moments of the climb to allow Bobby to reach the top of Mount Kennedy first. In the snow, he placed a copy of John F. Kennedy's Inaugural Address, PT-109 tie clips, and a medallion. He also planted what he described as "President Kennedy's family flag" —three gold helmets against a black background, with a silver and maroon border—for the first time unveiled and not to be found in the records of Irish heraldry.

In Washington, some of Bobby's Senate colleagues dismissed the ascent of Mount Kennedy as a publicity stunt, a gimmick, or complained that a Senator's place is on Capitol Hill, not on top of a mountain. But Bobby had made the climb to exorcise himself of the ghosts of Dallas, of the depression which had seized him. At the moment of success, he had felt "relief and exhilaration," and a sense of gratitude to the elements which had allowed him to stand at the peak finally and see the magnificent view that had, in effect, been dedicated by Canada to his brother. At the time, these reactions were more subconscious than conscious, but Bobby Kennedy's long trauma began to disappear as he started the descent to White Horse and to a world which had watched him remotely.

But if Bobby's Mount Kennedy adventure served an inner emotional need, his journey to Latin America seemed to have no relation to anything but that lust for controversy which increasingly seized him. His hair long, shaggy, and almost beatnik in style, Bobby ranged the South American continent less as an ambassador of goodwill or a Senatorial fact finder than as a kind of revolutionary evangelist, egging on those people who could understand him and courting trouble. Sometimes the crowds were sparse, sometimes large. When only a few people turned out, Bobby blamed it on the Johnson Administration and on the desire of embassy staffs to play up to the President by slighting him. When the turnouts were large, he attributed it to his appeal to youth. Some of the reporters covering him, whose Spanish was so feeble that their stories had the crowds shouting the French *vive* rather than the Spanish *viva*, quoted at length the sentiments of illiterate peasants and small children whose

English was nonexistent. And while with one ear Bobby listened to the cheers or boos of the *latinos,* with the other he waited for the reports from Wes Barthelmes, his press secretary, on the coverage the trip was receiving in the American press. That it was hardly page-one material deeply disturbed Bobby, and he complained long and petulantly.

The tour, typically, began in an atmosphere of acrimony. A briefing by Assistant Secretary of State Jack Hood Vaughn turned into a wrangle when Bobby refused to defend United States policy in the Caribbean or to present the official American view to Latin Americans. The United States had been wrong to intervene in the Dominican Republic, Bobby told favored reporters, and he would say so. The exchange was an angry one, but while there was no joy in the upper echelon of the State Department over the trip, the middle echelon was working diligently to make the trip an auspicious one—from a liberal-left standpoint. Foreign service officers, working secretly behind the scenes, began arranging quiet meetings between Bobby and the antigovernment leftists in the countries he was scheduled to visit.

"They hope," one reporter wrote, "to generate massive turnouts for him, particularly of professional students who are continual sources of trouble in Latin countries. This, they expect, will make headlines and 'prove' that he has inherited the mantle of John F. Kennedy. From the middle echelon's point of view, the major corollary of Mr. Kennedy's 'success' will be the implication that President Johnson's foreign policy has hurt America's image south of the border."

Arriving in Lima, Peru, on November 12, 1965, Bobby was met at the airport by government officials and hardly anyone else. This inauspicious start he unfairly blamed on United States embassy personnel who, fearful for Bobby's safety, had only that morning announced the time of his arrival. As his motorcade moved through the streets of the city, Bobby perched himself on the roof of his car, and the crowds began to form. His next stop was Cuzco, the ancient Inca city. Advance men, on his personal payroll, had spread the word and rounded up a sizable crowd which had to stand behind a barbed-wire "security barrier." As a police guard tried to lead Bobby to the reception committee, complete with bouquets of flowers, he broke loose and dashed for the crowd behind the barrier, his hand extended in the traditional politician's gesture. The people surged forward; the barbed-wire fence gave, scratching bodies and faces. Bobby's own cheek was cut and his trousers were ripped. Andrew Glass, who covered the trip, has reported that Bobby is "compulsively clean" and will change shirts ten times a day. But the torn trousers remained on him for the rest of that day.

Bobby's trip had been justified as an inspection of the success or failure of the Alliance for Progress. From Cuzco, therefore, he drove forty miles to an Alliance project set up to teach Indians better farming methods. When he spotted a group of workers, he would shout, "Stop the car" and leap out to greet them. Few knew who he was, but they could sense his importance by the size of the entourage. At one of these impromptu stops, a farm worker told Kennedy that he was compelled to pay very high prices for food being donated by the United States. On the basis of this complaint, Bobby told *Life en Español* that a "large landowner" in the Cuzco region was selling "powdered milk from the Food for Peace program which has been donated for free distribution among the people of Peru."

Senator Carlos Carrillo Smith, a noted Peruvian attorney, immediately wrote to Bobby "requesting information as to the grounds for this statement, in order to formulate the denouncement in legal form and thus bring to justice whoever is abusing in this manner this so-valuable program of assistance . . . [and] depriving the needy." Weeks later, Bobby answered Senator Carrillo. "Since the issue you raise requires more detailed information than I have immediately at hand," Bobby wrote, "I have referred your letter to the proper authorities. I shall be in further touch with you when I have received their reply." And that was the end of it.

It was in Cuzco that Bobby embarked on what the generally sympathetic Washington *Post* described as "pure mischief." Editorializing, the *Post* said: "The ubiquitous Senator Robert F. Kennedy of New York was being cheered loudly in the city of Cuzco. . . . In a burst of paternal enthusiasm, he challenged his audience to exceed him in procreation. Since the Senator has nine children, the crowd cheered him more loudly than ever. . . . The Senator had forgotten . . . that not all the world shares his comfortable circumstances. The Peruvian peasant's children do not enjoy the same assured prospects as Senator Kennedy's. His challenge to the crowd at Cuzco is not merely silly; it is dangerous."

The *Post*'s irritation derived from Peru's deep concern over a steadily rising birthrate. A year before Bobby's visit, the president of Peru had set up a Population and Development Study Center, necessitated by the twenty-year rise of the population to 10,000,000 from a little over 6,000,000. The government had warned that "the population of Peru in the year 2000 could be about 23,000,000, if no considerable change takes place in the birthrate." This population, coupled to a ten-percent decline in agricultural production over the past decade, had given the country a caloric intake average which was lower than what it had been fifteen years earlier. Bobby's remark, widely publicized and repeated by him in a number of variants whenever he introduced his wife, tended to undermine the Peruvian government's efforts to popularize the limitation of population. And it explained why Latin American leaders friendly to the Kennedys and in agreement with their politics had quietly expressed their fears to American diplomats of the forces that Bobby might unleash through his careless rhetoric.

A specific instance of what is usually muffled in diplomatic niceties was reported by Virginia Prewett in the Scripps-Howard newspapers a month before Bobby's trip. "Senator Robert F. Kennedy's trip to Latin America is making more than one government nervous," she wrote. "Venezuela's government is anxious lest the combination of the Kennedy name and the New York Senator's penchant for taking sensational positions on U.S. foreign policy may strike sparks in the tinderbox of Caracas' university leftism. . . . [His] views, repeated in Latin America by the brother of President Kennedy—who is revered there—will inevitably be taken as encouragement by that region's extreme left. . . . The Venezuelans have unofficially indicated a wish that Senator Kennedy bypass their inflammable student population. But he is reportedly determined to make contact with them."

It was a realization of this fear that had led the American embassy to schedule as few explosive confrontations for Bobby as it could. But the Kennedy party was considerably cheered up when it reached Chile. The ambassador in that country was a New Frontiersman, Ralph Dungan, and he had seen to it that the government bowed to Bobby's wishes. He visited with Chile's liberal, though anti-Communist, president Eduardo Frei and happily agreed with him that to defeat Communism, democratic forces must outdo the Reds in their attacks on the prevailing social order. But as the tour of the country proceeded, the question uppermost in people's minds was: What is he trying to prove?

In a school near Santiago, he was introduced as "our" candidate for President of the United States. In his speeches, he supported the "peaceful revolution" to a large group of students who had just driven out Communist hecklers. And he praised Frei in extravagant terms, calling him the "most brilliant and able leader" he had ever met. He called on the people to achieve "the better life"—as lived in the United States. He introduced Ethel from the trunk lid of the embassy car (damage: $300) as the "mother of nine children." And he continued what members of his party sourly referred to as an "all-expenses-paid slum tour of South America."

Invading the *callampas* of Santiago and other cities, he picked his way among the litter of the streets and invited himself into slum homes, asking questions and handing out PT-109 tie clasps to men and boys who had never owned a tie in their lives, and speaking in a kind of "poetic" rhetoric which astonished the American press covering him.

"This is the time of trial," he told Santiago's students. "Throughout the hemisphere, men and nations argue the great questions, and freedom hangs in the balance. Throughout the hemisphere, entrenched privilege resists the demands of justice.

"In every American land, the dispossessed and the hungry, the landless and the untaught, seek a better life for their children. In every American land, in yours and mine no less than in others, a revolution is coming—a revolution which will be peaceful if we are wise enough, compassionate if we care enough, successful if we are fortunate enough—but a revolution which will come whether we will it or not. We can affect its character; we cannot alter its inevitability."

It was different in Concepción, an industrial city with a substantial Red population. The police warned the embassy and the Kennedy party that the reception being prepared for him would not be pleasant. Others argued with Bobby that he could accomplish little and might lose a great deal if he insisted on treating his appearances there like a Madison Square Garden rally. But Bobby brushed their objections aside. "What's there to worry about?" he said. "These people want to be our friends. All we have to do is show them that we want to be theirs. It's easy." His performance showed that when he was not surrounded by those seeking a view of the charisma that was John F. Kennedy's or a bobby-soxer's thrill, he could expose himself to a kind of humiliation which is undignified and benefits no one.

Hours before he was to appear before a large crowd of university students in Concepción, he met with young Communist leaders in his hotel suite to press them into giving him a civilized hearing and to prevent violence. The young Communist leaders rather contemptuously promised him nothing. Bobby argued, pleaded that he did not intend to deceive them, attempted to shame them by comparing the free discussion he sought with what was the rule in Moscow or Peking.

"We have nothing against you personally," the Red students answered him, "but as a representative of a government whose hands are stained with blood."

"I haven't had a Marine stick a bayonet in *you* yet," Bobby said. "Let me make a deal with you. You speak for fifteen minutes, I'll speak for fifteen minutes."

The Communist leaders wouldn't even shake hands with him when they left.

That evening, changing his shirt for the second time in a quarter of an hour, Bobby left for the auditorium. The police guard dropped back at the university grounds, barred from following him by a Latin American tradition which makes all institutions of higher learning privileged sanctuaries. Entering the auditorium, a converted gymnasium, Bobby walked slowly in front of the stands. When he passed the Communist rooting section, he was pelted with eggs, garbage, and the crowning Latin insult, small coins. "Go home," shouted the Communist students. "Go home, you son of a Yankee whore." As students chanted the Chilean hymn, the Cuban hymn, and a stamped refrain of "San-to Do-min-*go,* San-to Do-min-*go,*" Bobby sat on the platform, smiling nervously. When the hall had filled with people and pandemonium, he leaped on the table and, microphone in hand, shouted at the students. "I believe in freedom," he shouted. "I will speak. I do not come tonight and say that the United States is without fault. All human beings make mistakes. But we support your revolution with our hearts because we are making the same effort in the United States." He was now talking at the top of his lungs. "If they are right," he said jabbing a finger in the direction of the Communists, "let one of them come down here and debate me. Let one of them speak for his side and let the rest of you decide."

The answer from the Communists was a string of obscenities. Bobby by this time was in a fury, all dignity gone. "Come down," he shouted. "Come down. I challenge you to a debate. I am willing. Do you want me to come up there?" Leaping off the platform, he forced his way through the crowd to the section where the uproar was greatest, stood on a chair to reach the stands, and raised his right arm. A student spit at him, hitting him squarely in the eye. Another student kicked at his hand. Then Bobby retreated, mumbling, "Let's go. We've done what we came to do." The Communists set an American flag on fire. Bobby returned to the hotel, changed his clothes, and went to a party.

The next day, Bobby and his entourage visited a coal mine. "Can we go down the shaft?" Bobby asked. "No, no," said the mine manager. Bobby joined a group of miners and proceeded to force his way in. Down in the mine, he asked a company official, "Would you be a Communist if you worked here as a miner?" With mine officials pleading with him to return, Bobby tramped for half an hour to the end of the tunnel.

Bobby's next stop was Buenos Aires. When security police tried to hold back the crowd at the airport, Bobby got out of Ambassador Edward Martin's Cadillac and plowed into the mob, grinning and shaking hands. The crowd was still shouting *"El Presidente"* when embassy officials got Bobby back into the car and drove him to the ambassador's residence—graciously described by the visitor as "a Versailles occupied by Babbitts." On November 20, his birthday, he landed at Congonhas, São Paulo's airport. The streets were virtually deserted as Bobby's motorcade moved into the downtown area, and Bobby remarked sadly, "I counted almost one hundred people." There was, however, a birthday party that Ethel had arranged. According to Andrew Glass' *Saturday Evening Post* account, "Ethel had written a half-dozen satirical—even libelous—songs based on the Kennedy trip and its imagined impact on some well-known U.S. political figures. . . . Ethel, holding a large paper bag, pulled out a series of party favors and explained what each one signified. There was, for example, a toy airplane that she described as a U-2 plane that Lyndon Johnson had ordered to spy on Bobby's progress."

But from that point on, there were no more horrendous mass demonstrations against him, no more of the degradation of being spat upon. In São Paulo, he defended the Alliance for Progress to a group of student leaders. In Rio de Janeiro, he attended a soccer game, went to mass on the anniversary of his brother's death, and insisted on visiting slums so noisome that security police assigned to guard him held back. In Natal, as he rode on the top of a truck, he yelled to those lining the road, "Every child an education! Every family adequate housing! Every man a job! As long as there is a Kennedy alive in the United States, there will be a friend of northeast Brazil." He tramped the searingly hot sugar-cane fields, asking labor leaders how much the workers made and then lecturing the owners of the fields when they disputed union figures. On one side trip, he entertained peasant farmers with "We Shall Overcome" and "The Marine Corps Hymn" in his off-pitch voice. Hot and sweaty, he asked some of the people in his audience where he might swim. They recommended a nearby lake. Bobby dashed to the lake shore, tore off his clothes, and plunged in. Only after he had emerged from the water did he discover that the lake was alive with piranhas, the viciously predatory and man-eating fish.

"Piranhas," he remarked, "have never been known to eat a United States Senator." [1]

As Bobby's plane was flying to Caracas, cruising at 30,000 feet, the intercom came to life. "Senator and Mrs. Kennedy," the Brazilian pilot said, "it has been a great pleasure to have you aboard. We are now crossing the Brazilian-Venezuelan frontier, and it is time to say goodbye."

"What's he going to do now?" Bobby asked. "Get off here?"

In Caracas, as the Venezuelan government had warned, the Communists threatened trouble—announcing that they would kidnap Ethel and machine-gun Bobby. The threat, Central Intelligence agents said, was serious. But the major weapon aimed at Bobby turned out to be a stink bomb, exploded in a hall as he arrived. Then it was back to Washington's National Airport where eight of the nine Kennedy children awaited him. "The people aren't going to accept the kind of lives they now lead," Bobby said to those who gathered at the airport to greet him. "I found affection and admiration and the desire to understand and many misunderstandings. Does that make sense?"

The reporters did not answer. Six months later, they might have asked the question themselves. For in an encyclopedic speech to the Senate, taking up two separate days, Bobby discussed at tremendous length his views on Latin America. The facts and figures in his speech did not come from direct observation or from his conversations with Latin leaders, but rather from library research. They were not extreme; they were not hysterical. And where they touched on such matters as land reform, they took into account circumstances which the "revolutionists of youth" would have found highly offensive.

---

[1] Bobby must have developed an affection for piranhas. When he returned home, he added one of them to the large collection of pets he kept at Hickory Hill. In the summer of 1966, an assistant to the producer of a major television program called a Washington columnist with a request. "I've been told that you can help us," the assistant said. "We're doing a show on famous people who have unusual pets, and we'd like to have somebody important from the government." The columnist suggested that Bobby Kennedy was the only prospect he could think of. "Well," said the assistant, "we heard he kept a pet piranha, so we called his office. They told us that this was true, but that the piranha had died." She paused a moment, then giggled. "I guess Senator Kennedy had a hard time getting human meat for it."

Land reform, which is so prominent in the propaganda of the liberal-left in underdeveloped nations, would fail, Bobby noted, if the large holdings were split up into the minute parcels which extremists demanded. The production of food would decline and the troubles of these countries would increase, Bobby said. The division had to be economically feasible. This made sense, but it was not what the thousands who heard him in more public places had been told.

If it was difficult to discover what Bobby was trying to prove in Latin America, his determination to visit South Africa was even more obscurely motivated. Latin America, at least, was tied to the United States and its problems were frequently those of the Senate. But South Africa had no connection with any of Bobby's various projects. At best, he would accomplish nothing for the Africans or for whites who opposed the apartheid policies of the Vervoerd government. At worst, he could inspire bloody riots which could turn sub-Saharan Africa into the cockpit of another major war. Bobby, moreover, was not wanted by either the government or its more mature opposition. The progovernment newspaper, *Die Vaderland,* accused him of making the trip "to draw world attention to himself." The antigovernment Johannesburg *Star* said, "Americans will be tickled to death. . . . And when they stop laughing, writers and columnists will proceed to take the hide off us."

But Bobby persisted in going, even after South African authorities had excluded the usual entourage of newspapermen who travel with a Kennedy party. Bobby's intentions were questioned when he bypassed Rhodesia, the one country in that area which was at the sharp end of America's policy stick. He remained silent over the rash of bloody civil wars that had engaged "democratic" Africa in the year before his journey and the dictatorial regimes imposed by Africans on the newly independent states they governed. There was nothing he could say after going to South Africa that he had not said before. And he had opened a Pandora's box for the United States. As the veteran columnist David Lawrence pointed out, Bobby had set out to break a tradition whereby officials of one government do not journey to other countries to criticize directly their peoples, their leaders and their policies. The Kennedy approach, Lawrence said, "will be pointed out in the future as an example of the right to stump a foreign country and discuss questions of internal policy. . . . It might develop now that officials of other countries . . . which have controversies with the U.S. may feel justified in addressing the American electorate in the hope of changing the policies of our government."

This described precisely what Bobby set out to do in South Africa, a country whose stability was necessary for the wellbeing of Great Britain and the United States—as both countries knew. Preaching a revolution of color, he told South African students that apartheid was one of the evils of the world. Other evils, he said, were "discrimination in New York, serfdom in Peru, starvation in India, mass slaughter in Indonesia, and the jailing of intellectuals in the Soviet Union." In Johannesburg, he told Africans, whites and Indians that "where men can be deprived because their skin is black, in the fullness of time, others will be deprived because their skin is white." He criticized the South African government for, he said, its belief that Africa is too primitive to develop.

For University of Natal students, he dragged out an old chestnut. "Suppose God is black," he said. "What if we go to Heaven and we, all our lives, have treated the Negro as an inferior, and God is there, and we look up and he is not white. What then is our response?" The response might have been that those were strange words to come from someone who took his Catholicism seriously. But Bobby was not exactly interested in doctrinal matters. "Maybe there is a black man outside this room who is brighter than anyone in this room; the chances are that there are many," he cried out. "Was Stalin black? Was Hitler black? Who killed forty million people just twenty-five years ago? It wasn't black people, it was white." This was a *non sequitur* to which he repeatedly returned, in a variety of forms.

"It was not the black man of Africa," he added, "who invented or used poison gas and the atomic bomb; who sent six million men, women, and children to the gas ovens and used their bodies as fertilizer." But it was not all cheering and oratory. Students challenged America's right—as exercised by Bobby—to interfere in South African affairs. The United States was not interested in dictating to South Africa or in telling its government how to run the country, Bobby countered. It merely wanted "one sign" that greater freedom was being planned for people of all races.

In Soweto, as Bobby shook hands or made speeches from the roof of a car, he noticed that the homes in what he described as a "black ghetto" were "pleasant, far more attractive than those in Harlem or Southside Chicago," but he nevertheless felt constrained to describe it as a "dreary concentration." He visited Albert Luthuli, a South African chief and winner of the Nobel Prize for Peace, who had been restricted to his farm for antigovernment activities. Bobby found him "impressive," "strong yet kind," with a smile "illuminating his whole presence, eyes dancing and sparkling" but looking "hurt and hard" when South Africa's racial separation was mentioned. Bobby presented him with a portable record player and recordings of President Kennedy's speeches. They played excerpts of a civil rights speech and, according to Bobby, the government officers who had accompanied him "stared fixedly at the floor" to hide their shame. Afterward, Bobby told reporters that Luthuli "feels the only change for the better will be brought about by God, and that alone can improve the situation."

For Ian Robertson, president of the National Union of South African Students, Bobby had a copy of John Kennedy's *Profiles in Courage*, inscribed "in admiration" by Jacqueline Kennedy. Robertson had invited Bobby to South Africa, but by government decree he was not permitted to accompany him or be present when he spoke. Robertson was, in effect, under a kind of house arrest. From Robertson and from other students to whom Bobby spoke he collected a variety of "facts" and "statistics," some of them of dubious validity, which he published later in *Look* magazine.

According to Stanley Uys, a London *Observer* correspondent familiar with the country, Bobby left South Africans of all political views puzzled when he said in one speech, "The worldwide contest of ideology, along with awesome developments in the speed, range, and impact of modern weaponry, have made the very notion of isolationism obsolete. Even the traditional distinctions of diplomacy— between belligerents and neutrals, between external and internal affairs, between a state of war and a state of peace—are slowly losing their meaning."

Then he departed for Negro Africa and the triumphal marches of its dictators. Had the South African government been the dictatorial regime that Bobby thought it to be, he would have left those who greeted him to face very unpleasant music. But the students, enthusiastic in their reception, had long second thoughts. They had heard him say things which they knew were not so. As a result, within forty-eight hours after his departure, their former enthusiasm had badly soured. It was Bobby's happy belief that he had struck terror into the hearts of faculty members and government leaders. Instead, they smiled indulgently, assured that the net effect of Bobby's passionate utterances had in fact hurt the opposition that Bobby had hoped to aid and comfort. To American reporters who subsequently visited South Africa, they had only gently ironic comments to make. "We have heard more eloquent undergraduates in our time," one professor remarked.

But there were echoes and repercussions—and criticism from men who have made diplomacy their life work. Ambassador Ellis O. Briggs, who had devoted forty-one years to furthering his country's interests at home and abroad, bided his time. Then, in a speech delivered in October 1966 before the Americas Foundation in New York, he scathingly summarized his views of the "revelations" reported to Latin America—and, by extension, to South Africa as well —by "this "voluntary emissary" and "youthful Senator."

"The first," Briggs said, "presumed to explain to the citizens and officials of successive South American countries—as to candidates for Boy Scout indoctrination—the intricacies of North American hemisphere politics. There was a comforting aside to the effect that Wall Street no longer dominates the Potomac." Moving to the Dominican situation, Briggs criticized Kennedy for the "loud forensic drumbeats that echoed across the area where the responsible United States official—the Secretary of State—was at the moment tiptoeing across Copacabana Beach, doing his utmost not to arouse the congregation assembled in Rio de Janeiro for the first formal Pan American reunion in nearly a decade. Unsolicited advice was then added to the prescription, and the neighbors were told how to comport themselves in their domestic responsibilities. . . .

"Sour are the abuses of hospitality. A worse way to promote international goodwill would be hard to imagine. In a reverse situation, an invading foreigner who presumed to harangue a North American audience about civil rights . . . or inadequate taxes would be lucky to escape with his shirt on his back. He would almost certainly have lost his *bombachas*"—his britches.

14

The Man Who Would Be President

THERE are men who climb high mountains or swim wide rivers. They are driven by ambition or the simple need to stand above their fellows. There are men who go into politics because they believe in the efficacy of their ideas, because they want money, or because it is the best way they know for passing the years from adolescence to senescence. None of these motivations applies to Robert Francis Kennedy. Unlike others of that wonderfully outgoing people who brought Ireland to America, Bobby Kennedy is not by nature a political animal. He is a politician because death and fate—and the desires of his father—moved him up in the line of succession. Of the Kennedy sons, only Joe Jr. was politically activated by temperament. In the Kennedy family, the ancient law of primogeniture applied, and so the dynastic crown passed eventually to Bobby's hands.

"Just as I went into politics because Joe died," Jack Kennedy had said when he was still in the Senate of the United States, "if anything happened to me tomorrow, my brother Bobby would run for my seat in the Senate. And if Bobby died, Teddy would take over for him." This calm, almost arrogant, insistence on what the family clearly considered to be its manifest destiny summed up the Kennedy mystique. Joe Jr., openly extroverted and carrying in his genes the steel and blarney of the saloon-keeping Kennedys and Fitzgeralds, would have been the ideal first Catholic President of

America. The torch fell from his hand and was picked up almost as a matter of course by Jack. An assassin ended his career when it was at its zenith. It was now up to Bobby, introverted and with an immigrant bitterness in him, to pick up the Presidential seal and run with it. Of the three brothers, he was the least suited, the least equipped emotionally and intellectually, to assume the Presidency. But there was seldom very much doubt that he would make a try for the nation's highest office, and he could be relaxed about it.

At a time when he was being assailed as a "carpetbagger" seeking to use New York as a stepping stone to the White House, he could take his political successes at the polls lightly enough to say to a group of women reporters in Washington, "I can't tell you how happy I am to be representing the great state of . . . of . . . uh . . . uh," and then, when the laughter had subsided to add, "I want to assure you that I have no Presidential ambitions—nor does my wife, Ethel Bird." This kind of self-directed irony, and his almost self-effacing campaigning style, are no measure of a steely determination to succeed where his brother "Johnny" had to prove what his father taught him—that the rewards and privileges of the world are clearly labeled "Kennedy" with only the shipping date unspecified.

But in politics, determination is not enough. There must be a political machine on which to ride. The makings of such a machine existed. It had been put together by Bobby in the drive to win the 1960 Democratic Presidential nomination for John F. Kennedy. It had been strengthened by the careful use of patronage. "Kennedy men" held high office in the Johnson Administration. They sat in state houses and ran cities. They were represented in state committees and on the precinct level where convention delegates are made and unmade. Though control of the Democratic National Committee had been taken away from John Bailey, its nominal chairman, he was still on the scene, biding his time for a return to status and the shared power he had held when President Kennedy was alive and Bobby ruled from the Justice Department.

As the 1966 primary contests began erupting, talk could be heard of "Kennedy men" seeking public office—governorships, House seats, Senate seats—and campaigning with the secret approval of the junior Senator from New York. Bobby wisely refrained from open commitments to them, but his loyal political operatives turned up with hardly concealed regularity when "Kennedy men" declared for office. The results of these contests was a mixed bag. In Florida, the mayor of Miami challenged the governor in a primary battle hailed as a test of Bobby's strength. The Kennedy man won. In Tennessee, however, an anti-Kennedy, pro-Johnson candidate easily took the gubernatorial primary. There was, as the professionals finally confessed, no clear pattern to prove that Bobby could transfer to "his" candidates, and by remote control, any guarantee of victory.

The test, if Bobby intended to make a show of power, could only be in his "home" state of New York. And there, the advice he received was contradictory. Some urged him to make a show of force in order to prove conclusively that the Democratic organization in the vote-rich state was subservient to him. Others pointed out that he had lost in his first attempt at kingmaking when his choice for mayor of New York had been defeated by a Republican. Given the overwhelmingly Democratic complexion of the city, that had taken some doing. But the defeat had not hurt Bobby, and those who urged him to lie doggo pointed out that he was still the most important man in the state's Democratic organization.

Bobby sided with the activists. To win his Senate seat, he had made common cause with the so-called "Regulars"—the machine politicians organized under Charles Buckley in the Bronx and J. Raymond Jones, the Negro leader of Tammany Hall. By supporting Abraham Beame in the mayoralty race, he had antagonized the "Reformers" and the Liberal party. The Liberals, in fact, had shown their displeasure with Bobby by throwing their support to John V. Lindsay, the Republican candidate. Having seen which way the wind seemed to blow, Bobby decided to dump the "Regulars" and make an alliance with the "Reformers" and the Liberal party. The "Regulars," under Tammany Hall's Ray Jones, had named State Supreme Court Justice Arthur Klein as their candidate for the patronage-rich post of surrogate. The "Reformers" and the Liberals hoped to challenge that choice in the primary, and their candidate was another Supreme Court Justice, Samuel Silverman.

It would have been a fairly even contest had the Reform-Liberal group not enlisted Bobby. In public statements, however, he played coyly for a time. But there were important reasons for him to make common cause with New York's liberal-left. He had been under criticism for his association with the machine politicians. As the spokesman for the "revolution of youth," moreover, he could not afford being identified with the "old" political forces in New York. Bobby therefore plunged into the battle for an office which seldom merited much attention and usually went to a party hack as reward for years of faithful service. From that moment on, the streets of New York reverberated with the babble from Silverman sound trucks. Every night those trucks roamed the city, at a cost not yet divulged. And back from his African trip, Bobby ranged the city, appealing to the strong minority vote. There were some bad moments for him when Ray Jones accused him of racism and made himself the issue. But this was forgotten in the uproar over Bobby's generalized accusations of "deals" and other skulduggery among the opposition.

When Samuel Silverman won by a substantial majority, New York and Washington rang with talk of Bobby's great coup. The New York Democratic party, the pundits insisted, was now safely in his pocket—and the first step toward capturing the Democratic nomination in 1972 had been taken. There was some truth to this, but it was compromised by various exaggerations. To begin with, the "Reform" group in the Democratic party, when allied to the Liberals, had won many victories in New York. This combination had been the mainstay of Mayor Robert Wagner, and his power had vanished when he lost its support. Secondly, Bobby's exclusionary alliance with the liberal-left of the city's Democratic party, and his rejection of his former friends among the "Regulars," had cost him much in local goodwill. In Presidential politics, the stakes are so great that this kind of "betrayal" is possible and necessary. On the local level, personalities and prerogatives loomed far larger.

On second thought, stock-taking politicians wondered if Bobby had not lost more than he had gained by putting so much into a minor city primary. "Lots of people in the party still haven't gotten over the way Bobby moved his carpetbags into the state," one politician said. "Upstate and in New York City you'll find some who feel that he deprived them of jobs and influence that is rightfully theirs. You can bet they'll be waiting for a chance to get back at him." Another said, "Bobby's moving too fast and too hard. I think he's riding for a fall."

The chance to take on Bobby Kennedy came in the summer of 1966. The stakes were high: possible control of the New York State delegation to the 1968 Democratic convention and the governorship of New York. It was a situation requiring tact, however, and it was this element which finally booby-trapped Bobby. He, of course, might have stayed out of the battle that began late in the spring. But the Liberal party and the "Reform" Democrats thought differently, and Bobby agreed to work with them.

In question was the future of Frank O'Connor, president of New York's City Council and a power among the "Regulars." Seeking higher office in the past, O'Connor had been put off with a promise that the Democratic gubernatorial nomination of 1966 would be his, and he assumed that this commitment would be honored. The "Reformers" and the Liberals, however, did not like him or want him. To them, he was just another Irish politician, up from the club-house. As such, he had the support of the machine politicians. But efforts to get O'Connor to withdraw failed. With Governor Nelson Rockefeller's decline in popularity, the Democratic nomination had become truly meaningful, and O'Connor was not stepping down.

A man more experienced in the ways of politics would have realized that in a situation such as this, you either join them or fight them. Bobby chose to do neither. Instead he suggested that the choice of candidate be an open one and invited all comers to plead their cases to the state's Democratic voters. He wrapped this up in shiny foil by "confiding" that he did not want to be accused of dictating the party's choice. Privately, he argued that the Democratic party had to lose the "Knights of Columbus image" by discarding O'Connor and nominating a candidate cut to the pattern of the New Frontier. O'Connor, Bobby said, lacked class. To further antagonize Frank O'Connor, Bobby encouraged Franklin D. Roosevelt Jr. and Eugene Nickerson to campaign for the nomination.

Had Bobby known New York better, he would have realized that the men he picked to give O'Connor a fight could never make it. "Frankie" Roosevelt had been elected to Congress from New York City by running on the Liberal party ticket against a Democrat, thereby antagonizing the "Regulars." He had lost the support of the "Reform" group and the liberals—both upper and lower case— once by accepting as a client the Dominican Republic of dictator Trujillo, and again by leading the hatchet squad against Senator Hubert Humphrey in the West Virginia Presidential primary of 1960, impugning Humphrey's war record and implying that he was a draft dodger. Nickerson was Bobby's real choice, but he was considered too conservative by Alex Rose and the Liberal party, and he lacked even the full support of the Democrats in his home district on Long Island. Had Bobby openly endorsed Nickerson, his candidacy might have constituted a real threat. But as the Washington *Post*'s Flora Lewis reported, "the Senator wanted to put his horse at the other end of the cart and join a Nickerson bandwagon after it gathered speed. It never got up to a good roll."

Bobby's rejection of O'Connor invited a series of damaging rumors about his motivation. It was said by the professionals and by many political observers that Bobby's opposition had little to do with principle. He was afraid, they said, that O'Connor would not give him full control of the New York delegation to the 1968 convention where the preliminary deals for the 1972 Presidential nomination would be made. In fact, it was argued, Bobby had no desire to see a Democratic governor who could challenge him now for party leadership and deprive him of the governorship in 1970—when it would make a better base for a Presidential campaign than the United States Senate. Bolstering this argument was the seemingly suicidal eagerness of the Liberal party to run a candidate of its own, thereby splitting the anti-Rockefeller vote and almost guaranteeing a Republican victory.

Those less partisan saw no great conspiracy in Bobby's actions. To them it seemed that he had simply been unable to assess the forces at work in the state and, again quoting Flora Lewis, that he had "goofed, miscalculating the way the contest would develop." Bobby's plea that he had merely wanted to remain "neutral" convinced few. At the time that he was proclaiming his "hands off" policy in New York, he was jumping into the battle for the Massachusetts gubernatorial nomination—against the wishes of his brother, Senator Edward M. Kennedy. Teddy had also claimed neutrality, but his close political allies were working for former State Attorney General Edward J. McCormack, nephew of Speaker of the House John W. McCormack—the man Teddy had beaten for the Senatorial nomination. Bobby's candidate was Kenneth P. O'Donnell, a White House assistant in the Kennedy Administration.

Whatever the reasons for Bobby's feeble performance in New York—and however they were interpreted—there was general agreement that O'Connor's success in winning the nomination was a blow to Bobby. A Presidential bandwagon must roll steadily. Any slowdown usually gives those who had climbed aboard the chance to do some more thinking—and to jump off. They could contemplate the primary victory in Tennessee of former Governor Bufford Ellington, a Johnson man, by 50,000 votes over John Jay Hooker, who had Bobby's tacit blessing and modeled himself and his campaign along Kennedy lines. But Bobby was counting on other factors in his drive for the Presidency.

Late in August 1966, there were signs that his New York setback did nothing to tarnish his national reputation. A Gallup poll taken then showed Bobby running ahead of the President among both Democrats and independents. In February, fifty-two percent of the Democrats polled had favored Lyndon Johnson, with twenty-seven percent going to Bobby. The summer poll, however, gave Bobby forty percent to Johnson's thirty-eight percent. Among independents, the shift had been even more marked—thirty percent for Johnson and twenty-seven percent for Bobby in February, to thirty-eight percent for Bobby and twenty-four percent for Johnson in the more recent sampling. The Gallup poll also showed that Bobby would make a stronger showing than the President against Michigan's Republican Governor George Romney.

More significant than any poll were the demands on Bobby from Democratic candidates. He was, by all accounts, the most sought-after speaker in the Democratic party. And responding to this, he set out on a stumping trip of the nation. More than 100 requests for his help sat on his desk when he announced that he would tour at least eighteen states in order to campaign for governors, Senators, and Congressmen. At every one of these appearances, Bobby mended fences and made deals. At every one, he was also putting future officeholders in his debt and reaching out to the lower-echelon party workers, all vitally important to him in any campaign for the Presidential nomination. The focus of Bobby's Presidential ambitions also shifted.

In the past, he had made it clear to friends and advisers that he was aiming at the 1972 nomination. But as the press continued to report strong feeling for him, Bobby permitted speculation on the possibility of challenging President Johnson in 1968. He was encouraged by the break-out of bumper stickers calling for "Kennedy-Fulbright in '68"—linking him with the Senate's major voice for the withdrawal of American troops from Vietnam and the adoption of a neo-isolationist foreign policy. Democratic Congressmen agreed on Bobby's electoral strength although they minimized his chances for overturning an incumbent President. In time, the rumors took another form. *U.S. News & World Report* summed them up in one brief item on August 15, 1966:

"From a Midwestern Democratic Senator: 'I'll make you a bet. The day is not far off when the President calls Hubert Humphrey to the White House and says: "Hubert, things at the U.N. aren't going well. I'm naming Arthur Goldberg to be Secretary of State and want you to go up and straighten out the U.N." Then he'll call in Bobby Kennedy and say: "Robert, we've had our differences, but let's bury those. I want you on the ticket this time." ' "

The "Midwestern Democratic Senator" was indulging in political whimsey. Johnson was not enchanted with Humphrey but turning to Bobby was another matter. That the Kennedy campaign should have taken that form spoke eloquently of the prevailing atmosphere in Washington. From a long-shot 1972 candidate, Bobby had moved up to a 1968 threat against an incumbent President of his own party. The professionals shook their heads in wonderment. Could the Kennedy millions have done it? Was the memory of John F. Kennedy so deeply rooted that it would still exert a hold on the electorate? Did Bobby Kennedy, for all his ability to antagonize, have the personality to take over a convention singlehandedly—and to violate all political tradition? Could a candidate so wedded to a position of liberal extremism and to the excesses of youth win over the vast American electorate? Did the stricture of professional politicians and professional analysts—that the United States stick to the center—become meaningless between 1964 and 1966? Or was Bobby simply taking advantage of the changing nature of the electorate—from middle-aged to young, from middle class to lower class? Did he represent the wave of the future, or would a surf now running high slip back to its ebb by 1968 or 1972?

By the time the votes in the November 1966 election had been counted, those questions were being asked with a new emphasis. For Bobby had campaigned long and arduously, placing his reputation as a vote-getter on the line. He had achieved little. And the politicians, who still subscribed to the formulation, "What have you done for me lately," reacted sourly to the results. In California, Governor Edmund (Pat) Brown, in what was considered a tight race against Republican Ronald Reagan, had called on Bobby to give him a hand. "We need help wherever we can get it," he had said of the possibility that the President might campaign for him, "but the guy I'd really like to see out here is Bobby Kennedy."

Bobby had accepted the invitation, but he had campaigned in a manner that would most hurt Brown. He appeared before a hysterical group of students at Berkeley and expressed his support of the lawless behavior that had made the campus a focus of the New Left and its Communoid associates. Berkeley, once the crown of the University of California's many schools, was a major issue in the gubernatorial campaign, and Brown had been trying to shake himself loose from charges that his weak policies had encouraged student extremists there. Bobby pleased the far left, the beatniks, and the Vietniks by his performance, but he antagonized California voters who flocked to Reagan—consolidating a plurality of a million votes.

In New York, the polls had given Frank O'Connor a slight edge over Governor Nelson Rockefeller. Although Franklin Roosevelt, running on the Liberal ticket, was expected to siphon off some of the O'Connor vote, experts noted that this would be balanced by the Conservative party's raid on the G.O.P. In a situation such as that, Bobby's pulling power, if it really existed, could be the factor that would give O'Connor a margin of victory. At least on the surface, the O'Connor-Kennedy rift was patched up and Bobby went to work with a will. Belatedly, he realized that to lose in New York would eliminate O'Connor as a rival for state power, but it would also be a blow to Kennedy prestige.

And that's what counted most for Bobby. To a team of *Newsweek* reporters who interviewed him late in October, Bobby talked more about his Presidential ambitions than about the campaign then reaching its highest decibel level. "Obviously I feel strongly about certain things," he told them, "and the Presidency is the place you can do most to get things done." So while he ranged the state, he made sure that his own image was the last one left on the political retina of the voters. He talked mostly about *his* issues, not those which the candidate was pressing. Usually, it was the poverty program and the "revolution of youth" that he discussed—to the point that one of his Senate colleagues, bogged down on Capitol Hill, snapped: "If he really wanted to win that poverty fight, he'd have stayed right here in town nailing down votes and coordinating pressure groups all over the country. Instead, he's been a hit-and-run Senator. If you're running for the Presidency, you don't have time to do anything solid on the legislative front." Nor, as both Bobby and O'Connor discovered on the night of November 8, on the electoral front. Despite Bobby's speechmaking and handshaking, his tugs at political strings and his efforts to capitalize on the Kennedy name, O'Connor was badly defeated.

And so it was throughout the country. His handpicked candidate in Florida, a superliberal, was defeated by a conservative who became the first Republican governor the state had elected since Reconstruction days. The results were equally discouraging for Bobby in other states. He could not even score a success in the Senate and gubernatorial races in Massachusetts, the Kennedy bailiwick. In all, he campaigned for eleven gubernatorial candidates, only three of whom won. He campaigned for ten senatorial candidates, and only four won. In the congressional races, where Bobby had also pushed hard, the Republicans gained forty-seven seats. And this was only a small part of the bad news. After the election, the complexion of both House and Senate had changed—from liberal to conservative. An analysis of the new Congress, prepared by *U.S. News & World Report,* indicated that the split in the House would be 196 conservatives, 163 liberals, 59 middle-of-the-road, and 17 uncertain. The

Senate breakdown of newly elected members was 16 conservatives, 9 liberals, 9 middle-of-the-road, and 1 uncertain.

Perhaps of greater significance was the picture the nation's politicians got of Bobby as a campaigner. Like Adlai Stevenson, who had been stiffly criticized by Bobby for this lack, he failed to meet his schedules, he was unprepared to speak the right word for his candidates, his staff was disorganized. As one observer remarked, "What Bobby needs now, if he's going to make the Presidency, is Bobby." A lawyer who takes his own case has a fool for a client, the old saw goes. And the same, some began saying, applied to a candidate who was his own campaign manager.

But Bobby did not see this. Nor did he realize that at the grass roots, precinct workers and county chairmen are very sensitive to mavericks. They may turn out to cheer, but they live by party regularity. However appealing Bobby may have been, it was the "regulars" who dispensed the patronage. The election returns once in, however, Bobby continued on his course of attacking the President at Senate hearings and accusing him of "turning his back" on the nation's poor. In the last weeks of November and the first week of December 1966, the political professionals sensed that Bobby's Presidential bandwagon had slowed again, no matter what the polls said. They predicted that his irascibility and his insistence on always having his way might in the end be his Achilles' heel as a Presidential candidate.

But this was all conjecture. Everywhere within the upper ranks of the Democratic party, there was uncertainty and worry. The Johnson Administration had obviously run into a buzzsaw of rebellion against its policies, but Bobby wanted to pursue them with additional vigor and cash. And then, what every politician fears struck. Bobby Kennedy found himself at the center of two controversies, two battles which he could not win. The first was with J. Edgar Hoover, director of the Federal Bureau of Investigation. The second was with the nation's sense of fair play—aided and abetted by its love of scandal.

Bobby's J. Edgar Hoover caper was typical of his approach. It demonstrated his supreme conviction that once he had said something it became the truth. But in this instance, he was dealing with documentary proof—the painstaking record compiled by the FBI in its dealings with all comers, particularly when they were highly politicized Attorneys General like Robert Francis Kennedy. The roots of the struggle between the two men dated back to the beginnings of the Kennedy Administration. Bobby had felt then that the FBI's files could be put to great use for the advancement of the Kennedy cause. Hoover, on the other hand, had fought over the years to prevent his agency from becoming a kind of American Gestapo. Bobby's growing commitment to the New Left had sharpened the issue between them.

A cloud no bigger than a legal brief had been the first sign of a growing confrontation. In May of 1966, long after Bobby had left the Justice Department, the Solicitor General of the United States informed the Supreme Court that FBI agents had planted an electronic listening device in the hotel suite of Fred B. Black, Jr., a former business associate of Bobby Baker. This had caused an uproar in government and legal circles. It was widely surmised that the Solicitor General, since he could not have taken such an unprecedented step without the knowledge of the President, had been throwing procedural cold water on the entire Bobby Baker case. The Supreme Court took a dim view of "bugging"—and with the Solicitor General's confession, it might throw out the litigation still pending against Bobby Baker.

Shrewder minds in Washington realized that the fallout from the admission of electronic surveillance would be far more radioactive for another Bobby—the Attorney General who had sanctioned it. This, they suggested, was what President Johnson had in mind, not a whitewash of the Baker case. But Bobby, forgetful of his past enthusiasm for telephone taps and electronic listening devices, used the opportunity to continue his attacks on Hoover and the FBI. To hear him tell it, the practice was a pernicious one and entirely the fault of the Federal Bureau of Investigation. This, too, was the line taken by civil-liberties organizations and those segments of the press which drew their inspiration from the Kennedy underground. Other disclosures—in a Nevada court trying an extortion case, of FBI use of bugs to ferret out underworld connections with Las Vegas gambling and the practice of "skimming" the take of the casinos in order to deprive the Internal Revenue Service of its taxes —kept the anti-FBI campaign alive. A further disclosure before the Supreme Court seemed to open the door for legislation against the bureau.

This was the situation on December 5, 1966, when Representative H. R. Gross, a fighting conservative from Iowa, dictated a letter to J. Edgar Hoover. He cited the news stories which had charged that the FBI had engaged in electronic eavesdropping and wiretapping without the authorization of the Attorney General. He further noted that it had been his "impression" that such practices had been engaged in only with the knowledge and permission of the Attorney General. "I would appreciate it if you would send me any documentation that you have that authorized the FBI 'eavesdropping' that resulted in the overhearing of the conversations of Robert G. [Bobby] Baker, Fred B. Black and others," Gross wrote. "If there is some reason why the documentation itself cannot be sent to me in any of these cases, I would appreciate your assurance that such documentation exists with the name of the Attorney General, Deputy Attorney General, or other Justice Department official who gave the authorization."

This was Hoover's opportunity to clear the FBI of charges being made against it that it was indiscriminately using wiretaps and electronic devices without the knowledge of the Attorney General, as Bobby Kennedy had contended. Reliable sources insist that he answered Gross without consulting the President. But suspicion persisted that the White House was at least aware of the step about to be taken, and that Hoover's rebuttal was somehow linked to the Solicitor General's "confession" to the Supreme Court.

"Your impression that the FBI engaged in the usage of wiretaps and microphones only upon the authority of the Attorney General of the United States is absolutely correct," Hoover wrote. "All wiretaps utilized by the FBI have always been approved in writing, in advance, by the Attorney General. . . . Mr. [Robert F.] Kennedy, during his term of office, exhibited great interest in pursuing such matters and, while in different metropolitan areas, not only listened to the results of microphone surveillances but raised questions relative to obtaining better equipment. He was briefed frequently by an FBI official regarding such matters. FBI usage of such devices, while always handled in a sparing, carefully controlled manner and, as indicated, only with the specific authority of the Attorney General, was obviously increased at Mr. Kennedy's insistence while he was in office."

With his answer to Representative Gross, J. Edgar Hoover enclosed a number of corroborating documents. One of them was a letter from Assistant Attorney General Herbert J. Miller, Jr., dated May 25, 1961, in which he informed Senator Sam J. Ervin that the FBI at the time had sixty-seven electronic listening devices in operation, employed in internal-security cases and against organized crime.

Believing that the best defense is a good offense, Bobby countered typically by denying everything. "Apparently Mr. Hoover has been misinformed," he said in a statement issued by his office. And he enclosed a letter from Courtney A. Evans, a former FBI liaison man (and the man who would have succeeded Hoover as director had Bobby won out), which stated, "I did not discuss the use of these devices with you in national security cases or other cases, nor do I know of any written material that was sent to you at any time concerning this procedure, or concerning the use, specific location or other details as to installation of any such devices in Las Vegas, Nevada, or anywhere else." Since the Evans assignment was to the Attorney General's office, this seemed like a clincher.

The controversy was now spread all over page one of the Washington newspapers. Hoover issued a statement to the press in which he said that it was "absolutely inconceivable" that Bobby could deny knowledge of the use of wiretaps and electronic listening devices. Bobby countered by charging that the FBI director was completely wrong. But the documents were on Hoover's side. To drive home his point, he released two memoranda from Courtney Evans. One of them discussed a conversation with Attorney General Kennedy "relative to his observations as to the possibility of utilizing 'electronic devices' in organized crime investigations. . . . The Attorney General noted that he had approved several technical surveillances . . . but that he had not kept any record and didn't really know what he had approved and what surveillances were currently in operation. He said that for his own information he would like to see a list of the technical surveillances now in operation. . . ." The second Evans memorandum noted that "the Attorney General was contacted on the morning of August 17, 1961, with reference to the situation in New York concerning the obtaining of leased lines from the telephone company for use in connection with microphone surveillances."

This disposed of the Evans disclaimer. But there was one more document which went to the heart of the matter. It was an August 17, 1961, memorandum outlining procedures for the use of the leased lines in New York that the second Evans memorandum had mentioned. "In the New York City area the telephone company has over the years insisted that a letter be furnished to [it] on each occasion when a special line is leased by the FBI. It is required that such a lease arrangement be with the approval of the Attorney General. In the past we have restricted the utilization of leased lines in New York City to situations involving telephone taps, all of which have been approved by the Attorney General. We have not previously used leased lines in connection with microphone surveillances because of certain technical difficulties which existed in New

York City. These technical difficulties have, however, now been overcome. . . . Accordingly, your approval of our utilizing this leased line arrangement is requested. . . ."

Alongside the word "Approved" is Bobby Kennedy's signature.

In spite of this cold and clear evidence, Bobby continued to deny any knowledge of the facts. Skiing in Sun Valley at the time, he issued still another press release arguing that it was "nonetheless true" that he was ignorant of FBI microphone surveillance. "Perhaps I should have known," he said piously, "and since I was Attorney General I certainly take the responsibility for it, but the plain fact of the matter is that I did not know."

Newspapermen in Washington who had known Bobby during his Senate Labor Rackets Committee days smiled. "This was his technique when he was caught leaking a story—high indignation, denial, a meaningless admission, and a fast fadeout," one reporter remarked. But now he was a candidate for the Presidency, and the fast fadeout was impossible. Fortunately—or otherwise—the story was knocked out of the newspapers by a new controversy, one which, in the long run, might prove even more damaging to the Kennedy posture of virtue. It had been brewing for some time, along with other stories which a benevolent press kept out of the papers. There had been reports that Bobby had attempted to coerce a publisher into dropping a book on Senator Edward Kennedy. There had been talk of a $12,000 bill to a Fifth Avenue shop for a mink coat for Jacqueline Kennedy which had suddenly been reduced to $7,000 after pressure from Bobby, then still Attorney General. But it was more than rumor when the case of William Manchester and his *The Death of a President* splattered across the nation's front pages.

Many issues were involved, as the story developed. But the major issue, insofar as Bobby and Jacqueline Kennedy were concerned, seemed to be their passionate conviction that anything concerning the late President Kennedy, whether public or private, was their property. This attitude had manifested itself in both Bobby's and Jackie's anger at the publication of a small memoir by Paul Fay, a friend of Jack Kennedy, called *The Pleasure of His Company*. It had been an affectionate book of small consequence, but Mrs. Kennedy had taken sufficient umbrage over it to refuse a contribution from Fay to the Kennedy Memorial Library in Cambridge, Massachusetts.

The Manchester book was something else again. The idea for it had come from Bobby and Mrs. Kennedy. They had approached Theodore White, author of *The Making of a President* and other highly successful books, but he had refused to accept the straitjacket conditions of control over the literary product that they demanded. Later they chose William Manchester, author of a book about John F. Kennedy which the New York *Times* had described as "adoring." He agreed to write what was described to him as a complete account of the assassination and accepted the proviso that it would not be published without the approval of Bobby and Mrs. Kennedy. Harper & Row had signed a contract with Manchester and the two Kennedys to publish the book. *Look* magazine had paid $665,000 for the first serial rights. And the Kennedys had opened every door for Manchester. Jackie, in fact, had given him a ten-hour taped interview in which she had unburdened herself in a manner usually reserved for the most intimate of friends. She had turned over to him her letters to Jack Kennedy. And other members of the family had acted with the same abandon—including Bobby. The first hours of Lyndon Johnson's tenure as President, right after the assassination, as well as descriptions of the allegedly stormy relations between Vice President Johnson and the President, received considerable mention from both Jacqueline and Bobby.

For a time, the project moved ahead smoothly. But in the two years that Manchester worked on the manuscript, times changed. Bobby became a strong contender for the Presidency and regretted his words. Mrs. Kennedy, divesting herself of her widow's weeds and accepting an honored place in the International Set, regretted her highly personal confidences to Manchester. And both of them realized that their account of Lyndon Johnson's behavior on the Presidential plane which flew John F. Kennedy's body back to Washington would not stand up to objective scrutiny. There were others present, such as Charles Roberts of *Newsweek*, who could challenge the Kennedy account. (In fact, Roberts did.)

Though what the New York *Times* described as "a gaggle of New Frontiersmen" read the manuscript and imposed their suggestions for revisions, Bobby and Jacqueline decided that they did not want it published. Bobby tried quiet pressure on Harper & Row and on *Look*, which had excerpted 80,000 words for serialization. But he was not dealing with a worried witness before his committee. Considerable sums of money had already been spent, on the basis of a telegram Bobby had sent the publishers in which he assured them that "members of the Kennedy family will place no obstacle in the way of publication of the book." He later could claim that he had not read the book and therefore could not approve publication, but this was a quibble. He had, in fact, read a substantial part of it—

117 galleys, if the Washington *Post* was correct. Mrs. Kennedy also claimed that she had not seen the book, but her insistence that it was an "invasion of privacy" and "in bad taste" spoke for a fairly good knowledge of its contents.

When the first *Look* installment was on the presses, she filed suit for an injunction to stop publication. Very reluctantly, Bobby made himself a party to the suit, although he remained in Sun Valley, skiing while New York burned with the story.[1] There were long negotiations between the lawyers for Harper & Row and *Look* on one side and Simon Rifkind, Mrs. Kennedy's attorney, on the other. The Bobby-Jacqueline desire for an injunction, however, cooled off when they discovered that a $5,000,000 bond would have to be posted before the injunction could be granted. And if *Look* won its case, that money would be forfeit to make up the magazine's losses. Eventually, in an atmosphere of *opéra bouffe*, a face-saving arrangement was worked out which made it seem that the publisher and the magazine had capitulated. In truth, only small revisions and deletions were made in the text. But in the course of this, every sordid episode, deleted before the Bobby-Jackie onslaught had begun, found its way into the press.

Much of what became public knowledge was grim, and some of it was grimy. The washing of historical linen is not a pleasant business. And it allowed reporters who had remained silent, out of deference to the memory of the late President, to speak up, to place what had happened against the carefully nurtured Kennedy myth. It became known, for example, that the rumors and reports in the press in 1963 that President Kennedy hoped to find a new running-mate in 1964 had been inspired by Bobby, to bring about what his brother never intended.

U.S. News & World Report was able to quote a former White House official on this subject: "Bobby Kennedy was trying to use the Bobby Baker case, and the Billie Sol Estes case, and Lyndon's TV station in Austin, and everything else, in an effort to convince Jack to 'dump' Lyndon. Bobby and Kenny O'Donnell were hoping to turn the Texas trip into an anti-Johnson show, to prove that Lyndon had lost political influence in his own home state, and that he didn't control Texas any more. . . . Vague hints that Lyndon John-

[1] There were some who did not believe that Bobby's participation was so remote. William Attwood, editor of *Look* and John F. Kennedy's Ambassador to Guinea, remarked bitterly that one night's negotiations with Jackie Kennedy's lawyers had been protracted because of difficulties in reaching Bobby in Sun Valley. "I know who calls the shots now," he said. "As I got it, the theme of the evening was, 'He'll be right to the phone. He's waxing his skis.'"

son was somehow responsible for Jack Kennedy's death—the Kennedys could have come out forthrightly and put a stamp of disapproval on the books and magazine articles fomenting this kind of speculation over the assassination. But they didn't. The Kennedys wanted to keep it going."

The Manchester book, based on the accounts given to the author by Mrs. Kennedy and Bobby, tried to obscure the fact that Johnson had taken the oath of office as President in Texas at Bobby's suggestion. Instead the impression was created that Johnson was pushing himself into the Presidency. It is customary for the oath to be administered to the Vice President as soon as possible when a President dies in office. There was Kennedy resentment that Johnson had been taken to the Presidential cabin in "Air Force One," though this had been done at the insistence of the Secret Service. While Johnson waited for a federal judge to arrive to administer the oath, Kenneth O'Donnell repeatedly gave the pilot orders to take off—and the order had to be countermanded.

On the flight back, the Kennedy party made it a point to ride in the rear of the plane, as far from Johnson as possible. One aide told a reporter, "Make sure that you report that we rode in the back with our President, and not up front with him." But the real blow at Johnson came when "Air Force One" arrived in Washington. President Johnson had asked that a ramp be brought up to the plane so that he and Mrs. Kennedy could leave together with the President's body. ("He felt," a Johnson aide later said, "that it was necessary to show himself to the nation and the world, so that everyone could see that the traditional transfer of power had taken place.")

But Bobby had made different arrangements. The moment the plane came to a stop and steps were pushed up to the forward entrance, Bobby raced into the plane and down its entire length to join the Kennedy party. At the rear door, he had arranged for a forklift to lower the casket. When President Johnson tried to make his way to the rear of the plane, he was blocked by Kennedy aides. Bobby Kennedy, and not Johnson, escorted Jacqueline Kennedy off the plane. By the time Johnson was able to emerge, the casket which bore Kennedy's body had been loaded into the ambulance, with Bobby and Jacqueline, and started for the naval hospital at Bethesda. And while the nation grieved, Bobby, Jacqueline, and the Kennedy staff held a council of war at the White House to plan ways to use the funeral as a means to "build up the Kennedy image."

In the controversy over the Manchester book, participants and observers recalled that Johnson had done everything within his power to make things easier for the Kennedys. Mrs. Kennedy remained at the White House for fourteen days, while the President of the United States worked in the inconvenience of his Spring Valley house and the Vice Presidential offices in the Executive Office Building. Yet Bobby stridently objected when President Johnson proposed to address a joint session of the Congress, four days after the assassination. Bobby argued that by speaking to the Congress, Johnson was trying to "seize" the powers of the Presidency—powers which the Constitution gave him without the permission of his Attorney General. At the end of the thirty-day mourning period declared by Johnson, he invited Bobby and Mrs. Kennedy to an interfaith memorial service—but they pointedly failed to attend.

This was the record which the Manchester book brought to light. For a man who would be President, Bobby had thrust himself into a controvery in which he was ranged on the side of censorship and suppression in order to cover up his own indiscretions. Worse, he had somehow tarnished the *beau idéal* that John F. Kennedy had been to many people by involving him in an undignified wrestling match over the rights to his last hours. In the anteroom of Simon Rifkind's office, as the press waited for hourly bulletins on the course of negotiations, Murray Kempton, the New York *Post* columnist, expressed the attitude of many when he said, "One of the Kennedy people spoke to me on the phone the other night and he just lied and said, 'You know, Mrs. Kennedy is nearly as upset over this as she was when he died.'" Bobby, in Sun Valley, would have shuddered over the nuances of those words.

After the Hoover controversy and the Manchester litigation, questions could be asked which had never entered the minds of his followers or his enemies. Those who had observed his measurable rise looked about them for the equal and opposite reaction which his personality and the political posture he affected were sure to prompt. If the polls ranked him high, the conversation of newspaperman and politician in Washington found little that was good to say of him. There was admiration, perhaps, for the uses he had made of organized feistiness and sheer disregard for others. But there was also hatred and fear—the hatred personal, the fear more generalized into speculation about the effect of his dictatorial, almost nihilistic, approach to an American system reeling from the impact of legal anarchy and popular disregard for law.

Bobby Kennedy had made his way in the political jungles by carefully marking himself off from the policies of the Democratic party to which he presumably owed his loyalties and of the President who led that party. His attitude plainly said that Lyndon Johnson was an interloper, and even when he took positions similar to those of the White House, there was an edge of contempt to his formulations which neither Lyndon Johnson nor the Washington press corps missed. On foreign policy, for example, he encouraged the coalition of pacifists, appeasers, and left extremists who wished to see the United States withdraw from Vietnam under any pretext. By arguing for the inclusion of the Communists in the government of South Vietnam, he made the President's burden that much heavier and encouraged the "negotiate now" pressures of America's putative allies and friends.

Like a linebacker at a tea party he plunged into the touchy, dangerous, and highly complex questions of nuclear disarmament, creating the impression that the Johnson Administration was committed to the status quo and insensitive to the consequences of nuclear proliferation. But calling for what almost amounted to the unilateral nuclear disarmament of the United States and the West, he offered nothing concrete that could be measured against past and present policies.

At a time when the Great Society's domestic program was pushing the country into inflation, he called for more—not less—economic profligacy. He demanded more spending for welfare programs that had not been tested or had already bogged down in maladministration or open corruption. He was cutting and ironic to those who presented the unpalatable alternatives, but his hit-and-run attacks, though damaging to the Administration, failed to present his own views.

On civil rights, as violence racked the nation's cities, he continued to speak in glittering and generalized support of more and more concessions to the Negro extremists. In his trips abroad, he used friendly or unfriendly governments as sounding boards for criticism of his own country, for stirring up "revolutionary" zeal. His heart—or at least the public heart that was his political symbol —belonged to those whose excesses were stirring up a backlash that could, in time, destroy all the advances that the Congress and the people had made in race relations. It almost seemed that, like the "black power" proponents, he wanted to tear down everything in sight so that he could rebuild it according to his own ideas and in his own image.

In short, Bobby Kennedy and his followers did not move like an advancing army, determined on conquest, but like battalions of paratroopers who descend from the skies to sabotage and destroy, to convulse a territory and paralyze it, and then withdraw. As a semideclared belligerent in the battle for the Presidential nomination, he could afford to deal in negatives, to propose nothing constructive, to offer only doubt and suspicion of the Johnson Administration, and to badger the loyal Republican opposition. But once he had crossed his political Rubicon, stating what everyone knew was on his agenda—after he had changed the tense, from "want to be" to "would be" President—could Bobby continue to hold his following? Dealing in specifics might win over some of the dubious, but it would also lose those who rallied to him previously because he was against the Establishment and its responsible critics.

Admittedly, Bobby was a maverick and a phenomenon. He had piled up big votes in the past and he knew the techniques for keeping his name in the limelight of television and press. The pundits had been wrong about him in the past. Had they really measured him properly for the role he had chosen? Did they really understand his radical view of political operation? They had scoffed at the thought of a Kennedy dynasty. They had smiled indulgently when Bobby had suggested that one of his children might also be President. Yet every day, Bobby's pugnacity had paid off. As the 1968 campaign approached, the professionals and amateurs of politics began to realize that Bobby Kennedy might well be the next President of the United States. Certainly they wondered if it was not too late to stop him. Their hope for this lay in the thousands of small and large hurdles that a Presidential candidate must take, as well as the millions of pits which history and current events dig for the front runner in a political race.

Working for Robert Francis Kennedy was his overwhelming need for the Presidency. He wanted it so badly that, as the saying goes, he could taste it. Against this ambition, this determination, only an equal ambition and determination could prevail. For the man who would be President—fingering in his secret hours the inscription on a cigarette box that "Johnny" had given him in 1960—this was his secret weapon. "When I'm Through, How About You?" the inscription read. Robert Francis Kennedy could hardly disagree.

INDEX

Index

Lodge, Henry Cabot, Jr., 47-48, 164, 293
Lodge, Henry Cabot, Sr., 47
Loevinger, Lee, 178-79
Long, Edward V., 229
Louis, Joe, 85-86
Lovett, Robert, 274
Luciano, Lucky, 223
Luthuli, Albert, 347-48

Macapagal, Diosdado, 287
Macdonald, Torbert, 148, 243
McCarthy, Eugene, 161
McCarthy, Joseph R., 27, 40, 46-57, 65-69, 73, 82-83
McClellan, John, 54, 55, 59, 67, 72-82, 87, 118-19, 128-32, 318
McCone, John, 262
McCormack, Edward J., 355
McCormack, John, 50-51, 141, 174
McCulloch, William M., 250
McDonald, David J., 214
McElroy, Robert, 66
McGee, Gale, 315
McGill, Ralph, 306
McGovern, Jack, 104
McGrory, Mary, 283
McInerney, James, 51
McKeon, William H., 309
McMullen, Richard, 121
McNamara, Pat, 83
McNamara, Robert, 207, 257, 272, 275, 282, 317-18
McNiff, John, 310
Mafia, 220
Manchester, William, 363-67
Mann, Floyd, 182
Mann, Thomas, 333
Mansfield, Mike, 331
Manuel, Robert, 127
Marshall, Burke, 178, 187, 192, 195
Martin, Dean, 21
Matsinaga, S. M., 243

Mazey, Emil, 110-14, 120-24
Mazo, Earl, 72, 174-75
Mboya, Tom, 316
Meissner, John, 92
Meredith, James, 187-88, 190-91
Miller, Herbert J., Jr., 179, 361
Miller, William E., 232
Mitchell, James P., 87
Molik, Frank, 122
Mollenhoff, Clark, 78
Monroe, Marilyn, 21
Moore, Eddie, 34
Morgenthau, Robert, 227, 282
Morrill, Mary, 68
Morris, Robert, 46, 191
Morse, Wayne, 148, 243, 314
Moss, Annie Lee, 55, 59-61
Motsinger, Jess F., 122-23
Mozer, Robert, 310
Mundt, Karl, 61, 65, 83, 103, 130
Murphy, Charles, 256
Murrow, Edward R., 65, 255, 265, 270
Myers, Deb, 138-39

Nathan, Robert, 164
National Insurance Association, 20
National Labor Relations Board, 82
National Negro Association, 20
Nickerson, Eugene, 354
Nixon, Richard, 70-72, 164, 168-69, 288, 300
Nkrumah, Kwame, 270
Norton, Howard, 150, 154
Novak, Rodbert D., 174
Nunan, Joseph D., 46

Oberdorfer, Louis, 179
O'Brien, Lawrence, 145, 152-53, 167, 251, 286
O'Connell, William Cardinal, 27
O'Connor, Frank, 353-54, 357-58